Gulshan-i Rāz

SUNY series in Islam

Seyyed Hossein Nasr, editor

Gulshan-i Rāz

The Rose Garden of Divine Mysteries

Maḥmūd Shabistarī

Translated and with commentary

by Seyyed Hossein Nasr

Compiled by Rana Shieh and Collaborators

SUNY
PRESS

Cover Credit: Rosette bearing the name and title of Emperor Aurangzeb from the Shah Jahan Album. Calligrapher Mir 'Ali Haravi. The Met Collection, https://www.metmuseum.org/art/collection/search/451288.

Published by State University of New York Press, Albany

Printed in the United States of America

EU GPSR Authorised Representative:
Logos Europe, 9 rue Nicolas Poussin, 17000, La Rochelle, France
contact@logoseurope.eu
For information, contact State University of New York Press, Albany, NY
www.sunypress.edu

Library of Congress Cataloging-in-Publication Data
Names: Shabistarī, Maḥmūd, author. | Nasr, Seyyed Hossein, translator. | Shieh, Rana, compiler.
Title: Gulshan-i rāz : the rose garden of divine mysteries / Maḥmūd Shabistarī, author, Seyyed Hossein Nasr, translator, and Rana Shieh, compiler.
Description: Albany: State University of New York Press, [2025]. | Includes bibliographical references and index.
Identifiers: ISBN 9798855804362 (hardcover : alk. paper) | ISBN 9798855804379 (paperback) | ISBN 9798855804386 (ebook)
Further information is available at the Library of Congress.

Contents

Preface, vii
Compiler's Introduction, ix

[Exordium], 3
Question [1], 29
Question [2], 43
Question [3], 97
Question [4], 105
Question [5], 129
Question [6], 137
Question [7], 143
Question [8], 153
Question [9], 163
Question [10], 175
Question [11], 195
Question [12], 215
Question [13], 219
Question [14], 239
Question [15], 253

Glossary of Persian and Arabic Technical Terms, 283
Notes, 291
Selected Bibliography, 301
Index, 303

بِسْمِ اللهِ الرَّحْمٰنِ الرَّحِيْمِ

Preface

I have been engaged with the *Gulshan-i rāz* for many decades and have taught it in a traditional manner from cover to cover in both Persia and the United States. The last time this exercise was carried out was in Washington, and those present were all advanced students of religion in general and Islamic studies in particular. They recorded the classes, and two of them, Rana Shieh and Nicholas Boylston, asked me to publish my translation and commentary, an invitation that I accepted. The present work includes the version of the Persian text I established on the basis of several well-known editions of the book, my own new translation of the poem, and my commentary.

Shieh has compiled the work with the help of Boylston and others for which I am grateful. As it stands, this opus is both a translation of the text kept as close to the meaning of the original verses in Persian as possible and a commentary that draws from my humble knowledge of the whole Sufi tradition and also the commentaries written on the text of *Gulshan-i rāz* over the centuries. My goal has been not only to present a masterpiece of Persian Sufi literature in English but, most of all, to bring out the metaphysical, cosmological, and general sapiential teachings of one of the most important Islamic spiritual texts. May the work succeed in achieving this goal.

In conclusion I wish to thank, in addition to Shieh and Boylston, all those who helped in the preparation and presentation of this work in book form, especially Munjed Murad. I also wish to thank Nariman Aavani and Syed Amir Hamza Zaidi for their assistance.

Wa'Llāhu a'lam
And God knows best
Seyyed Hossein Nasr

Preface

Compiler's Introduction

In the month of Shawwāl of the year 717 of the Hijra,[1] a letter containing seventeen questions on the most profound matters of metaphysics and Sufi doctrine reached the circle of Shaykh Maḥmūd Shabistarī in the northwest of Persia. The letter had traveled from the other end of Persia, sent by the eminent Sufi Mīr Ḥusayn Harawī, who would leave this world almost exactly a year later.[2] By his own admission, Shabistarī was not a poet—he had hardly composed any poetry before this point—but he was already renowned for his knowledge of Sufism. Within a few days, he answered all of these questions, each of which demanded knowledge of the most subtle aspects of Sufism, and sent them back with the messenger to Harawī. Some time later, inspiration struck him again, and he developed the answers to these questions into one of the most important Sufi poems ever written, naming it *Gulshan-i rāz, The Rose Garden of Divine Mysteries.*

Gulshan-i rāz quickly gained popularity in Persian-speaking Sufi circles, drawing a broad readership as a result of its combination of depth, beauty, and concision. The text became the subject of tens of commentaries over the centuries and has continued to be read widely by seekers of Sufi wisdom and literary aficionados in Persia and the subcontinent of India until today. The importance of *The Rose Garden of Divine Mysteries* was also recognized by Western scholars. In the early eighteenth century; the French travelers Chardin and Bernier had noted its importance in Persian scholarly circles,[3] and it was translated into German by von Hammer-Purgstall in 1838 ,into English by Whinfield in 1880, and more recently by Robert Abdul Hayy Darr in 2007,, among others.[4]

However, although *Gulshan-i rāz* has been translated into English several times, the book you are now reading is quite different from any other work written in English on this text. In order to understand this issue, we need to recognize first that Sufi thought and literature, reflecting Sufism itself, are more than simply textual traditions. Texts are certainly important, whether they be literary masterpieces such as Rūmī's *Mathnawī-yi ma'nawī* (*The Spiritual Couplets*), or prose expositions of Sufi doctrine, such as Ibn 'Arabī's *Fuṣūṣ al-ḥikam* (*The Ringstones of Wisdom*). However, these texts live and breathe within a broader context of discussion, quotation, and teaching, in which readers contemplate their teachings in order to deepen their awareness of the nature of reality and cultivate their characters. As such, although texts of theoretical Sufism sometimes appear to present an abstract philosophy that can be mastered with the mind alone, they in fact present the conceptual doorway to a world that includes much more than the mind.

Although the numerous books, manuscripts, and translations of works of theoretical Sufism suggest otherwise, the life of this tradition is not only the written word itself, but in fact the oral commentary, or as it is expressed in Persian, the knowledge passed 'chest to chest' (*sīnah bi-sīnah*). A work of theoretical Sufism, whether poetry or prose, creates the framework for the transmission of something more than just the text. Certainly, explanation of the literal meaning of the text itself, including both its grammar and the meaning of its technical terms, has its place. Likewise, exposition in detail of teachings that a text presents in brief, the clarification of recondite expressions, and elaboration on the broader significance of ideas presented all play an important role in this oral transmission. But the teaching of theoretical Sufism traditionally embraces more than can be contained within a written commentary. The presence of the teacher and the ambiance that he or she creates is crucial to this process, as the teacher represents the living transmission and the embodiment of the ideas presented in the text, transmitting the non-verbal aspects of Sufi doctrine in a chain that links the students not only to the author of the texts but also to the origin of Sufism itself, in the inner reality of the Prophet Muḥammad and the revelation of the Quran. To paraphrase the commentator of this work, referencing his own teacher

'Allāmah Muḥammad Ḥusayn Ṭabāṭabā'ī, to master theoretical Sufism one not only has to learn how to interpret the black ink of the writing on the page but also learn how to "read" the white of the page itself.

It was this awareness that we could not understand theoretical Sufism by simply sitting with the books on our own that motivated us to approach Seyyed Hossein Nasr in 2015 to request that he teach us the *Gulshan-i rāz*. These classes would be offered to a small group of students outside of his ordinary teaching schedule at The George Washington University, in the same way that his own teachers in Persia had offered such extracurricular classes (*dars-i khārij*) in order to transmit the knowledge of theoretical Sufism in a context that was freer than either the jurisprudence-based focus of the seminary or the curricular and time-based limitations of the university system. Our request was precisely that he teach this text in the same way that he had been taught by such masters of theoretical Sufism as 'Allāmāh Ṭabāṭabā'ī, Ilāhī-Qumsha'ī and Ḥā'irī. Nasr accepted our request graciously, and taught the entire text of the *Gulshan-i rāz* over the course of fifteen sessions, each several hours long, which took place in Washington, DC, and Northern Virginia between 2015 and 2018. Soon after these sessions began, it became clear that we were experiencing something that could benefit a much broader audience. In our studies of Sufi literature, we had already experienced that in order to receive an oral commentary on a text of theoretical Sufism such as this, one would have to know Arabic and/or Persian fluently and then travel to the Islamic world to find one of the rare living masters of this tradition. Yet, here we were in the United States, receiving such a commentary in English. Without doubt, there were aspects of those sessions that were impossible to record in writing, as our engagement with Shabistarī's text led to a wide range of responses, from moments of contemplative seriousness to expressions of wonder at the beauty of the poetry or the depth of the poet's insight, as well as many moments filled with joy and laughter. However, given the scarcity of records of the oral transmission of theoretical Sufism, we again approached Nasr to allow us to transcribe the recordings of these sessions and submit them to him to transform them into a written work. It is his edition of both those lessons and the Persian text of *Gulshan-i rāz* that you are reading now.

The choice of *Gulshan-i rāz* as the text at the center of these lessons turned out to be a happy one. From one point of view, the exposition of the text itself was not the only goal, for the white page behind the writing of all works of theoretical Sufism is in a sense the same. As such, in this commentary, and in the tradition of the oral exposition of theoretical Sufism, Nasr often uses a verse in the text as a pretext to express a fundamental point of Sufi metaphysics. Likewise, rather than simply reading *Gulshan-i rāz* as a work that belongs only to the eighth/fourteenth century, Nasr shows its timeless relevance, as well as its relevance to the contemporary world, and in doing so connects this work to a wide range of topics about which he has written elsewhere, from the environmental crisis to modern physics.

However, from another point of view, the choice of *Gulshan-i rāz* was of course crucial to the lessons and the book that emerged. In requesting that Nasr teach this particular work, we were aware that he had taught this text several times over the decades in both Persia and the US, and that he felt a particular affinity for it. As a metaphysician and poet himself, Nasr values both the philosophical depth of Shabistarī's work as well as the beauty and concision with which it is expressed. As such, before explaining the details of how the book is presented, a few words about Shaykh Maḥmūd Shabistarī and *Gulshan-i rāz* are in order.

Maḥmūd Shabistarī

Despite the fame of *Gulshan-i rāz* we know surprisingly little with certainty about its author, Sa'd al-Dīn Maḥmūd ibn 'Abd al-Karīm Yaḥyā Shabistarī. As the name Shabistarī indicates, Shaykh

Maḥmūd was born in northwest Iran in the village of Shabistar, which lies roughly between Tabriz and Lake Urumia. The biographical information we have about him dates generally from at least a century after his lifetime and contains some contradictions. For example, although his death date is usually listed as 720/1320 CE, it is actually more likely that he died closer to 740/1340, as he requested to be buried at the foot of his teacher Shaykh Bahā' al-Dīn who died in 737/1336-7, and whose tombstone is visible in the mausoleum of Shabistarī, which still stands in Shabistar today.[5]

The one date we know with a high degree of certainty is the date of composition of *Gulshan-i rāz* itself, since Shabistarī mentions at the beginning of the poem that the aforementioned letter he received from Mīr Ḥusayn Harawī reached him in the month of Shawwāl 717 AH (December 1317 or early January 1318).

In another of his works, *Sa'ādat-nāmah* (*The Book of Felicity*), Shabistarī mentions that he traveled widely in search of knowledge, stating, "I spent a long part of my life studying the science of Divine Unity, travelling through Egypt, Turkey, and Arabia, day after day, night after night. Year in and year out, for months on end, like time itself, I trekked through town and country, sometimes burning the midnight oil, sometimes making the moon my bedside lamp."[6] The names of two of Shabistarī's spiritual teachers are known, the abovementioned Shaykh Bahā' al-Dīn, regarding whom little is known, and one Shaykh Amīn al-Dīn, whom Shabistarī mentions in *Sa'ādat-nāmah*. As Leonard Lewisohn points out, this figure may be either Ḥājjī Amīn al-Dīn Tabrīzī (known as Ḥājjī Dādā) or Amīn al-Dīn 'Abd al-Salām Khunjī, and there is not sufficient evidence available to decide between them. However, since both of these figures were most likely disciplines of the famous Kubrawī master Nūr al-Dīn Isfarāyinī (d. 717/1317), we are still able to associate Shabistarī's spiritual genealogy with the Kubrawī Sufi order.[7]

Some of the biographical texts suggest that Shabistarī had neither physical nor spiritual offspring, indicating that later *silsilah*s (the initiatic chains of Sufism) do not pass through him, but this is uncertain; a lineage emerged in Kerman around five hundred years later that claimed both spiritual and physical descent from him.[8]

However, Shabistarī's intellectual and literary legacy is without question, as he left behind him three works that have survived to today, one in prose and two in poetry. The prose work is titled *Ḥaqq al-yaqīn fī ma'rifat rabb al-'ālamīn* (*The Truth of Certainty on Gnosis of the Lord of the Worlds*), and though fairly short is considered a masterpiece in theoretical Sufism. Given that in the *Gulshan-i rāz* Shabistarī states that he had previously written on theoretical Sufism in prose but never in poetry, it is likely that *Ḥaqq al-yaqīn* predates the former poem, and there are certain similarities in content.[9]

Shabistarī's last extant work is the aforementioned *Sa'ādat-nāmah* (*The Book of Felicity*), which Lewisohn suggests was written in the last period of the poet's life. Though possessing passages of high literary quality, this work is considered to be more conservative in its expression of Sufi teachings, favoring the precedent of Abū Ḥāmid al-Ghazzālī over the more daring turns of expression found in the writings of Ibn 'Arabī or indeed the *Gulshan-i rāz* itself.[10]

Between these two works, Shabistarī of course wrote the *Gulshan-i rāz*, which is rightly considered his *magnum opus* and sealed his fame as one of the greatest exponents of Sufi teachings in the Persian language.

Gulshan-i rāz, The Rose Garden of Divine Mysteries

As mentioned above, *Gulshan-i rāz* was written in response to a letter containing seventeen questions, sent to the Sufi of Azerbaijan from Khurāsān by Mīr Ḥusayn Harawī, who as his name indicates, hailed from Herat in present-day Afghanistan.[11] The response to this letter was composed in two separate versions, one that was immediately returned with the messenger bringing the original letter, which contained short versified answers to Harawī's questions, and another, longer version, based on the same questions that Shabistarī composed later when inspiration moved him, or as he puts it, when 'the parrot of my speech began to speak.'[12]

The product of this inspiration is a poem of over a thousand verses written in the *mathnawī* (or rhyming couplet) genre, using a meter known as *baḥr hazaj maḥdhūf*.[13] Following a versified prelude and description of the circumstances of the composition of the work, *Gulshan-i rāz* is organized according to the seventeen questions posed by Harawī. The answer to each question is them subdivided into sections with titles such as *tamthīl* (meaning illustration) or *qā'idah* (meaning here principle). As such, the work can be classified as 'didactic,' in the sense that its purpose is to convey directly specific teachings, and like other didactic poems, which have been common in the majority of Islamic languages, is written in a way that lends itself to easy memorization and concision of expression. However, this label should not lead us to think that the work is lacking in poetic quality, for it is both its beauty and its precision that have led to its fame, and indeed many of its lines have entered into the Persian language as proverbs or aphorisms.[14]

These questions around which *Gulshan-i rāz* is composed broach a wide range of topics, including metaphysics, cosmology, ethics, and aesthetics, and deal with some of the most difficult questions of theoretical Sufism, such as what it means to attain union (*waṣl*) with God, or what Manṣūr al-Ḥallāj meant when he declared "I am the Truth" (*ana'l-Ḥaqq*). In discussing Shabistarī's responses to these questions, scholars have often endeavored to trace the influences of prior authors on him, pointing in particular to the literary influence of Farīd al-Dīn 'Aṭṭār and the intellectual influence of Muḥyī al-Dīn ibn 'Arabī. While these influences, and others, are certainly present—for we hear Shabistarī himself apologizing that his poetic skill cannot match that of an 'Aṭṭār,[15] and we do see terminology and teachings characteristic of Ibn 'Arabī amply represented—it is important to note also that *Gulshan-i rāz* is really sui generis in the history of Persian literary and theoretical Sufism. Though the ideas found in the text share a family resemblance with other texts written by interpreters of Ibn 'Arabī, and though the poetic beauty of the Persian has much in common with the finest Sufi love poets who wrote in the language, Shabistarī's approach is quite different from anything that has come before or after.

The unique character of *Gulshan-i rāz* is particularly evident from the beginning and end of the text. The work begins with questions on the nature of thought (and also meditation or contemplation, that is, *tafakkur*) and the nature of selfhood, or the question "Who am I?" While this topic is certainly of great importance for theoretical Sufism, it is more common for the nature of selfhood to be dealt with indirectly and by way of allusion. Likewise, the *Gulshan-i rāz* also ends with Shabistarī casting aside the veils of allusion so common in Sufi literature, this time through an exposition of the symbolism of the various features of the female face as well as other esoteric symbols found in the Persian poetic tradition, such as idol worship, Christian symbols, and the "tavern of ruins" (*kharābāt*). This section of the work is introduced by one of the most important passages ever written on the Sufi philosophy of language.

The breadth, depth and originality of the *Gulshan-i rāz* make it an extremely rewarding text to study; yet, the terseness and richness of the texts is such that it is only with considerable contemplation and commentary that its depths can be penetrated.

The Present Work

As mentioned above, this book developed from lessons given by Seyyed Hossein Nasr in which he translated and commented on the entire text of the *Gulshan-i rāz*. The recordings of these sessions were transcribed and then edited in order to conform more closely to standards of written expression, and with the exception of a few tangential discussions all of the material of those classes was included. Nasr then edited the entire English text a second time, adding further material to the commentary in order to make it more useful for a general readership. During this process, he produced a new edition of the Persian text of the *Gulshan-i rāz*, which is also presented here and is particularly suited to the needs of teaching and commenting on this text. For this task, the edition of Ghulāmriḍā Kaywān Samī'ī published in his edition of Lāhījī's commentary on the *Gulshan-i rāz* was used as the base text, since this is the Persian version that is most commonly studied in Persian intellectual circles today. However, certain lines from the critical edition of Jawād Nūrbakhsh were selected in favor of those found in Kaywān Samī'ī's edition, particularly when they were judged to be more accurate or were clearer of expression. In these cases the version found in the Kaywān Samī'ī edition is presented in a footnote.[16]

Nasr's commentary is intended for a general audience interested in gaining a deep knowledge of Sufi metaphysics, and hence each concept and idea is explained from the ground up. However, given that there will be readers with some level of familiarity of Persian or other Islamic languages, the original Persian is given in transliteration for the most important terms as well as certain idiomatic expressions. This book thus presents not only a new edition and translation of one of the most important texts of Persian Sufism ever written, but it also provides a rare point of access to the oral tradition of theoretical Sufism in the English language, an exposition of the whole gamut of topics of that tradition—an explanation both accessible and detailed, with an overview of Sufi terminology in Persian, which can act as a bridge to studying the Persian text itself for those who wish to pursue it.

The Persian text of the *Gulshan-i rāz* is presented in a readable *naskh* font in order to make it accessible to readers who know some Persian or another Islamic language but do not have experience reading the traditional Persian *nasta'līq* script. The orthography (*rasm al-khaṭṭ*) of the Persian has been adapted to the needs of contemporary readers, and hence is slightly different from that found in the Kaywān Samī'ī edition. When the original Persian or Arabic version of texts other than the *Gulshan-i rāz* is mentioned, it is presented in Latin transliteration in order not to be confused with the *Gulshan-i rāz* itself.

I would like to conclude by thanking Seyyed Hossein Nasr himself, who not only dedicated his time and energy to teaching this text but also accepted at our request to undertake the painstaking task of editing it for publication. I apologize to both him and the readers for any printing errors in the text. I also wish to express my deepest gratitude to my dear friend and colleague Nicholas Boylston for his assistance throughout the editing process, to tireless friends for their tireless work typing Nasr's amendments to the text and transcribing the lessons themselves, and to Syed Amir Hamza Zaidi and Munjed Murad for their help in this task.

Rana Shieh
Washington, DC
Tāsū'ā, 1444

The Rose Garden of Divine Mysteries

[Exordium]

بِسْمِ اللهِ الرَّحْمٰنِ الرَّحِيْمِ

In the Name of God

Most Merciful, Most Compassionate

به نام آن که جان‌را فکرت آموخت
چراغ دل به نور جان برافروخت

In the Name (*bi nām*) of Him who taught the soul (*jān*) how to meditate (*fikrat*),
And illuminated the lamp of the heart with the light of the soul (*jān*).

Islamic books usually begin with the Names of God, *bismi'Llāh al-Raḥmān al-Raḥīm*, and some praise of God and the Prophet, and then comes the phrase *ammā ba'd*.[1] But here Shabistarī does not mention one of the revealed Names of God directly, but indirectly. This practice is seen in some other major works of Persian poetry, where only allusion is made to God and His Acts, sometimes in a very daring way. The *Dīwān* of Ḥāfiẓ begins with an Arabic line (originally by Yazīd ibn Mu'āwiyah) followed by a Persian one:

> O Saki, give us the cup and fill it (with wine),
> For He made love easy at first, but then came difficulties.[2]

The *Dīwān* of Ḥāfiẓ thus begins with the Saki pouring the wine, which symbolizes the receiving of Divine Knowledge and Love, but it does not speak about God directly.

Turning now to the commentary on the *Gulshan-i rāz*, first of all, *bi nām*, "In the Name": *Nām* in Persian, which is an Indo-European language, is similar to *nāma* in Sanskrit, "name" in English, and *Namen* in German.

So Shabistarī says, "In the Name of." Why does he begin with the Name? That itself is a very important question. In traditional metaphysics, and traditional thought in general, the name of something is related to the reality of that thing. This fact is considered to be true even for human names. In the old days, people were very careful about what names they would give to their children. It was considered a very profound act. We have a *ḥadīth* attributed to the Prophet, *nazzala al-asmā' min al-samā'*, that is, "The names [given to people] descend from Heaven."

Now, this way of considering a name is a continuation of a very important metaphysical teaching: that the name is not just an accident but rather corresponds to the essential reality of a being. This truth should not be confused, however, with ordinary names in modern languages that may not possess this metaphysical significance. And then there is a third possibility: the case of something that is transcendent so that any name you give it to it is not really its name. This doctrine is asserted at the beginning of the *Tao Te Ching*, "The name that can be named is not the name."[3] These cases should not be confused with each other. There is the positive significance of a name, and the negative significance of a name. Metaphysically, the name is that which is identified with the named in its inner reality, and especially in the case of God. So the Names of God *are* God. This is the foundation of all of *taṣawwuf* (Sufism). You say *Allāh*, you invoke the Name of God, but also God is present in His Name. In the deepest sense the Name of God, as revealed in sacred languages, *is* God.

In the Abrahamic world this truth is very much emphasized. The Lord's Prayer, which Christ recited, says, "Hallowed be Thy Name." Why "Name"? That term goes back to the same truth. When you say, "Hallowed be Thy Name" it refers to this reality. It is calling upon God: "Hallowed by Thy Name," meaning "Thy Reality as manifested in human language." The Name of God in sacred languages is sacred. It is so sacred that the Jews do not write it anymore; they say that they are not allowed to write the Name of God until the coming of the Messiah. So, we must understand this universal teaching that we see in different ways in Judaism, Christianity and Islam of what the Name is. The Name, traditionally understood, is not just like saying the name "camera," and you invent a gadget and call it "camera." Rather, the name is something that relates to the inner reality of a being.

As for the word that I translated as "meditate," *fikrat*, it derives from *fikr*, which has two meanings in Arabic, "to think" and "to meditate." When the Qur᾽ān commands *tafakkarū*, it does not mean only "think," it means most of all "meditate." Unfortunately, this point is lost upon many people, including some modernized Muslim commentators of the Quran. For those who know French, one can mention that unlike English in French you have the term *penser*, used as a title of one of the most famous books of philosophy in French, the *Pensées* of Pascal, which does not mean just thinking—it is the *Meditations* of Pascal. So, the word *penser* is like *fikr*; it has both meanings. Here, since this is a spiritual text, it is not "In the Name of God, who taught the soul how to think," but rather " . . . to meditate," to meditate upon the Divine Realities, as is shown by the words that follow, "the lamp of the heart" (*chirāgh-i dil*), which is illuminated with the light of the soul.

Now, we could also translate the second "soul" (*jān*) as spirit. The word *jān* is a Persian word, which has also entered into Turkish and many Indian languages but is not found in classical Arabic. *Jān* can mean life, like *anima*; an animal is called *jāniwar* in Persian. Moreover, *jān* can also mean soul, and in certain cases it can also mean spirit. It is also a term of endearment, as when you say *jānam* in Persian, meaning dear, or literally, my soul. If someone is close to you and they call your name, you answer, *jānam*, instead of yes. This is a very strong term of endearment. And sometimes God is called *jān-i jānān*, "the Spirit of spirits," "the Soul of souls."

Now, in Arabic there are various specific distinctions, such as between *nafs* and *rūḥ*, that is, between "soul" and "spirit"—"soul" here in the sense of "psyche." But "soul" in English does not only mean psyche. "Soul" can also mean spirit because when you talk about the immortal soul, you are really talking about the spirit, not about the psyche. So, the translation and interpretation of the word *jān* in English can be very complicated.

Here, if I wanted to be very exact, with the word *jān* being repeated twice in this verse I would translate the first *jān* as "soul" and the second as "Spirit," so it would be: " . . . taught the soul meditation" and then "illuminated the lamp of the heart with the light of the Spirit."

One more point: the comparison of the heart to a lamp, to a source of light, refers to a universal symbol. You even have in English, "light-hearted." Of course, that is against heavy-hearted, but it also signifies light in the sense of feeling elated and joyous. Christian mysticism makes many references to the illumination of the heart. This understanding is not unique to Islam but rather, it is universal. Why? Because at the center of the heart resides the Divine Reality, the Presence of God. As the famous *ḥadīth* mentions, *Qalb al-mu'min 'arsh al-Raḥmān*. "The heart of the believer is the Throne of the Most Merciful." So, right at the center of our heart resides God, and God is Light. Therefore, those who have faith, who have Divine Knowledge, who are good human beings, who have virtue, have light in their heart, and one speaks of heart knowledge. Also, we see the reverse of this positive aspect of the reality of the heart when we say, "I feel as if my heart is darkened," that is, in a sense, goodness and light has departed from it. When you feel depressed psychologically, there is always a kind of contraction of the heart, as if the light has left it. When you have light in your heart, you feel an expansion of your breast. You know you are not depressed anymore because of the joy that is combined with the expansion of the breast, *inshirāḥ al-ṣadr*, at whose center resides the heart. The heart of an illuminated person has been enlightened by *jān*.

ز فضلش هر دو عالم گشت روشن
ز فیضش خاک آدم گشت گلشن

> From His Divine Generosity (*faḍl*), the two worlds became illuminated,
> And from His Emanation (*fayḍ*), the dust of man became a rose garden.

Faḍl means both virtue and knowledge. A person is called *fāḍil* who is learned, implying also having pursued and attained virtue and knowledge. But *faḍl* also means bestowal—the bestowal of light, of goodness, of knowledge, of being, of everything positive, when it refers to God. So, *zi faḍlash* is translated as "from His Divine Generosity," emphasizing this sense of *faḍl*, this aspect of giving.

The word *fayḍ*, which means emanation, manifestation, and grace, can also mean in certain instances the same thing as *faḍl*. In technical Islamic philosophy *fayḍ* means emanation in a Neoplatonic sense. When you study Ibn Sīnā, you read about the *fayḍ* or emanation of the Second Intellect from the First Intellect. But its meaning, especially in Sufism, is wider, and also has to do with grace. For example, in Persian, in very polite language, if you want to say to somebody that you really benefited from his presence, you say *az ḥuḍūritān fayḍ burdam*, that is, "from your presence, I derived *fayḍ* (that is, a kind of *barakah*, a grace, a spiritual presence, a light—and all of these realities combined)."

Both of these words, *faḍl* and *fayḍ*, are very difficult to translate, because there is a cluster of meanings related to each. So, we could say: "From His *faḍl*, from His Generosity, His Virtue, and Power of bestowing existence, the two worlds became illuminated." Therefore, we could say everything in the world is illuminated through the *faḍl* of God, through what God has given. "And through the emanation, *fayḍ*, of His Reality the dust of man became a rose-garden."

I have translated *gulshan* as "rose garden," not just "garden." *The Rose Garden of Divine Mysteries* is how I translate the title *Gulshan-i rāz* into English. Some people have translated *gulshan* as only "garden," which is a possibility. My book, *The Garden of Truth*, the title of which I chose in light of Shabistarī's work, is called *Gulshan-i ḥaqīqat* in its Persian translation. As "garden" you can relate *gulshan* to *jannah* and *firdaws* and all the other Quranic terms for the paradisal garden, but more specifically it means a rose garden.

This next verse is remarkable, from the point of view of poetry:

توانائی که در یک طرفة العین
ز کاف و نون پدید آورد کونین

> The All-Powerful, who in the blink of an eye (*ṭurfat al-'ayn*),
> From "b" and "e" brought into being the two worlds (*kawnayn*).

Ṭurfat al-ỳayn means the blink of an eye, that is, in an instant beyond duration, and is an Arabic term, which is translated into Persian as *chishm bi ham zadan* (though the Arabic term also exists in Persian).

Now to what is he referring? He is referring to the Qur'ānic verse, *Kun! fa-yakūn.* "(God said) *Kun!* (the command form of 'Be!') and there was" (Q. 36:82), and so, I have translated the *k* and *n* of *kun* as the b and e of "be." God does not need time or any intermediary to do anything (although He can and sometimes does use an intermediary agent, such as sending an angel to do something). The Command of God is something that has immediacy. It is beyond time. So the *fā'* (and) in the Qur'ānic verse, *"Kun!" fa-yakūn,* does not imply time. It implies consequence — cause and effect. God said *Kun!*, "Be!," and *fā'*, immediately, *yakūn*, "there was."

In Arabic the word for to be, *kāna*, *yakūnu*, is not usually used as a copula. You connect the subject and the predicate together without the use of a copula, which is implied. In English, you say, "The door is open." "The door" is the subject, "open" is the predicate, and "is" is the copula, which relates the subject to the predicate. Now, if you wanted to say "the door is open" in Arabic, you would do not say *yakūn al-bāb maftūḥan*. You say, *al-bāb* (the door) *maftūḥ* (open). You skip over *yakūn* and do not use the verb "to be." There is a very profound philosophy connected to this linguistic usage. As I have written somewhere, in Arabic the whole language is plunged in God, plunged in being. Everything is already plunged in *wujūd* (being)—so you do not need to use the verb "to be" as copula, as you do in Indo-European languages.

The word *kawn* (existence) comes from the verb "to be" (*kāna*), but it is also used in another sense to mean the world, *'ālam al-kawn*, namely that which has received existence. So, *kawnayn*, (literally, "the two existences") going back also to the Quran, means this world and the next.

We have then, "The All-powerful, who in the blinking of an eye, From 'k' and 'n'"—which I translated as "b" and "e"—"brought into being the two worlds." The problem is that in Arabic and Persian you have the dual form *kawnayn*, but in English it is not possible to have a dual form in the same way; rather, you have to use the plural or say "two worlds."

The next verse uses the power of sounds and onomatopoeia, using *qāf,* the hardest of all the Arabic letters, though its sound is softer in Persian:

چو قاف قدرتش دم بر قلم زد
هزاران نقش بر لوح عدم زد

When the "P" of His Power (*Qudrah*) breathed upon the Pen (*Qalam*),
It cast thousands of patterns upon the tablet of nothingness (*lawḥ-i 'adam*).

This verse refers, of course, to creation. In the numerical system of Arabic letters, the letter *qāf* corresponds to the number 50, and *Qāf* is also the name of the fiftieth chapter of the Quran, in which there is discussion of the creation of the world by God. All of these ideas go together in a cluster, and *qāf* itself symbolizes in fact both the creation of the world, the Power of God (*Qudrah*), and also the cosmos itself or more precisely the cosmic mountain, known as Mount Qāf. Now, one of the ways in which the Quran describes the creation of the world is through the symbolism of the Pen, *qalam,* because the Quran is a book as is the cosmos, as in the verse, "And if all the trees on earth were pens, and if the sea and seven more added to it [were ink], the Words of God would not be exhausted." (Q. 31:27) That verse means that if all the seas and oceans were to be ink, all of that ink could be used by the writing of the *qalam*, but the creative Power of God would not be exhausted.

Creation itself is seen in Sufism as the result of the writing by the Divine Pen upon the tablet of nothingness (*lawḥ al-'adam* in Arabic), because there cannot ultimately be anything other than the Being of God. There can thus only be the casting of forms upon the tablet of nothingness, which is what the world is. The form comes from God, but it is "nothing" in itself indendependent of God. Everything is a reflection, a theophany of the Divine Names and Qualities.

Here we see the symbolism of the Pen (*qalam*), to which the Quran refers—*nūn wa'l-qalam* ("[By the letter] *Nūn*. By the pen," Q. 68:1). God thus even swears by the Pen. The Pen symbolizes the creative Power of God. It is a symbol of Divine Power, of Creative Power. It is remarkable how religions meet in different ways, on a certain level. In Hindu India, in a very different context, that symbol is the phallic symbol associated with Shiva, which also geometrically and physically looks like a pen. You see this symbol all over India, which for us Muslims and for others might appear very strange. But it is similar to the role the pen plays in Islamic cosmology; it is the vertical element of creation. You always have a vertical and a horizontal element, a masculine and a feminine element, *purusha* and *prakriti*, in Sanskrit; and in Islam, you have the *qalam* and the *lawḥ* (the Tablet). The *qalam* and the *lawḥ* in a sense correspond to the supreme male and female principles, the supreme principle of activity, and the supreme principle of receptivity and passivity. So, this symbolism is used.

The word *naqsh*, which means pattern, refers actually to existing things, the world of forms.

از آن دم گشت پیدا هر دو عالم
وز آن دم شد هویدا جان آدم

> From that moment (*dam*) the two worlds appeared,
> And from that moment (*dam*), the soul of man became manifest.

"From that moment" refers to the moment that was mentioned in the previous verse, the single moment in which through His Power (*Qudrah*) of the Pen, God cast a thousand patterns upon the tablet of nothingness. So, the important point here is that as soon as the Divine Power moved the Pen, you might say, the two worlds appeared, instantaneously. The word (*dam*) which I have translated as "moment" also means breath, and this verse can be also understood as referring to the "Breath of the Compassionate" (*nafas al-Raḥmān*) through which God created the world according to Sufi cosmology.

This verse is very significant from another point of view: We learn of the appearance of both worlds, or creation, at once and not gradually. This verse is a direct rejection of Darwinian evolution. There are some Muslims who believe that Islamic teachings can accept the theory of Darwinian evolution. Absurdities from the traditional Islamic point of view such as this belief are now being propagated in certain eastern circles especially in the subcontinent of India, because of the long British teaching of Darwinism in the nineteenth and early twentieth centuries in that land. Most Islamic defenses of evolution have come out of India and Pakistan, and very few out of the Arab world or Iran. That fact is one of the positive aspects of modern Persian and Arabic intellectual life. There are many negative elements there, but at least nobody of any consequence has defended Darwin in Tehran or Damascus.

As I mentioned, *dam* means technically breath and also moment. In Persian it has other meanings, including "nearness," "proximity," and "intimacy." *Dam* is also used in *taṣawwuf* in relation to techniques of breathing and remembering God at the very moment when one breathes. And it can also mean the ordinary moment, when you say for example, *dam bi dam*, "from moment to moment" or "continuously." So, it has many different meanings, but here it means "from that moment or instant of creation," indicating that there is no time, sequence or separation between the Supreme Cause and Its effects. That is to say, there is no separation between the Breath of God identified with His Word through which everything was created. Metaphysically we are dealing with that which is above the flow of time and in the principial order. If I speak to you now, it takes a second for my voice to come from my mouth to your ear. But here in this verse we are still above time; so, everything is taking place immediately and instantaneously. It is not a question of sequence in time. The author is referring to the creation of the world and of man metaphysically and in the principial order.

"From that moment, the soul of man became manifest"; that is, the soul was created by God. *Huwaydā* means literally apparent, manifest, to be something that can be seen. *Huwaydā shudan* is an eloquent Persian expression, which means to "appear," to be "seen," to be "manifested." Now, we have the world, and we have man. Of course, "man" means "men" and women—the human being—and before turning to the cosmos or the world, Shabistarī delves into the inner nature of man.

در آدم شد پدید این عقل و تمییز
که تا دانست از آن اصل همه چیز

> There appeared in man this intelligence and discernment (*tamyīz*),[4]
> Through which he came to know the principle of all things.

It is important to pay attention to the fact that Shabistarī begins with "through intelligence" or "through the intellect" (*'aql* meaning both). This fact is an indication of the gnostic and metaphysical nature of this text, which always emphasizes the primacy of knowledge and discernment. Frithjof Schuon used to say concerning the *Gulshan-i rāz*, "I have never seen a Sufi text like this, which is pure metaphysics, and based so directly on the power of discernment." This work is the most Vedanta-like Sufi text in a certain sense. It is like the Advaita Vedanta, which always emphasizes the importance of knowledge and discernment, as in the famous work of Shankaracarya, *The Crest Jewel of Discernment*. So, in that very moment or *dam* of the creation of Adam, there appeared in man, through his intellect, through the God-given *'aql*, intelligence, the power of discernment or *tamyīz*.

The Arabic word *tamyīz*, which we translate here as "discernment," or "discrimination" in its positive sense, implies discernment and distinction between good and evil, between truth and falsehood, between beauty and ugliness. In its highest sense *tamyīz* means discernment or discrimination between the real and the illusory and also between various levels of reality. So, there appeared in man, through the intellect, the power of discernment.

It is thanks to this God-given faculty that we can know "the principle of all things." Now, there is a very important point that is implied here. In principle, man can know all things. We cannot set a limit to what human beings can know, except that which is called unknowable. But even to know that something is unknowable, you have to know something about it in order for this statement to be true. So, we say that God's Essence is unknowable, but that means that we already know something about the Divine Essence to be able to know that it is unknowable. That is the truth to which Meister Eckhart and certain other sages have referred. Frithjof Schuon also used to allude to it often.

Certain Sufis have referred to unknowable realities, and in Christianity the Divine Mysteries are called Mysteries because they are considered to be unknowable, hence the famous Christian mystical work, *The Cloud of Unknowing*. But such assertions are based on the ordinary understanding of knowledge not metaphysical and gnostic knowledge. Actually, in principle there is nothing that the inner Intellect cannot know, nothing that they eye of the heart cannot see. It is in a sense like our external eye. There is nothing that our eye cannot see if it is put before it—of course if we have healthy eyes, not if we are blind, God forbid. The actualized intellect within is like the eye but with infinitely greater power of vision. There is no limit in principle to its power to know, not that everyone can know everything. Some people are more intelligent, some people are less so, but human intelligence in principle has no limit. Our body does. Your height is this much, you can only throw a stone so many feet, you can only run at such a speed. There are all kinds of limits set for our bodily and mental faculties. But from the Sufi point of view there is no limit to intelligence per se.

And therein in a sense lies the great tragedy of our times. When ordinary intelligence becomes cut off from its principle and turns against God, turning solely toward the world, it then becomes, as I have written before, like an acid that burns the whole texture of the world around man and leads as we see in the modern world to endless curiosity and desire for possession. Modern and postmodern man are never satisfied with what they have and seek something else. This is the reverse of the person in whom the intellect that can know and be in the ultimate sense is actualized. But even the fact that this endless inquietude exists itself points to the fact that there is no limit to human intelligence. There is nothing that we cannot think about, and not know, if it is put before us and the conditions are right to grasp the meaning and to understand what is involved.

چو خودرا دید یک شخص معیّن
تفکّر کرد تا خود چیستم من؟

When he saw himself as a distinct being,
He meditated, asking himself, "What am I?"

With this verse Shabistarī comes in reality to the end of the exordium. This is a very key verse of the *Gulshan-i rāz*, for the reason I shall mention for you.

Shakhṣ here means individual being, a distinct individual being. He, that is man, meditates, asking, "Who am I?" or "What am I?" *Chīstam?* Some of texts have *kīstam man*? *Kīstam* means "Who am I?" whereas *chīstam man* means "What am I?" in Persian. These versions amount to the same thing, because *chīstī* includes *kīstī*. ("What-ness" includes "who-ness.")

"What or who am I?" You see here that the *Gulshan-i rāz* begins in earnest, like the famous Hindu sage Shri Ramana Maharshi, with the question "Who am I?" It begins from the human side, not with the Divine Reality. There are two ways to begin metaphysics. One is, "Who is God?" The other is, "Who am I?" From the Subject and from the Object.

In a sense as I have discussed before elsewhere, this subjective path was the one that Descartes was trying to follow, and the famous dictum, "I think therefore I am"—*cogito ergo sum* in Latin and *je pense donc je suis* in French—is the assertion of my thinking I-ness as that which determines my being. Now, the Cartesian understanding is a caricature of what Shaykh Maḥmūd Shabistarī is saying here, or as was said in our own days by Shri Ramana Maharshi, the great saint of India, who all of his life when disciples came to him would say, "Ask yourself who you are." "Who am I?" And this approach is like dealing with an onion that you peel layer by layer, saying "I am not only this body," "I am not this psyche," "I am not even my thought." "At six o'clock in the evening I may get angry at something, but tomorrow morning I am somewhere else in a happy state; so, this or that aspect of me as a subject that experiences is not my real self. Those layers are an accident, in the philosophical sense, like the coat I wore, and I took off." I should ask over and over again about my I-ness—this is a spiritual method—until I reach who the real I is, which is the *Ātman*, the Divine Reality. "Who am I?" I am *Ātman* in the Hindu sense. I am none other than a drop in the ocean of Divinity. My I is ultimately *Ātman*.

And so Shaykh Maḥmūd Shabistarī turns to answer the basic question, "Who am I?" As soon as man realizes that he is an individual being, he becomes aware of his individual consciousness. This fact is itself quite remarkable if one thinks about it in depth. You are now reading this book, and you have individual consciousness. You know that you have a distinct consciousness of your own self. Otherwise, you would not be mentally normal. But at the same time, you can go beyond your consciousness and are able to have contact with other consciousnesses. That is why you are able to talk to others and understand what Shabistarī wrote centuries ago. We are able to speak together, to have discourse together, because ultimately there is but one Consciousness in which our individual consciousnesses participate. So, many mystical texts try to wrestle with this issue. They begin with this question, 'Who am I?' or 'What am I?' That is so because we meditate, we are thinking beings. Here in the text in fact *tafakkur kard tā khud chīstam man*, means that we began by thinking and asking ourselves "Who am I?," "What am I?" Here, however, the question goes deeper than what we ordinarily think. In his *Meditations* Descartes also pondered about

"Who am I?," "What am I?," "What is this seat of consciousness?" But he limited himself to the individual "I," whereas Shabsitarī sees these questions as leading to the Divine Self or *Dhāt*.

I want to point out something simple but essential. You are sitting here reading this book. You can think, and through memory remember last year; then the year before; then the year before that year. Then your memory becomes dimmer. You remember certain events of your childhood. But you can never remember the origin of your remembering. Have you ever thought of that? Your remembering has no origin. Your consciousness has no temporal origin because it is rooted in the Divine. It comes from God. It is, therefore, timeless. Now, some people try to use the idea of transmigration and reincarnation to explain this matter. Islam does not accept this perspective except in the metaphysical sense of there being only the One transmigrant. But even if that were to be the case, it does not change what I am trying to say here, namely that there is no origin to our consciousness.

So, man asks himself, "What am I?," "Who am I?" After he asks himself, "What am I?," the next verse says:

ز جزوی سوی کلّی یک سفر کرد
وز آنجا باز بر عالم گذر کرد

> He made a journey from the particular to the Universal,
> And from there looked upon the world again.

Pay attention to what an important metaphysical statement this is: to learn what the world is, he journeyed from the particular to the Universal. As Plato also asserted, you have to look at the world of manifestation from the universal point of view, the world of the Platonic Ideas, to understand the real nature of the particular. And so from that universal point of view, he looked upon the world.

جهانرا دید امر اعتباری
چو واحد گشته در اعداد ساری

> He saw the world as contingent being (*amr-i i'tibārī*),
> Like the [number] one that flows through all the numbers.

This verse needs much explanation. In fact every one of the verses in this section of the *Gulshan-i rāz* has so much metaphysical and philosophical content in it that I could spend the rest of the book just on one verse. "He saw the world as contingent being" (*amr-i i'tibārī*): One could also translate *amr* as "thing" in the philosophical sense like the Arabic term *shay'*. *Amr* here does not mean command as it often does. There are words in Arabic that you can use in many contexts, such as *amr.* So, one could also say, "He saw the world as contingent thing."

In Islamic philosophical vocabulary, *i'tibārī* means contingent, not to be confused with other meanings it has in other contexts. What is he saying? He sees the world as contingency while ordinary human beings see it as reality. What he is implying is that when you are looking at the world from a universal rather than a particular point of view, you realize that this world is contingent. The word "contingent" as used here is a philosophical and also gnostic term. It is not an ordinary English word. In philosophy, it means that which depends on something else for its being in the ontological sense. "Contingent" means not having a reality of its own. That is what "contingents" or *i'tibāriyyāt* means in Islamic philosophy and Sufism. So, he realized that the world is a contingent and not independent reality.

"Like the [number] one that flows through all the numbers." This is one of the key verses of the *Gulshan-i rāz* having to do with numerical symbolism in the Pythagorean sense. Now, what does he mean? You have the number 10 or 86 or whatever. But if you really look at it, it is nothing but the number one repeated. It has no existence of its own. It has *māhiyyah* (quiddity)—it has characteristics. Let us say, 81 is divisible into 9, but 82 is not divisible into 9; yet, it is divisible into 2, and so forth and so on. But its *wujūd*, its reality, is nothing but the number one. So, what he wants to say is that he saw the world was contingent and everything in the world nothing but the Divine Reality manifesting itself, just as all numbers are but the number one repeated.

جهان خلق و امر از یک نفس شد
که هم آن دم که آمد باز پس شد

> The world of creation and Divine Command became of the same breath,
> For the very moment that it would come, it would return again.

These verses are so amazing because they synthesize pages and pages of philosophical and metaphysical explanation. "The world of creation and Divine Command became of the same breath." *Nafas* here means moment, pointing to the eternal Now. *Nafas* means literally breath, but it also alludes to a single moment.

Jahān (world) means the same thing as *'ālam*, and so the verse asserts that *'ālam al-khalq wa'l-amr*, the world of creation and Command, that is, the Divine Command mentioned in the Quran (Q. 7:54), became a single moment, a single breath, a single reality. Now, first of all I want us to learn the Quranic expressions *khalq* and *amr*. *Khalq* means creation, whereas *amr* means order or command, from which comes *amīr*, commander or prince, and also the name of the part of the soul that directs us to evil, *al-nafs al-ammārah*. These terms are all from the same root, not to be confused with words derived from the root *'ayn-mīm-rā*.

In Islamic cosmology and metaphysics we distinguish between *'ālam al-amr* (the world of Divine Command) and *'ālam al-khalq* (the world of creation). *'Ālam al-amr* means the spiritual and archetypal world. So, *amr* here is not just an ordinary command or order; rather it is related to the *fiat lux* that created instantaneously the principial world, and therefore means the spiritual and archetypal world. Why *amr*? Because by the Command (*amr*) of God, *yaqūla lahu 'Kun!' fa-yakūn*, "(God) said to it *Kun!* (the command form of 'Be!') and it was" (Q. 36:82), everything came into existence. And the metaphysicians say it is the root reality of things that preexist in God's Knowledge that came into existence. The world of compounds then came through the actualization of that original creation, not that every tree in the garden out there came into existence when God said "*Kun!*" God brought the *'ālam al-amr* into being, the *'ālam* that is the principle of *'ālam al-khalq*. Therefore, Shabistarī makes this distinction.

So, *'ālam al-amr*, is the world of the principial reality of creation and by extension *jabarūt*, the first thing created by God, the highest level of reality below God. And *khalq* means this world of creation in which we live. In a sense, *amr* is also *makhlūq* (created), of course, because everything is created except God. From another point of view, *khalq* itself is also from the Divine Command. If God had not commanded, this tree would not have grown in the garden. Nonetheless, this metaphysical distinction, *'ālam al-amr* and *'ālam al-khalq*, is very important. Sometimes the *'ālam al-amr* is identified with the intelligible world, the *ma'qūlāt* (intelligible realities), and the *'ālam al-khalq* with the *maḥsūsāt* (the sensible realities). All kinds of coordinations and correlations have been associated with these key terms.

In one moment, that world and this world became the same. The world of creation and the Divine world, the spiritual world became the same, that is, their oneness was realized.

As for the verse, "For the very moment that it would come, it would return again," to understand it first of all we have to realize its symbolism. We breathe in and out: one breath in; one breath out. This rhythmic action is itself symbolic of the creative Act of God. The Sufis consider the real substance of this world to be *nafas al-Raḥmān*, "the Breath of the Compassionate." We think that the world is just standing out there, like the trees in the garden, while we are reading this book. But at every moment, the world is breathed in and breathed out again. At every moment, the world returns to God. This is called *tajdīd al-khalq fī kulli 'l-ānāt* in Arabic, "the renewal of creation at every moment." Anyone reading this book is the same person now as ten minutes ago. But that is not the whole truth. Rather, at every moment he goes back to God and comes back, except that it occurs so quickly that he does not realize it. This is the very famous doctrine of *tajdīd al-khalq fī kulli 'l-ānāt*.[5]

So, from one point of view, God created the world so many eons ago, and various creatures have existed in it during the long period of its history. From another point of view, God is creating and re-creating the world every minute right now. The world is new at every moment. And that is also the secret of the efficacy of *dhikr* (the remembrance of God). The reason the *dhikr* is efficacious is that at every moment we renew our whole existence with it, returning to God with every breath. And this is a replica of creation itself. In a sense you might say, in the deepest sense, that the Universe is the *dhikr* of God, *dhikr Allāh*. And the essence of the breath of that *dhikr* is *nafas al-Raḥmān*. Every moment the Universe returns to God and comes back. There is also a *barakah* (blessing) in this doctrine that is not usually discernable. Five minutes from now you could be in another *ḥāl*, in another state of mind. You could be happy or sad. You do not know now. These *aḥwāl* come and go. In the deepest spiritual sense, this is because we return to God at every moment without full awareness, but it is for us to be aware of this reality.

This verse can be interpreted to be a reference to *nafas al-Raḥmān* and the two phases of "cosmic breathing," like our own breathing, which comes in and out, in and out, expansion and contraction. Every moment, God "breathes in" the whole world, and we return to God, and then He breathes us out. But it is so rapid that we do not see it and are only aware of our temporal continuity.

This is another kind of cosmology that we have in Islam, different from the ordinary kind that we have in Ibn Sīnā or others. There you have the world out there; you explain the various levels of reality, the stars, the heavens, the *falak al-aflāk* (the outermost cosmic sphere), the *thawābit* (the sphere of the fixed stars), and so on and so forth. But what we are talking about here is a kind of mystical cosmology, which binds the origin of the Universe to God, not only at the temporal origin of creation but at every moment. That is the significance of it. From one point of view, the world is old—we are near the end of time. From another point of view, the world is always renewed and fresh, just as every morning when you awaken it is a new day. You feel fresh physically and rejuvinated. One morning you might have a headache or something like that, but usually you feel as if a new cycle has begun in your everyday life. All of these cycles that we have in life go back to the fundamental cycle of the *qabḍ* (contraction) and *basṭ* (expansion) of the whole Universe, through the Divine Breath. It is to this reality that Shabistarī is alluding.

ولی آن جایگه آمد شدن نیست
شدن چون بنگری جز آمدن نیست

But in that place, where there is no coming and going,
Going, if you look closely, is nothing but coming.

"But in that place, where these is no coming and going," means in the Divine Reality, in that place where there is Pure Being and no coming or going. "Going, if you look closely, is nothing but coming," means that from the Divine point of view there is not even coming and going which belong to the cosmic or manifested order and determine the rhythm of cosmic existence.

به اصل خویش راجع گشت اشیا
همه یک چیز شد پنهان و پیدا

All things returned to their Principle.

All things became one reality, both hidden and manifest.

What a lesson for all of us to learn. *Yarji'u kullu shay'in ilā aṣlih*, is an Arabic proverb: "All things return to their principle." This verse is the Persian version of the same dictum. Everything goes back to its roots, to its source. *Aṣl* in Arabic means root—the root of a tree—but it also means principle and ultimately the Principle.

"All things became one reality." At the highest level of realization one sees that all reality becomes one Reality. That is the realization of *tawḥīd*, when one returns to one's Principle, when one returns to one's *aṣl*.

"Both hidden and manifest" (*pinhān-u paydā*) means the inward and the outward, the hidden and the manifest, are all the same reality when one realizes *tawḥīd* at the highest level.

تعالی الله قدیمی کو به یک دم
کند آغاز و انجام دو عالم

Allah, the Transcendent, the Eternal, Who in one breath,
Determines the beginning and end of both worlds.

The Transcendent Supreme Principle, who is also the Eternal, manifests the whole of existence, both this world and the next and in fact all the worlds, all the levels of reality, and determines them, and all in a single breath or moment (*dam*) that is beyond time. All transformations in time are determined by the Reality that is beyond becoming, and becoming is nothing but the unfolding of what God has created in that single breath or moment.

جهان خلق و امر آنجا یکی شد
یکی بسیار و بسیار اندکی شد

There, the world of creation (*khalq*) and of Divine Command
(*amr*) became the same,
The One (*yik*) became many (*bisyār*), and the many became small.

These verses contain the whole mystery of creation. Shabistarī says that in the Divine Reality, "the world of creation and Divine Command (this world and the principial order) became the same," became one, and metaphysically it is now as it was.

"There, the world of creation and of Divine Command became the same." The One became "many, and the many became small" means that in the Divine Presence, these two worlds are one. There is a play between unity and multiplicity. Multiplicity flows out of Unity and goes back to Unity. *Yik* means one in Persian, *bisyār* means many, and *andak* means little, which indicates that the One becomes many, and the many became One again, *andak* being used from the point of view of the worldly seen in relation to the One. There is the cycle of the generation of the many from the One, and the return of the many to the One.

همه از وهم توست این صورت غیر
که نقطه دایره است از سرعت سیر

It is all from thy apprehension, this form of otherness,
For the point becomes the circle because of the speed of its movement.

The symbolism of the line, "For the point becomes the circle, because of the speed of its movement" is difficult for some Western students to visualize and understand, as it is even for most modernized Persians. When we were children, however, there was something called *ātash-gardān*. If you wanted to operate and use a samovar or a water pipe, you would put a few pieces of coal in a little metallic container that had a handle on it. You would light one of the pieces of the coal and take the handle and swing it in a circle. Because of the speed, the coal would not fall, and gradually all of the coal would begin to glow, tracing an illuminated circle in the air. When I was teaching at Tehran University, I used to be able to give that example, but now many people have not seen such a thing. In any case, if you take a light, attach it to a string, and start making it go around very fast, it will trace a circle. It is to this phenomenon that Shabistarī is referring. This seems to be far-fetched for us, but for those living in Tabriz in the eighth century AH, it was very common to observe the *ātash-gardān*. In any case, it is a beautiful and powerful image.

As for the first line, "It is all from thy apprehension (*wahm*), this form of otherness," *wahm* is a technical, philosophical and mystical term, which can also refer to imagination, but here it means apprehension. This is one of the faculties of the soul in Avicennan faculty psychology, and it is used also by the Sufis as well as Islamic philosophers but with a somewhat different meaning. According to Ibn Sīnā, it is one of the five internal senses. In Sufism, *wahm* is used in a more general sense, as it is used also in everyday Persian and Arabic, indicating something unreal. For example, you say *mawhūm* in Arabic, something based on *wahm*, meaning something that is not true, that is not real, but nevertheless appears to be so.

"This form of otherness" refers to multiplicity. Everything you consider to be "other than" or "otherness" is from your *wahm*, your apprehension. So, he says, all otherness—*hamah* "all" here means everything other than God; the *hamah* goes back to *ṣūrat-i ghayr*, that is, "all the form of otherness"—all the things that are other than the Divine Principle, come from thy apprehension, this power of *wahm*, and are therefore ultimately unreal. It is just like a single point; once it moves fast in a circular fashion, we apprehend it through our *wahm* to be a circle. We see it as a circle, but it is really a single point.

یکی خطّ است از اوّل تا به آخر
بر او خلق جهان گشته مسافر

There is a single line, from Origin to End,
On which all creatures of the world are journeying.

These outwardly simple but inwardly very rich and beautiful verses involve the symbol and the image of the spiritual journey, the ultimate human journey, and also the cosmic journey, for everything is journeying toward God.

The road from the very beginning to the end is like a single line. *Huwa'l-Awwal wa'l-Ākhir*, "He is the First and the Last," as the Quran says (Q. 57:3). There is "a single line" upon which all beings are journeying, from the ant and the mollusk in the sea, to philosophers and angels. Everyone is journeying in a line from God to God.

And now Shabistarī turns to prophecy, which makes the journey possible for man and guides him on it.

در این ره انبیا چون سارباناند
دلیل و رهنمای کاروانند

On this path, the prophets are like leaders of the caravan;
They are the guides and the directors of the caravan.

The leader of the caravan, or *sāribān*, is the person who leads the first camel in the caravan and the rest of the caravan follows. So, he compares the life of man—and, more generally, the whole journey of creation—to a caravan moving in the desert. And among all those who are moving in the desert of existence, the prophets are those who guide the caravan. Without prophecy the caravan could not reach its destination safely.

وز ایشان سیّد ما گشته سالار
هم او اوّل هم او آخر در این کار

Among them our Sayyid has become the Patriarch (*sālār*),
He is both the beginning and the end of this endeavor.

These lines refer to the inner reality of the Prophet of Islam to which the Sufis refer as the Muḥammadan Reality (*al-ḥaqīqah al-muḥammadiyyah*), a reality that is manifested in all the prophets culminating in the last Prophet, that is, Muḥammad. "Our Sayyid" is the Prophet—*alayhi 'l-ṣalātu wa'l-salām*—and *sālār* means patriarch, the head.

What is he saying here in these cryptic verses? Of course, what Shabistarī is saying is that prophecy associated with the Prophetic Reality or the Muḥammadan Light (*al-nūr al-muḥammadī*), begins its function in the temporal order with Adam, and manifests itself fully in the Prophet of Islam. This is one of the most famous verses in Persian poetry. The Muḥammadan Reality is both the first and the last in the matter of guidance of creation toward its Ultimate Source.

احد در میم احمد گشته ظاهر
در این دور اوّل آمد عین آخر

Aḥad, the One, became manifest in the M of Aḥmad.
In this circle, what came first was exactly the same as what came last.

This is a very esoteric verse. First of all, *Aḥad*, the One, is a Divine Name, *qul huwa'Llāhu Aḥad*, "Say, He, God, is One" (Q. 112:1). It is a Name of the *Dhāt* (*ism al-Dhāt*), the Divine Essence, not a Name of Attributes (*ism al-ṣifāt*), nor a Name of Actions (*ism al-af'āl*). Being an *ism al-Dhāt*, it points to the very Essence of God.

"Aḥmad" is the esoteric name of the Prophet Muḥammad, *ṣallā'Llāhu 'alayhi wa sallam*. It comes from the same root as "Muḥammad," *ḥā'-mīm-dāl*, but is another form of it. In Sufism it is associated particularly with the inner reality of the Prophet. Now, when you write *Aḥad* in Arabic, all you have to do is add the letter *mīm* in the middle and it becomes Aḥmad, as in English. So, between Aḥmad and *Aḥad*, there is only the difference of one *mīm*. The numerical value of *mīm* in the science of the numerical symbolism of letters or *jafr* is forty, which is also the age of the Prophet when he was chosen as prophet. It is also the first letter of *mawt* or "death" and symbolizes the point of return to God in human life as is also mentioned by Dante in the *Divine Comedy*. And so, the One becomes manifest in the m of Aḥmad.

The verse, "In the circle, what came first was exactly the same as what came last," refers to the Muhammadan Reality (*al-ḥaqīqah al-muḥammadiyyah*). To summarize, according to Sufism, all prophets beginning with Adam carry the Muḥammadan Light (*al-nūr al-muḥammadī*) and the Muḥammadan Reality (*al-ḥaqīqah al-muḥammadiyyah*), which is the first reality that God created, within themselves. This reality is also the Logos in the Islamic context. This issue is one of the most complicated matters when discussed in the context of religions in general—what about Christ being the Logos and so forth—but I am not going to go into that issue now. In Islamic metaphysics the first being that God created is the Muḥammadan Reality (*al-ḥaqīqah al-muḥammadiyyah*). The various *ḥadīths* such as *awwalu mā khalaqa'Llāh nūrī* (The first reality that God created was my Light), *awwalu mā khalaqa'Llāh al-'aql* (The first reality that God created was the Intellect), *awwalu mā khalaqa'Llāh al-kalimah* (The first reality that God created was the Word), all refer to the same Muḥammadan Reality. And so, the prophetic function begins with God's creation in a sense, and it manifests itself in the beginning with Adam, the first prophet, and comes at the end of the prophetic cycle with the Prophet of Islam. This includes all of the 124,000 prophets, covering the whole cycle of history.

ز احمد تا احد یک میم فرق است
جهانی اندر آن یک میم غرق است

Between *Aḥmad* and *Aḥad* (the One) there is only the difference of an M.
The Universe is drowned in that one M.

The reality of the whole Universe is rooted in that M which refers at once to the Muḥammadan Reality and also alludes to the point of return to God.

بر او ختم آمده پایان این راه
در او منزل شده ادعوا الی الله

With him the end of this path has been reached;
And to him has been revealed, "call upon God" (*ud'ū ilā'Llāh*).

With him, that is, with the Prophet of Islam, this path has come to its end, namely the path of prophecy and so, he is called in Islam *khātam al-anbiyā'*, the "Seal of Prophets."

"To him has been revealed, 'call upon God,'" *ud'ū ilā'Llāh*. That call is at the heart of the function of the Prophet, to call upon God. As the Quran asserts so eloquently and intimately, *Idhā sa'alaka 'ibādī 'annī fa-innī qarībun, ujību da'wat al-dā'ī idhā da'āni*, that is, "When My servants ask thee about Me, truly I am near. I answer the call of the caller when he calls Me" (Q. 2:186). "Call upon God," that is what the prophets brought us as their central message. So, Shabistarī quotes the above verse of the Quran.

مقام دلگشایش جمع جمع است
جمال جانفزایش شمع جمع است

His heart-pleasing station (*maqām-i dilgushā*) is the synthesis of all syntheses (*jam'-i jam'*).
His life giving beauty is the candle of every assembly (*sham'-i jam'*).

The cadence of this verse and its music is very difficult to translate. *Dilgushā* is something that expands the heart. So, *maqām-i dilgushā* is translated as "his heart-pleasing station." In the first hemistich, *jam'* means synthesis: *jam'-i jam'*, "the synthesis of all syntheses." It refers to a reality that contains everything. The word *jam'*, however, also means assembly or gathering, which is the meaning in the second hemistich. In the old days there was of course no electricity, so one would light a candle that would be put in the middle of an assembly, thus becoming the heart of an assembly.

شده او پیش و جانها جمله در پی
گرفته دست جانها دامن وی

He is at the forefront, and all souls are following him,
The hand of the souls have grasped his skirt.

This verse is a reference to the Prophet. "The hand of the souls" refers to the hands of men and women. "Skirt" is used since the Prophet wore a long robe, a *thawb*, so that he had a skirt. This is not a woman's skirt, as one would think of the word in English. It means the long traditional Arab male dress. "In Arabic and Persian "to hold on to someone's skirt" means to ask for help. I am sure you have seen in plays, when some poor person comes and grasps somebody's robe and asks for help. This is the image Shabistarī is depicting. All Muslims seek to grasp his skirt for help.

در این ره اولیا باز از پس و پیش
نشانی داده‌اند از منزل خویش

On this path the friends [of God] (*awliyā'*), standing before and after,
Each gives an indication of his own spiritual station (*manzil-i khwīsh*).

This is a very significant verse and is the key to understanding why there are different perspectives in Sufism. Each friend of God or each saint describe the spiritual mountain from the point where he is located and the vision he has of the mountain. Therefore, "On this path the friends [of God], standing before and after, each gives an indication of his own spiritual station," means that each saint speaks from where he is. Now, as for the word station: it is the translation of the word *manzil* here. Though I would usually use the word "station" to translate *maqām*, here I am also using it to translate *manzil*, which of course, means the place of descent. We also use this term in such expressions as *asbāb al-nuzūl* (the causes or occasions of the descent of the revelation) in Arabic. It comes from the verb *nazala*, *yanzilu*, and *manzil* is the *ism maḥall*, the place name of the verb *nazala*. *Manzil* also means house in Arabic, but it also refers to where the caravan rests for the night, that is, the place of *sukūn*, of stay, of rest. When we used to have caravans, wherever they stopped, it was called a *manzil-gāh*, in Persian. So, here, using the term spiritually, *manzil* means *maqām* in the technical Sufi sense.

Az manzil-i khwīsh, "of his own spiritual station," that is, where they stood before God because not all saints are in the same station, and not all of them have the same perspective. That is why there are different perspectives, even among the *awliyā'*.

به حدّ خویش چون گشتند واقف
سخن گفتند در معروف و عارف

When they became aware of their own limits,
They began to speak of that which is known and he who knows.

"Of their own limits" means of their station and where they are standing on the spiritual path. From there, each began to speak from the point of view of where he was, the worldview(not only *Weltanschauung* but also *Gottanschauung*) that he had.

یکی از بحر وحدت گفت انا الحقّ
یکی از قرب و بعد سیر زورق

One from the ocean of unity said "I am the Truth."
Another spoke of the nearness and distance of the journey of the ship.

"I am the Truth" is of course a reference to the famous saying of Ḥallāj. "The ship" refers to the spiritual vessel that takes us to the other world.

یکی‌را علم ظاهر بود حاصل
نشانی داد از خشکی ساحل

One had attained knowledge of the outward (*'ilm-i ẓāhir*),
And gave indication of where the coastline was.

"Knowledge of the outward" (*'ilm-i ẓāhir*), could also be translated as exoteric knowledge. "Of where the coastline was" refers, of course, to where dry land was to be found, because he was still at sea looking for a place to land.

یکی گوهر برآورد و هدف شد
یکی بگذاشت آن نزد صدف شد

One brought out precious jewels (*guhar*) and [it] became its aim.
Another left it there, so it turned into a pearl.

One Sufi, one sage, "brought out...," which means implicitly "out of the sea of Unity." *Guhar* means jewel, something precious. For those of you studying philosophy, you should know that this word is Persian but has also entered into Arabic and became the word *jawhar*. In its Arabic form, it means "substance" in Islamic philosophy. But the meaning of "precious jewel" still exists in the Arabic term *jawāhir*. In Persian, the original form, without the *gāf* becoming *jīm* as in Arabic, that is, *gawhar*, has been preserved, and so has *jawhar*. So, if you are studying Ibn Sīnā, you will hear about *jawhar* and *'araḍ* (substance and accident). But *guhar* (more correctly *gawhar*) here means jewel, as something precious, not the Avicennan meaning of the term. Anything precious in Persian can be called *guhar*, even a wonderful person or a precious scholar. We might then translate it as "treasure" or something like that.

یکی در جزو و کلّ گفت این سخن باز
یکی کرد از قدیم و محدث آغاز

> One person spoke about the particular and the universal.
> Another began to talk about the eternal and the created.

This verse shows that Shaykh Maḥmūd Shabistarī knew a lot about Islamic philosophy since there are all of these philosophical references here. "The particular" and "the universal" are philosophical terms.

"The eternal and the created": the word *qadīm*, means old in ordinary Arabic, and is related to *qidmah*, "coming before" and so forth. But in philosophy it means eternal, without temporal origin, whereas *muḥdath* means having temporal origination. There is a major debate in Islamic philosophy as to whether the world is *qadīm* or *muḥdath*, and the verse is referring to that discourse. So, people began to debate whether the world is created or not created.

But while someone was speaking about particular and universal, a Sufi uses a completely different set of symbols:

یکی از زلف و خال و خط بیان کرد
شراب و شمع و شاهدرا عیان کرد

> Another began to speak about the hair, the mole, and the line of her face,
> Explaining the meaning of wine, the candle, and the witness (*shāhid*).

Now, there is one word here in particular that needs explanation. *Sharāb* means "wine," from *shurb* (drinking) in Arabic. *Sham'* means "candle." But what does the word *shāhid* mean?

The word *shāhid* means "witness." But in Sufism, this term is very much debated, and I want to make its significance clear for you because a lot of orientalists have written all kinds of inappropriate things about this term. *Shāhid-bāzī* was considered by some to be a sort of "play with young boys," or even pedophilia, and some people accused the Sufis of practicing it, but this is not true in serious Sufism. In the old days women were often not present in Sufi gatherings. So, some orders would bring handsome young boys to serve in the *majālis* (gatherings) to try to test the dervishes and teach them to control themselves, as a test of their *nafs*. I once asked this question of my great teacher Sayyid Muḥammad Kāẓim 'Aṣṣār concerning this very verse, and he said the same thing. He said that this was a kind of test for the *fuqarā'*, because, as I said, they could not invite the young women or something like that because of social conditions. This is what *shāhid,* which appears so often in Ḥāfiẓ and in classical Persian poetry in general (and also in Arabic Sufi poetry), means. It also means to witness, but in Sufi poetry it is not an ordinary witness. This verse in fact alludes to explains what is meant by *shāhid* in a Sufi context.

یکی از هستی خود گفت و پندار
یکی مستغرق بت گشت و زنّار

> One spoke of his own existence and thought.
> Another became drowned in the idol and the belt.

Again, Shabistarī refers to different states and stations from the perspective of which the sages have spoken. In the second stage he goes beyond the Islamic perspective to refer to "idol worship," the deeper meaning of which he explains later in the text, and also to Christianity.

سخن‌ها چون به وفق منزل افتاد
در افهام خلائق مشکل افتاد

> Since words [were uttered] in accordance with the stations [from which they were uttered],
> Difficulty began to arise in the understanding by creatures.

He explains why there is this difference in perspectives and explanations, and why ordinary people think that there is contradiction in them. There is no contradiction; the differences come from differences of perspective.

Afhām is the plural of *fahm* or "understanding." *Khalā'iq*, means "creatures," or here it refers to ordinary people. *Mushkil* means "difficulty." So, "Difficulty began to arise in the understanding by creatures" because of this difference in angles of vision and perspectives.

کسی‌را کاندر این معنی است حیران
ضرورت می‌شود دانستن آن

> He who is bewildered in this matter,
> It is necessary for that person to come to know it.

He (*kas*) could also be translated as "he or she," or "person," since Persian has no gender and *kas* literally means "person." "To come to know," could be translated as "to come to understand."

I want to add a side note here. Traditionalists explain that Truth is one, but its expression and crystallization are not always the same. Although the peak of the mountain is the same, the paths that lead to it do not always describe the same landscape of the road leading to the summit. The higher you go, the more similar the landscape becomes. The symbolism of mountain climbing is, for that and other reasons, quite powerful. We are on the base of the mountain: we are, let us say, looking north toward Kashmir when we are in the Himalayas, and somebody is in the north of the mountains, looking south. We see different sceneries. But as we climb the mountain range gradually differences diminish, until at the very top, we realize that there is only one mountain peak and all these different sceneries were different perspectives of the same truth, of the same reality.

Now one of the great achievements of Shabistarī in the *Gulshan-i rāz* is to explain this matter in the verses that I laid out for you. Furthermore, the commentary on the *Gulshan-i rāz* by Lāhījī has a very cogent explanation of this matter and is one of the best explanations that we have in Islamic literature of it, that is, about why there are these different viewpoints among Sufis on different matters. The simple explanation he gives is that each Sufi is standing like a person on the slope of a mountain, exalted, but speaking from his own *manzil*, from where he is, from the depth of his own perspective about the way reality is. One says *ana'l-Ḥaqq* ("I am the Truth"), and somebody else speaks of the *sayr-i zawraq* (the journey of the ship taking us to the other world), and so on or so forth, but they are all right. Inwardly, they do not contradict each other. That is what Shabistarī is trying to bring to us in these verses.

On the Purpose of the Composition

of this Book and its History

We really do not know exactly why, but a well-known shaykh from Khurāsān sent a number of questions to Shaykh Maḥmūd Shabistarī who was from Azerbaijan, in Western Persia. The questions, therefore, traveled a long way from eastern to western Persia, over a distance of about 1000 km, but we really do not know exactly why this happened. Nevertheless, it did happen, and the *Gulshan-i rāz* is the answer to these questions. The questions are by a shaykh called Hirawī Sayyidī-yi Ḥusaynī, who was probably from Herat, but we do not know very much about him. The present work is not, however, a book on the history of Persian literature but on the philosophical and gnostic meaning of the text. I am, therefore, just mentioning this matter incidentally. What is important to note here is that the *Gulshan-i rāz* is the result of this remarkable exchange. The subject that concerns us is the metaphysics, gnosis, cosmology, and symbolism of this poem.

گذشته هفت و ده از هفتصد سال
ز هجرت ناگهان در ماه شوّال

When 717 years had passed from the *Hijrah*,
Suddenly there appeared, during the month of *Shawwāl*,

Shawwāl is one of the months of the Islamic lunar calendar.

رسولی با هزاران لطف و احسان
رسید از خدمت اهل خراسان

A messenger (*rasūl*), with a thousand kindnesses and virtues (*luṭf-u iḥsān*),
Arrived from the service (*khidmat*) of the people of Khurāsān.

Rasūl, of course, means primarily messenger, in the sense that the Prophet of Islam—*'alayhi'l-ṣalātu wa'l-salām*—is called a messenger, but in Arabic or Persian it can also mean an ordinary messenger, that is, one who brings a message. *Khidmat*, which I translate here as "service," actually implies that he was a disciple of the Khurāsānī master who formulated the questions.

بزرگی کاندر آنجا هست مشهور
به اقسام هنر چون چشمهٔ نور

A great man, who is famous there,
And in the different arts like a spring of light.

همه اهل خراسان از که و مه
در این عصر از همه گفتند او به

All the people of Khurāsān, old and young,
Said that he was the best of this age.

This verse shows that he must have been a very respected shaykh from Khurāsān and known to Shabistarī.

جهان‌را سور و جان‌را نور اعنی
امام سالکان سیّد حسینی

Nourishment (*sūr*) to the world and the light of the soul,
Imam of those who follow the spiritual path,
Sayyid Ḥusaynī.

Sūr here means nourishment more than anything else, though it can also mean banquet, but in any case the reference is to spiritual nourishment.

نبشته نامه‌ای در باب معنی
فرستاده بر ارباب معنی

He wrote a letter concerning the inner meaning of things,
And sent it to those who are masters of the
inner meaning of things.

در آنجا مشکلی چند از عبارت
ز مشکلهای اصحاب اشارت

In it [he had written] a few difficult phrases and sentences,
Among the difficulties confronted by the people of indication
(*aṣḥāb-i ishārat*).

Aṣḥāb in Arabic or Persian often refers to the companions of the Prophet, the *ṣaḥābah*, but it also means "people of" in general, as in "the people of the Cave" (*aṣḥāb-i kahf*) in the Quran, and "the people of art" (*aṣḥāb-i hunar, aṣḥāb-i ṣanāyi'*) or "the people of knowledge" (*aṣḥāb-i 'ilm*). These meanings are also related to the root meaning of the word for "speech," *ṣuḥbah*.

The term *ishārat* is very significant here. In general *ishārah* means indication, but what does it mean here? The answer is that the people who follow the spiritual path, the Sufis, are called *aṣḥāb al-ishārah*, in Arabic, and we use the same phrase in Persian. The reason for this usage is that much of the teaching of Sufism is carried out by means of *ishārah*, by indication, rather than by the direct expression and analytical exposition of something. Of course, one of the most famous books of Islamic philosophy, that is, *al-Ishārāt wa'l-tanbīhāt* of Ibn Sīnā, uses this term in its title, and he uses it for that reason: because the book is full of indications of philosophical and even in certain parts of Sufi teachings, particularly in the ninth chapter (*namaṭ*), entitled "The Stations of the Gnostics" (*maqāmāt al-'ārifīn*), which deals with *ishārah* in the spiritual sense. So, you should learn the meaning of the word *ishārah* on three levels: first the ordinary level, in Persian and Arabic, that is, to indicate something (*ishārah kard bi fulān chīz*); second, as it is used by Islamic philosophers, as indicating a concept pointing to other ideas; and third, the Sufi understanding, where just with an *ishārah* a teacher will impart an understanding of something hidden to his disciples. The *ishārah* then appeals to a reality that is already inside the persons for whom it is meant. And so *mushkil-hā-yi aṣḥāb-i ishārat* means "the difficult doctrines or teachings of the Sufis."

به نظم آورده و پرسیده یک یک
جهانی معنی اندر لفظ اندک

He put [these difficulties] into verse, and one by one he asked.
A world of meaning within a pithy expression (*lafẓ-i andak*).

رسول آن نامه‌را برخواند آنگاه

فتاد احوال آن حالی در افواه

The messenger read the letter, and then,
A spiritual state (*ḥāl*) was created among those who were present (*afwāh*).

"The messenger read the letter" before Shabistarī and his disciples. *Afwāh* means here the people present, or one could say addressed to the minds of the people present.

در آن مجلس عزیزان جمله حاضر
بدین درویش مسکین گشته ناظر

In that gathering (*majlis*), all the dear people (*'azīzān*) were present,
They looked at this poor darvish [i.e. Shabistarī himself].

'Azīz means dear, but it also means powerful. It has two opposite meanings in Arabic, and is related to the word *'izzah* (might, glory), which on the highest level belongs to God. *'Azīz* is also used sometimes as a title for a ruler or high authority, as in the case of Joseph who became the *'azīz* of Egypt for a while as mentioned in the Quran. But the word *'azīz* here does not mean powerful. It means dear people, people who were intimate, that is, the *fuqarā'*, the disciples who were present. They began to look toward Shabistarī.

یکی کو بود مرد کاردیده
ز من صد بار این معنی شنیده

One of the disciples, who was a man of experience (*kār dīdah*)
And had heard the inner meaning (*ma'nā*) from me a hundred of times,

"Inner meaning" here refers to the esoteric Sufi teachings. This is now Shabistarī himself speaking.

مرا گفتا جوابی گوی در دم
کز آنجا نفع گیرند اهل عالم

Said to me, "Provide an answer this very moment (*dar dam*),
In such a way that will benefit the people of the world (*ahl-i 'ālam*)."

بدو گفتم چه حاجت کین مسائل
نبشتم بارها اندر رسائل

I said to him, "For what purpose should I do this?
For I have written about these questions many times in my treatises."

This assertion means most likely that Shabistarī must have written several Sufi works that have been lost. There are only three extant works by him[6] (though there are other works attributed to him). But we do know that he had written texts that have been lost. Since he says here that he had written many times about these questions, that means that he most likely wrote more than three or four works.

بلی گفتا ولی بر وفق مسؤول
ز تو منظوم می‌داریم مأمول

"Yes," he said. "But in accord with having responsibility,
We hope to [receive] from thee [the answers] in poetry."

By saying "yes," the messenger confirms his mission, adding that the Sufi shaykh and his followers who sent the questions would like to have the responses in poetic form, and it is implied that Shabistarī accepted the request although he did not consider himself to be a poet.

پس از الحاح ایشان کردم آغاز
جواب نامه در الفاظ ایجاز

After [the disciples'] insistence I began,
Answering [the questions] of that letter in brief form.

به یک لحظه میان جمع احرار
بگفتم این سخن بی‌فکر و تکرار

So, in one moment, amidst the assembly of noble people (*aḥrār*),
I uttered these words, without deliberation and repetition.

Aḥrār comes from the Arabic word *ḥurr*, meaning free. But here *aḥrār* does not mean free men in the sense of those who are not slaves. Rather, it is a very positive term in Arabic and Persian, referring to people of spiritual quality, people who are free spiritually.

Now, Shaykh Maḥmūd Shabistarī addresses us as readers.

کنون از لطف و احسانی که دارند
ز من این خردگیها در گذارند

Now, considering the kindness and virtue (*luṭf-u iḥsān*) that they have,
I hope they will not be critical (*khurdagīhā dar gudhārand*) of me.

Iḥsān can also mean kindness, generosity and beauty, but here I have translated it as virtue, which is also one of its primary meanings. *Khurdagī* here means criticism in Persian, and *khurdah giriftan* means literally to hold into little pieces, but here it means definitely to criticize.

همه دانند کین کس در همه عمر
نکرده هیچ قصد گفتن شعر

Everyone knows that this person [that is, I, Shaykh Maḥmūd Shabistarī]
throughout all of my life (*'umr*),
Has never attempted to compose poetry (*shi'r*).

This verse does not rhyme very well because *'umr*, which means life, and *shi'r*, meaning poetry, do not rhyme; so, you have to read one of these terms with an irregular pronunciation. This type of structure happens sometimes in both Arabic and Persian poetry.

بر آن طبعم اگر چه بود قادر
ولی گفتن نبود الا به نادر

Although my nature (*ṭab'*) had the power,
Only very rarely did I compose a poem.

Ṭab' means nature but can also be used in relation to the gift for poetry so that it can also mean having the nature of composing poetry, as we say in Persian *ṭab'-i shi'r dāshtan*, that is, having a poetical gift or poetic nature.

ز نثر ارچه کتب بسیار می‌ساخت
به نظم مثنوی هرگز نپرداخت

Although many books were written [by me, that is, by Shabistarī], in prose,
I never turned to the composition of rhyming couplets (*mathnawī*).

This verse indicates again that he must have written many prose works before writing the *Gulshan-i rāz*. "I never turned" is expressed in the third person in the Persian text, but of course he is referring to himself.

The word *mathnawī*, which is well known in English because of the famous book of Jalāl al-Dīn Rūmī with this title, is actually a form of poetry in Persian, Arabic, and some other Islamic languages such as Turkish. It means rhyming couplets, from *thanā* meaning two. This form developed gradually in Khurāsān, after the ninth/tenth century, and culminated with Sanā'ī and 'Aṭṭār, and of course after them by Mawlānā Jalāl al-Dīn Rūmī, who composed the six-volume *Mathnawī-i ma'nawī*, which is so famous that it came to be known as *The Mathnawī*. So, when we say in Persian *Mathnawī*, it usually refers to that work. Many Persians do not even know that *mathnawī* is a general poetic form and not just the famous work by Rūmī. We have, however, many *mathnawī*s. *The Conference of the Birds* (*Manṭiq al-ṭayr*) of 'Aṭṭār, another great Sufi masterpiece, is in *mathnawī* form, as is the *Gulshan-i rāz*. It is the *mathnawī* form to which Shabistarī is referring here and not a work such as Rūmī's *Mahnawī*.

عروض و قافیه معنی نسنجد
به هر ظرفی درون معنی نگنجد

Rhyme (*qāfiyah*) and rhythm (*'arūḍ*) cannot contain spiritual meaning.
Not every container is able to contain spiritual meaning.

Qāfiyah means the rhyme of verses of poetry, and *'arūḍ* means the meters. But *'arūḍ* and *qāfiyah* together mean the science of prosody, including both rhyme and rhythm.

Now, the word "meaning" (*ma'nā*) is not confined just to the ordinary sense of the term. It connotes in the deeper sense "inner meaning." Ananda Coomaraswamy once said that "God is meaning," which is a remarkably profound statement if one understands the profound sense of the term "meaning."[7] It is this sense of inner meaning that Shabistarī intended, not just the external meaning of a word written on a traffic sign or something like that. So, throughout this work, *ma'nā* means "the inner meaning," "the inner reality of something."

معانی هرگز اندر حرف ناید
که بحر قلزم اندر ظرف ناید

Meanings can never fit into words,
For one cannot pour the Red Sea (*baḥr-i qulzum*) into a container.

This verse might appear enigmatic because words can convey inner meaning. Otherwise, there would be no *Gulshan-i rāz*. What Shabistarī means is that words understood in their ordinary sense cannot exhaust their inner meaning.

چو من از حرف خود در تنگنایم
چرا چیزی دگر بر وی فزایم

When I myself am already tired of my own words,
Why should I add anything to them?

Again, Shabistarī is seeking to express humility in writing this work.

نه فخر است این سخن کز باب شکر است
به نزد اهل دل تمهید عذر است

This word is not through bragging (*fakhr*), but it is to be grateful [to God].
Among the people of the heart, it is the way of making an apology.

Fakhr means pride but also refinement in Arabic and Persian, and can have a very positive meaning, but it can also mean pride in the negative sense. Here *fakhr* means bragging or showing off and so forth. So, he is saying that this work is not meant to show off, but to be grateful to God (*az bāb-i shukr ast*). And among the people of the heart, that is, everybody who will be able to understand this work, it is a way of making an apology.

مرا از شاعری خود عار ناید
که در صد قرن چون عطّار ناید

I am not embarrassed to be called a poet,
But in a hundred centuries, there does not come the like of 'Aṭṭār.

This line is one of the most famous verses of the Persian language. Both Shabistarī and Rūmī paid the supreme homage to Farīd al-Dīn 'Aṭṭār as the greatest poet before them.

Rūmī is reported to have said:

'Aṭṭār traversed the seven cities of love.
We are still stuck on the turn of the first street.[8]

This verse of Shabistarī has very much the same purport as the quoted verse of Rūmī. Some versions of the text have "a hundred years" (*ṣad sāl*) instead of "a hundred centuries" (*ṣad qarn*).

The word *'aṭṭār* means actually perfumer or pharmacist. But it is of course also the proper name of one of the greatest poets of Sufism, Farīd al-Dīn 'Aṭṭār, who lived during the Mongol invasion in Nayshapur, and whose tomb is found outside of that city. Though the Mongols destroyed everything in Nayshapur, fortunately his tomb is outside the city and it is still extant. Along with Khayyām, it is the only tomb of a poet of the pre-Mongol era that has survived in Nayshapur. There is a beautiful garden where the two tombs are located. If you ever go to Mashhad, you owe it to yourself to visit it. The tomb of 'Aṭṭār has a wonderful spiritual perfume. I spent a lot of time there in my younger days.

اگر چه زین نمط صد عالم اسرار
بود یک شمّه از دکّان عطّار

Although there is contained in this chapter (*namaṭ*) a hundred worlds of mysteries,
It is but a single sample from the store of 'Aṭṭār.

Namaṭ usually means a section or chapter of a book, but here it refers to the whole of the *Gulshan-i rāz*. In this couplet, Shabistarī is paying supreme homage to Farīd al-Dīn 'Aṭṭār while humbling himself.

ولی این بر سبیل اتّفاق است
نه چون دیو از فرشته استراق است

This [i.e. the writing of this book] is happening accidentally;
It is not like the devil trying to eavesdrop (*istirāq*) on the angel.

علی الجمله جواب نامه در دم
نبشتم یک به یک نه بیش نه کم

To summarize, instantly I began to respond to the letter.
I began to write [a response] one by one [that is, one question after another], neither more nor less.

This verse indicates clearly that the inspiration to write the work came to Shabistarī quickly and also that the text was rapidly written.

رسول آن نامه‌را بستد به اعزاز
وز آن راهی که آمد زود شد باز

The messenger took the letter respectfully,
He returned soon by the same road from which he had come.

I'zāz, here means "respectfully." "He returned by the same road from which he had come," refers to the fact that he went back directly to Khurāsān, it being understood that he would give the response to his Sufi master immediately.

دگرباره عزیزی کار فرمای
مرا گفتا بر آن چیزی بیفزای

Then again, another of those who are dear (*'azīz*), who was experienced in affairs,
Asked me to add something to it.

همان معنی که گفتی با میان آر
ز عین علم با عین عیان آر

"The inner meaning that thou expressed, bring it forth.
From the *'ayn* of knowledge (*'ilm*), bring the *'ayn* of manifestation (*'ayān*)."

Here he is using poetically the letter *'ayn*, which is the first letter of the word *'ilm* (knowledge), and also the term *'ayān* (manifest). What he means is, "Manifest outwardly the knowledge that is within thee inwardly."

نمی‌دیدم در اوقات آن مجالی
که پردازم بدو از ذوق حالی

I did not find time on that occasion (*majāl*)
To turn to it based on a spiritual taste (*dhawq*) creating [within me] a spiritual state (*ḥāl*).

This somewhat enigmatic verse implies that Shabistarī was being humble, and so stated that he did not have the inspiration to compose the text of the *Gulshan-i rāz* because he certainly did have both *dhawq* and *ḥāl* to do so.

که وصف آن به گفت و گو محال است
که صاحب حال داند کان چه حال است

For the description of that [spiritual state] is impossible.
Only a person who has a spiritual state (*ḥāl*) knows what that state is.

Only a person who has experienced *ḥāl* knows that it is only with *ḥāl* that one can compose an inspired work such as the *Gulshan-i rāz*.

ولی بر وفق قول قائل دین
نکردم رد سؤال سائل دین

Nevertheless, in accordance with the saying of the speaker of religion (*qā'il-i dīn*), [that is, the Prophet],
I did not reject a question about religion that was asked of me,

This verse implies that despite what he said in humility above, he followed the Prophetic command not to refrain from answering a religious question posed to a person if that person is able to provide the correct answer.

پی آن تا شود روشن‌تر اسرار
درآمد طوطی نطقم به گفتار

Following that [injunction], to make Divine Mysteries (*asrār*) clearer,
The parrot of my speech began to speak.

The eloquence of the poem was the result of the Divine Imperative and a gift from Heaven to Shabistarī to elucidate the Divine Mysteries.

به عون و فضل و توفیق خداوند
بگفتم جمله‌را در ساعتی چند

With the Help, Grace and Succor of God,
In a few hours I composed the whole work.

This is the clearest indication of the very short period in which the work was composed. A few hours must not be taken literally. Rather, it means a very short time.

'Awn (help), *faḍl* (grace), and *tawfīq* (succor) are all very important Arabic and Persian Sufi terms, which point to God's role in any positive human achievement.

دل از حضرت چو نام نامه درخواست
جواب آمد به دل کین گلشن ماست

When (my) heart asked God (*Ḥaḍrat*) what the name of this work should be,
The answer came, "This is Our Rose Garden (*gulshan*)."

Ḥaḍrat in Sufi metaphysics means Divine Presence, but can refer also to various levels of being. Its meaning on various levels was central to Ibn 'Arabī's doctrine and received its deepest exposition in his hands. This is a key verse since it explains the reason for the title of this book, which came from Divine Inspiration.

چو حضرت کرد نام نامه گلشن
شود زو چشم دلها جمله روشن

Since the Divine Presence (*Ḥaḍrat*) named this work *Gulshan*,
May the eye of hearts become illuminated by it.

This part of the book gives a sense of the almost miraculous conditions under which this work was composed. Many people have discussed this point, including Javad Nurbakhsh, who worked on the manuscripts and edited this text, and with whom I used to have hours of discussion and argument about it. He suggested that it was not composed in a few days, and that such a thing was impossible, but he really had no cogent line of reasoning. Why is it not possible? After all, Suhrawardī wrote *Ḥikmat al-ishrāq* (*The Philosophy of Illumination*) in forty days in prison under the sentence of death, which is almost unimaginable. We cannot even read it in depth in forty days. If they condemned us to death tomorrow morning, could we write one single line? Can you imagine the catharsis of the soul (*tajrīd*), the detachment from worldly things, of Suhrawardī to be able to do such a thing? But it did happen, and similarly for Shabistarī. I am not going to say that it is impossible to accept the traditional account of how the *Gulshan-i rāz* was composed as being true.

So, this work was composed in only a few days and yet has been read widely for seven centuries across the Persian-speaking world, which includes not only Iran and Afghanistan but also Pakistan and Muslim India. This book was as famous in Lucknow as it was in Isfahan for hundreds of years. There was a kind of miraculous eruption causing the appearance of a work of extraordinary power and beauty by someone who before this event had not composed any other book of poetry. He was not like Sa'dī or Ḥāfiẓ who composed beautiful poetry all their life, or Mawlānā for that matter, who so suddenly became a poet at midlife but continued to write sublime poetry until the end of his earthly existence.

Question [1]

نخست از فکر خویشم در تحیّر
چه چیز است آن که خوانندش تفکّر؟

First of all, I am in bewilderment concerning my thought (*fikr*).
What is it that is called *tafakkur*?

Tafakkur means both thought and meditation and is not to be identified only with ordinary thinking about everyday matters. It is important to note that this verse is somewhat enigmatic. Where does he begin? He begins with bewilderment about his own thinking, which means himself, his own consciousness. He is really asking the question, "Who am I?" like Śrī Ramana Maharshi, the great saint of India of the twentieth century.[1] The questioner does not begin by asking about God or the Prophet.

Coming back to *tafakkur*, it is one of the words that I would have preferred not to translate because it means both "thinking" and "meditation" on all levels of meaning. Here perhaps "meditation" would be a more appropriate translation, but it depends how you look at it. There is more distinction in English between the two terms, but in Arabic and Persian there is more unity between them. So, we say *tafakkur-i falsafī*, which could be "philosophical meditation" and "philosophical thinking." And so, in asking the question, "What is *tafakkur*?," he is asking a basic question: What is the process of knowing itself, implying who is the agent who knows and indirectly what is it that is known? So, we begin not with the object of knowledge but with the subject. And how does the subject of knowledge know? That is the problem with which he begins here.

Now, the next section reveals that Shaykh Maḥmūd Shabistarī knew logic and Islamic philosophy in addition to Sufism.

Answer

مرا گفتی بگو چبود تفکّر؟
کز این معنی بماندم در تحیّر

Thou hast asked me, "What is *tafakkur*?
For I have become bewildered in [understanding] its meaning."

"It" here refers to the inner meaning of the term, not its outward meaning, which could not be the cause of bewilderment. The word *taḥayyur*, which I have translated as "bewilderment" is also a very rich term in Arabic and Persian. It can have a pejorative meaning, as in "I am bewildered by what you are saying," that is, "I do not understand what you are saying." But it has also a very positive aspect, that is, to be bewildered spiritually. The Prophet prayed, *Yā rabb zidnī taḥayyuran fīk!* "O Lord, increase me in *ḥayrah*, in bewilderment, in Thee!" And the word *ḥayrah* is discussed by Ibn 'Arabī extensively in the sense used here in the *Gulshan-i rāz*. So, it is important to know that the words *ḥayrah* and *taḥayyur*, can be understood on different levels.

تفکّر رفتن از باطل سوی حقّ
به جزو اندر بدیدن کلّ مطلق

Tafakkur is going from falsehood to the truth,
To see in the particular the Absolute Universal.

This is a famous verse and has been quoted extensively by various authors. For example, in the Philosophy Department of Tehran University we often cited it in the context of teaching students the meaning of *tafakkur*, as understood metaphysically as distinct from rationally.

Here Shabistarī is expressing a metaphysical understanding of what *tafakkur* is: to go from the false to the true, or from falsehood to the truth, and to see in the particular (*juzw*), the Absolute Truth (*kull-i muṭlaq*). This verse is another one of those important syzygies: *kull wa juz'* in Arabic, "particular and universal," which is found in logic, philosophy, and other disciplines. The terms are often cited together. We also have *kullī* and *juz'ī* (also meaning "universal and particular"), but there is a difference in Islamic philosophy between *kull* and *kullī*, and *juz'* and *juz'ī* into which I shall not go now.

حکیمان کاندر این کردند تصنیف
چنین گفتند در هنگام تعریف

When philosophers (*ḥakīmān*) began to write about this,
This is how they defined it:

And now he begins to give the definition of *tafakkur* as related to earlier stages of mental activity that lead to it.

که چون حاصل شود در دل تصوّر
نخستین نام وی باشد تذکّر

When in the heart conceptualization (*taṣawwur*) comes into being,
At first its name is called *tadhakkur* (reminding).

Here he begins to define several technical Sufi and philosophical terms. *Tadhakkur* is not exactly the same as *dhikr* (invocation, remembrance) as used in Sufism, although it has the same root. Rather, *tadhakkur* means that the mind is made to remind or recall something.

وز او چون بگذری هنگام فکرت
بود نام وی اندر عرف عبرت

When, during thinking (*fikrat*), thou traversest it,
In ordinary language it is called "learning a lesson" (*'ibrat*).

When one goes through the process of thinking, one goes through the stage of *tadhakkur*, leading to *'ibrat*.

تصوّر کان بود بهر تدبّر
به نزد اهل عقل آمد تفکّر

When conceptualization is used for learning (*tadabbur*),
Among the people of intellect (*ahl-i 'aql*), it is called *tafakkur*.

Tadabbur means to learn, to gain experience or to control one's thought. *Ahl-i 'aql*, "the people of intellect" means philosophers or thinkers. So, he is defining these different stages of thought in a philosophical way in using this terminology.

ز ترتیب تصوّرهای معلوم
شود تصدیق نامفهوم مفهوم

Through the order of known concepts,

> The affirmation (*taṣdīq*) of that which is incomprehensible becomes comprehensible.

In logic we have *taṣawwur* and *taṣdīq*, or concept and judgment. *Taṣdīq* means both affirmation and judgment. In our thought process we go from concept to judgment. We first of all conceive ideas of things and then we make a judgement about them, that is, we gain knowledge of certain concepts in our mind and with the help of them then go from something we do know to knowledge of something that we did not know, and we do so through the process of judgment of those concepts.

مقدّم چون پدر تالی چو مادر
نتیجه هست فرزند، ای برادر

> The first premise is like the father, the second premise like the mother,
> And the result, o brother, is like the child.

Here Shabistarī is referring to the classical Aristotelian syllogism. In a syllogism, we have the major premise and the minor premise, and then we have the result or conclusion. For example, if you say, "All trees are green," this is the major premise. "This is a tree" is the minor premise. "Therefore, this tree is green," is the result. This is a very simple Aristotelian syllogism (*qiyās*), which we use all the time without usually calling it "syllogism."

ولی ترتیب مذکور از چه و چون
بود محتاج استعمال قانون

> But the order given above, concerning how to do it,
> Is in need of the use of law (*qānūn*),

Qānūn (law), which is the Arabization of the word "canon," is originally of Greek origin which entered into Arabic and other Islamic languages. It is, however, to be distinguished from *shar'*, which means Divine Law, while *qānūn* means law in the general sense. Here, the verse means that you have to use the law of logic.

دگرباره در آن گر نیست تأیید
هر آیینه که باشد محض تقلید

> But if there is no [intellectual] affirmation in it,
> It will be simply pure imitation.

In the perspective of Shabistarī even in the rational or syllogistic manner of thinking, the intellectual element, as distinct from the rational, is necessary. Otherwise, the result would be mere imitation.

رهی دور و دراز است آن رها کن
چو موسی یک زمان ترک عصا کن

> This is a long path, let it go.
> Like Moses cast away thy staff.

Having devoted several verses to the syllogistic method of knowing, the author suddenly advises the reader to leave that manner of thinking, throwing it away as Moses cast away his staff according to the Quran.[2]

درآ در وادی ایمن زمانی

شنو «انّی انا الله» بی‌گمانی

Come to the Valley of the Right for one moment.
Hear without any ambiguity, "Verily, I am God." (Q. 28:30).

This is a reference to the Quranic saying where it is mentioned that Moses heard from the right side of the sacred valley the Voice of God. The Valley of the Right (*wādī-yi ayman*) was where Moses went, the sacred valley of Ṭuwā.

محقّق‌را که وحدت در شهود است
نخستین نظره بر نور وجود است

The verifier (*muḥaqqiq*) who is on the path of vision (*shuhūd*),
The first thing he sees is the light of Being.

Muḥaqqiq, literally "verifier," means here a person who is very advanced in Sufi knowledge, from the word *taḥqīq* (verification), which Ibn ʻArabī often uses. For Ibn ʻArabī, the *muḥaqqiqūn* comprise the highest class of Sufis.[3] In this verse Shabistarī is using the term in its Ibn ʻArabian sense. So, the advanced Sufi does not see things and then is led by them to the light of Being; rather, he first sees the light of Being.

دلی کز معرفت نور و صفا دید
ز هر چیزی که دید اول خدا دید

A heart that has been filled through knowledge (*ma'rifat*) by light and purity,
In whatever it sees, it first sees God.

The ordinary believer is often led to God through the reflection of His Names and Qualities in created beings, but the purified heart sees God first and then His Names and Qualities and their reflections in creatures.

بود فکر نکورا شرط تجرید
پس آنگه لمعه‌ای از نور تأیید

The required condition of good thought (*fikr*) is catharsis (*tajrīd*),
And then a spark of Divine Affirmation (*ta'yīd*).

Fikr, again, means meditation or thought. *Tajrīd,* "catharsis," means disentanglement from potentiality, materiality, and imperfection. Moreover, man can do nothing without *ta'yīd*, a Quranic term meaning the Help of God, the Affirmation of God. Reaching the Truth must have ultimately God's *ta'yīd.*

هر آنکس‌را که ایزد راه ننمود
ز استعمال منطق هیچ نگشود

Whoever has not been guided by God,
No door will open for him through the use of logic.

To reach the Truth, reason and logic are not sufficient. Divine Affirmation is necessary to open the door. This verse should be inscribed on the doorway of every university these days. Can you imagine the import of this verse? It means the total rejection of all secular and rationalistic philosophy.

حکیم فلسفی چون هست حیران
نمی‌بیند ز اشیا جز که امکان

The philosophical *ḥakīm*, because he is bewildered,
Does not see anything in things except contingency.

He is referring here mainly to the Peripetetics, not the *Ishrāqīs* (the Illuminationist philosophers). The term *imkān* (contingency), which is paired with *wujūb* (necessity), is an Avicennan concept. What Shabistarī is indicating is that by limiting oneself to rational philosophy, one becomes unable to see the Divine Presence in the created order. He does not deny that *ashyā'* or things are contingent if considered only in their quiddity.

از امکان می‌کند اثبات واجب
از این حیران شد اندر ذات واجب

He tries to prove the Necessary through the contingent,
For this reason, he is bewildered when it comes to the Essence of the Necessary.

This verse means that the Peripatetic philosopher tries to prove God through the world. One should note here that Shabistarī does accept the philosophical term *wājib* (the Necessary) which came to be used widely in Islamic discourse for God.

گهی از دور دارد سیر معکوس
گهی اندر تسلسل گشت محبوس

Sometimes, through a vicious circle (*dawr*) he travels in reverse.
Sometimes, he gets imprisoned in a series *ad infinitum* (*tasalsul*).

Dawr used as a technical philosophical term means a vicious circle, *circulus vitiosus* in Latin, that is, B is proven through A and then A is proven through B. Here, allusion is made to the Peripatetic use of this term in the pejorative sense of going in circles, "circle" being the literal meaning of *dawr*. If you prove A by B, then you cannot prove B itself on the basis of A alone. You have to have a C in order to do so.

Tasalsul, means infinite regress, that is, A is proven by B, B by C, C by D, and so on, without there being an end to this chain. *Dawr* and *tasalsul* are both rejected as means of proof in Islamic philosophy, as also in Latin texts and traditional Western philosophy. For example, St. Thomas Aquinas has a long discussion in his rejection of both of these methods.

چو عقلش کرد در هستی توغّل
فرو پیچید پایش در تسلسل

Since his reason became enmeshed in [the question of] being,
His legs became tied in the series *ad infinitum*.

The verse thereby criticizes the manner in which reliance on reason alone in seeking knowledge of Being leads to the impasse of infinite regress.

ظهور جملهٔ اشیا به ضدّ است
ولی حقّ‌را نه مانند و نه ندّ است

The appearance of all things is through their opposite,
But the Divine Truth has no like and no opposite.

This verse is again one of the most remarkable metaphysical verses of any literary work that I have seen. It contains the basic principle of manifestation and its contrast to the Principle. Let us consider the quality "tall." How do you know something is tall? Vis-à-vis what is short. Big is known vis-à-vis small, black vis-à-vis white, light vis-à-vis darkness. We know everything in this world through its opposite. That is how things appear: hence, "The appearance of all things is through their opposite." Your shirt has checkered blue and red patterns on it, for example. If everything were just of one color, you could not even see the pattern distinctly. The distinct pattern is revealed by the contrast of colors. The same is true for one's hair and face. If all of your face were covered by just black hair and nothing else, one could not distinguish any of your features. All distinction in this world comes from opposites of various qualities and elements; "But the Divine Truth has no like and no opposite."

چو نبود ذات حقّرا ضدّ و همتا
ندانم تا چگونه دانی اورا

> Since the Essence of the Truth has no opposite and no like,
> I know not how thou shalt know It.

And so the Shaykh poses the basic metaphysical dilemma. In light of what has been said above, how is one going to know that Reality that has no opposite and also no like?

ندارد ممکن از واجب نمونه
چگونه دانیش آخر چگونه؟

> Contingent being has no trace in itself of the Necessary Being;
> How then shalt thou know the Necessary Being, how?

Contingent being, of course, means everything except God. There is nothing in it like the Necessary Being. Therefore, "How then shalt thou know the Necessary Being" if you rely solely on contingency? We just limit ourselves to the contingent, to this world if we follow such a path. He then ends with what is really the intellectual disease of many people.

زهی نادان که او خورشید تابان
به نور شمع جوید در بیابان

> There is many a fool who seeks the light of the shining Sun,
> In the middle of the desert with a lamp in his hand.

This verse is an unbelievably powerful description of the intellectual state of affairs in a secularized world such as ours, although it also of course concerns certain people of Shabistarī's day. "There is many a fool": that is really what some Muṣlim opponents of *ḥikmah* as well as many modern philosophers can be seen to be as from the point of view of Tradition. That state of affairs is what characterizes the modern world. Modernists are looking for the Sun with the lamp in their hand in the middle of the desert while the Sun's rays are already shining down upon them.

Illustration (*tamthīl*)

This *tamthīl*, which means illustration ("to illustrate a certain principle"), is one of the apogees of the *Gulshan-i rāz* from a poetical point of view. The art of poetry of the verses in this section is quite remarkable, as is the depth of what is written.

In this *tamthīl*, he has recourse to a remarkable image, which I will explain before the translation. We usually perceive things as distinct objects through differences of form, color, position, contrast with what surrounds them, etc. If there were no contrasts of any kind or change in anything, we would not detect that thing. Of course, you could say that there is no change in a vase that I put in the kitchen years ago, for example; it has been there for a long, long time, and

I still see it. But that is not the same thing because the differences from what surrounds it persist whether there is any change or not. This point is important also metaphysically. We detect the day and night, because the Sun sets. If the Sun were never to set, we would have no experience of the light of the Sun as a distinct reality separate from other elements in the world about us. That is what Shabistarī wants to say here. This truth is recounted in the famous story of the baby fish who asked its mother, "What is water? Everybody talks about water. What is this water?" And the mother fish replied, "Show me what is not water, and I shall tell you what water is." So, it is discontinuity in the manifestation of being that allows us to know something separately in itself, and it is on the basis of that truth that Shaykh Maḥmūd Shabistarī expands this illustration.

اگر خورشید بر یک حال بودی
شعاع او به یک منوال بودی

If the Sun were to be in a single state,
And its rays would always be the same,

That is, if there were no change in the shining of the rays of the Sun.

ندانستی کسی کین پرتو اوست
نبودی هیچ فرق از مغز تا پوست

No one would know that this light is from the Sun.
There would be no difference from the kernel to the crust.

"From the kernel to the crust" means between the inward and outward. This is the first principle that he mentions, as I explained above. We know the Sun as a distinct reality because it sets. If the light of the Sun were always the same, we would never detect any change and not even remain aware that it is there. We would not even notice it as a distinct reality.

جهان جمله فروغ نور حقّ دان
حقّ اندر وی ز پیدائی است پنهان

Consider the whole world to be the reflection of the Light (*furūgh-i nūr*) of the Truth (*Ḥaqq*).
The Truth is hidden because it is so manifested in it.

Furūgh here is another word for the reflection of light, or rather it is the derivative manifestation of that Light. We come back to this idea that God hides Himself from us by that which is nothing but Himself, because God is both *al-Ẓāhir* (the Outwardly Manifest) and *al-Bāṭin* (the Inwardly Hidden) as the Quran asserts (Q. 57:3). As Ibn ʿArabī has said in a famous utterance, "Glory be unto Him Who Hides Himself from us with that which is nothing other than Himself."[4]

Where is God? We do not see Him anywhere. He seems to be hidden, and yet He is so manifest. Everything is a manifestation of God. And, therefore, we do not detect this external manifestation, like the light of the Sun if it were never to set. If it were to shine all the time, this reality would hide the presence of the Sun from us. If God were to take away His Light from us for a moment and then give it back, we would then realize the presence of that Light.

But why is it that there are many human beings who are atheists? Because they neglect completely the continuity of the grace, the *barakah*, the acts of existentiation that they receive from God all the time. So, they take this continuity for granted, and yet, they do not know where the source is. So, the best way God could make us all devout people would be to stop for a moment, being God, *astaghfiru'Llāh*, in which case of course we would all die, we would all disappear and we would not be around anymore to be good Muslims or bad Muslims, good Christians or bad Christians; but if He were to return and reexistentiate us with our memories intact, we would all be aware of His Presence and there would be no one who could deny the Light of Being. This is a very important point. The neglect on the part of human beings of Divine Theophany and the Blessings of God is because of their continuity in this world. So, the human mind does not find a contrast, and many take that Divine Presence for granted as simply part of the material and living reality that constitutes their own reality and what surrounds them.

You have to understand that this existential situation is itself a Divine trial. Many people become pious when they are sick, or when their father dies. At least they become pious for a short while. Why? Because they took their health for granted, or they took the father's well-being for granted as part of their experience of life. And for those who have a spiritual nature (not for everyone), when a trial like that comes to an end, it makes them aware that they were receiving blessings from God without realizing it. It is not accidental that so many people at the moment of distress turn to God. It is because the comfort of ordinariness and the forgetting of God is jolted. Ordinary human beings are comfortable in forgetting God, but they are uncomfortable in remembering God. They do not want to remember God, but rather are comfortable in forgetting Him and are only concerned with their *nafs* (the lower self or ego) and its demands. It is that state of mind that is jarred when a difficult experience comes in life, whether it be death, divorce, failure in one's profession, or all the other kinds of difficulties that can occur in life. This is one consequence of the fact that God is hidden in this world while in reality everything is His manifestation and He is present. The deaf cannot hear that all creation hymns the praise of God.[5]

The word that is used for manifestation in Persian is *paydā'ī*. The word *paydā kardan* means to find, to discover, to know. *Paydā'ī* means to be visible, to be manifest, that is, something that you can see, that you can find out, something that is out there and is real.

چه نور حقّ ندارد نقل و تحویل
نیابد ذات او تغییر و تبدیل

> Because the light of the Truth does not have any transport and change of state (*taḥwīl*),
> No change and transformation exists in Its Essence.[6]

تو پنداری جهان خود هست دائم
به ذات خویشتن پیوسته قائم

> Thou thinkest that the world exists continuously,
> That it subsists through its own essence.

The world appears to be always there. That is how one usually conceives it, thinking that its abiding reality comes from its own essence and nature. But then Shabistarī responds to this error with one of the most famous verses of Persian poetry, which I admire greatly and which is very popular.

کسی کو عقل دوراندیش دارد
بسی سرگشتگی در پیش دارد

> He who possesses a reason (*'aql*) that seeks that which is far-fetched (*'aql-i dūrandīsh*),
> A lot of bewilderment (*sargashtagī*) stands before him.

Dūrandīsh (lit. "far-thinking") is seen usually as a positive quality in Persian. It means to stop and think of the future and the consequences of what is occurring in the present moment, not being satisfied with only immediate effects of a cause. But here it does not mean that at all. Here *'aql-i dūrandīsh* means unlimited reason—something that can understand everything and keeps going from step to step to step without a finality based on certitude. A person with such a mindset will always be in bewilderment, not in the Sufi sense of *ḥayrah*, but in the sense of confusion.

There are some manuscripts that have *darmāndagī*, "to be stuck," instead of *sargashtagī*, but *sargashtagī* is very appropriate here. *Sargashtagī*, means to be lost, as if you are lost in a bazaar or something like that, and you do not know where to go—or if you are lost in life. So, we could call a person who is a rationalist someone with *'aql-i dūr-andīsh*, or one who thinks that everything can be solved by human reason alone, but he experiences a great deal of bewilderment. He will be lost in the maze of life.

Here in the text Shabistarī turns to a discussion that is famous in Persian literature and, in fact, in the whole of Islamic literature: the characterization of the different deformities of the human mind and soul. He explains the different excesses, exaggerations, or deviations of the human mind, which are particular to different schools of thought, such as *kalām* (Islamic theology), *falsafah* (philosophy), and so forth.

As I stated before, when he says *falsafah*, he really means *mashshā'ī* (Peripatetic) philosophy, to which he was opposed. This opposition needs some explanation. When you look at the history of Islamic thought, during the time of Avicenna, in the fourth and fifth Islamic centuries, Sufis and Islamic philosophers were not so opposed to each other. But at that time, Sufism did not speak much about the doctrinal and intellectual aspects of the truth asvmuch as it did about the practical dimension and virtues. So, there was little conflict between the two. You might have heard of the supposed meeting of Avicenna and the famous Sufi Abū Sa'īd-i Abū'l-Khayr and the stories that surround it.

Then a major change takes place. From the Seljuq period onward, for two or three centuries, as al-Ghazzālī and others attack Islamic Peripatetic philosophy; it becomes fashionable for many Sufis to also attack philosophy. Mawlānā Jalāl al-Dīn Rūmī does it, as do Sanā'ī and 'Aṭṭār before him. They were, however, true philosophers themselves in the deepest sense but attack rational philosophy. Shabistarī belongs to that trend. Since philosophy disappeared practically as a distinct school in most of the Arab world outside Iraq after this period terminating with Ibn Rushd (Ibn Khaldūn being an exception), the problem of criticizing rational philosophy does not even arise there. But in Persia, India, and the Ottoman world where philosophy survived, you have another phase in which from about the seventh or eighth Islamic century, Islamic philosophy and Sufism began to have more in common and are even integrated together mostly on the basis of the *Ishrāqī* or Illuminationist school of Suhrawardī that had been established earlier. So, one finds a person such as Dāwūd al-Qayṣarī, who was a Turk, or the Persian Ṣā'in al-Dīn ibn Turkah, who were both great philosophers and Sufis. And this trend toward synthesis is what leads finally to Mullā Ṣadrā and his transcendent theosophy (*al-ḥikmah al-muta'āliyah*), which is the synthesis of *taṣawwuf*, *ishrāq*, *kalām* and rational philosophy.

This explanation helps us to understand where Shaykh Maḥmūd Shabistarī stood and particularly the verses that follow, which of course do not concern later Islamic philosophy. Shabistarī comes at the end of that period, the eighth Islamic century, when there was still this opposition, and it was fashionable for Sufis to attack the philosophers. This is different from both the period before and the period after. Of course, a very interesting fact is that in the middle of this period comes Suhrawardī, who in fact represents a synthesis of Sufism and philosophy. So, this period of Islamic thought is very complicated. Here, however, I just want to locate Shaykh Maḥmūd Shabistarī intellectually for you.

ز دوراندیشی عقل فضولی
یکی شد فلسفی دیگر حلولی

As a result of this ever-meddling reason (*dūrandīshī-yi 'aql-i fuḍūlī*),
One has become philosophical (*falsafī*) and the other incarnationist (*ḥulūlī*).

'Aql-i fuḍūlī is very difficult to translate into English. *Fuḍūlī* here means the colloquial English word "nosy," as in "to put your nose into everything," or "being overinquisitive." So, we could say "nosy reason," though it is not very elegant English; but it does suggest the mind that is inquisitive, always meddling in matters where it has no business being. The words *fuḍūlī* and *faḍl*, to which the former is related and shares the same root in Arabic, have very different meanings in this context, and some make mistakes about their distinction. The word *faḍl* itself means "virtue" or "grace," but *fāḍil* also means "learned." But *fāḍilah* can also mean "trash," and yet words such as *fāḍil-āb* (sewage) in Persian derive from it. In Iran, *fuḍūlī* is used, for example, when a child is sitting among elders and keeps asking all kinds of questions that do not concern him or her. The father might say "*Fuḍūlī nakun*!"; that is, stop being nosy, and do not meddle in things that are not your concern—keep quiet and do not go beyond your boundaries. That is exactly what *fuḍūlī* means here. It has nothing to do with the word *faḍl*, and some Western orientalists have misunderstood this word because they went to a dictionary and chose the wrong meaning. So, *'aql-i fuḍūlī* means an *'aql*, reason, that meddles in things that are beyond its ken, as we all do in life sometimes, getting into something that is none of our business. It is transgressing beyond the boundaries of where one should be.

Shabistarī is also criticizing different schools that *taṣawwuf* opposes. *Falsafī* means proponent of rational philosophy, and *ḥulūlī* is in reference to the Christian theological doctrine of incarnation, and also to certain people within the Islamic world who presented similar ideas. They were called *ḥulūlī*. *Ḥulūl* means for something to become manifested in, literally "entering into," something else. It is related to the word *ḥall* (dissolve), as when you take some sugar, put it in tea and stir it; the sugar is dissolved (*ḥall shudah*) in the tea. Technically in Islamic thought, *ḥulūlī* is usually used in reference to Christian theologians but not always. There are certain Muslim thinkers who were considered by others to be *ḥulūlī*.

خردرا نیست تاب نور آن روی
برو از بهر او چشم دگر جوی

> Reason (*khirad*) cannot bear the light of that Face;
> For it [that is, the Face of God], go and find another eye.

Here the word *khirad* must be understood as "reason" rather than "intellect." You need another eye than that of reason to be able to see God; therefore in order to be able to see the Face of God go seek another eye, which alludes to the inner eye or the eye of the heart (*chism-i dil/'ayn al-qalb*).

At this point Shabistarī alludes to different schools of Islamic thought and criticizes them, explaining why each falls short of the Ultimate Truth, except gnosis.

دو چشم فلسفی چون بود احول
ز وحدت دیدن حقّ شد معطّل

> Since the two eyes of the philosopher are squinting eyes (*aḥwal*),
> He was kept waiting (*mu'aṭṭal*) to see the Unity of the Truth.

"Philosopher" here refers to the rationalists, not the general class of the *ḥukamā'* (sages). "Squinting eyes" (*aḥwal*) means eyes that see double; that is, people who are cross-eyed or have squinting eyes see everything double. They cannot see the oneness of any reality. The author is making use of this symbol philosophically to explain why rationalists cannot see God as the One.

ز نابینایی آمد رای تشبیه
ز یک چشمی است ادراکات تنزیه

It was from blindness that came the opinion of similitude (*tashbīh*).[7]
From one-eyedness comes understanding of things as utterly beyond (*tanzīh*).

Tashbīh, meaning similitude, analogy, likeness and immanence is a very important technical theological and metaphysical term with multifarious meanings. As for *tanzīh*, it not only means "being beyond" but also "transcendent" and like *tashbīh* has several meanings. So, it is best to concentrate on the Arabic terms. *Tashbīh* and *tanzīh* are now in fact entering the English language since they are very common terms in Islamic studies. They are both opposite and complementary and often used together. Often, *tashbīh* will be translated as "immanence" and *tanzīh* as "transcendence," which are the more profound meanings of these terms. *Tanzīh* means to be beyond (*munazzah*), transcendent vis-à-vis something. *Tashbīh* is to be like (*shabīh*) something. So, there are those who liken the Divine Qualities to human qualities or human qualities to Divine Qualities, and they are called *ahl-i tashbīh* (the folk of *tashbīh*). Those who say, "No, God is beyond all things and one cannot understand him using human language," and so forth are called *ahl-i tanzīh* (the folk of *tanzīh*). Both of these concepts, if taken by themselves and in exclusion of the other, can lead to a theological cul-de-sac, a dead end of the worst kind.

It is said that some people asked Imam Ja'far al-Ṣādiq about this question, and he said *lā al-tashbīh, wa lā al-tanzīh bal ḥaqīqat al-amr baynahumā,* "Neither *tashbīh* nor *tanzīh*, but the truth of the matter is in between," that is, God is both transcendent and immanent, the Divine Qualities are both beyond and within. If you say, for example, "God is Beautiful," and if you say, "This garden is beautiful" or "This person is beautiful," what does that mean? Is this person beautiful as God is Beautiful? If you say, "No, God's Beauty has nothing to do with this earthly beauty," you cannot even talk about God. This is one extreme view. But if you say "yes," you fall into materializing God (*tajassum*) and so forth. So, you have to have both *tanzīh* and *tashbīh* in order to reach the truth concerning God and the manifestation of His Qualities in His creation. Therefore, Shabistarī says that the view of *tashbīh* has come from blindness, that is, not being able to recognize the transcendent dimension.

When you close one eye and see with only the other eye (*yik chismī*), you really only see two dimensions. Because we are used to seeing with both eyes, we still have a feeling of three dimensions, but that is from experience and memory, not from the vision of only one eye. Once you only have one eye you really only see two dimensions, and three-dimensional reality is reduced to two dimensions. The reason we can see three dimensions is because we have two eyes. If you have a view that only *tanzīh* is true, then either only God is good, for example, and the phrase "good man" does not mean anything, or "good man" means something and "God is good" does not mean anything except in an anthropomorphic sense, because you do not know what good is when it concerns Him. "Seeing with one eye" means that you lose the third dimension, which makes it impossible to understand that God's goodness is both beyond all things but also manifests itself in this world, such that there are people who are good or things that are good, while God is the Supreme Good.

تناسخ زان سبب کفر است و باطل
که آن از تنگ چشمی گشت حاصل

Reincarnation is considered infidelity and falsehood (*bāṭil*),
Because it is the result of myopia (*tang-chismī*).

Tang-chismī means "not having correct vision" or "seeing things in a limited way, in a small way." *Tang* means literally "tight," "narrow." *Chishm* means "eye." So *tang-chismī* means "to see the things in a narrow way." Why is this so? What is he saying?

Like Shabistarī and other Muslim authorities, we as traditionalists reject reincarnation. René Guénon has written about this matter, as has Frithjof Schuon, and Ananda Coomaraswamy has a remarkable essay called "On the One and Only Transmigrant," in which he says in fact that the correct Hindu doctrine is not what is found popularly in India that individual souls transmigrate, but it is the Supreme Principle associated with *Ātman* that does so.[8] There is only one transmigrant, which is ultimately the Supreme Self. He transposes and understands the idea of reincarnation metaphysically. But we know that ordinarily Buddhists and Hindus all believe in reincarnation, which the Abrahamic religions reject it.

Why is it that this view is rejected in Islam? It is because what it does is in a sense to reduce the higher levels of reality to the earthly and involves the repetition of God's theophany, whereas *lā takrār fī'l-tajallī* (there is no repetition in theophany). When you and I die, we shall go into another world, which has certain relations with this world but is not this world. In fact there are many other worlds. If you reject all the other worlds (or at least do not pay attention to them, as Hindu cosmology does not reject the other worlds, but does pay attention to them both cosmologically and eschatologically), then you consider that after death people fall back to the same state, which is the earthly state. That is reincarnation that exists in popular Hinduism despite the presence of authentic sapiental knowledge at the heart of that tradition. So, this is a key verse, explaining something very profound, which is one of the great issues in the "new spiritualities" sprouting in the West today. This phenomenon as far as the West is concerned is also due to the fact that theologically a lot of Westerners are becoming interested in popular Hinduism and Buddhism, and they now believe in reincarnation, as do members of new cults in the West, such as the Wiccans and the new Druids in England, many of whom believe in reincarnation. This belief is due to the misunderstanding of the principle *lā takrār fī'l-tajallī*, which is the metaphysical reason why there is no reincarnation: God's *tajallī* (theophany) never repeats itself. You cannot come into the same state twice. The same being cannot come into the same state twice.

چو اکمه بی‌نصیب از هر کمال است
کسی کورا طریق اعتزال است

> Since the person born blind (*akmah*) is deprived of every perfection,
> This person is like one who follows the Mu'tazilite position.

Akmah means a person who is blind from birth and therefore has never seen anything external to him or her. "Deprived of every perfection" means that he does not see forms and colors, and therefore does not see the forms' realities and qualities. By saying "deprived of every perfection," Shabistarī is not referring to inner perfection but rather to the perfection that sees the spiritual reality of the world of nature or God's creation. "This person is like one who follows the Mu'tazilite position," refers to the Mu'tazilite position being one that rejects the Divine Presence in the created order. Here, Shabistarī is criticizing well-known Islamic schools of thought with which he disagrees one by one.

رمد دارد دو چشم اهل ظاهر
که از ظاهر نبیند جز مظاهر

> The two eyes of the people of outwardness are afflicted with ophthalmia (*ramad*),
> So, in the outward they see nothing but that which is the manifestation of the outward.

Ramad is an ailment of the eye called "ophthalmia" in English. It is a disease of the eye in which the eyes become very watery and therefore do not see things exactly as they are—everything is blurry. "In the outward they see nothing but that which is the manifestation of the outward," means that they do not see the inward dimension of things, the archetype of which the outward is an external manifestation. They do not see that the outward is the outward of the inward. Therefore, they try to understand the outward in terms of the outward alone. This is a problem with much of the modern study of religion today, particularly phenomenology as popularly understood. When it began with Husserl it tried to distinguish between the noumenal and the phenomenal, between the *ẓāhir* (the outward) and the *bāṭin* (the inward), but then stuck to understanding the *ẓāhir qua ẓāhir* forgetting the noumenal or the *bāṭin*. That is exactly what Shabistarī is criticizing here.

کلامی کو ندارد ذوق توحید
به تاریکی در است از غیم تقلید

A theologian (*kalāmī*), since he has no taste of unity (*tawḥīd*),
Is lost in darkness, as a result of simple imitation.

Kalāmī means a person who follows Islamic *kalām*, or "theology," and "theologian" in the Christian sense. *Kalām* is one of the traditional sciences, but from the point of view of metaphysics it is considered to be a limited way of understanding things. He is "lost in darkness, as a result of simple imitation," points to the fact that he is just repeating things but does not see or experience the Truth.

از او هرچه بگفتند از کم و بیش
نشانی داده‌اند از دیدهٔ خویش

Concerning Him, whatever they have said, more or less,
They have all given a sign of their own vision of things.

I wish all the people reading this book could memorize this verse because it applies to all of life. Usually what we say about the truth is not the truth itself but what we see of it, what our vision of it is. And this is especially true in our world today where the objective crystallizations of the truth have been put aside in so many fields. This verse also means that even those who have spoken of the Truth spiritually and metaphysically, such as the Sufis, have done so from their particular spiritual stations.

منزّه ذاتش از چند و چه و چون
«تعالی شأنه» عمّا یقولون

His Essence is transcendent (*munazzah*) vis-à-vis quantity, quality and state (*chand-u chi-u chūn*),
His Station (*sha'n*) is beyond (*ta'ālā*) everything they say (*'ammā yaqūlūn*) of Him.

The second part of this verse has a two-part Arabic phrase from the Quran. *Ta'ālā sha'nuhu* declares the transcendence of the Station of God. The second part, *'ammā yaqūlūn* means "from what they say." This is part of Quran 17:43. *Munazzah* means "to be pure," "to be beyond," "to be transcendent," that is, to be qualified by *tanzīh*. *Chand-u chi-u chūn*, that is, "quantity, quality and state," are Persian translations of three of the categories of Aristotle, and the other categories are presumed to be understood as being included. So, God is beyond all of the categories used in ordinary thinking. After this verse Shabistarī turns to the next question.

Question [2]

كدامين فكر ما را شرط راه است؟
چرا گه طاعت و گاهی گناه است؟

What kind of thought [or meditation, *fikr*] is the condition for the path?
Why is it that sometimes it is obedience, sometimes sin?

Fikr, as mentioned already, can mean both thought and meditation. So, why in following a spiritual path should one sometimes make use of thought and not think at other times? This is a very pertinent issue in following the Sufi path because in practicing Sufi methods of realization sometimes one has to use mental activity and sometimes cast it aside as a great obstacle.

Answer

در آلا فکر کردن شرط راه است
ولی در ذات حقّ محض گناه است

To meditate upon blessings is the condition of the path,
But to meditate upon the Essence of God is pure sin.

This is again one of the remarkable verses of this work. It formulates with such simplicity and clarity a major metaphysical truth.

Ālā means blessings or kindnesses. Many know that in Islam we are prohibited from meditating upon the Essence of God. This verse is an almost direct translation of a *ḥadīth* of the Prophet, *tafakkarū fī ālā'i'Llāh wa lā tafakkarū fī Dhāti'Llāh.* "Meditate upon the blessings of God, but do not meditate upon the Essence of God." There is also a version, "Meditate upon the Names and Attributes of God . . ." If one really thinks about one's meditating upon God, one realizes that one cannot meditate upon God's Essence. It is always a Quality and Aspect of God upon which one can meditate. One can meditate on God as Beauty, God as Love, God as Power, and so on; or one can meditate upon an image, such as the image of the calligraphy of a Divine Name; or on the sound of a piece of sacred music. But none of these Divine Qualities and theophanies are the *Dhāt*, the Essence of God. They are manifestations of the *Dhāt*.

So, Shabistarī asserts that to try to meditate upon the Divine Essence is pure sin. There is no Sufi order that has its members meditating upon the Divine Essence because it cannot be done. The only thing we can do vis-à-vis the Divine Essence is to drown in it. In relation to the Essence we are either nothing or everything, depending on who we are. There is no "I and" when it comes to the Essence. Why in relation to the Essence we are either everything or nothing? Nothing because He is the Absolute Reality, and everything because that reality is right in the center of our being. This assertion is in a sense the heart of all metaphysics.

بود در ذات حقّ اندیشه باطل
محال محض دان تحصیل حاصل

To meditate upon the Essence of the Divine Truth (*Ḥaqq*) is false.
Consider it to be impossible to attain that which has already been attained (*taḥṣīl-i ḥāṣil*).

Here Shabistarī keeps using the word *Ḥaqq*, the Divine Name "the Truth," which is a Name of Essence (*ism al-Dhāt*, as opposed to the Names of Acts, *asmā' al-af'āl*, or the Names of Attributes, *asmā' al-ṣifāt*). So, "the Divine Truth" refers to the Essence of God.

In the phrase *taḥṣīl-i ḥāṣil*, *ḥāṣil* means "something that has been accomplished," "something that is already done." *Taḥṣīl* is "to attain," so *taḥṣīl-i ḥāṣil* is "to attain that which has already been accomplished." But if something is already accomplished, it is pure impossibility to then try to accomplish it. It is already there. Then Shabistarī gives a wonderful reason for this affirmation:

چو آیات است روشن گشته از ذات
نگردد ذات او روشن ز آیات

> Since the signs (*āyāt*) [of God] have become illuminated through His Essence,
> His Essence will never become illuminated through them.

Āyāt (plural of *āyah*) means "signs of God." Esoterically everything in the Universe is a sign of God as are the verses of the Quran. So, the faculty of man that tries to meditate upon the Essence of God is itself illuminated by the Essence of God and so cannot illuminate the Essence for us. The relationship goes the other way; it is the Essence that is the ultimate source of illumination of the *āyāt*. That is why I said that vis-à-vis the Essence we are either nothing or everything. That is the end of it. But we can meditate *qua* human beings upon the Divine Qualities.

همه عالم به نور اوست پیدا
کجا او گردد از عالم هویدا

> The whole world is manifest (*paydā*) through His Light.
> How can then He ever become visible (*huwaydā*) through the world?

Paydā, "manifested," is very similar to *phainómenon* in Greek, that is, to be outwardly manifested. Here, however, the Sufis part ways from those Peripatetic philosophers, whether Islamic, such as Avicenna, or Christian, such as St. Thomas Aquinas, who believe that you can go from the world to God, that is, you can prove God from His signs in the world. Most Westerners know the famous painting of Michelangelo in Rome, in which Plato and Aristotle are walking together. Plato has his finger pointing upward, while Aristotle has his finger pointing downward. What this means is that Plato is saying that the reality of beings are the Divine archetypes, and Aristotle is saying that the forms of beings are within themselves. Aristotelianism tried to go from the existent to the Unmoved Mover, whereas Plato said that you have to start with the archetypes, with the Divine Ideas, and not with the world. On this issue, Sufism sides, of course, completely with Platonism as does *Ishrāqī* philosophy. So, Shabistarī is saying that if the world appears through the Light of God, how can you expect that which appears through the Light of God then to be the light by which God is seen in His unmanifested Reality?

نگنجد نور ذات اندر مظاهر
که سبحات جلالش هست قاهر

> The Light of His Essence does not fit (*nagunjad*) into any manifestations (*maẓāhir*),
> For the Glory of His Majesty is victorious.

The Divine Essence is too great to fit (*nagunjad*) into or be located in any of Its manifestations (*maẓāhir*) or forms in this world. The reason is that, "the Glory of His Majesty is victorious." The Quran states, *Allāh al-Wāḥid al-Qahhār*, God is the One, the Victorious (Q. 12:39). What does this mean? It means that, if the Light of the Divine Essence were to become present in this room, everything would be shattered into nothingness, and God alone would be victorious (*qāhir*). The Light of the Divine Essence would just destroy every relative existent by virtue of the fact that it is the Light of the Divine Essence and of the Divine Essence alone. In fact, the world exists because God has allowed His Light to become gradually dimmed through gradation. If the Light of God in its original purity were to become present everywhere ontologically speaking, there would no longer be a world that is characterized by its separation from God on its own relative level of existence, although emanation of the Light of God is present in the world. Otherwise, it would not exist.

رها کن عقل‌را با حقّ همی باش
که تاب خور ندارد چشم خفّاش

Let reason go. Be always with the Truth.
For the eye of the bat cannot bear the light of the sun.

Of course, bats always live in dark places and only come out at night, for the eye of the bat cannot bear the light of the sun. Shabistarī uses this fact as a metaphor to bring out the point that using reason alone is like being a bat that cannot bear the light of the sun. So, he gives the advice to free oneself from the shackles of reason and thereby be constantly with the Divine Truth.

در آن موضع که نور حقّ دلیل است
چه جای گفتگوی جبرئیل است

In that place where the Light of the Truth is itself proof (*dalīl*),
What place is there for the discourse of Gabriel?

Can you imagine what a daring poem this is? There is a possible direct discourse between man and God that is even above the archangelic level, even above the agent of revelation, that is, Gabriel, who brought the Quranic revelation to the Prophet. *Dalīl* is used here in the sense of metaphysical proof.

فرشته گرچه دارد قرب درگاه
نگنجد در مقام «لی مع الله»

Although the Angel has proximity to the Divine Threshold (*dargāh*),
It cannot be contained in the station of "I am with God" (*lī ma'Allāh*).

Dargāh here indicates "the Divine Presence"; this Persian word also exists in other Islamic languages such as Urdu and many other Indian languages, and is usually used for the palace or court of kings, but is also used in Sufism. As for *dargāh-i ilāhī*, it means actually "the door opening to the Presence of God." *Dar* means "door" in Persian, and *gāh* means "place," so literally the phrase means "the place of the door," that is, where you enter into a place. Here, *dargāh* means actually the locus of entrance into the Divine Presence. During the Prophet's *mi'rāj* (celestial ascent), he ascended all levels of cosmic reality and even went beyond all of the angels and archangels. Therefore, he reached a stage that even the archangel Gabriel, could not reach. According to a *ḥadīth*, "I have a time with God which I do not share with any angel brought nigh, nor any prophet sent forth."

چو نور او ملک‌را پر بسوزد
خردرا جمله پا و سر بسوزد

Since His Light will burn the wing of the Archangel,
It will burn reason from head to toe.

This is again in reference to when the Prophet—*'alayhi 'l-ṣalātu wa 'l-salām*—went on the *mi'rāj*. Gabriel was of course accompanying him, and the Prophet reached a stage in which Gabriel said, "I cannot go any further, because if I do so, my wings will be burned," that is, the Prophet reached a stage which transcended the archangelic level, which is the highest reality below God (*dūn Allāh*). The Prophet ascended even beyond that level. So, in reference to that fact Shabistarī says that when even the Archangel's wings would be burned if it tried to go a step higher, surely if you try to understand God through reason alone, human reason would be burned from head to toe (*sar tā pā*). It would be reduced to ashes.

بود نور خرد در ذات انور
به سان چشم سر در چشمهٔ خور

> The light of reason, when seen in relation to the Most Luminous Essence (*Dhāt-i anwar*),
> Is like comparing the eye that is in the head to the spring (*chishmah*) of sunlight.

First of all, although the Persian word *khur* is used, it should be pronounced here as *khawr*, and it refers to the Sun. The Pahlavi word *khora* or *khera* means light and also it means wisdom, and has very important meanings that pertain to this double sense of the term. The word *khurshīd*, therefore, really means "the ray of the *khera*," but is used to refer to the Sun itself in Persian. Here we have to pronounce it *khwar* to rhyme with *anwar*. In the first hemistich, *Dhāt-i anwar*, "the Most Luminous Essence" can also be translated "the Essence of the Most Luminous One." Both are correct. But why does he use this image? It is because it clarifies a very important metaphysical truth, which he explains in the next verse.

چو مبصر با بصر نزدیک گردد
بصر از درک او تاریک گردد

> When that which is to be seen comes very close to the eye that sees,
> The eye becomes darkened in apprehending it.

That verse means that if something comes very close to one's eye, it becomes dark, a darkness that comes not from distancing from the eye but from extreme proximity to it. Now, having said this, he turns to the positive symbol of the color black and darkness.

سیاهی گر بدانی نور ذات است
به تاریکی درون آب حیات است

> Blackness, if thou wert to know, is the Light of the Divine Essence,[1]
> A darkness within which there is the water of life.

This is one of the key verses of the *Gulshan-i rāz*, coming back to the symbolism of black light. The Light of the Divine Essence is black, according to Sufism, and some of the most important verses about the symbolism of black light appear in the *Gulshan-i rāz*. "The water of life" flows and originates from this principial darkness. According to mythology, the spring of eternal life (*chisma-yi āb-i ḥayāt*) flows from a dark place, which Alexander tried to find. The water of eternal life always originates from a dark place.

This issue is very significant metaphysically and religiously. Look at the religions of the world. They are like the spring of life, the fountain of life, but they originate in darkness: we do not have external evidence about their origins except that they come from God. What was Christ doing when he was three years old? Of course, we know about a few moments of his life, but the origin of his inner being is hidden in a meta-historical reality. But it is a darkness from which flows life and light. The principle of manifestation is always like that. All of us were conceived in the darkness of our mothers' wombs. We came from that darkness and then gradually grew and came to the world of light. So, the word "darkness" here has this aspect of the unmanifested, not that which is below light, but that which is the unmanifested world above the light of ordinary existence. It is not *ẓāhir* (outwardly manifest) as is light. So, darkness here really corresponds to the inner and hidden reality before it becomes manifested outwardly.

سیه جز قابض نور بصر نیست
نظر بگذار کین جای نظر نیست

Blackness is nothing other than the contraction of the light of vision.
Put opinion aside, for this is not the place for opinion.

Naẓar here means "rational discourse" or "opinion" and should not be associated with vision or view, which are also meanings connected with it.

چه نسبت خاکرا با عالم پاک
که ادراک است عجز از درک ادراک

What relation is there between the dust (*khāk*) and the world of purity (*'ālam-i pāk*)?
For to understand the inability to perceive is itself perception.

This first hemistich is one of the most important sentences that all of us need to learn throughout life. The juxtaposition of *khāk* (dust or earth) and *'ālam-i pāk* (the world of purity) appears often in Persian literature. *'Ālam-i pāk* means the world of the Spirit. What relation is there or can there be between the dust and the world of purity?

The second hemistich is also very notable. "To understand the inability to perceive is itself perception." The inability to understand and to know that one cannot perceive is itself a form of knowledge or perception (*idrāk*). The fact you come to know that you do not know is itself a mode of knowing, a very important mode of knowing.

سیه رویی ز ممکن در دو عالم
جدا هرگز نشد والله اعلم

The state of being blackfaced from contingent being in the two worlds,
Is never separated, and God knows best.

Here Shabistarī uses the word *siyah-rūyī* "blackface" in the ordinary sense, not black as referring to the Black Light of the Divine Essence. To become blackfaced in Persian means to be sorry that something has gone wrong or the state of not having fulfilled what one should be fulfilling. It means to apologize for something or be ashamed. All of these ideas are combined in the idea of *siyah-rūyī*. *Mumkin* means contingent being. "And God knows best," *Allāhu a'lam*, is a traditional term of humility to denote that one seeks to express the truth of something to the best of one's ability, but perfect knowledge belongs to God alone.

سواد الوجه فی الدارین درویش
سواد اعظم آمد بی کم و بیش

O darvish, there is the blackness of the face in both worlds,
And then comes Supreme Blackness, without more or less.

With the term "Supreme Blackness," Shabistarī is referring to the Divine Essence while ordinary blackface in the sense of humility is the life of the Sufi who is aware of the grandeur of the Black Light of God's Essence. This verse brings Shabistarī to some very sensitive issues. So, he says:

چه می‌گویم که هست این نکته باریک؟
شب روشن میان روز تاریک

What can I say? For this point is very delicate,
An illuminated night amidst a dark day.

This is again one of the famous verses of Persian Sufi poetry and contains a stunning and profound symbolism. Day here symbolizes manifestation, outwardness. It also has a positive aspect because of the association of day with light. In ordinary human life the daytime has a positive character, and then when there is no light, it becomes dark, and night is seen as being negative as far as human activity is concerned. We do all of our activities during the day. But from a spiritual point of view, night represents absence of outwardness and the presence of the reality of the inward. And so, what appears to be a light day is not so spiritually. The only time that is really light is the illuminated night. Why not "an illuminated day"? Because a person given to the spiritual life experiences more concentration, feels close to God, to his own inner thoughts, at night when he goes more deeply within himself. In the evening and at night we interiorize a lot of things that occur during the day. So, night is the time for contraction, but also concentration and inwardness. It has a positive meaning for those who seek to discover the inner dimension of their being.

In Persian the language of this verse is simple yet very profound. "An illuminated night amidst a dark day" means to be with God, to be immersed in spiritual practice, which shuns the world of outward manifestation that is seen as darkness. What appears as light for others is darkness for a spiritual person, and what appears as darkness for others is light for him or her. The spiritual person likes to be alone at night. The ordinary person runs away from this solitude, and will do whatever he or she can not to be alone until he or she retires. But a spiritual person experiences, in this concentration at night, the Divine Presence and Luminosity. So, the night here is not a negative symbol, but a positive one. The reason that he writes this verse here is that the night is dark, and he relates this darkness to the darkness of the Divine Essence; therefore, the positive symbolism of darkness. Do not confuse this truth with the ordinary experience of the night as dark and to some gloomy, and then the Sun rises and everything becomes luminous and full of life. The dark here is really a stage above and beyond manifested light. The ordinary symbolism of light connotes being, clarity and luminosity (*rawshanā'ī*). But we should also understand that above this light stands a darkness that is even higher than this light. That is what he is trying to bring out.

در این مشهد که انوار تجلّی است
سخن دارم ولی ناگفتن اولی است

In this stage of discourse (*mashhad*), in which the Divine Lights are manifested,
I have much to say, but it is better to remain silent.

The word *mashhad*, literally meaning "place of witness," is also used for the divisions or chapters of many Islamic texts, or the place of a particular discussion. Of course, it also means the tomb of a saint, of which the most famous is the city of Mashhad in Khurāsān, Iran, which is called Mashhad because the eighth Shi'ite Imam 'Alī al-Riḍā is buried there. The word *mashhad* can be the place name (*ism maḥall*) for both the words *shuhūd* (witnessing) and *shahīd* (martyr). Since the Eighth Imam was martyred, the name of the city means where he dies is Mashhad, a place where a person is martyred. We also say *mashhad-i Imām Ḥusayn* in Karbalā' in that sense of the term.

Illustration[2]

اگر خواهی که بینی چشمۀ خور
تورا حاجت فتد با جسم دیگر

If you want to see the spring of sunlight (*chishmah-yi khwar*),
You are going to need another body.

This verse from the point of view of poetry does not rhyme well. So, خور is pronounced as *khwar* instead of *khur* to rhyme with *digar*. *Chismah* literally means spring or fountain, and is related to the word "eye" (*chism*), but here *chishmah-yi khawr* means the full Sun or source of sunlight. "You are going to need another body," because you cannot look directly into the Sun with the ordinary eye.

چو چشم سر ندارد طاقت تاب
توان خورشید تابان دید در آب

Since the eye of the head cannot endure the shining of the Sun,[3]
Thou canst see it as [reflected] in water.

That verse states that one can see the reflection of the Sun in water. The eye can bear to see the reflection, but it cannot look at the Sun directly.

از او چون روشنی کمتر نماید
در ادراک تو حالی می‌فزاید

Since, from that reflection, less light issues forth,
It increases the condition for your perceiving it.

عدم آیینۀ هستی است مطلق
کز او پیداست عکس تابش حقّ

Non-existence is the mirror of the Absolute,
In which is manifest the reflection of the shining forth of the Truth.

This verse refers back to the symbolism that I have explained before, which is essential for understanding Islamic metaphysics and philosophy, namely that nonbeing is conceived of as a mirror in which is reflected the Light of Being.

عدم چون گشت هستی‌را مقابل
در او عکسی شد اندر حال حاصل

When non-existence was placed in front of Being,
A reflection was produced in it at that moment.

Nonexistence is like a mirror so that when, "A reflection was produced in it," that is, in nonexistence; when it was placed before Being, it could reflect Being while being nothing in itself.

شد آن وحدت از این کثرت پدیدار
یکی‌را چون شمردی گشت بسیار

That unity became manifested through this multiplicity [that nonexistence reflects].
If you count one many times it becomes many.

Since Being is reflected in the mirror of nonexistence, although One in Itself, it produces many reflections and therefore multiplicity. As for the second hemistich, it means that if you count 1, 1, 1, 1, 1 and keep counting in this way, you reach multiplicity although you are simply repeating unity.

عدد گرچه یکی دارد بدایت
ولیکن نبودش هرگز نهایت

Number, although it has only one beginning,
It does not ever have an end.

This is the indefiniteness of number, of the numerical series, which has a beginning in one or unity, then goes on indefinitely and has no end. This verse is a reference to the basic metaphysical truth that although the Origin of existence is One, there is no limit to the manifestations of the One.

عدم در ذات خود چون بود صافی
از او با ظاهر آمد گنج مخفی

Non-existence, since in itself is purity (*ṣāfī*),
The Hidden Treasure was made apparent through it.[4]

Non-existence in itself is like a mirror that is *ṣāfī*, purity and simplicity, thus enabling the Divine Reality, hidden in Itself, to become manifest. The second hemistich refers to the *ḥadīth* of the Hidden Treasure, which Shabistarī explains in the next verse:

حدیث «کنت کنزاً»را فرو خوان
که تا پیدا ببینی گنج پنهان

Go read the *ḥadīth* of "I was a Hidden Treasure" (*kuntu kanzan*)
So that thou wouldst be able to see manifested the Hidden Treasure.

The *ḥadīth* of the Hidden Treasure is a *ḥadīth qudsī*, that is, a *ḥadīth* in which God speaks in the first person. God Himself speaks, but it is not in the Quran. There are only about a hundred *aḥādīth qudsiyyah*, in which God speaks through the mouth of the Prophet without it being part of the Quran. This famous *ḥadīth* is not in the canonical collections, but it is very common among Sufis, and goes back to at least Abū Ḥāmid al-Ghazzālī. Sufis considered it to be one of the most important *ḥadīth*s, which was transmitted orally in the early centuries of Islam and therefore is not to be found in Bukhārī, Tirmidhī, Muslim and other *Ṣiḥāḥ* (collections of sound *ḥadīth*s).

The *ḥadīth* is as follows, *Kuntu kanzan makhfiyyan fa-aḥbabtu an u'raf fa-khalaqtu'l-khalq li-kay u'raf.* God says, "I was a Hidden Treasure, and loved to be known. Therefore, I created the world so I would be known." Many Western scholars have translated it as "I wanted to be known," but the word used is *aḥbabtu*, "I loved," and not "I wanted." It is difficult to surmise how profound this *ḥadīth* is, particularly in the fact that it combines God's Knowledge and God's Love. When some do not mention *ḥubb* and translate *aḥbabtu* as "I wanted to," they ignore a major part of the meaning of the saying. God *loved* to be known. So, His Knowledge is related to His Love, and it is God's Love for being known that brings about the manifestation of the world, so that God can be known through the world. He externalizes Himself for that reason.

This saying is perhaps the most important *ḥadīth* in Islam to explain why God created the world. Every religion tries to have an answer to this basic question: Why did God create the world? In Hinduism, the answer is Divine Play (*līlā*), and so there is no reason needed. You do not ask a child, "Why are you playing?" The playing itself is the purpose. The purpose is in the play itself. This is the Hindu answer. In Christianity the reason for creation is primarily that God could send His only Son to the world and is one of the mysteries about which many Christian theologians have written. Islam brings the answer back to the element of Divine Knowledge, which is very different from both the Hindu and Christian answers. There is nothing like the "*Ḥadīth* of the Hidden Treasure" in Christian or Jewish religious literature, nor in Sanskrit sources. In Buddhism, generally the question is not even posed because Buddhism generally does not address the question of creation and cosmogenesis, but that is another story. In Confucianism it is the same. But for those religions which have dealt with the creation of the world, such as Hinduism, Islam, Christianity or Judaism, the question always arises, "Why did God create the world?" And Islam has this remarkable answer: because He wanted to be known. This truth shows the gnostic and metaphysical nature of Islam itself. But this knowledge is one that is combined with love: *Aḥbabatu an uʿraf*, "I loved to be known," from *ḥubb*, which is a Quranic term. The Quran does not use the word *ʿishq* which means "intense love," but uses the words *ḥubb*, *wadd* and other Arabic terms. So, Shabistarī says, "Go read the *ḥadīth* of 'I was a Hidden Treasure.'"

عدم آیینه عالم عکس و انسان
چو چشم عکس در وی شخص پنهان

Non-existence is a mirror, the world a reflection, and man,
Is like the eye of the reflection in which the person is hidden.

This complicated symbolism needs some elaboration. When you look in a mirror, you see yourself. When you look at your eye in the mirror, inside the pupil of the eye, you also see yourself, your whole self. If you have not experienced this fact, you should try to do so. This fact is that to which this incredible verse refers.

تو چشم عکسی و او نور دیده است
به دیده دیدهرا دیده که دیده است

Thou art the eye of that reflection, and He is the light with which thou seest.
Who has ever been able to see (*dīdah-ast*) with the eye (*bih dīdah*) which
[itself] sees the seen (*dīdah*)?

In the first hemistich, Shabistarī is affirming that God is not the Object of vision; He is in the deepest sense the Subject, the Light of the eye with which you see your own eye. That is why we cannot see God. God, he says, is the Light with which we see what is real. He is not an Object out there to be seen in the ordinary sense. He is the Light with which we see everything. The version presented here is the common recension of this verse, but there is also another version.[5]

جهان انسان شد و انسان جهانی
از این پاکیزهتر نبود بیانی

The cosmos has become man, and man has become the cosmos.
There is no purer explanation than this.

This verse is again one of the most famous in the Persian language. The cosmos has become man (*insān*), the human being, *mensch*, that is "man" in the traditional sense, not the male. This verse summarizes the correspondence between the macrocosm and the microcosm. "There is no purer explanation than this," claims that there is no clearer explanation of this whole doctrine.

Illustration[6]

چو نیکو بنگری در اصل این کار
هم او بیننده هم دیده است و دیدار

If thou lookest well into the roots (*aṣl*) of this matter,
Thou wilt see that God is both the seer, the seen and the vision.

"If thou lookest well into the roots of this matter" means that if you look well into the principles, the heart of this matter, then you will realize that God is both the seer, the active noun of to see, what is seen, and the vision itself.

حدیث قدسی این معنی بیان کرد
«فبی یسمع و بی یبصر» عیان کرد

The sacred saying (*ḥadīth-i qudsī*) has explained this meaning;
"And through Me he hears and through Me he sees" was made evident.

This verse is a reference to the *ḥadīth qudsī* that says, "If My servant draws nigh unto Me with supererogatory works (*nawāfil*), I become the ear with which he hears (*yasma' bihi*), and the eyes with which he sees," and so forth. God becomes the eye with which we see. and the ear with which we hear; that is, when you hear a word or a piece of music, it is God who is hearing it according to this *ḥadīth*. When you see an object, it is God who is seeing it.

As mentioned above, a *ḥadīth qudsī* is a *ḥadīth* in which God speaks in the first person through the Prophet. Many people have asked why this *ḥadīth* is not part of the Quran, and this matter has been discussed a great deal by orientalists and also by Islamic scholars. The answer is that it was God's choice, that is, God directed the Prophet that such sayings not be part of the Quran. Otherwise, since God is speaking in the first person, it might be taken to be a verse or verses of the Quran. For example, we have the verse *Naḥnu aqrabu ilayhi min ḥabl al-warīd*, "We are nearer to him than his jugular vein" (Q. 50:16). So, here God is speaking to us, and stating that He is closer to us than our jugular vein. Why is it that this verse is part of the Quran, whereas *wa yasma' bihi* is not? This is God's decision revealed through the Prophet. So, the Prophet ordered his Companions not to include the *aḥādīth qudsiyyah* in the Quran.

This *ḥadīth* has a very special status in Islam and is extremely important for the understanding of Sufism.[7] The *aḥādīth qudsiyyah* are esoteric. They have nothing to do with public life, taxation or simply external acts. They are all of a very spiritual nature, dealing with our relation with God. Martin Lings has translated the *ḥadīth* as follows: "My slave ceaseth not to draw nigh unto Me with devotions of his free will until I love him; and when I love him, I am the Hearing wherewith he heareth, and the Sight wherewith he seeth, and the Hand wherewith he smiteth, and the Foot whereon he walketh."[8] And the *ḥadīth* continues, "If he taketh one step towards me, I take a hundred steps towards him. If he taketh ten steps towards me, I take a thousand steps towards him." If we take one little step towards God, He takes many steps toward us.

جهان‌را سر به سر آیینه میدان
به هر یک ذره‌ای صد مهر تابان

Consider the whole world, from beginning to end, as a mirror.
In every single atom, (there exists) a hundred shining suns.

God is reflected in the mirror of non-existence and His Light shines forth like a hundred suns at the heart of all His creation.

When the atom was split in 1944 and earlier the model of the atom was revealed as a nucleus with electrons revolving around it like the solar system, a few articles were written in Persian claiming that Shaykh Maḥmūd Shabistarī had already predicted this truth, as had Hātif Iṣfahānī (d. 1783) who said,

If thou splitest the heart of any atom,
Thou wilt find therein a light of the Sun.[9]

This verse seems to correspond to the Fermi model of the atom, and there was a lot of debate going on about its origin at the time of Fermi and soon thereafter. I do not, however, look at these matters in the same way. Nevertheless, these Sufis had an intuition about the nature of the manifested order that was and remains very significant. Understanding the structure of reality metaphysically did not require the Fermi laboratory at the University of Chicago or the work of Oppenheimer. That being said, when the model of the atom was presented with the nucleus and various electrons moving around it, which is exactly like the solar system, and people noticed these remarkable resemblances, they were astounded that these Sufis had said these things centuries before.

اگر یک قطره‌را دل بر شکافی
برون آید از آن صد بحر صافی

If thou takest a single drop of water and split it,
A hundred seas will flow from it.

These verses refer to the same cosmological and metaphysical reality as in the above verses.

به هر جزوی ز خاک ار بنگری راست
هزاران آدم اندر وی هویداست

Thou lookest at any part of dust correctly,
Thou wilt see thousands of human beings therein.

Man is made of dust into which God breathed His Spirit and returns to dust when he dies. These verses refer to both of these realities.

There is also a lesson here similar to what one finds in the quatrains of Khayyām, in which he mentions so often that the body turns to dust after death, and so if you make a vase, *kūzah*, out of dust you may be making it out of the dust of the body of a human being. There is also an implication here of the doctrine that in a sense, everything is in everything. This doctrine is referred to as *tadākhul* (interpenetration) in Arabic, which means that the reality of everything exists in everything else. This is a view that is different from the Aristotelian cosmology of Ibn Sīnā and others.

به اعضا پشه‌ای همچند پیل است
در آسمان قطره‌ای مانند نیل است

In the parts of its body a gnat is like an elephant.
In the sky a drop of water is like the Nile.[10]

It might be interesting to mention that there are about fifty thousand combinations of DNA in the simplest living cell, of both a gnat and an elephant. So, it is as if Shabistarī were predicting this later scientific discovery, although his words are not meant to be scientific in the modern sense but metaphysical. And so, the gnat and the elephant in a certain sense share on the deepest level the same reality of life. One is very big, and one is very small, but there is great complexity in the structure of a gnat, or even a trilobite and not only in big animals. It is not as Darwin said, that life goes from simplicity to complexity. Life begins with extreme complexity. The scientist Michael Behe makes this point clear in his book, *Darwin's Black Box*, which has caused so much stir since it was written by a microbiologist who simply rejected the whole of the theory of Darwinian evolution on the basis of the fact that in contrast to what Darwin said, life begins with complexity and not simplicity.[11] A little gnat, a little mosquito, is just as complex as an elephant, microbiologically speaking, chemically speaking.

And how did Shaykh Maḥmūd Shabistarī come to such a conclusion? This is a very interesting matter to consider. These are intuitions that come from traditional sciences that reveal the hidden nature of things, but I do not want to go into that now. There are other ways of gaining knowledge of the nature of reality than through methods used in mainstream modern Western science from Galileo to today.

درون حبه‌ای صد خرمن آمد
جهانی در دل یک ارزن آمد

From the heart of a single grain comes a hundred harvests.
A whole world is contained in the heart of a grain of millet.

Here, Shabistarī is emphasizing the same truth mentioned above but through different examples.

به پر پشه‌ای در جای جانی
درون نقطهٔ چشم آسمانی

There is life in the wing of a single gnat,
And inside the point of the eye a sky.

This verse is again another highly poetical image expressing the abovementioned principle.

بدین خردی که آمد حبهٔ دل
خداوند دو عالم راست منزل

With all the smallness of the middle of the heart (*ḥabbah-yi dil*),
It is the place of descent of the Lord of the two worlds.

Now, he turns to man. *Ḥabba-yi dil*, in both traditional and modern anatomy, is an empty space in the very middle of the heart, which is also called *dihlīz* in Persian. So, *ḥabba-yi dil* is considered as the very center of the heart. And it is there where the seat of the Divine Presence is to be found, following the *ḥadīth*, *Qalb al-mu'min 'arsh al-Raḥmān*, "the heart of the believer is the Throne of the Compassionate." So, Shabistarī says, "It is the place of descent of the Lord of the two worlds." God resides at the center of the heart of the human being.

در او در جمع گشته هر دو عالم
گهی ابلیس گردد گاه آدم

In him [*ū*, that is, man] is assembled both worlds.
Sometimes he becomes the Devil, sometimes Adam.

Although God resides in the center of the heart of man, some men forget that center and become like the Devil, while others remember it, becoming the Adamic reality. The fact that both possibilities are there means that God has given man freedom, which presents him with the peerless opportunity to ascend to the Divine or fall into infernal states.

ببین عالم همه در هم سرشته
ملک در دیو و شیطان در فرشته

Look how in the world everything is mixed together;
The angel in the demon, and the Devil in the angel.

This truth continues what was said in the verses above. We see this reality clearly in the world today, and it must have been like that in Shabistarī's time also. What does he mean? He means that we have all the elements of good and evil potentially within ourselves. Every possibility exists potentially within the human being. Sometimes he or she is angelic, sometimes demonic. Sometimes he or she is good, sometimes evil. All the different forces exist within the human being, and that is what makes life so challenging.

همه با هم به هم چون دانه و بر
ز کافر مؤمن و مؤمن ز کافر

All are mixed together like a seed and what grows from it.
From the infidel comes the believer, from the believer the infidel.

Mu'min (believer) and *kāfir* (infidel) constitute one of those complementary and at the same time oppositional terms that one finds often in Islamic thought, like such terms as *tashbīh* and *tanzīh*.

به هم جمع آمده در نقطهٔ حال
همه دور زمان روز و مه و سال

All of these are assembled together in the present moment,[12]
All periods of time, days, months and years.

"All of these are assembled together," means all these different contradictory traits that we have in us and exist in the world are assembled together right here and now, "in the present moment," when we find ourselves. Then Shabistarī makes a profound metaphysical point:

ازل عین ابد افتاد با هم
نزول عیسی و ایجاد آدم

Post-eternity (*abad*) has become the same as pre-eternity (*azal*);
The descent of Christ and the creation of Adam.

To clarify what the first hemistich means, Shabsitarī turns to Abrahamic sacred history. Christ was called the second Adam. Adam was created from clay into which God breathed His Spirit. Christ was not created from clay, but was born with the Spirit of God (*Ruḥ Allāh*), and was therefore in a sense a second Adam. Christ was, thereby, the Eternal Adam. This verse shows that Shabistarī had a profound knowledge of prophetology. Also, Adam, in a sense, represents *azal* (pre-eternity). Christ represents *abad* (post-eternity), and as the second Adam, *abad* goes back to *azal*. They become the same reality. So, the second hemistich is really an example of what the poet is saying in the first hemistich.

ز هر یک نقطه زین دور مسلسل
هزاران شکل می‌گردد مشکّل

From every point in circuitous reasoning and infinite regress,
A thousand forms become formalized.

Here, Shabistarī is referring to the nature of false reasoning from which numerous formal errors arise.

ز هر یک نقطه دوری گشته دایر
هم او مرکز هم او در دور سایر

From a single point a circle is generated,
That point is both the center and the moving point of the circumference.

"From a single point a circle is generated" refers to the single Principle generating the circle of existence while remaining the center of that circle. This verse is referring to the metaphysical principle of manifestation that I mentioned before.

اگر یک ذره‌را برگیری از جای
خلل یابد همه عالم سراپای

If a single speck of dust were to be removed from where it belongs,
The whole world would collapse.

Everything in this world has its place. Do not say, "Oh, I have moved a brick from the wall of my house, and nothing collapsed." That is something different. The point is that ontologically speaking, everything has its place in the Universe; its *makān* (location) can change, but its ontological reality cannot be taken out of the Universe. Ṭūsī refers to the same reality when he says,

Whatever exists must be what it is.
Whatever is not meant to exist is not.[13]

همه سرگشته و یک جزو از ایشان
برون ننهاده پا از حدّ امکان

[In this whole world] all beings are wandering, but not a single part of them,
Has set foot beyond the world of contingency (*imkān*).

Here he is using the philosophical terms formulated by Ibn Sīnā. God is the Necessary Being (*wājib*), and everything else is contingent (*mumkin*). No existent can, therefore, go beyond contingency to necessity in its own nature. Only God is the Necessary Being.

تعیّن هر یکی‌را کرده محبوس
به جزویّت ز کلّی گشته مأیوس

Determination has imprisoned each being,
Because of particularity, it has lost hope of the Universal.

"Determination has imprisoned each being" refers to the fact that all beings are imprisoned by the determination of being the particular being that they are in the realm of contingency.

تو گوئی دائما در سیر و حبسند
که پیوسته میان خلع و لبسند

It is as if you were to say that all creatures are always in movement, and at the same time imprisoned,
For they are constantly going between unveiling (*khal'*) and veiling (*labs*).

In this world creatures are in movement, yet confined within their limits. *Khal'* means to take off one's clothing, and *labs* means to put on clothing. What does that mean? It means that forms are taken away from the creatures of this world and new forms are imposed by God upon them. Yet, they remain the same contingent beings.

همه در جنبش و دائم در آرام
نه آغاز یکی پیدا نه انجام

[In this world,] all are in movement and yet constantly at peace,
Neither the beginning of a being is manifest nor its end.

There is both movement and rest in the created order, the origin and end of which is not evident.

همه از ذات خود پیوسته آگاه
وز آنجا راه برده تا به درگاه

All the creatures have an awareness of their own essence.
Through this self-awareness, they have found the path to the Divine Threshold (*dargāh*).

This verse points to an important but often forgotten truth. Do not think that animals have no awareness or consciousness of themselves. They do, and that is why the creatures of God all pray to Him. The Quran says, *wa in min shay'in illā yusabbiḥu bi-ḥamdihi*, "And there is no thing save that it hymns His praise" (Q. 17:44). All creatures praise the Glory of God. "Through this self-awareness, they have found the path to the Divine Threshold" refers to finding the Divine *dargāh*, the Divine Proximity.

به زیر پردهٔ هر ذرّه پنهان
جمال جانفزای روی جانان

Behind the veil of every single atom there is hidden,
The Life-giving Beauty of the Face of God (*Jānān*).

The inner reality of every creature reveals the Beauty of God, but to see that Beauty we must not only cast aside the veil of creatures but also penetrate into our own inner being.

Principle

This *qā'idah*, this principle, asks very important questions about different aspects of the world, with reference to certain *ḥadīth*s.

تو از عالم همین لفظی شنیدی
بیا برگو که از عالم چه دیدی؟

Thou hast only heard concerning the world a phrase.
Come and recount, what hast thou seen of the world?

"A phrase" refers to the outward appearance of the world, and so Shabistarī questions what meaning a person has drawn from only hearing about the world, thus asking what one has really seen of its essential reality. Here, "seen" must be also understood as "come to know."

چه دانستی ز صورت یا ز معنا؟
چه باشد آخرت چون است دنیا؟

What hast thou come to learn about form (*ṣūrat*) and meaning (*ma'nā*)?
What is the other world (*ākhirat*)? And what is this world (*dunyā*)?

Shabistarī is asking these questions one after another to bring about awareness of the need for deeper understanding even of this world. Here, he uses the word *ṣūrat* and *ma'nā*. I want you to make sure that you understand that we have two different usages of the word *ṣūrah* (in Arabic) or *ṣūrat* (in Persian) in Islamic thought that many confuse with each other. One is when we talk about form and matter in the Aristotelian sense of *morphos* and *hylé* or *forma* and *materia*, for which the terms *ṣūrah* and *māddah* or *hayūlā*, are used in Arabic and Persian. In that case *ṣūrah* is the formal principle, the actualized aspect of something. It is the higher aspect of the reality of a thing. However, when used in Sufism it is the other way around: *ṣūrah* is juxtaposed with *ma'nā*. *Ma'nā* is a very important word in Arabic, and means "meaning." Arabs will often use the related word *ya'nī* when they speak, which means "it means." Now, "meaning" here is not just what one thinks of in ordinary English usage, for example when we say *la porte* in French means door. "Meaning" (*ma'nā*) in Sufi usage means again the inner essence of something, the spiritual principle. So, the word *ṣūrah* here plays the opposite role to that it does in the form-matter distinction used by the Peripatetic philosophers. For the Sufis *ṣūrah* is the outward form. The inner principle is the *ma'nā*.

بگو سیمرغ و کوه قاف چبود؟
بهشت و دوزخ و اعراف چبود؟

Tell what is the Sīmurgh? And what is Mount Qāf?
What is Paradise? What is Hell? What is Purgatory (*a'rāf*)?

The Sīmurgh, *al-'Anqā'* in Arabic, is usually translated as "Griffin" in English, and Mount Qāf is the cosmic mountain in Islamic cosmology. I shall explain these terms below. The word *a'rāf* comes from the Quranic *sūrah* by that name and means a place in the intermediate state between Heaven and Hell. And so it is often translated as "Purgatory," although it is technically only a part of Purgatory, the whole of which is usually referred to as *barzakh*. Without providing answers, Shabistarī is posing questions about both cosmological and eschatological realities to make the reader become aware of the importance of gaining knowledge of them.

كدام است آن جهان کو نیست پیدا
که یک روزش بود یک سال اینجا؟

Which is that world that is not visible,
One day of which is like a year here?

In this verse, set again in the form of a question, Shabistarī is alluding to Quranic verses such as "And truly a day with your Lord is as a thousand years of that which you reckon" (Q. 22:47), and "Unto Him ascend the angels and the Spirit on a day whose measure is fifty thousand years" (Q. 70:4), that is, in the other world, time is not the same as it is here, and a day there is equivalent to a year or a thousand years or even fifty thousand years. With this question Shabistarī is persuading the reader to seek the invisible world and the different experiences of time in various levels of reality.

همین نبود جهان آخر که دیدی
نه «ما لا تبصرون» آخر شنیدی؟

What thou hast seen then is not the whole Universe.
Hast thou not heard, "[I swear by] what you see not"? (Q. 69:39).

بیا بنما که جابلقا کدام است
جهان شهر جابلسا کدام است؟

Come and show where *Jābulqā* is.
Where is the world of the city *Jābulsā*?

This verse needs some explanation, but before proceeding any further, I want to explain the Sīmurgh and Mount Qāf, which are in a sense related to *Jābulqā* and *Jābulsā*. These are all metaphysical, cosmological, and/or mythical terms in the Islamic tradition. First of all, the Sīmurgh: The word itself is found in Pahlavi, *semargha*, and dates back to the Achaemenid period.[14] It entered modern Persian as *murgh*, "bird." As for *sīmurgh*, it consists of two words, *sī* (thirty), and *murgh* (bird). So, *sīmurgh*, which is the proper name of a mythical bird residing on top of Mount Qāf, the cosmic mountain, could also mean thirty birds, because in Persian when you say something in the plural preceded by a number you do not use the plural form of the noun. In English you say, "one door," "two doors," but in Persian it is as if you say "one door," "two door," and so on. I mention this point because the word *sīmurgh* entered into Sufi literature in which some played on the words *sī* and *murgh*, especially Farīd al-Dīn ʿAṭṭār. The great masterpiece that deals with this term is his *Manṭiq al-ṭayr* (*The Conference of the Birds*), which has been translated into English several times,[15] and is one of the greatest masterpieces of the Persian language, and in fact of all Sufi literature.[16] In brief, in this narrative, a large number of birds set out to meet the Sīmurgh, which resides on Mount Qāf. *Qāf* is both the name of one of the letters of the Arabic alphabet and the name of the fiftieth *sūrah* of the Quran as well as the cosmic mountain. This *sūrah* deals with many important cosmological and eschatological matters, and in it God speaks about a new creation (*khalq jadīd*, Q. 50:15). There are all kinds of symbols related to the letter *qāf*, but it is considered primarily to be the name of the cosmic mountain.

But what does "cosmic mountain" mean? In nearly every traditional civilization there is a sacred mountain, which is considered to symbolize the cosmos itself, with all its states of being. The pyramid has the same symbolism. The peak of this mountain touches the void. It touches "infinity." From that one point cosmic existence is generated, going from unity to multiplicity, such that all the points in multiplicity meet in that one single unity. Many of the traditional writers, including Frithjof Schuon and René Guénon, have discussed this symbolism, and Marco Pallis has a book called *The Way and the Mountain*, in which there is a wonderful discussion of the symbolism of the cosmic mountain.[17] I will not go into the details of this matter now, but will only add that, for example, the Hindus believe in Mount Meru, the Greeks have Mount Olympus, and so on. In Islam, although it is a non-mythological religion, the idea of Mount Qāf, the cosmic mountain, is very prevalent in Arabic, Persian, Turkish and Urdu literature. In ancient Persia the cosmic mountain was considered to be represented by Mount Damavand, just outside of Tehran, which is a majestic conic mountain, nearly nineteen thousand feet high, and is the highest mountain in Western Asia. In the Zoroastrian period this mountain itself was considered to be sacred as the cosmic mountain, and many Persians even after the coming of Islam have continued to believe that Mount Damavand symbolizes the cosmic mountain. This belief is something symbolic. No one knows where the central cosmic mountain really is, but nearly every civilization has this idea and identifies a physical mountain with it.

Another example is Mount Fuji, Fujiyama, in Japan, which is the cosmic mountain in Japanese civilization. That is why nobody climbs to the very top of it, for the top belongs only to the gods. If today you look at the Japanese climbing Mount Fuji, you will see that the traditional Japanese do not go to the very top, which they consider to be reserved for deities. The first civilization that began to go to the top of mountains was the modern secular civilization of Europe. The Nepalese never went to the very top of the mountains in the Himalayas. They considered them to be sacred, to belong to God. I did a lot of mountain climbing in the Alps in my young days, and saw that even today the traditional Swiss shepherds do not go to the very top of a mountain, believing that it is a sacred precinct that belongs to God. Can you imagine this attitude persisting in Europe in the middle of a secularized country like Switzerland? But the shepherds up there are not modernized. They are traditional Swiss and have a very different mentality from those who try to "conquer" mountain peaks and subjugate mountains.

So this is a very important matter from a religious point of view. The top of the cosmic mountain belonged to the Divinity. That is where manifestation touches the void. The mountain symbolizes the cosmos. The sky symbolizes the Divine Infinity. The very top of the mountain symbolizes Being, from which existence is manifested. And the space beyond the top of the mountain points to the infinity of Non-Being or Beyond Being. So, there are very powerful symbols associated with the mountain, and all the rites performed for example at several sacred mountains in northern India go back to this fundamental and primordial symbolism, to which Shabistarī is alluding here.

Yes, the top of the mountain belongs to God, to the Divinity, to the metacosmic Reality, you might say. At the top of the mountain, according to this Persian mythology, resides the Sīmurgh. Now, who is the Sīmurgh? Until 'Aṭṭar wrote the *Manṭiq al-ṭayr*, the Sīmurgh was usually seen as a symbol of the Logos, the link between the metacosmic and cosmic reality, and in a sense, the creative act of God Himself. It was not identified with God. But in 'Aṭṭār's poetry the Sīmurgh is transformed into the Divine Reality itself, to God Himself, not the Logos. The Sīmurgh in *Manṭiq al-ṭayr* is a symbol of the Divine Itself, and in fact alludes to the highest level of the Divine Reality. Therefore, of course, in that poem no one can see the Sīmurgh. In the *Manṭiq al-ṭayr*, when the Sīmurgh reveals Itself, only thirty of the birds that journeyed to see It are left, and 'Aṭṭār plays with the word *sī*, which, as I mentioned means thirty in Persian, and *murgh* (birds). And so when the birds reach the end of their journey and seek to see the Sīmurgh, they see a mirror, in which they see themselves as thirty birds. When they see the Sīmurgh, they do not see themselves as *sī murgh* but as Sīmurgh. When they see themselves as thirty birds, they do not see the Sīmurgh.

I believe that although Shabistarī knew ʻAṭṭār's work, when he asks here if the reader knows what the Sīmurgh is, we can say that he means the Logos, that is, the reality that is the nexus between God and the created world, that is,. the Word of God, by which things were made as the Book of John says. However, in ʻAṭṭār the Sīmurgh is elevated to the Divine Reality Itself.

Now we come to *Jābulqā* and *Jābulsā*, which are also related to traditional cosmology. This issue again needs quite some explanation. These terms are famous in Persian literature, and they are mentioned by other poets such as Nāṣir-i Khusraw and Mawlānā Rūmī. But what are *Jābulqā* and *Jābulsā*? If you ask many Persian scholars today, few will not know their full meaning. Many will just say that they refer to some mythical cities.

So, let us explain it. As you know, according to ancient geography, there were seven climes or climates. This word comes from the Greek word *climata*, which also entered into Arabic and Persian as *iqlīm*. The Greek geographers divided the habitable world, the world in which human beings live, into seven regions, each of which was called a *climata*. When you say, "the climate is good," there is an indirect meaning of it implying that this is the condition of the *climata* in which you live. Otherwise, in English today we do not use the word "climate" in the same way as did Greek or Muslim geographers.

So "clime" or "climate" was a geographical division of the world. Since the known world was envisioned as a flat piece of land extending from Europe to Western Asia, this land was divided into seven regions from north to south, which were called the seven *climata*. The regions that were not known in medieval geography were Siberia and Northern Asia, Central and South Africa, lands in the Indian Ocean, and of course Australia and the Americas; so those areas were not considered. It was said that all habitation, all human life, is in these seven climates. You might be a Swede, you might be a Persian, you might be an Arab, you might be an Indian: all with different features and skin color living in one of these *climata* or *iqlīm*s. The Ikhwān al-Ṣafāʼ have a lengthy discussion about this matter, considering why for example, Indians are more contemplative than Persians, and Persians learn things more quickly than them (and similar matters depending upon the *iqlīm* in which they lived). These discussions are related to the *climata* (the climate), which also has an anthropological and spiritual sense.

These climates, therefore, determined all the different conditions of life in this world. This world is not, however, the only world. There are other worlds, and our souls come into this world from those higher worlds and after death return to the worlds beyond. Gradually there developed this mythology (I use the word in a positive sense), especially in Persian literature, but also in Arabic and other forms of Islamic literature, of the eighth clime (*iqlīm-i hashtum*). The eighth clime cannot be in this world, since there are only seven climes in it. Consequently, the eighth clime was seen as the intermediate world, the world immediately above this world, the imaginal world of which Suhrawardī speaks and about which Corbin wrote.[18] The eighth clime does not belong to the physical world: but the reason the term clime was used was because it gives a sense of reality, like the geography of this world. It is part of the *géographie imaginaire*, as Corbin called it, that is an imaginal geography, a geography that embraces a world beyond this earth and that has its own cities, life and characteristics.

Now, the place from which one descends from the eighth clime into this world, whether one is born in England or in India, is called *Jābulqā*. That is the last stage of our descent into this world. We begin to cry when we come out of our mother's womb; where have we come from? From *Jābulqā*. That is why we cry. We do not want to leave *Jābulqā* and come to this lowly place into which we have fallen. You have never seen a child born who was laughing (Christ being an exception). The child already has intelligence and it still has the reality of the other world in its mind, and so, it realizes its fall. It is not only because it hurts to be born, for after a short while the pain goes away. But it takes some time before the baby laughs and smiles. It always begins, however, by crying. It asks, "Where in the world have you brought me?"

And then on the way back when we die, the first "city" that we visit is *Jābulsā*. Therefore, *Jābulqā* and *Jābulsā* belong to the imaginal world, to *'ālam al-khayāl* in Islamic philosophy, but this is not at all *khiyāl* (imagination) in the sense of being unreal. On the contrary, it is very real, and more real than the physical world. It is *khiyāl* in the sense that Suhrawardī, Mullā Ṣadrā and other Islamic sages understood it.

مشارق با مغارب هم بیندیش
چه این عالم ندارد جز یکی بیش

Meditate (*biyandīsh*) also upon the easts and the wests,
For this world has only one of each.

Andīshīdan, which ordinarily means "to think" here means "to meditate." The fact that "the easts and the wests" are in the plural is very important. When the Quran says, God is *rabb al-mashāriq wa al-maghārib*, "Lord of the easts and the wests" (Q. 70:40), it means that there must be other easts and other wests; that is, there must be other worlds. It is to this truth that Shabistarī is alluding.

بیان «مثلهنّ» ز ابن عبّاس
شنو پس خویشتن‌را نیک بشناس

The explanation of "the like thereof" by Ibn 'Abbās
Harken to it, then know thyself well.

This is in reference to a time when the Prophet commented to Ibn 'Abbās in commentary on the verse of the Quran, "God it is Who created the seven heavens, and from the earth the like thereof (*mithlahunna*)" (Q. 65:12). When the people asked Ibn 'Abbās what the Prophet told him, he said, "If I told you what the Prophet told me, you would kill me." Outwardly this seems to be a very strange report, that the cousin of the Prophet would say that if he were to reiterate what the Prophet had told him, he would get himself killed. Many Sufis take this as a reference to the esoteric meaning of verse twelve of *Sūrat al-Ṭalāq*. The Arabic word *mithlahunna*, "like them" in this verse by Shabistarī is in reference to this episode.

تو در خوابی و این دیدن خیال است
هر آنچه دیده‌ای از وی مثال است

Thou art asleep and what thou seest is imagination.
Whatever thou seest is a symbol (*mithāl*) that comes from Him.

Mithāl should be translated as "symbol" in this context, and not "example," which is another meaning of this term. There is also the implication that the ordinary person, one who has not awakened spirituality, sees symbols but does not realize that what he sees is not just a fact but a symbol that comes from God.

به صبح حشر چون گردی تو بیدار
بدانی کان همه وهم است و پندار

On the morning of resurrection, when thou wakest up,
Thou wilt discover that all those things are apprehension and [thine own]
thought.

"All those things" means "the whole world"; that is, this world is not truly real; reality belongs to elsewhere. You all have heard the *ḥadīth* of the Prophet that says *al-nāsu niyām wa idhā mātū intabahū*, "People are asleep, and when they die, they awaken." Shabistarī is referring to this teaching. We are asleep here, but we think that we are awake. When we really wake up, we find out that, as Shakespeare said, "Life is but a dream."

Now, this doctrine does not mean that this earthly life is completely unreal. Again, we have to understand the ontological levels that metaphysicians talk about, and realize that a dream itself has a reality. It is not completely unreal; rather, it is a lower level of reality. You have a very exceptional case in one form of Hindu metaphysics, in which, in fact, the higher levels of reality are associated with deeper levels of sleep. There are four different levels, and the deepest level of reality is identified with deep sleep. So, that understanding of sleep must not be confused with sleep in the sense that one finds in both mainstream Islamic and Christian thought.

In any case while we are asleep in this world, what is going on has consequences and a reality, but not the reality that fallen man attributes to it. In sleep sometimes we are afraid, sometimes we see things, sometimes we think of things. When we wake up, we enter another state of consciousness, and then we realize that in our sleep we were dreaming and what we saw did not possess the reality that we experience while awake. If we never woke up, we would not know that we were dreaming. The reason we know we are sleeping is that we wake up. This is the truth to which Shabistarī is alluding on the spiritual level, that is, death is a waking up. But since we have not died, we take this life to be reality itself. It is not totally unreal, but it is like the reality of a dream, to be contrasted with the reality we experience in the morning when we wake up.

چو برخیزد خیال چشم احول
زمین و آسمان گردد مبدّل

When the imagination (*khiyāl*) of the squinted eye is lifted,
The earth and heaven become transformed.

Here he is not using the *khiyāl* in the creative sense of *khiyāl* that Ibn 'Arabī and Mullā Ṣadrā also use, but just imagination in the ordinary sense. If you could only see, if you did not have all the abnormalities of the eye that we mentioned before, which for Shabistarī represent particular metaphysical errors, you would see that the whole world, both the earth and the heavens, will be transformed.

چو خورشید جهان بنمایدت چهر
نماند نور ناهید و مه و مهر

When the Sun of the world shows its face to thee,[19]
Nothing will remain of the light of Venus, the Moon and the Sun.

"The Sun of the world" is in reference to Being and not the astronomical Sun. We see the light of the stars when the Sun is not there. During daytime the stars are still shining, but we do not see them because during the day the light of the Sun covers everything and overwhelms the lesser light of all the stars.

فتد یک تاب از آن بر سنگ خاره
شود چون پشم رنگین پاره پاره

If one ray of that [Sun] were to be cast upon a piece of rock (*sang-i khārah*)
That rock would turn into a piece of colored wool, all torn up.

This verse means that if the Light of the Divine Reality were to be totally present in anything, it would demolish the apparent separative existence of that existent completely.

بدان اکنون که کردن می‌توانی
چه نتوانی چه سود آنگه که دانی

Know, now when you [still] can do so.
When you cannot, what benefit does it have to know then?

This point is something important for all of us to learn. There is a warning here about death, about how important life is. In this world we can gain awareness, we can become knowledgeable, but when we die, we are cut off from the possibility of attainment of principial knowledge and truth although we realize that they are real. And then he castigates himself:

چه می‌گویم حدیث عالم دل
تورا ای سرنشیب پای در گل؟

What am I saying concerning the story of the world of the heart,
For thou hast thy head downward and thy feet stuck in the mud (*sar-nashīb-u pāy dar gil*)?

The phrase *sar-nashīb-u pāy dar gil* means someone who has fallen with his head cast low and his feet stuck in the mud. So, why do I say these things to such a person? He is asking himself.

جهان آن تو و تو مانده عاجز
ز تو محرومتر کس دید هرگز؟

The world belongs to thee, but thou remainest helpless.
Has one ever seen anyone more deprived than thee?

The world is in a sense under our dominion in the spiritual not material sense, but we do not realize that reality. We are, therefore, helpless because we do not realize the truth and act on it. Can anyone be so deprived?

چو محبوسان به یک منزل نشسته
به دست عجز پای خویش بسته

Like prisoners [thou art] sitting in a single house,
Having tied thine own feet with [the rope of] helplessness.

Man has become a prisoner of his own *nafs* unable to go to states beyond it. He has tied his own feet because of ignorance of who he really is and can be; so, he sits in a corner helpless, whereas he should be, he could be, the spiritual master of the whole world.

نشستی چون زنان در کنج ادبیر
نمی‌داری ز جهل خویشتن سیر

Thou art sitting like women in the corner of misfortune (*idbīr*);
Thou dost not become satiated with thine own ignorance.[20]

Now, this verse has to be understood not literally but socially and historically. In the days of Shabistarī when one said *zanān* (literally "women") it also meant someone who was weak, who could not do something by herself and needed someone to help her. Be we are not to confuse *zanān* with only the female gender; it is important to recall the *ḥadīth* that on the Day of Judgment,

God commands, "All the *rijāl* (literally 'men') step forward," and the first person who steps forward is the Virgin Mary (Sayyidah Maryam)—*'alayhā al-salām*. This statement means that *rijāl* is not concerned only with gender, but with spiritual quality. So, one should not be offended by this verse at all as being sexist and applying present day notions to another historical situation. At the end of this book we are going to read about the beauty of a woman's face, which represents God's Qualities and see the exalted state of femininity in Sufism.

The use of the term *zan* in the old days was also reference to certain social qualities found in both genders. The word *zan* was used to refer to someone who could not help another human being and could not even help herself or himself, who was weak and this kind of thing. That is what it means here, not at all as reference to every woman, especially not spiritually. For example, *idbīr* means misfortune; so, Shabistarī says, "Thou art sitting like women in the corner of misfortune" because in those days, not only in the Islamic world but also in India and other places, often when a husband or brother died and a woman did not have any protector, she would go to some relatives and sit in the corner of their house and not meddle in anything. When I was in Iran, in the house of my uncles there was often an old woman, the mother-in-law or an aunt for example, who would just sit in some corner of the house all the time and was supported by the rest of the family. They would feed her in her room until she died. She would read the Quran during the day and pray. That situation represents a social aspect of this matter to which one has to pay attention. Old men in such situations were also treated the same as old women. Applying value judgments of the future to this century's might result, for example, in many getting extremely angry at us because we did not give the same rights that they would give at their time. But you cannot blame the people of this century because they were not living in that ambiance. So, one has to consider this basic fact.[21]

"Thou dost not become satiated with thine own ignorance" uses a very important Persian expression, to have had enough of one's ignorance (*az jahl-i khwīsh sīr shudan*). *Sīr shudan* in Persian means "to become full" after eating, or to have had enough of something. Human beings who are ignorant have never had enough of their own ignorance. If I keep serving you food, after the third helping, you would say, "*sīr shudam*," "I have had enough, I cannot eat anymore," but when it comes to ignorance, no matter how much of it we have, we usually continue in our state and often become even more ignorant as time passes by.

دلیران جهان آغشته در خون
تو سرپوشیده ننهی پای بیرون

The heroes of the world are drowned in blood,
Thou art hiding thy head and refuse to take a step outside,

"The heroes of the world are drowned in blood," alludes to the result of the spiritual battle that men of God are carrying out. To be hiding at home to avoid the spiritual battle of life means to refuse to face reality in its deepest sense.

چه کردی فهم از این دین العجائز
که بر خود جهل می‌داری تو جائز؟

What hast thou learned from the religion of infirm old people (*'ajā'iz*)
So that thou considerest ignorance to be acceptable for thyself?

The word *al-'ajā'iz* means "infirm old people," who cannot think or act well. So, Shabistarī criticizes those who try to imitate the religion of such people and, therefore, consider ignorance to be acceptable for themselves. If you accept to be ignorant, then what have you understood of religion?[22]

زنان چون ناقصات عقل و دین اند
چرا مردان ره ایشان گزینند؟

> Women are like those infirm in intellect and religion.
> Why should men choose their path?

I have already commented on this issue above. I could add that a reason for this verse is that in days of old, there were very few women who were knowledgeable in the sciences and, moreover, many women followed folk practices and were interested in talismans and magic and all kinds of things like that, which we still see in the Islamic world. They rarely studied the intellectual aspects of religion firmly. The verse does not state that they lacked faith. In Islam most women had very strong faith. It is they who have brought up children and taught them the first steps of being a Muslim, and many continue to do so today.

When I was a small child, for example, every Nawrūz (the Persian new year) we would go on pilgrimage and spend it in a sanctuary, either in Qom or Ḥaḍrat-i ʻAbd al-ʻAẓīm near Tehran, at the moment of the vernal equinox. Thousands of people were there, and the experiences of those occurrences are some of the very clear memories that I have of my childhood. With whom did I go? My mother. I never went with my father, not even once. So, Shabistarī is not talking about faith and the transmission of love of God and matters like that. He is talking about the intellectual aspect of religion, Islamic law, philosophy, and so forth. In the old days, women usually did not study these subjects; so, that fact is a reality to which he is referring. This verse is not to be taken as a general insult against women, to whose spiritual qualities the poet turns at the end of this work. As I told you, one cannot evaluate historical figures on the basis of criteria that have now become prevalent. It is like saying, why does Shakespeare use sexist language by referring to men, or Christ was called the Son of Man. He was born of a mother, but he was called the Son of Man, that was the title of Christ. Now, some are trying to change it to "the child of humans," which does not make the same theological sense in the English language. This verse of the *Gulshan-i rāz* must be understood in the context of the worldview held at the time when it was composed.

اگر مردی برون آی و نظر کن
هر آنچ آید به پیشت زان گذر کن

> If thou art a [real] man (*mard*) come out, and cast your glance;
> Whatever happens before thee, pass it by.

"Come out," that is, from the corner in which you have been hiding from the truth. *Mard* here means *rajul* ('man' in the sense explained above) and does not mean male. It means be a person who is active in following the spiritual path. Of course, a female can also hide herself from the spiritual battle or engage in it as can a male; it is not a question of gender. Then he advises the seeker to come out of the prison of his ego and whatever happens, to experience it, then to pass it by, going beyond it.

میاسا یک زمان اندر مراحل
مشو موقوف همراه رواحل

> Do not rest for a moment in the steps of the path,
> Do not stop from accompanying the caravan (*rawāḥil*).

Rawāḥil is the plural of *rāḥil*, and includes the camels and those who are journeying together with them. The caravan stops from time to time, and the person on the spiritual journey should not discontinue his journey at any way station and not leave the caravan.

خلیل‌آسا برو حقّ‌را طلب کن
شبی‌را روز و روزی‌را به شب کن

Like Abraham (*Khalīl-āsā*), go and seek the Truth.
Pass the night into the day and the day into the night.

Khalīl is the title of Abraham (Khalīl Allāh, Friend of God), and *āsā* means "like" in Persian, so *Khalīl-āsā* means "like Abraham." Let us remember the story of Abraham in the Quran, in which he did not want to do anything day and night until he found the Truth. And then let us recall the three episodes that occurred when he was looking for God and a star appeared, and he said that cannot be God because the star set, and "I love not that which sets" (*lā uḥibb al-āfilīn)*, and likewise when he saw the Moon and the Sun. Having passed beyond these stages, he finally reached God (see Q. 6:75–79).

ستاره با مه و خورشید اکبر
بود حسّ و خیال و عقل انور

The star, the Moon and the greater Sun,
Correspond to the senses, the imagination and the illuminated intellect,

He is again referring to the story of Abraham that is mentioned in the Quran. These stages also symbolize the means and levels of seeking God.

بگردان زین همه ای راهرو روی
همیشه «لا احب الافلین» گوی

Pass by all of these, O thou who art walking upon the path.
Always say, "I do not love that which sets" (*lā uḥibb al-āfilīn*). (Q. 6:76)

Here he is referring to the fact that Abraham was not fooled by any of the abovementioned experiences and knew that they cannot be God. So, man is advised to be like Abraham and not become fixated upon any theophany, mistaking it for the Origin of the theophany.

و یا چون موسی عمران در این راه
برو تا بشنوی «انّی انا الله»

Or, like Moses son of 'Imrān, walking on this path,
Go until thou hearest, "Truly I am God" (*innī ana'Llāh*). (Q. 28:30)

You see how enmeshed the *Gulshan-i rāz* is with the Quran and the stories it contains. Some people think that Sufism came from Neoplatonism, India or some source like them foreign to the Quran, but they do not really know what they are talking about. Sufism has grown out of the inner meaning of the Quran and the power of *walāyah/wilāyah* that goes back to the Prophet of Islam, who is the supreme exemplar for the Sufis.

Here reference is to the famous account of Moses hearing a bush utter "I am God." When Moses went into the sacred valley, *wādī al-ṭuwā*, he heard from the right side of the valley God speaking through the bush this *āyah*, *innī ana'Llāh*.

تورا تا کوه هستی پیش باقی است
جواب لفظ «ارنی» «لن ترانی» است

As long as the mountain of existence remains before thee,
The response to "show me," is "thou shalt not see Me." (Q. 7:143)

According to the Quran, when Moses wanted to see God, God said to him, *lan tarānī* "Thou shall not see me." As long as we live in a separative state of existence, we cannot have a vision of God. His response to our request to see Him in our separative state will be, "Thou shalt not see Me."

حقیقت کهربا ذات تو کاه است
اگر کوه توئی نبود چه راه است

The truth is like a magnet and thy essence is like iron-filing,
If the mountain of thy thyness were not to be there, the road would be very short.

In the Persian original *kahrubā* (amber) and *kāh* (straw or blade of grass) are used, which I have rendered as "magnet" and "iron filing," which are more common in English. What prevents us from reaching God, or that filing being attracted to the magnet, is what he calls *tu'ī* or thyness, that is, the *nafs*, which could also be understood as I-ness, depending on how one translates the term. It is our ego that prevents us from being pulled by God unto Himself very quickly, like the magnet pulling iron-filings to itself.

تجلّی گر رسد بر کوه هستی
شود چون خاک ره هستی ز پستی

If theophany were to reach the mountain of existence,
Existence would become through abasement like the dust of the road.

If God were to unveil His Reality to this world of separative existence which we take to be reality, it would turn into dust.

گدائی گردد از یک جذبه شاهی
به یک لحظه دهد کوهی به کاهی

A beggar can become through a single attraction [to the Divine] a king.
In a second, he would give a mountain for a dried blade of grass.

Once a person, even a lowly beggar, is attracted to God, he becomes like a king, and he would exchange the whole of his existence, which appears to him like a mountain, for a blade of grass or iron filing that is drawn to the magnet.

And then Shabistarī advises the reader,

برو اندر پی خواجه به اسرا
تفرّج کن همه آیات کبرا

Follow the Master (*khwājah*), in the celestial ascent
Study all the great signs [of God].

"The Master" here refers to the Prophet and *isrā* to the first part of his celestial ascent (*al-Mi'rāj*) in which he, riding the "mythical" horse *Burāq*, was taken by Gabriel to Jerusalem and from there ascended to the Divine Presence.

برون آی از سرای «امّ هانی»
بگو مطلق حدیث «من رآنی»

Come out of the house of Umm-i Hānī.
Recite in an absolute way the *ḥadīth* of "Whoever has seen me" (*man ra'ānī*).

Umm-i Hānī was the sister of 'Alī ibn Abī Ṭālib, and it is said that when the Prophet went on the *mi'rāj*, he left from her house. And so, in the esoteric understanding of this central episode in the life of the Prophet her house represents this world, and to leave the house of Umm-i Hānī means to leave this limited world for the Divine Abode.

"Whoever has seen me" (*man ra'ānī*), refers to a very famous *ḥadīth*, *anā Aḥmadun bi-lā mīm, anā 'arabun bi-lā 'ayn, man ra'ānī fa-qad ra'ā'l-Ḥaqq*. "I am Aḥmad without the m, [that is, *aḥad,* 'the One'], I am Arab without the *'ayn* [that is, *Rabb*, 'the Lord']; whoever has seen me, verily, he has seen the Truth." This is a very daring and outwardly enigmatic *ḥadīth*, which is in reference to the inner reality of the Prophet as a mirror of all of God's Names and Qualities, the Prophet being *al-insān al-kāmil* (the Perfect Man) par excellence.

گذاری کن ز کاف کنج کونین
نشین در قاف قرب «قاب قوسین»

Pass through the [letter] *Kāf* of the corner (*kunj*) of the two worlds (*kawnayn*),
And sit in the [letter] *Qāf* of the proximity of "the length of two bows." (Q. 53:9)

The words *kunj* (corner) and *kawnayn* (the two worlds) both start with the letter *Kāf*. This verse means pass through this world and the next. "The length of two bows" (*qāba qawsayn*) refers to when the Prophet went on the *Mi'rāj* and reached the highest station of Proximity to God, referred to in the Quran as *qāba qawsayn*, the length of two arches of the bow, this being the station nearest to God that even the Prophet could attain. So, Shabistarī says put yourself in this station of foremost proximity to God.

دهد حقّ مرتورا از آن چه خواهی
نمایندت همه اشیا کما هی

God will thereby give thee everything thou wantest,
He will show thee things as they really are.

The poem presumes the phrase "if thou doest so," then God will provide all that thou desirest, revealing to thee the reality of beings as they really are, *kamā hiya* referring to the famous prayer of the Prophet, "O Lord, show us things as they really are."

Principle

The short section that follows compares the Quran to the cosmos in relation to the language of the sacred revelation. This discussion is in a sense a reference to *al-Qur'ān al-tadwīnī* (the collated Quran) and *al-Qur'ān al-takwīnī* (the cosmic Quran).

به نزد آن که جانش در تجلّی است
همه عالم کتاب حقّ تعالی است

For the person whose soul is in theophany,
The whole world is the Book of the Transcendent Truth.

For the person whose soul has been illuminated by God, the whole of creation is seen as Sacred Scripture, as the Quran in its inner reality and cosmic reflection.

عرض اعراب و جوهر چون حروف است
مراتب همچو آیات وقوف است

Accidents [of this world] are like declensions and the substance like letters.
The different stages [of existence] are like pauses in the verses.

Shabistarī is using Arabic grammar to refer to traditional cosmology in which everything in nature consists of substance and accidents. For example, you have a painting on the wall. The material part itself is in itself a substance, but the color red on it is an accident. The length of one meter is an accident, while the material itself that is a meter long is substance. The accidents are called *'araḍ* in Arabic, and substance is called *jawhar*.

In the text of the Quran, unlike most Arabic writing, all of the declensions, the *i'rāb*, are written so that you know exactly how to pronounce each letter. Here, Shabistarī is comparing the written Quran to the cosmic book. In the cosmos there is a tree here, a mountain out there, and the sky above. They all consist of substance and accidents, while the Quran consists of letters (*ḥurūf*) and declensions (*i'rāb).*

The different creatures in the world, whether they be in the mineral, plant, animal or human realms, are like the verses of the Quran and the *wuqūf*, the stops that separate either words or verses in the Quran from each other like the elements that separate creatures from each other.

از او هر عالمی چون سوره‌ای خاص
یکی زان فاتحه دیگر چو اخلاص

From Him [has issued] each world, like a particular *sūrah* [of the Quran],
One is *Sūrat al-Fātiḥah* (Q. 1), the other *Sūrat al-Ikhlāṣ*. (Q. 112)

In these verses he makes the comparison more explicit. The *Sūrat al-Fātiḥah* comes at the beginning of the Quran and *Sūrat al-Ikhlāṣ* at the end.

نخستین آیتش عقل کلّ آمد
که در وی همچو باء بسمل آمد
The first *āyah* [of God] was the Universal Intellect,
Which appeared like the *Bā'* of *Bismi'Llāh*.

The very first letter with which the Quran begins, is *Bā'*: *Bismi'Llāh al-Raḥmān al-Raḥīm (In the Name of God, the Compassionate, the Merciful)*, and the first thing that God created was the Universal Intellect, and so he compares the two together.

دوم نفس کلّ آمد آیت نور
که چون مصباح شد در غایت نور

Second came the Universal Soul in the Light Verse. (Q. 24:35)
Which became like a lamp in the intensity of its light.

According to traditional accounts of the cosmic hierarchy, the highest created reality is the Universal Intellect and the second the Universal Soul. Like the above verse, Shabistarī compares it to an *āyah* of the Quran, the famous Light Verse.

سوم آیت در او شد عرش رحمان

چهارم آیت الکرسی همی خوان

The third *āyah* that appeared in it was the Throne of the Divine
Compassionate (*Raḥmān*).
The fourth, the Pedestal Verse (Q. 2:255). Read it.

Shabistarī is showing the correspondence between different verses of the Quran and different cosmic realities. The word *Raḥmān* indicates that he is referring to *Sūrat al-Raḥmān* (Q. 55), and of course *āyat al-kursī* is from *Sūrat al-Baqarah* (The Cow), the second *sūrah* of the Quran.

پس از وی جرمهای آسمانی است
که در وی سورۀ سبع المثانی است

After that come the celestial bodies,
In which are contained the *sūrah* of the *sab' al-mathānī* (The Seven
Oft-Repeated).

Only after those higher cosmic levels does one reach the heavenly bodies. *Sab' al-mathānī* (The Seven Oft-Repeated) is usually understood to refer to the opening chapter of the Quran, *Ṣūrat al-Fātiḥah*, which has seven verses.

نظر کن باز در جرم عناصر
که هر یک آیتی هستند باهر

Observe again (*naẓar kun bāz*) the body of the elements.
Each one is a sign of God made evident (*bāhir*).

Naẓar means "observe" here, and *bāz* means "again," but also implies "keenly" or "closely." "The body of the elements" refers to the creatures of this world.

پس از عنصر بود جرم سه مولود
که نتوان کردن این آیات محدود

After the elements, there is the body of the three kingdoms (*mawlūd*),
The number of whose signs one cannot limit.

The traditional elements become mixed together and the result is the bodies of the three kingdoms. Now, *mawlūd* in Arabic is translated as "kingdom" in English, but not in the political sense. Our use of the term "three kingdoms" goes back to the medieval period; in French also the term *royaume* is used. By the three kingdoms is meant the mineral, the plant, and the animal realms, which are called in Arabic *al-mawālīd al-thalāth*, that is, the three realms that are born of the elements, earth, water, air and fire in different proportions.

"The number of whose signs cannot be counted," because you have an indefinite number of beings in the world. You have only three kingdoms, but you do not know how many plants, how many animals, how many minerals there are in this world.

به آخر گشت نازل نفس انسان
که بر ناس آمد آخر ختم قرآن

The descent of the human soul came at the end (*bi ākhar gasht*).
That is why the Quran ends with [the *sūrah*] *al-Nās*. (Q. 114)

The last being to be created in this world was man. So, the Quran, which ends with *Sūrat al-Nās*, the last word of which (*al-nās*) means mankind, corresponds to the process of generation of the world of creation. There is one point that I want to mention here, and that is how well-versed so many Sufi writers were in cosmology as well as the Quran, such that they knew both in depth better than most of the *fuqahā'* (jurists). In his commentary on the *Gulshan-i rāz*, Lāhījī has dealt quite extensively with the implications of this section, because it is very cryptic and in just a few lines Shaykh Maḥmūd Shabistarī summarizes a vast subject.

Principle on Meditation (*al-fikr*) upon the Horizons

Now, we come to a section that might be a bit difficult for many modern readers because it includes some traditional astronomy, and one of the lacunae in modern education is this subject. In the old days every student used to study at least some astronomy, but such is not necessarily the case today, even as far as modern astronomy is concerned. So, in order to understand what he is saying, I will give a brief introduction to the subject. Although I am not an astronomer myself, I have studied Islamic astronomy and have written on traditional astronomy in "The Wedding of Heaven and Earth in Astrology" in my *An Introduction to Islamic Cosmological Doctrines*.[23] This might appear to have nothing to do directly with the *Gulshan-i rāz*, but it might help in understanding such verses as those discussed below and elsewhere.

Consider the Earth with its North-South axis. The Earth does not actually revolve around this axis, but rather revolves with a tilt. This angle is what causes the seasons and the different kinds of weather in different parts of the world. Now, the axis around which the earth actually revolves tilts some twenty degrees from the straight North-South axis.

You have all heard of the signs of the zodiac. What are the signs of the zodiac? If you are living on earth you see the sky at night filled with stars. There is a belt right in the middle of the earth where are found all the stars that we include in the signs of the zodiac. So, the zodiac does not include stars that are outside of this equatorial belt. Furthermore, this belt is divided into twelve parts, forming the twelve zodiacal signs. The Sun moves in this belt, and so do the Moon and the other planets. In Persian and Arabic each sign of the zodiac is called a *burj*, which means literally "tower" in Persian and Arabic. So, the belt in which the twelve signs of the Zodiac are located is called *manṭaqat al-burūj* (the region of the "towers") in Islamic astronomy.

As everyone knows, there are twelve signs of the zodiac, starting with Aries, which marks the beginning of the solar year when the Sun enters it. In the Persian solar calendar Aries corresponds to Farvardīn, the first month of the year, and all the other months correspond to the other signs of the zodiac. The Western calendar of course begins on January first, which does not have any astronomical significance. In the West the periods of each sign of the zodiac begin around the twenty-first day of the solar month.

So, we have this belt around the Earth with the twelve constellations of the zodiac. But we might ask who invented this? This is one of the great mysteries of the history of science. No matter how far back we go historically, we still see the signs of the zodiac nearly everywhere, including the Chinese zodiac. The Chinese zodiac also has twelve signs, except one of the signs is different from ours and the other eleven are the same. The Chinese have in addition a twelve-year cycle of the zodiac which includes relations to twelve animals, which we do not have in the Mediterranean world, in the Islamic world, in the West, in Greece or in India. But that exception should not be seen as refuting the worldwide presence of the zodiac. The actual Chinese zodiac is just like the Greek, Roman, Persian, Babylonian or Mesopotamian zodiac except for the sign of one animal.

The question arises concerning how this global view came about. Why is it so widespread, cutting across such boundaries as Hindu civilization, Far Eastern civilization, Mediterranean civilization, Persian civilization, and so forth? It must have been extremely old, going back probably to about ten thousand years ago, long before Babylonian science began. In their book, *Hamlet's Mill*, the late Giorgio de Santillana, my teacher at MIT, and the German scholar von Dechend show how ancient these ideas are.[24] In the oldest Sumerian Tablets of about five thousand years ago, in Mesopotamia, one sees the signs of the zodiac. So, this idea is something very ancient, and the signs obviously correspond to cosmic forces. In the old days astrology and astronomy were not separated from each other. So, the zodiac had to do with the symbolism of cosmic relations and not only with physical astronomy.

The signs of the zodiac symbolize archetypes. Today, such archetypes are usually studied only microcosmically because modern science does not permit that they have any meaning macrocosmically. For example, Jung writes about psychological types that correspond to signs of the zodiac, but Jung just mentions this word and does not really understand what an archetype is metaphysically, his perspective being psychological. In our sense of archetype, it is the cosmic archetypes to which the signs correspond.

Jungian psychologists speak a great deal about this subject these days. Interestingly enough, this subject has such a hold on human beings that even in the age of modern science many newspapers still have a section on astrology. This deep hold on the human psyche is not going to go away. In fact interest in it has increased a great deal in recent decades. For example, in France, the cradle of Western rationalism and agnosticism, the number of books on astrology that are sold every year is many times more than those on astronomy. Astrological symbols concern realities ingrained in the depth of our whole being, and traditional astrology deals with our functioning not on the everyday level but on the highest level, in relation to the archetypes that are above the world of facts. The idea that if a person wants to go on a date he can use a horoscope to see if it is going to be a good date or not, and matters like that, are really a popularization that turns to superstition in a certain sense, but deep down there is something very significant in traditional astrology if properly understood.

Now, the planets move through these twelve signs of the zodiac, and each has a house (or *manzil* in Islamic astrology). The way the planets move through the houses affects the cosmic forces below. That is really the philosophical foundation of astrology. It is important to understand the symbolism of astrology and astronomy, and this next section of this book deals precisely with their cosmological significance beyond the material realm.

مشو محبوس ارکان و طبایع
برون آی و نظر کن بر صنایع

Do not become a prisoner of the elements (*arkān*) and natures (*ṭabāyi'*).
Come out and take a look at God's creation (*ṣanāyi'*).

Arkān is the plural of *rukn*, which in Arabic and Persian means column and foundation. But *arkān* also means the foundations of nature: the four elements. *Ṭabāyi'* are the four natures. The four elements are fire, air, water and earth, and the four natures are wet, dry, hot and cold. He says, "do not become a prisoner" of these realities, that is, come out of this material world, out of your body, out of the external aspect of the world of nature.

Ṣanāyi' is the plural of *ṣinā'ah* meaning craft or skill, but here means the creative Power of God. One of God's Names is al-*Ṣāni'*. Today in Arabic and Persian it often means industries in the modern sense, but the original meaning of the Arabic word *ṣun'* is artistic creation, generation and production, a meaning that is still alive, as in contemporary Persian a craftsman is still called *ṣan'atgar.* Its theological meaning pertaining to God's creative Power is of course also very much alive.

تفگر کن تو در خلق سماوات
که تا ممدوح حقّ گردی در آیات

Meditate, o thou, upon the creation of the Heavens,
So that thou wilt become praised by the Divine Truth (*mamdūḥ-i Ḥaqq*) in the signs (*āyāt*).

The signs (*āyāt*), that is, the symbols that God has created refers to creation itself wherein everywhere are to be found the "signs of God." *Mamdūḥ* of course means praised, but *mamdūḥ-i Ḥaqq* implies that one is already praising the Lord, and becomes praised by the Lord as a consequence.

ببین یک ره که تا خود عرش اعظم
چگونه شد محیط هر دو عالم

See a path (that goes) itself to the Supreme Throne [of God],
How it became encompassing of both worlds.

Here, Shabistarī is referring actually to *'arsh al-Raḥmān* (the Throne of the All-Merciful), to the Divine Throne, and the fact that it is also the heart of man. As the *ḥadīth* states, *Qalb al-mu'min 'arsh al-Raḥmān*, "The heart of the faithful is the Throne of the All-Merciful," to which he is going to refer. That is why the distance from this *'arsh* (the heart) to that *'arsh* (the Divine Throne) "encompasses" the whole of the Universe.

چرا گردید نامش عرش رحمن؟
چه نسبت دارد او با قلب انسان؟

Why has its name become the Throne of the All-Merciful?
What relation does it have to the human heart?

He is asking the basic question, why is this reality called the Throne (*'arsh*), and why of all the possibilities of the Divine Names, the All-Merciful (*al-Raḥmān*)? And then, why is this exalted reality related to the human heart? No question is more basic concerning the relation of the *anthropos* to the cosmos and the Divine Itself.

چرا در جنبشند این هر دو مادام
که یک لحظه نمی‌گیرند آرام؟

Why is it that both are always (*mādām*) moving?
And not for one moment do they rest?

These two questions both involve the dynamic aspect of both the heart and the Throne. From *'arsh al-Raḥmān* (the Throne of the All-Merciful) is manifested existence, whose substance is the Breath of the Compassionate (*nafas al-Raḥmān*). The angels are always moving around it, and it has a dynamic aspect as well as a static one. *Mādām* comes from the Arabic *mā dāma*. *Mādām* has become a single word in Persian, meaning continually or always. And so the question is why there is this constant dynamism.

مگر دل مرکز عرش بسیط است
که این چون نقطه آن دور محیط است

Is the heart the center of that expanded Throne,
So that this is like a single point while the Throne is like the circumference?

This verse refers to a remarkable symbolic meaning. There is the relation between our heart and the Divine Throne. Our heart always beats. If it stops, we die. Our head does not beat, it stands still. If it were to start beating we would get a headache. But if our heart stops beating that would be the end of us. It is this dynamic reality that makes possible life, thought and action. Our blood circulates through the heart, and the heart is central like a point in the center of a circle, while the Throne is the circumference of both microcosmic and macrocosmic reality. The two are, therefore, related together.

برآید در شبانروزی کما بیش
سراپای تو عرش ای مرد درویش

One day (*shabānrūz-ī*) [this truth] will become more or less manifest,
[Thou shalt realize that] from head to foot, o dervish, that thou art thyself the Divine Throne.

This daring comparison is the result of this correspondence between the heart and the Divine Throne.

از او در جنبش اجسام مدوّر
چرا گشتند؟ یک ره نیک بنگر

Through that [the Divine Throne both inward and outward] round bodies are moving.
Look carefully at this path; ask yourself, why are they moving.

"Round bodies" means the stars and the planets. One should look carefully and try to understand why those bodies are moving as they do.

ز مشرق تا به مغرب همچو دولاب
همی گردند دائم بی‌خور و خواب

From the East to the West, like moving wheels (*dūlāb*),
They are always going around without eating or sleeping.

Dūlāb means the moving wheels of a mill, which go around continuously without interruption.

به هر روز و شبی این چرخ اعظم
کند دور تمامی گرد عالم

In one day and night, this supreme wheel,
Makes a complete turn around the world.

This obviously refers to the daily turning of the highest astronomical heaven in the solar system around the earth.

وز او افلاک دیگر هم بدین سان
به چرخ اندر همی باشند گردان

By means of it in the same way, the other spheres (*aflāk*),
Are moving circularly, constantly turning.

Aflāk is the plural of *falak*, which means "orbit of a heavily region" the orbit in which a star or planet moves. Here, it means that circle in which the celestial bodies move. "The other spheres" here means the other planets and stars below the highest heaven.

ولی برعکس دور چرخ اطلس
همی‌گردند این هشت مقوّس

But contrary to the movement of the supreme sphere (*charkh-i aṭlas*),
These eight arches (*hasht-i muqawwas*) move constantly.

Falak al-aṭlas is the supreme sphere according to traditional astronomy. We have the seven planets, each of which has its own orbit or *falak*, and then we have the eighth, which is the sphere of the fixed stars. Beyond this sphere there is *falak al-aṭlas*, the supreme sphere, which is invisible and separates the world of cosmic manifestation from the Divine Reality.

In contrast to that supreme *falak al-aṭlas*, which moves, "these eight arches" move in another way. *Hasht-i muqawwas* (the eight arches) refers to the arch of the orbit of the seven planets in addition to the sphere of the fixed stars. *Muqawwas*, which comes from the word *qaws* (arch), means literally "arched." Each heavenly body has its own orbit or arch, its own trajectory on which it moves.

معدّل کرسی ذات البروج است
که آنرا نه تفاوت نه فروج است

The ecliptic of the Footstool is the possessor of the Zodiac (*dhāt al-burūj*),
In which there is no difference, no holes.

The *dhāt al-burūj* (that which possesses the signs of the Zodiac) is the single belt around the middle part of the sky that I described above.

حمل با ثور و با جوزا و خرچنگ
بر او بر همچو شیر و خوشه آونگ

Aries with Taurus and with Gemini and Cancer
Suspended to it like Leo and Virgo.

Here, Shabistarī is mentioning the names of these various signs of the Zodiac. First of all, *thawr* is Taurus, *ḥamal* is Aries. *Jawzā* is Gemini and *kharchang* is Cancer. Then there is *shīr*, Leo, and *khūshah*, Virgo.

دگر میزان عقرب پس کمان است
ز جدی و دلو و حوت آنجا نشان است

After it come Libra, Scorpio, then Sagittarius.
There are sign of Capricorn, Aquarius and Pisces.

Mīzān (the balance) is Libra, *'aqrab* is Scorpio, and *kamān* (the bow) is Sagittarius. *Jadī* is Capricorn, *dalw* is Aquarius, and *ḥūt* (the fish) is Pisces, which is the last of the twelve signs.

ثوابت یک هزار و بیست و چارند
که بر کرسی مقام خویش دارند

The fixed stars are a thousand twenty-four,
Each of which has its own station on the Footstool.

According to many traditional works on astronomy, there are 1024 fixed stars in the sky. Of course, there are many, many more, millions of them, but those counted were the ones that were easily visible to the eye. So, the number 1024 became more or less established. Needless to say, Muslim astronomers did not take into account the stars that are only visible from the southern hemisphere. Later on, when Islamic astronomers heard about them, they changed this number.

به هفتم چرخ کیوان پاسبان است
ششم برجیس را جا و مکان است

The seventh wheel is governed by Saturn (*kaywān*),
And the sixth is the place and position of Jupiter (*birjīs*).

These names, *kaywān* for Saturn and *birjīs* for Jupiter are Persian names, whereas today in Persian we use the Arabic names, *zuḥal* and *mushtarī*. Nowadays, the older Persian names are not used often in Persian.

بود پنجم فلک مرّیخرا جای
به چارم آفتاب عالم‌آرای

The fifth heaven is the place of Mars (*mirrīkh*),
The fourth the Sun, which embellishes the world.

سیم زهره دویم جای عطارد
قمر بر چرخ دنیا گشت وارد

The third is Venus and the second the place of Mercury,
The Moon [then] entered the circle of the world.

"The Moon [then] entered the circle of the world" means in a sense completed the planetary order.

According to astrology each planet has a *manzil* or a house within the twelve signs of the Zodiac. So, the planets move through the signs and the houses. Shabistarī wants to point out how complicated the order of creation is, and how these movements in a sense govern what goes on in the sublunar region.

The seven planets that he mentions are the planets that can be seen with the human eye. So, they are the planets that could be seen before the discovery of new planets with the help of the telescope. Planet means "wanderer" in Greek, *sargardān* in Persian. That means that if you look at the sky for many nights, you see a large number of lit points, the stars, which do not move vis-à-vis each other. They only move as a whole, as if you had a ceiling full of lights and the ceiling itself moved, but the lights do not move vis-à-vis each other. That is why the starry sky is called the heaven of the fixed stars. But when you look at the sky long enough, you will see that there are seven bodies that are an exception and that have a movement of their own in addition to their diurnal movement. And of these seven bodies, two of them are big and seen by everyone, namely the Sun and the Moon, and the others are small, so that one needs more observation to detect them. These moving bodies start closest to Earth with the Moon, then Mercury, Venus, the Sun, Mars, Jupiter, and finally Saturn. There are thus three above the Sun, and three below the Sun. As I said, these are celestial bodies that are visible to the naked eye globally, and so astronomy everywhere speaks of seven planets, whether it be Hindu, pre-modern Islamic or Western and so forth.

These seven celestial bodies were often considered to correspond to seven levels of being, seven prophets, and seven stages of perfection. When the Prophet went on his *Mi'rāj*, the Nocturnal Ascent, he went through seven heavens and met seven prophets each corresponding to a heaven. Christ was in the fourth heaven, the heaven of the Sun, which is at the center of the seven planetary spheres, and so he is metaphysically speaking a "solar" figure. All of these meetings with prophets are very meaningful from the point of view of the symbolism of numbers, in relation to prophetology.

There are then seven planets, or "wanderers," and each has its own orbit. The three below the Sun, of course, have shorter orbits than 365 days, and the orbits of those above the Sun have longer orbits because of the distances they have to traverse, but their trajectories all are within that belt; so, they move through the Zodiac. It is the interaction between the planets and the signs of the Zodiac that supposedly determined one's destiny, one's natal chart and events that happen during one's life. The two have to be combined together. For example, when you are born, that determines your horoscope and it cannot be an accident. No one is born at any time or any place when and where God does not want him or her to be born. That moment is when that being enters into the earthly level of the cosmos. Suppose we go to a big department store. The particular door of the store where we enter determines where we shall be in that store and the order of all the things we would see there. So, the point of entrance into this life determines where we are going to go. It is the beginning of the road. Later on, other factors come into play, how we take the road for example, but the starting point is related to the positions of the planets at the time of birth. Obviously, there are also many other factors, such as the culture into which each individual is born. But astrology is based on the correspondence between the microcosm and the macrocosm, and that particular moment when a microcosmic being comes into this world. One's horoscope corresponds to the condition of the macrocosm at that time.

زحلرا جدی و دلو و مشتری باز
به قوس و حوت کرد انجام و آغاز

The house of Saturn is in Capricorn and Aquarius, and Jupiter,
It waxed and waned in Sagittarius and Pisces.

حمل با عقرب آمد جای بهرام
اسد خورشیدرا شد جای آرام

The place of Mars is in Aries and Scorpio,
In Leo is the place of rest of the Sun.

چو زهره ثور و میزان ساخت گوشه
عطارد رفت در جوزا و خوشه

As Venus made Taurus and Libra her house,
Mercury abided in Gemini and Virgo.

قمر خرچنگرا همجنس خود دید
ذنب چون رأس شد یک عقده بگزید

The Moon saw Cancer as akin to itself,
When the tail became like the head, a knot was chosen.

This section contains reference to the domicile of each of the planets in the twelve signs of the Zodiac.[25]

قمررا بیست و هشت آمد منازل
شود با آفتاب آنگه مقابل

The Moon has twenty-eight stations,
Then it comes face to face with the Sun.

The symbolism of this couplet is very important. *Qamar*, the Moon, orbits the Earth in twenty-eight days. The reason that it can take twenty-nine days for the lunar cycle to be complete is that during those twenty-eight days, the earth has also moved or the Sun has also moved, depending on the perspective of geocentrism or heliocentrism. But actually, in Sufi cosmology it is always said that the lunar month is twenty-eight days and the moon has twenty-eight mansions. Now, this should not be confused with the Arabic lunar calendar, which has months of twenty-nine or thirty days.

So, there are twenty-eight *manāzil*, or lunar mansions, and these correspond in Islamic astrology to the twenty-eight letters of the Arabic alphabet. On the basis of that correspondence, an elaborate astrology was developed based on the symbolism of the *manāzil* of the Moon. There is a revealing discussion of this issue in the book of Titus Burckhardt, *Clé spirituelle de l'astrologie musulmane d'après Mohyddîn ibn 'Arabî,* which was translated into English as *Mystical Astrology According to Ibn 'Arabī*.[26] There, Burckhardt talks about the twenty-eight mansions of the Moon in relation to the twenty-eight letters of the Arabic alphabet, as well as the reason for this symbolism and how this accords with the letters of the sacred language of the Quran. Just to allude to how exact these correspondences are, in Arabic we have the *ḥurūf shamsiyyah* (solar letters) and *ḥurūf qamariyyah* (lunar letters). *Ḥurūf shamsiyyah* are those letters which, if you put the definite article *al-* before them the "l" disappears and the letter is made into a *shaddah* (i.e., it is doubled). For example, you pronounce *ash-shams* instead of *al-shams*. *Ḥurūf qamariyyah* are those in which you do pronounce the *al-*; so, you say *al-qamar* not *aq-qamar*. There are fourteen *ḥurūf shamsiyyah* and fourteen *ḥurūf qamariyyah* in the Arabic alphabet, and Ibn 'Arabī says that fourteen represent manifest realities and fourteen represent hidden realities. This is a complex topic into which I cannot go further here. What is important for the understanding of the spiritual message of the *Gulshan-i rāz* is not to get lost in this maze of astrological technicalities.

پس از وی همچو عرجون قدیم است
ز تقدیر عزیزی کو علیم است

Then [the Moon] becomes like a little thin stalk of a palm tree
(*'urjūn-i qadīm*).
As a result of the predestination of the Most Powerful One Who is
All-Knowing.

This verse refers to Quran 36:39, "And for the moon, We have decreed mansions, till it returns like an old palm stalk," describing the crescent moon.

اگر در فکر گردی مرد کامل
هر آیینه که گوئی نیست باطل

If you turn to think, o perfect man,
Surely you will say, "This is not false."

Once one meditates upon the order of the heavens, one realizes that it was not created falsely. As the Quran says, *Rabbanā mā khalqta hādhā bāṭilan*, "Our Lord, Thou hast not created this in vain" (Q. 3:191).

کلام حقّ همی ناطق بدین است
که باطل دیدن از «ظنّ الذین» است

The Word of God speaks precisely of this,
For to look at things falsely is from "the conjecture of those who [disbelieve] (*ẓann al-ladhīna*)."[27]

This is a reference to Quran 38:27, "And We did not create Heaven and earth and whatsoever is between them in vain (*bāṭil*); that is the conjecture of those who disbelieve (*ẓann al-ladhīna*). So woe before the Fire unto those who disbelieve!"

وجود پشه دارد حکمت" ای خام
نباشد در وجود تیر و بهرام

The existence of a gnat reveals wisdom, o unripe man,
Which does not even exist in Mars and Mercury.

There is another version of the first hemistich, as preferred by Nurbakhsh, which uses *ḥikmat-i tāmm* (perfect wisdom).[28]

ولی چون بنگری در اصل این کار
فلکرا بینی اندر حکم جبّار

But if thou lookest carefully at the roots of this matter,
Thou shalt see that all of the heavens are under the order of the Compeller (*al-Jabbār*).

God, Whose Will is absolute, determines all things. This is why one of the Names of God is *al-Jabbār*, the Compeller.

منجّم چون ز ایمان بی‌نصیب است
اثر گوید که از شکل غریب است

The astronomer, since he is devoid of faith,
Says that the effect is from a strange configuration.

Shabistarī does not want to imply that all astronomers were devoid of faith, but that in their astronomical discussions many neglected the presence of the Divine Will and Wisdom, especially those who simply followed Greek astronomy. One only needs to read al-Bīrūnī to see that this verse does not apply to all astronomers.

نمی‌بیند که این چرخ مدوّر
ز حکم و امر حقّ گشته مسخّر

He does not see this revolving sphere,
Is dominated by the command and order of the Truth.

This last couplet of the present section contains an important lesson for those who are astronomers today.

Illustration

تو گوئی هست این افلاک دوّار
به گردش روز و شب چون چرخ فخّار

Thou couldst say that these rotating heavens (*aflāk-i dawwār*)
Going around day and night are like the potter's (*fakhkhār*) wheel.

Fakhkhār, an Arabic word meaning "potter," has also another meaning, that is, "someone who is very boastful," someone who has a lot of *fakhr* or boasting. There are in fact several meanings in Arabic for the root *f-kh-r*, but here the word *fakhkhār* is the name of the profession of one who makes pottery.

I want to allude here to the symbolism of the potter in Persian poetry, which you also find elsewhere. In Islamic anthropology, of course, God molded the body of Adam from clay (*ṭīn*) and therefore, a potter in a sense emulates the creative Act of God. There are in fact two aspects to this issue: One is the creative aspect of making things out of clay, in a sense emulating the Divine Act. But there is also the reverse implication in the fact that pottery made by man disappears so easily. The poet Khayyām, who talks all the time about this symbolism, usually implies strongly the second view and compares so much of life to the making of pots and pans that break and disappear. He uses the Persian terms *bādah-kish* and *bādah-furūsh* and so forth, referring to one who makes the cup of wine from clay and who sells it and the one who drinks from it, pointing out that they all soon disappear, turning to the dust from which the cup is made. This is a way to express the fleeting aspect of the world. But the other aspect related to this term is the creative aspect. I am sure you have seen potters, who have a wheel that revolves and is worked with their feet, while with their hands they mold the clay into various shapes, such as a cup or a bowl. This symbolism of the potter's wheel is met with in many places in Persian poetry. One also comes across it occasionally in English literature, but it is more common in Persian. So, Shabistarī is comparing the movement of the heavens with the movement of the potter's wheel. *Dawwār* means that which makes a *dawr* (circle), that is, that which goes in circles, so the *aflāk-i dawwār* are 'the heavens that move in circles'. They are like the wheel of the potter, which also moves in a circle.

در او هر لحظه‌ای دانای داور
ز آب و گل کند یک ظرف دیگر

From it, every second, the Knower, the Judge (*dānā-yi dāwar*)
Makes another pot from water and clay.

"It" refers not to the will of the *fakhkhār*, the potter, but to that moving wheel of the heavens, and therefore by extension to God's creation. *Dānā* means knower and *dāwar* means judge, but here these terms refer to two Divine Names; so, they are written with capital letters. He "makes another pot from water and clay" refers to the continuity of God's creation.

هر آنچه در زمان و در مکان است
ز یک استاد و از یک کارخانه است

Whatever exists in time and in place,
Comes from one Master (*Ustād*) and one workshop (*kārkhānah*).

Here, going back to the symbolism of making pots, Shabistarī is again describing God as the Divine Potter. So, he suggests that we should envisage the whole Universe as a potter's workshop with only one *Ustād*, one Master Potter, Who from the clay of this world continues to create everything. After having stated that truth, Shabistarī poses certain vexing questions.

کواکب گر همه اهل کمالند
چرا هر لحظه در نقص و وبالند

The planets, if they possess perfection,
Why is it that every moment they are waxing and waning (*naqṣ-u wabāl*)?

Naqṣ-u wabāl can be translated as "waxing and waning," or "twinkling." *Naqṣ* means "the lessening of light" and *wabāl* means the reverse. A variant of this verse has *naqṣ-i wabāl*, which could be translated as the "defect of setting."

همه در جای و سیر و لون و اشکال
چرا گشتند آخر مختلف حال؟

All are in place, movement, color, and forms.
Why then at the end have they such different states?

He is inviting us to ponder the question of where this being comes from in different configurations and conditions and why they are in different states.

چرا گه در حضیض و گه در اوجند؟
گهی تنها فتاده گاه زوجند؟

Why are they sometimes in the perigee and sometimes in the apogee?
Why is it that sometimes they are alone and sometimes in pairs?

The perigee is the lowest point of the curve and the apogee the highest point of the trajectory of a heavenly body. Look at the different phenomena of the heavens. Why is it that these celestial bodies are in these different states in the place where they belong?

دل چرخ از چه شد آخر پر آتش؟
ز شوق کیست او اندر کشاکش؟

From where then hast the heart of the wheel become full of fire?
From whose intense desire (*shawq*) is it in tumult?

The wheel again refers to the cosmic wheel, the heavens: Why are they moving? *Shawq* means desire or intense desire; so, Shabistarī is alluding to the fact that the heavens are seeking the Divine and this *shawq* for God is what makes them move.

همه انجم بر او گردان پیاده
گهی بالا و گه شیب اوفتاده

All the stars are like one moving on foot moving around Him.
Sometimes they are elevated, sometimes they fall low.

This refers back to what was said in the above couplet.

عناصر آب و باد و آتش و خاک
گرفته جای خود در زیر افلاک

The elements, water, air, fire and earth,
Each has taken its place under the heavens.

Here, Shabistarī is completing his account of the main tenets of traditional cosmology. *'Anāṣir* (sing. *'unṣur*) in classical Islamic texts means "element" in the old cosmological sense. When modern chemistry came, that word continued to be used in Arabic and Persian for the elements such as oxygen, hydrogen or sodium, but originally it meant the four elements, water, air, fire, and earth. Here, for poetic reasons instead of "air" (*hawā*) the poet uses the word *bād*, that means literally wind, which here is used to mean the same reality.

"Each has taken its place under the heavens" refers to traditional cosmology in which you have the heavens from the Moon above, with each planet having its own orbit, and then you have the sublunar region, which begins below the Moon (that is why it is called sublunar). This region is comprised of the four elements, which by nature are always in transformation. That is why you have generation and corruption below the level of the Moon, whereas above the level of the Moon, there is no generation and corruption. This assertion refers to what is visible in the world about us. If you concentrate on what you see directly by looking at the heavens, you do not see the same thing there as you see in the mountains, seas, animals, and trees here below. For example, you see leaves growing on trees and trees blooming, and then the leaves become yellow and fall. You do not see the same type of phenomena in the heavens. The fact that you experience this world of generation and corruption is related to the fact that the sublunar region of the world consists of the four elements, whereas the level above the Moon is considered to be composed of the *quintessentia*, the quintessence, which means the fifth element. The word quintessence in English, which we use to mean the heart of something, the real essence of something, is related to this distinction. So, the heavens are composed of the quintessence, sometimes called *athīr* in Arabic and Persian, or ether in the classical Greek cosmological sense. The fifth element, ether, is incorruptible, whereas the four elements participate in corruptibility.

ملازم هر یکی در مرکز خویش
که ننهد پای یک ذره پس و پیش

Of necessity each is in its own center,
For it will not set its foot one iota forward or backward.

I have explained this subject extensively in my *An Introduction to Islamic Cosmological Doctrines*,[29] but I shall summarize this topic for you here. According to traditional cosmology, which the Greeks, Muslims, early Christians and Jews share together, in the sublunar region you have the earth, which is the lowest level, then water, then air, then fire. Each has what is called in Arabic *al-ḥayyiz al-ṭabī'ī*, which means "the natural place" of something. The natural place of earth is the lowest; so when we drop a piece of earth it falls down to its natural place. You do not see the natural place of fire, but it is just below the sphere of the Moon, reaching the heavens; so, it is the highest level, and therefore fire rises. Water also tries to reach its own level, which is above earth and below air. If you put a bottle of air under water it pops up. This is how traditional cosmology explains the natural place of everything.

That this view is refuted in modern physics is irrelevant to the present discourse. The traditional cosmology has a profound symbolic and cosmological aspect to it, namely that everything in the Universe has its proper place, including us. However, we are the only beings who have the free will to break that principle, to move out of our place. In Persian we say, *maqām-i khud-rā nadānad*, which means that a person does not know the place or station in which he or she should be. Traditional societies try to bring this natural order into human society as much as possible, whereas modern society has tried to disregard that teaching as much as possible in opposition to the natural order of things.

There are very important issues here into which I cannot delve further, but what I want us to learn is that in traditional cosmology each element has its place, and so it is for all things in this world, which are made of various elements. Their place depends on their composition and what predominates within them. So, for example, depending on the different proportions of elements in different bodies, some sink in water and some float. Likewise, the proportion of various elements in the human body also determines our health, our relation to food, our relation to the air we breathe, and the whole harmony that exists or should exist between the human being and its environment.

چهار اضداد در طبع و مراکز
به هم جمع آمده کس دید هرگز؟

> The four natures, which are opposite in nature and centers,
> Have become united together. Has anyone ever seen such a thing?

What does Shabistarī mean here? If you pour water over a fire, the fire will go out; but if the fire is very strong, the water will evaporate. The two cannot exist side by side. Now, *ṭab'* (nature) does not mean element but nature. The four natures, *al-ṭabāyi' al-arba'ah*, are hot and cold, wet and dry, going in pairs that are opposed to each other. As for the four elements, each has two of these natures. Water is cold and wet; earth is dry and cold; air is hot and cold; and fire is dry and hot. So, they go in pairs together like this, and the natures in each element cause them to be distinct from each other.

However, despite this distinction and opposition, in a miraculous way they all work together. Even talking in modern terms, one can say that there really is something like a miracle in how opposites work together in the world and in our bodies. We eat acidic food and then basic food, and we eat certain proteins, which are opposite to other proteins, and then there are all kinds of bacteria in us that are opposed to bacteria in the food we consume. There is this unbelievable contention and yet complementarity. If you analyzed all these elements, you would be amazed how, despite all these differences, we have one single concrete body that is alive. These components are all contending with each other often in opposition, but there is a balance and harmony that rules over them. Shabistarī is thus referring to the idea that our bodies have all four natures in them: heat and cold, wet and dry. These are opposite to each other, but we are a unity. We feel that unity as we function. If somebody takes your leg and your hand on one side, and your hand on the other side and pulls, you feel as if you are being pulled apart because they are opposite forces, but we do not feel that opposition within our bodies if they are healthy. It is only when one falls sick that the balance is threatened, and if it reaches past a certain stage, then one dies.

That is the medical implication of these verses, which I will not discuss further here, but Shabistarī is focused not on the medical but on the cosmological dimension. We share the four natures and elements with the whole world of nature around us. Everything in the sublunar region according to this cosmology is made of the four natures and the four elements, and then there is the balance between them. There is also in normal circumstances a balance, a harmony between our bodies and the world around us. These are ideas that are for the most part overlooked in much of modern science. But now these ideas are gradually making a comeback. As soon as you say eco-, as in "ecology," you come back to them; "eco-" implies the relation of a number of living beings together. If you only had one kind of life form in the world there would be no ecological system as this term is usually understood. So, ecology itself implies a multiplicity of life forms that function together. Now, this way of viewing nature is making a comeback, and people are realizing how remarkable the intertwining of us and the natural environment around us is.

مخالف هر یکی در ذات و صورت
شده یک چیز از حکم ضرورت

Each one is different in its essence and form,
But because of the principle of necessity (*ḥukm-i ḍarūrat*), they have become one thing.

"Each one" refers to the four natures and four elements. "The principle of necessity" refers to the fact that God has willed this order to take place. *Ḥukm* can mean "order" or "judgment," but it can also mean "principle" here. God has made it necessary for this combination to take place, that is *jam' al-aḍdād*, the *coincidentia oppositorum*. The great metaphysician from Italy, Nicholas of Cusa, says that God Himself is *coincidentia oppositorum*, the coincidence of opposites. This is a very profound metaphysical statement, for of course God is beyond the opposition seen in His creation. As Shabistarī said above, "The appearance of all things is through their opposite, but the Divine Truth has no like and no opposite." The answer to this enigma is, of course, given by the *Gulshan-i rāz*.

Shabistarī is explaining that the things in the sublunar world are composed of the combination of opposing natures and elements. We usually do not think about this matter, but if you take an apple and eat it, you experience a single thing; it has unity, even though it combines these different natures and elements. In nature beings have somehow both similar and opposite qualities and yet work in harmony. That is a difficult matter to understand rationally. That is why modern science evades this question. Every physician knows that you have opposite forces in the body that also work together. Sometimes you have to send one force into the body against another force. But a point is reached when those two that are against each other then work together to carry out a particular function. This is one of the most remarkable aspects of God's creation, one that is beyond our ken. One cannot really imagine how this "miracle" takes place.

موالید سه‌گانه گشت از ایشان
جماد آنگه نبات آنگاه حیوان

The Three Kingdoms have come into being through them:
The mineral, then the plant, then the animal.

This couplet simply asserts that all the three kingdoms comprised the same four elements and natures.

هیولی‌را نهاده در میانه
ز صورت گشته صافی صوفیانه

[He] has placed prime matter (*hayūlā*) in the middle,
While He is Himself free from form, in a Sufi manner.

The subject of the first hemistich is God, that is, He has placed in the middle the *hylé*, the *materia prima* or prime matter, *hayūlā*, which has come from Greek into Arabic and Persian. The Greek word *hylé*, is the origin of the term "hylic" in English.

Perhaps the most profound intuition of Aristotelian philosophy is the doctrine of form and matter, that is, the realization that everything in this Universe that we see is the result of the imposition of form upon matter. A very clear example of this doctrine of hylomorphism given over the ages, especially in preindustrial societies where everything was made by hand, is that of a carpenter. The carpenter takes a piece of wood, and if he wants to make a chair, he imposes the form of the chair upon that wood. For that chair, that wood is *materia*, its matter. But the chair is not only that matter: that wood could have also become a table or a door. So, it is the form that makes the chair a chair. This is a very profound understanding of how things are made, and societies that lived with handicrafts, that is, traditional societies without the modern machines, were very much aware of this reality because everything they made was done through the imposition of a form upon matter. This is even true of cooking. As a cook, you consider in your mind the dish you want to make: let us say here a kebab or the Persian dish *ghurmah sabzī*. You have the form of the dish in your mind, and you take the meat, chop it up, and put it in the stew with vegetables, etc. You are actually imposing a form upon that original meat, vegetables, and other ingredients, which before you began to cook were in a sense amorphous from the point of view of your *khūrish* (stew). But of course they also had their own form, because rice is different from wheat, or lamb from chicken, for example.

This investigation and analysis into the form and matter of each existent can be repeated until one gets to prime matter, which is below the four elements. Prime matter is pure potentiality and therefore difficult to conceive. It has existence but only potentiality and is not actualized. Its only quality is potentiality and the receiving of form. The reality and characteristics of all things come from the form, not from prime matter. This is the heart of the doctrine of hylomorphism. *Morphé* in Greek means "form," and the word form in English comes from the word *forma* in Latin, which is equivalent to the Greek *morphé;* and *hylé* of course, means "prime matter." Hylomorphism is thus the doctrine that things are made of form and matter (*ṣūrat-u māddah*). Everything in this world has to have *hylé*. So, "[He] has placed prime matter in the middle," means the middle of everything and everywhere. Everything has *materia prima*.

The second hemistich is somewhat enigmatic. Since it is God who has placed prime matter in the middle, since humans cannot do this, the second hemistich must refer to God. In this hemistich, the word form refers to the spiritual understanding of *ṣūrah*. In major Islamic languages such as Arabic and Persian, you have two very different understandings of the word *ṣūrat* in Persian, *ṣūrah* in Arabic, which mean both "form" and "face" in both languages. Philosophically, people such as Ibn Sīnā, Ibn Rushd or al-Ghazzālī, when they speak about *ṣūrah*, use the Aristotelian meaning of it. That which gives reality to something, that which actualizes something is called its *ṣūrah*, and everything is made from the wedding of *ṣūrah* and *hayūlā* (*hylé*) or *māddah*, form and matter, as explained above. Now, this understanding of the term *ṣūrah* is totally different from the way the Sufis understand the term. For the Sufis, *ṣūrah* is the external aspect of something. The inner reality is *ma'nā*. Mawlānā Rūmī, especially, talks about this dichotomy all the time. So the philosophical and the Sufi understanding are just the opposite of one another. If you are reading Ibn Sīnā, *ṣūrah* refers to the positive aspects of something, that which gives it reality, that which is actualized, that which gives it being. When you read Mawlānā, it is just the reverse. *Ṣūrat* is just the external form, and what gives a reality to a being is not its *ṣūrat*; it is its *ma'nā*. All of Sufi hermeneutics implies going from *ṣūrah* to *ma'nā*, to go from the external form to the inner meaning. That is all you have to do. Here the word *ṣūrah* is being used in the Sufi sense. *Ṣūfiyānah* means literally, "in a Sufi manner," or "as the Sufis say."

همه از امر و حکم و داد داور
به جان استاده و گشته مسخّر

Everything [in the Universe] as a result of the Command and Order and Justice of the Just Judge (*dād-i dāwar*),
Stands in perfect surrender (*bi jān īstādah*), and has become dominated by Him.

Dāwar, the Judge, of course, refers to God, one of Whose Names is Supreme Judge. *Bi jān īstādah* means literally "standing with his life at hand" implying fully or perfectly surrendered to God's Will. And then Shabistarī turns to poetic metaphors and says,

جماد از قهر بر خاک اوفتاده
نبات از مهر بر پا ایستاده

> The mineral [realm] through [God's] Domination (*Qahr*) has fallen down on earth,
> The [realm of] plants, because of the love (*mihr*) [of God], has stood up.

Qahr means Divine Power or Domination, and it can also imply victory. The word Qāhirah, Cairo, comes from the same word. See how beautiful this verse is: "Whereas the [realm of] plants, because of the love of God, has stood up." Why are those trees you see outside standing vertically? What is pulling them up? Shabistarī says that this force is *mihr*, the love of God, whereas for the earth it is just the reverse quality that is involved; it is subdued, surrendering to His Dominion.

نزوع جانور از صدق و اخلاص
پی ابقای جنس و نوع و اشخاص

> The regeneration of the [realm of] animals on the basis of truth and sincerity,[30]
> Is in search of preserving genus, species and individuals.

همه بر حکم داور کرده اقرار
مراورا روز و شب گشته طلبکار

> All have confessed to the rule of the [Supreme] Judge,
> Day and night, seeking what they are due (*ṭalab-kār*).

"They are seeking what they are owed" (*ṭalab-kār*) means that all creatures are expecting something from God. *Ṭalab* means seeking or yearning, but *ṭalab-kār* means someone who is owed something. It is not that God owes anything, but it means that they are yearning to receive something from God, He "owing" man or woman by virtue that He has created him or her as a human being.

Principle on Meditation on Souls (*Qā'idah fi'l-tafakkur fi'l-anfus*)

In the last two sections we have been dealing with the macrocosm, the world out there, also referred to as *al-āfāq* (the horizons). Now, Shaykh Maḥmūd Shabistarī turns to the inner being of human beings, according to the teachings of such verses of the Quran as 41:53, *Sanurīhim āyātinā fi'l-āfāq wa fī anfusihim ḥattā yatabayyana lahum annahu'l-Ḥaqq*, "We shall show them Our signs upon the horizons and within themselves till it becomes clear to them that it is the truth."

Most Islamic writers, especially Sufis, juxtapose the *āfāq* to the *anfus*, based on the above verse. *Āfāq* is the plural of *ufuq*, meaning "horizon," so *āfāq* means "the horizons" or the external world. *Anfus* is the plural of *nafs* meaning "soul," "inner being" or "spirit" depending on how the term is used. It is a very fluid term in Arabic and Persian, but here it means the human microcosm, the inner being of men and women. And so, now Shaykh Maḥmūd Shabistarī turns to this very important section of the *Gulshan-i rāz* concerning the in-depth understanding of the human self, the human being.

Before I start commenting on this section, I want to provide a prelude. As mentioned previously, there are two ways to discuss pure metaphysics: Is the principle the Divine Reality as completely other, the pure Object, or it is the Self, the pure Subject? Is the Supreme Reality viewed as transcendent or immanent? Many forms of mysticism begin with God as the Other, the Transcendent Reality out there beyond everything with which one then seeks to become intimate. For most Sufis this view is also the case, but there is in Sufism also a strong vein of looking at God as the Supreme Self. It is this dimension that is very much emphasized in Hinduism, although Hinduism is not bereft of the other dimension either. In the school of Shankara, of course, Reality is the Self or *Ātman*, the Supreme Self, and *Ātman* is Brahman. Now, the *Gulshan-i rāz* is one of the few texts of Sufism that emphasizes this same perspective, that is, of the reality of the Supreme Self, without, of course, neglecting transcendence. There are very few texts in Sufism that are so open to this perspective.

به اصل خویش یک ره نیک بنگر
که مادررا پدر شد نیز و مادر

> Look well for a moment (*yak rah*) at thine own roots (*aṣl*),
> For mother has become also father and mother.

This is one of the most enigmatic verses of the *Gulshan-i rāz*. *Yak rah* usually means one path, but here it means for a moment. *Aṣl* in Arabic means root, but it also means "principle" and "source." In Persian, its basic meaning is "principle," but it can also be translated as "the root." So, Shabistarī is saying, go back and look at yourself. Look at your roots.

The second hemistich is especially enigmatic and has been interpreted in several different ways. The more generally accepted meaning, which Lāhījī and other commentators discuss, is that this hemistich is a reference to the Universal Intellect. The Universal Intellect is the generator of the Universe, and through the Help of God generates the Universal Soul. So, in a sense it is the father of the Universal Soul. But it is also its mother, because the Universal Soul issues from it; that is, the Universal Intellect (*'aql-i kullī*) is, in a sense, both the father and mother of the Universal Soul. The Universal Soul, which is feminine in gender, is like our mother; our soul comes from it, and so, its father also "became" its mother.

جهان‌را سر به سر در خویش می‌بین
هر آنچ آید به آخر پیش می‌بین

> See the world from beginning to end (*sar bi sar*) in thyself.
> Whatever will come at the end, see it before.

Sar bi sar means "from one end to the other end" or "from beginning to end." One should pay attention to how the verse elevates the status of the human being. The whole Universe is contained within us.

در آخر گشت پیدا نقش آدم
طفیل ذات او شد هر دو عالم

> The role of man appeared at the end.
> [Yet] both worlds became dependent (*ṭufayl*) upon him.

In both the Bible and the Quran, God created the world in six days and at the end created man. In the Islamic perspective man was created on Friday after God had created all the other creatures. So, in this scheme of creation, we were created last, and also in the modern scientific view we are the last species to appear on Earth. Those people who believe in evolution do not ask why there is no other species after us. Why has the process of evolution stopped while so many people have come to believe in evolution? Have you ever thought of that? There have been no new species after us because we contain all cosmic possibilities within ourselves.

The word *ṭufayl* (dependent) is related to the word *ṭifl*, which means child, which clings to the mother, depends on the mother, feeds from the mother.

نه آخر علّت غائی در آخر
همی گردد به ذات خویش ظاهر؟

Is it not that the final cause comes at the end?
That it becomes manifest in its essence?

Supposing you want to make a chair. In the schema of the four Aristotelian causes, which Ibn Sīnā also accepts, the chair's material cause is the wood, its efficient cause is the carpenter, and the formal cause is the form of the chair. Its final cause is its raison d'être, that is, to be able to be sat on. That is what it was made for. Shabistarī is referring to this reality. The final cause always appears externally at the very end, but it is there in the archetypal world at the beginning. You do not see that final cause in the chair until the chair is made, put in your room, and then you sit on it. Yet all the other causes became operative so that this object could be created, but all the effort was made for this final cause. So, he asks you this question and then he mentions again a very enigmatic verse.

ظلومی و جهولی ضدّ نورند
ولیکن مظهر عین ظهورند

Persons lost in darkness (*ẓalūmī*) and in ignorance (*jahūlī*) are opposed to light,
But they are themselves the very locus of manifestation.

Ẓulm in Arabic and Persian can mean oppression and injustice, but it also means darkness. Arabic has so many profound roots like this; to be unjust is to be in darkness. And here *ẓalūmī* means somebody in darkness, because it is followed by *jahūlī*, which means "an ignorant person." They are against light, and yet they are both the locus of manifestation of the Divine; otherwise they would not exist. The being of an ignorant person is not ignorance. His being is being that belongs to God, and so one has to make a distinction between the two. *Shayṭān* can create evil, but evil in order to be active has to make use of creation itself that *Shayṭān* cannot existentiate. For example, you have to have a knife or a gun in order to steal from a bank. On that level *Shayṭān* cannot create the knife or gun but can lead you to misuse them; that is, *Shayṭān* cannot bring a creature into being. In the verse *kun fa-yakūn* ("Be! and it was") the *kun* (*Be!*) can be uttered by God alone.

You might ask, "What about those Sufis who would existentiate something seemingly out of nothing?" The answer is that God can lend His creative Power occasionally to make possible a miracle, but that is an exception that proves the rule. *Kun* belongs to God alone. The Devil has the power to create illusion that appears to be real but not reality itself on the objective level. So, even the ignorant and those lost in darkness, in evil, are still the *maẓhar*, the place of manifestation, of some Quality of God.

چو پشت آینه باشد مکدّر
نماید روی شخص از روی دیگر

Because the back of a mirror is opaque,
It is able to show the face of someone in its other face.

This verse uses a universal symbol common to Sufism. Shabistarī equates opaque (*mukaddar*) with evil, darkness, and lack of light. But if the back of a mirror were not *mukaddar*, were not opaque, if it did not have mercury or whatever substance you rub on the back of it, it would not be a mirror, and you would not be able to see yourself in it. So, even in this world, in a sense this darkness is necessary, without which the good could not be reflected.

Only God is good in Himself. In this world, goodness can only be discerned in relation to evil. Remember this famous verse of Shaykh Maḥmūd Shabistarī mentioned above:

The appearance of all things is through their opposite,
But the Divine Truth has no like and no opposite.[31]

Now, this is a very profound and important point. If you consider a group of people, some will be tall and others short, some fatter and some thinner, some more intelligent and some less intelligent. We can only judge all of these qualities by their opposite. If all human beings were six feet tall, there would be no short and no tall human beings. If all human beings were three hundred pounds there would be no fat people; if they all weighed a hundred pounds there would be no thin people. If all human beings had the same intelligence, there would be no intelligent person and no unintelligent person. We live in a world in which we understand qualities through their opposites.

So, here he is bringing out this argument again. *Ẓalūm* and *jahūl*, are two words from the Quran (Q. 33:72), characterizing the people who are lost religiously, who have turned away from God, who are in darkness and ignorance. But even they play a role in God's creation. They are like the opacity behind the glass that makes a mirror a mirror. They are themselves the loci of the manifestation of Divine Qualities. Otherwise, they would not play a function in the Universe and would not even exist. They are not nothing. He goes on to say that all of us, throughout our lives, are a series of theophanies of a particular Divine Name, or set of Names. Even people who have turned against God nevertheless play a cosmic function.

شعاع آفتاب از چارم افلاک
نگردد منعکس جز بر سر خاک

The ray of the Sun from the fourth heaven,
Does not become reflected, except upon the earth.

Remember that the Sun is in the fourth heaven according to traditional astronomy. Of the seven planets, the Sun is in the middle with its domicile in the fourth heaven (*falak*). It "does not become reflected, except upon the earth," means that you need the earth in order to see the sunlight. The earth itself is opacity, darkness, but reflects light. These are powerful images and symbols upon which one should meditate. As the rays of the Sun come down from the heavens, you do not see them until they hit the earth. So, that which itself is opaque is necessary in order for us to experience the light of the Sun, through its reflection.

تو بودی عکس معبود ملائک
از آن گشتی تو مسجود ملائک

Thou wert a reflection (*'aks*) of what the angels worship.
That is why thou becamest the [being] before whom the angels prostrated.

In this verse, referring to the Quranic account of the creation of man, Shaykh Maḥmūd Shabistarī is addressing all of us. This whole section is about human beings, the *anfus* not the *āfāq*. You are a reflection of God's Qualities, in the sense of having the Divine Names and Qualities reflected in your being.

"That is why thou becamest the [being] before whom the angels prostrated," reiterates the Quranic account. In the Quran, 2:34, God commands all the angels to prostrate before Adam, and all of them do so except Iblīs. What does this verse mean inwardly? It means that there must have been something in the creature whom God created and called Adam that is higher than the angels, and the angels understood that truth, all except Iblīs.

If we were to ask why it is so, the answer is given in the first hemistich of this verse: "Thou wert a reflection (*'aks*) of what the angels worship." *'Aks* in modern Persian means picture, but here it means reflection. Each angel represents only one aspect of God's Qualities. When God created Adam, He made him the mirror of all of His Names and Qualities. Since all the angels save Iblis understood that reality, they prostrated before Adam. They did not seek to use analogical reasoning, saying they were made of fire and Adam of clay, and so they held a higher station in the created scheme. Only *Shayṭān* used this kind of reasoning, and thus refused to obey God's Command.[32] As it is said in Arabic, "The first to use analogical reasoning was the Devil" (*awwalu man qāsa al-Shayṭān).*

بود از هر تنی پیش تو جانی
وز او در بسته با تو ریسمانی

From every body there is in thee a soul,
And from that [body] a rope has been tied to thee.

"From every body there is in thee a soul," means that thou containeth the soul or spirit, that is, the inner reality of all things within thyself. "And from that [body] a rope has been tied to thee" means that all creatures have been tied to thee; so, in a sense thou art connected to all the cosmos, to everything that exists.

از آن گشتند امرت‌را مسخّر
که جان هر یکی در توست مضمر

It was for this reason that they all obeyed thy order,
For the soul of every one of them is hidden in thee.

The Quran asserts that God has given the power of domination over creatures to man. That is why all creatures can be made to fall under our domination. We can force even big fish to jump through hoops. We have this power that is unique among earthly creatures. Why? Because from every one of them there is in us something of their own soul, a part of their own being.

تو مغز عالمی زان در میانی
بدان خودرا که تو جان جهانی

Thou art the pith (*maghz*) of the Universe, for that reason thou art in the
middle [of all things].
Know thyself, for thou art the life of the world.

Maghz means literally marrow or pith; so, man is in a sense the marrow of the bone of the Universe. He is the very heart, the essence of the Universe. "Know thyself," is, of course, the repetition of the famous Socratic dictum. Man is so because he is the soul (*jān*) of the Universe, the spirit of the world. The word *jān* can mean both life and soul, and can also mean spirit. As I have explained before, *jān* is a very rich Persian word which you also have in Urdu and almost all other Indian languages, and also in Turkish. It can also mean dear. For example, you refer to your mother as *mādar jān*, "dear mother." It can mean life, as in "he took his own life," *jān-i khod-rā girift*. Sometimes the word *jān-i jānān* is used for God, the Spirit of spirits. It is thus a very rich term, having a whole gamut of meanings all the way from ordinary biological life to the Spirit. In Arabic you have the word *rūḥ*, which plays a somewhat similar role, but the meaning of *jān* is even more extensive. It means also both *rūḥ* (spirit) and *nafs* (soul) and the two taken together.

Now, Shabistarī turns to a notable symbolism.

تورا ربع شمالی گشت مسکن
که دل در جانب چپ باشد از تن

The northern quarter (*rub'-i shimālī*) [of the Earth] became thy home,
Because thy heart is located on the left side of thy body.

In the understanding of geography of Shabistarī's time, most of the people lived in the northern quarter, *rub'-i shimālī*, of the Earth. *Rub'* means both "quarter," that is, a space or quarter of a city, and also means "quarter" in the sense of "one fourth." So, here it means both because it was known then that there were other parts of the Earth where nobody was living, behind known lands in the extreme north, south and so forth. So *rub'-i shimālī* refers here to the northern area or northern quarter of the Earth, which was the location of human settlement.

What is the connection between the north and the left in this verse? The word *shimāl* in Arabic means both north and left. This fact indicates the primordial orientation of traditional man, according to which if man stands facing the East or the rising Sun, the left hand points to the North, and the right hand (*yamīn*) to the South, hence the name of both the country Yemen and the right hand. That is the primordial orientation.

As Guénon has discussed in his work, there are two fundamental orientations that one observes in traditional societies.[33] One is facing North, in which case the right hand is the East, and left hand is the West. This involves the symbolism of *sharq* meaning the rising of the Sun and therefore the East, and *gharb*, meaning the setting of the Sun and therefore the West. The other orientation is the one that I mentioned above, that is, facing the East, in which case you have your right hand facing the South, your left hand facing the North, and your back facing the West.

Shabistarī says that we live in the northern part, *shimāl*, of the Earth, because microcosmically that is where our heart is. The heart is in the left or *shimāl* of the human breast.

جهان عقل و جان سرمایهٔ توست
زمین و آسمان پیرایهٔ توست

The world of intellect and of soul are thy capital (*sarmāyah*).
The Earth and the Heavens are thy robe.

Since man is endowed with both intellect or spirit and soul, the cosmos is like his robe, and there is a correspondence between him and the cosmic order.

ببین آن نیستی کو عین هستی است
بلندی‌را نگر کو ذات پستی است

Look at that nonexistence which is identical to existence,
Look at the height which is the essence of lowness.

As an example, Shabistarī mentions that which is ultimately nonexistent, that is, the ephemeral world that yet has existence at its heart, and the height of the creation, which is nevertheless lowness before the Divine Majesty.

طبیعی قوّت تو ده هزار است
ارادی برتر از حصر و شمار است

> By nature, thy power is ten thousand,
> But thy will is beyond count and number.

"By nature, thy power is ten thousand" refers to the truth that thou dost possess so many different capabilities and powers. Have you ever thought how many different things we can will and we can do? We get up every morning, we can do this or that, beyond being able to count how many things we can do by our nature. The power we have naturally in normal cases is very extensive. So, look at all the things we do during our life and the power that God has given us. And yet, the will that God has given us is even vaster than all the power we have by nature.

وز آن هر یک شده موقوف آلات
ز اعضا و جوارح وز رباطات

> Among them each has become constrained (*mawqūf*) by various means (*ālāt*),
> Including the limbs and organs and the arteries and veins.

"Among them" refers to the powers and forces that we have within ourselves. So, we operate with a knife or make glasses for our eyes; we can ride a steed; we do this, we do that by dominating over various instruments for our actions. And these actions also include the functioning of various parts of our physical body. Moreover, all kinds of instruments are then related to these different powers that we have.

حکیمان اندر آن گشتند حیران
فرو ماندند در تشریح انسان

> Immersed in this [question] philosophers fell into a state of wonder,
> And became bewildered in the dissection of the human body.

This verse refers to the complexity of the human body and how it functions, which if studied causes wonder and bewilderment.

نبرده هیچکس ره سوی این کار
به عجز خویش کرده جمله اقرار

> No one has found a way [of understanding] in this matter.
> Each has come to admit his inability.

"No one has found a way [of understanding] in this matter" refers to explanation of this complexity, the remarkable complexity of the human body and its functioning, having to admit the shortcoming to explain fully the workings of our bodies.

ز حقّ با هر یکی حظّی و قسمی است
معاد و مبدء هر یک ز اسمی است

> In relation to the Truth each one has a particular joy and a particular share.
> The return (*ma'ād*) and the origin of each person is through a Divine Name.

Here, we come to another important issue. *Ma'ād* means return, that is, our return to God or eschatology. This is a doctrine that Ibn 'Arabī also explains: that we issue from a particular Divine Name and return to that Divine Name. This is a subtle doctrine of Sufism, not to be confused with the doctrinal assertion that man is the theater of the reflection of all God's Names and Qualities.

از آن اسمند موجودات قائم
بدان اسمند در تسبیح دائم

All creatures subsist through that Divine Name.
They are all the time invoking (*tasbīḥ*) that Name.

Tasbīḥ also means rosary, but *tasbīḥ* here means the invocation of a Divine Name. Since all creatures owe their very existence to a theophany of a Divine Name, their very existence means that they are in constant invocation of God's Name. The very substance of existence is *dhikr Allāh*.

به مبدء هر یکی زان مصدری شد
به وقت بازگشتن چون دری شد

Each being has a source (*maṣdar*) in the Origin (*mabda'*).
At the time of return that [source] becomes like a door for him.

This verse again contains a very profound metaphysical issue. *Maṣdar* means a place of issuing or source and *mabda'* means origin. It is as if God were "a House," and each of us leaves this House from one of the doors to come into this world and at the time of return we go through that same door back to God.

از آن در کآمد اوّل هم بدر شد
اگرچه در معاش او در به در شد

Through the door from which he came he returned,
Although in making a living, he becomes lost (*dar bi-dar shud*).

Dar bi-dar shudan means losing one's normal bearings, to be in a state of loss of one's home and of all of the things that are contained in it.

از آن دانسته‌ای تو جمله اسما
که هستی صورت عکس مسمّا

The reason that thou canst know all of the Names of God,
Is that thou thyself art the image of the Named.

This verse again contains a basic metaphysical statement. Have you ever thought of this matter: We were taught how to invoke *Allāh*, but if the Divine were not already in the depth of our being, how would we be able to do so? Every time we say *Allāh* in a sense we are going back to the depth of our own being, to the Supreme Self Who is the center of our being. He is not just a Being out there. It is because we are unfamiliar with ourselves, with our inner being, because we do not know ourselves, that God seems unfamiliar and out there. The more we know ourselves, the more familiar we become familiar with God. That is what Shabistarī is saying here.

ظهور قدرت و علم و ارادت
به توست ای بندهٔ صاحب سعادت

The manifestation of power, knowledge and will,
Depends on thee, o servant [of God] who possesses happiness (*ṣāḥib-sa'ādat*).

The realization of the manifestation of the Divine Names and Qualities in us depends upon us. We are endowed with happiness because we have all these Divine Qualities reflected within us. Can you imagine what *sa'ādat*, what happiness, what joy, you have in being able to know God? Who are we sitting here to understand how God created the world? Have you ever thought of what a remarkable gift it is from God that we can sit here and even ponder about these matters?

سمیعی و بصیر و حی و گویا
بقا داری نه از خود لیک از آنجا

[Being] the hearer, the seer, the living, the possessor of speech,
Thou persistest not from thyself, but from "There."

Hearing, Seeing, Life and Speech are all Divine Qualities. So, Shabistarī is making sure that we know where these powers come from, not from ourselves but from God.

زهی اوّل که عین آخر آمد
زهی باطن که عین ظاهر آمد

How wonderful (*zahī*) that the beginning came exactly as the end.
How wonderful (*zahī*) that the inward came exactly as the outward.

This is again an enigmatic verse of the *Gulshan-i rāz*. *Zahī* means in a sense how glorious or how wonderful, and it can also mean many. This verse is a difficult one to translate because it has so many different meanings. "How wonderful that the beginning is exactly as the end" could refer to man. Or it could refer to the *ḥaqiqah muḥammadiyyah* (the Muḥammadan Reality) as "the first thing God created," according to the *ḥadīth*, which in different versions also refers to the Word, the Intellect and the Muhammadan Light as the first thing created. But the Prophet Muḥammad comes at the end of the prophetic cycle. Shabistarī has already alluded to that matter previously.

This hemistich could also mean the creation of man himself; that in a sense, we precede creation. God said, *alastu birabbikum, qālū balā*, "Am I not your lord, they said 'Yea'," (Q. 7:172) before He created horses, elephants, donkeys, trees and lakes. But our presence on earth comes at the end.

This verse could also have another meaning: that where we go finally is where we come from; our beginning and end are in the same place. The door that he spoke about before refers to the same truth. So, this verse can have all of those meanings, and commentators have different views about it.

"The inward is exactly as the outward" can also have many meanings. First of all, it can refer to God, *huwa'l-awwal wa'l-ākhir wa'l-ẓāhir,wa'l-bāṭin*, "He is the First, and the Last, and the Outward, and the Inward" (Q. 57:3). The one God cannot be four gods, and so the Outward must be related to the Inward and the First to the Last. But this hemistich can also refer to the perfected human being, whose inner reality is then totally manifested in his outer reality. So, this interpretation refers to the practical, spiritual, operative aspect of the path.

تو از خود روز و شب اندر گمانی
همان بهتر که خودرا می‌ندانی

Be it day and night, thou art doubting thyself.
It is then better that thou dost not know thyself.

This is a kind of caustic criticism, stating that people who do not know themselves are always in doubt. Of course, the verse implies that one should know oneself.

چو انجام تفكّر شد تحيّر
بدينجا ختم شد بحث تفكّر

Since the end of meditation (*tafakkur*) is bewilderment (*taḥayyur*),
Here, the discussion of meditation comes to an end.

As discussed previously, the terms *ḥayrah* and *taḥayyur*, both meaning "bewilderment," are important Sufi terms. There is a *ḥadīth* attributed to the Prophet, *Ya rabb zidnā taḥayyuran fīk*, "O Lord, increase our wonderment in Thee." So, *taḥayyur* can also be translated as wonderment. Our wonderment in God, our sense of wonder, is even beyond ordinary knowledge because this type of spiritual knowledge is itself of course a wonder. Wonder is a way of having us reach knowledge, but it is a wonderment or wonder that is beyond ordinary knowledge itself.

Question [3]

As a prelude to this section, I want to mention again that in all expositions of authentic metaphysics, one can start and end either from and with the pure Subject or the pure Object. As mentioned before, most of the basic metaphysical expositions in Hinduism are based on the pole of the Subject; they speak about *Ātman*, whereas in most of the Abrahamic forms of esoterism, metaphysics is based on the pole of the Object. Now, in Sufism, one sees both. This fact is true even in commentaries upon the *shahādah* (the testification of faith) *lā ilāha illa'Llāh*. Some Sufis, including Suhrawardī, have said that *lā ilāha illa'Llāh* can mean *lā anā illā Anā* (There is no I but I), *lā anta illā Anta* (There is no thee but Thee), *lā huwa illā Huwa* (There is no he but He), and so forth, going through all the pronouns.

As for the *Gulshan-i rāz,* it pays special attention to this Subject at the center of the being of *man* (meaning "I" in Persian), leading ultimately to the Divine Reality within the human being as "I," as will be explained below. This question is therefore being asked in the context of a metaphysics that is based on the Subject leading to the Divine, to our inner reality. So, Shabistarī begins this new section with this question that was sent to him.

که باشم من؟ مرا از من خبر کن
چه معنی دارد اندر خود سفر کن؟

Who am I? Inform (*khabar kun*) me about myself.
What does it mean, "travel within thyself?"

"Who am I?" is the exact question that formed the heart of the teaching of the famous Ramana Maharshi, the great Hindu saint, and was thereby made famous in contemporary writings on spirituality.

Khabar kardan means to give news, information, or knowledge. So, the sage from Khurāsān is asking to receive knowledge of himself, of the subject who knows, not the object being known. The word *man* in Persian is the ordinary pronoun in the Persian language for "I." As mentioned above, in order to avoid a sense of inflation of the ego in polite Persian we usually do not keep saying *man, man*. In fact in Persian we say that *man manī kardan*, "saying I, I" is pejorative, implying having a sense of pride or self-centeredness. When we say *man manī nakun* (Do not say I, I), it really means do not consider always your *man*, your I, to be the center of everything, confusing that "I" with the Divine "I."

Now, this is the negative aspect of this issue, but I want to turn back to the words to which this term is related. First of all, it is related to the foundation of all Hindu Law, *The Laws of Manu*. The famous *Laws of Manu* is the foundation of the whole caste system and the legal aspect of Hinduism. Manu is the Universal Man in a sense, and the name is related to the English word "man." The word "man" in English is also related to the Persian word *man* or "I."

It is also important to recall that Persian has no gender, and of course in English also the first-person pronoun has no gender. "I" can be masculine or feminine. In some languages that is not the case. The word *man* in Indo-European languages does not mean only "the male"; rather, it refers in its universal sense to the human state, both male and female. This must be understood clearly, and it is not altered by the fact that in English one says "to become a real man," which refers to the male, or manliness and terms like that, implying virtues such as honesty, endurance, magnanimity, etc., that can, however, also be found in the female.

Another point that needs to be mentioned is the unfortunate consequences from a traditional point of view of the metric system becoming popular. It made things easy, dividing quantities by ten and so forth, but it destroyed the relationality between measurement in relation to the human being. The metric system was invented by the French, and the Germans, Italians and other Europeans accepted it fairly rapidly save for the Anglo-Saxon world (including America and certain other British colonies and former colonies) that refused to do so and still resist it to a large extent. The measurements in the British system relate to the human body are similar to what one finds in traditional societies. The inch is supposed to be the measure of one part of the finger. The foot is of course related to the length of the human foot. The yard is the measure of a single step. Before the invention of the metric system, all units of measurements were related to the human body and therefore to the relationship between us and the world of nature, between the microcosm and the macrocosm. You can feel what a foot is like, but if you say "thirty centimeters" it does not mean anything existentially. We have all learned what it means in school, but it does not correspond to the human microcosm.

This correspondence is present in the Persian word *man* because, besides being the word for "I" it is a unit of weight in Persian and is still used widely. When I was in Iran, if I went to buy apples, in the fancy stores in the north of Tehran they would sell *yik kīlu, du kīlu* (one kilo, two kilos), but as soon as you went to downtown Tehran, they would say *yik man, du man* (one *man*, two *man*) *man* being equivalent to three kilos. So, the unit of weight was *man*, and the other units, such as *chārak* and *mithqāl* were subdivisions of it. This fact also held true for distance. For example, the word *farsakh* means a distance someone walks during a set number of hours. Traditionally everything is based on cosmic correspondence and relations with the human body. All of that correspondence and harmony with the natural world was destroyed with the complete quantification of nature by the modern metric system of measurement. Rather, one should perhaps say that it was the quantification of nature that permitted the destruction of human and cosmic correspondence.

So now, Shabistarī repeats, "Who am I?," the fundamental question. As mentioned above, you can always start your search for God or metaphysical understanding with one of two questions, either "What is Reality?" or "Who am I?" and of course they are not exclusive of each other. The approach you take depends on your mental structure. Some people look for Ultimate Reality and ask, "What is Real?" Some people try first of all to discover within themselves, "Who am I?"

There are many Arabic sayings that indicate this approach, for example the famous Arabic dictum, *al-insān numūdhaj al-wujūd*, "man is the pith, the supreme example, of all of existence," which reminds one of the *ḥadīth* of the Prophet, *man 'arafa nafsahu fa-qad 'arafa rabbahu*, "He who knows himself knows his Lord."

The question asked here was not at all alien to the Islamic perspective, and here we have one of the most important discussions of it in Sufi poetry.

Answer

دگر کردی سؤال از من که من چیست؟
مرا از من خبر کن تا که من کیست

Thou hast again asked me the question, "What is I?"
Give me (*marā*) knowledge about myself as to who I am.

In this verse Shabistarī uses the word *man* (I) four times. *Marā*, contains also *man*, since *marā* in Persian is the abbreviation of *man-rā*. "Thou hast again asked me this question," what question? The question of what *man* or "I" is. He returns to the question that he asked before, "What am I?" requesting a response.

چو هست مطلق آید در اشارت
به لفظ من کنند از وی عبارت

When Absolute Being (*hast-i muṭlaq*) is indicated,
They use the expression "I" (*man*) for it in the explanation.

This is an exceptional assertion for an Islamic text, asserting that when *ishārat*, meaning reference or indication, is to Absolute Being, the expression *man* (I) is used in the explanation and interprettion, because actually usually "He" (*Huwa* or *ū*) is used rather than "I" (*man*). This is remarkable because we do not see that usage usually, a usage that is similar to the formulation of Advaita Vedanta.

حقیقت کز تعیّن شد معیّن
تو اورا در عبارت گفته‌ای من

The truth, when through determination has become determined,
Thou hast called it in expression *man* (I).

Once the nondetermined infinite state becomes determined in expression, the term *man* is used for it, "thou hast called it *man* (I)." So, he is identifying *man* (I) with the Absolute Truth, which corresponds to *Ātman*. This assertion is very similar to the view of Shankara and the Advaita Vedanta in Hinduism.

من و تو عارض ذات وجودیم
مشبکهای مشکوة وجودیم

I and thou are accidents (*'āriḍ*) of the Essence of Being,
We are the lattices (*mushabbak*) of the niche of Being.

We encounter here a powerful and beautiful symbol. Imagine a lamp in which holes are formed in the brass or wood surrounding the light and the light shines through them. These lattices determine the way the light shines, but they are not the light itself.

'Āriḍ means "accident" here. We are accidents in comparison to the Essence or the Substance of Absolute Being. *Mushabbak* refers to those lattices of the lamps that I mentioned, used here for manifestation of Being Itself.

همه یک نور دان اشباح و ارواح
گهی ز آیینه پیدا گه ز مصباح

Consider shadows and spirits to be one light,
Sometimes manifest in the mirror, sometimes through the lamp.

Here, he is asserting through another symbol and image the transcendent unity of Being, that is, there is only one Being, only one Light.

Shabistarī adds, addressing the person who sent the questions:

تو گوئی لفظ من در هر عبارت
به سوی روح می‌باشد اشارت

Thou hast said that the expression *man* (I) in every sentence,
Is an indication pointing to the Spirit.

Of course, here he is referring to the *Gulshan-i rāz* and not to every text in general in which *man* is mentioned.

چو کردی پیشوای خود خردرا
نمی‌دانی ز جزو خویش خودرا

Once thou hast made reason (*khirad*) thy guide (*pīshwā*),
Thou no longer knowest thyself as part of thyself.

Pīshwā means here leader or guide. *Khirad* does not mean the intellect here, it means reason, used in ordinary rational thinking.

The second hemistich contains an enigmatic phrase. What Shabistarī is saying is that because a person has chosen reason as his guide or become a rationalist, he does not realize that his self is "part of" the Divine Self. So, one hides his self from the Real Self.

برو ای خواجه خودرا نیک بشناس
که نبود فربهی مانند آماس

O *khwājah* (O man), go and know thyself well,
For obesity is not the same thing as swelling (*āmās*).

Āmās is a medical term, meaning a special form of swelling. It is not used often in Persian. "Obesity is not the same thing as swelling" means that two realities could be different even if they might appear to be the same outwardly.

من تو برتر از جان و تن آمد
که این هر دو ز اجزای من آمد

Thy *man* (I) is beyond soul and body,
For both of these are actually parts of (I) (*man*).

Jān can mean life, soul and spirit. So, the first hemistich can also mean that thy I-ness is beyond life and body or Spirit and body. The "I" is transcendent vis-à-vis both body and soul, both of which are derived from it and dependent upon it.

به لفظ من نه انسان است مخصوص
که تا گوئی بدان جان است مخصوص

The expression I (*man*) is not particular to only the human being,
So that thou wouldst say by it is the Spirit (*jān*) particularized.

Here the word *jān* definitely means the Spirit, the most inner reality of the human being; our body never says *man* (I). It is the center of our consciousness that says "I," the very center of our being.

یکی ره برتر از کون و مکان شو
جهان بگذار و خود در خود نهان شو

Become a path beyond existence (*kawn*) and place (*makān*),
Leave the world behind and become hidden within thyself.[1]

Penetrate into thine own being. That is where thou wilt discover God. "The kingdom of God is within you" as Christ has said. Here, Shabistarī is emphasizing the inner I or *man*, the inner being.

In the next verse he plays with the form of the Arabic-Persian script:

ز خطّ وهمی های هویّت
دو چشمی می‌شود در وقت رؤیت

From the imaginary line of the "h" of identity (*huwiyyat*),
When thou lookest at it, thou seest it having two eyes.

One cannot understand this verse without knowledge of some Arabic orthography. The Persian word *huwiyyat*, which in Arabic is *huwiyyah*, comes from the Arabic third-person singular pronoun *huwa*. *Huwiyyah* itself means identity. The "h" in Persian can be written in two ways. Most often it is written in a way that creates two circles (ه); so, it has two eyes. It is to this fact that Shabistarī is referring, saying that as long as you identify your *huwwiyah* with your ego, you always see double, like the two eyes of the "h" of *huwiyyat*. You do not see unity.

The first hemistich refers to the imaginary line, in the philosophical sense of *wahm*, of the Persian orthography of the "h" of *huwiyyat*. One sees it with two eyes when one looks at it, meaning that once one gets stuck in individualistic *huwiyyah*, in identifying one's reality only with the individual *man*, one can never see unity. For most of us that is what we do all the time. When we say "I, I, I" we look at things from the point of view of our individual ego.

نماند در میانه رهرو و راه
چو های هو شود ملحق به الله

There no longer remains either the person who walks upon the path or the path itself,
When the "h" of him (*huwa*) becomes attached to *Allāh*.

Most people familiar with the Quran know the Quranic expression *huwa'Llāh*, "He is God" (Q. 112:1). On the inner level, *huwa* refers to God in His metaphysical Essence, and is identified with the last letter of *Allāh* itself. The Name *Allāh* (الله) contains the whole of reality. With the *alif* is a descent of Divine Reality, and with the *hā'* is the return. The form of *hā'* is like the female womb and the *alif* the male sexual organ, both of which must be understood here in their symbolic aspect. In the Arabic orthography of *Allāh* if you take the *alif* away, you have *li'Llāh*, which means "belongs to God." Then if you take the first *lām* away, you have *lahu*, "His," which indicates in a sense a closer, more intimate relation to God. And if you take the other *lām* away, all you are left with is "h," *huwa*, meaning "He." So the "h" at the end of *Allāh* is identified metaphysically with *huwa*, referring to the Divine Essence.

It is also interesting to note that in the orthography of the word *Allāh*, you can write the last letter in two ways. Sometimes it is written as a circle (ه) but you can also write it as a curved line (ـه), which is also a symbol of absorption back into the Divine. The feminine element, metaphysically speaking, absorbs everything back to God. Do not forget that the Essence (*Dhāt*) of God in Arabic is feminine. And so, the orthography of *Allāh* in a sense symbolizes all the levels of metaphysics and all the grades of both cosmogenesis and the return of the cosmos back to God.

Once that "h" of *huwiyyat* becomes the *huwa* that comes at the end of *Allāh*, then there is no longer a path nor journey upon the path. One is already there.

بود هستی بهشت امکان چو دوزخ
من تو در میان مانند برزخ

Being is Paradise and contingency like Hell,
Thy I (*man*) is in the middle like Purgatory (*barzakh*).[2]

Now, Shabistarī is discussing *man*, our ordinary I-ness. So, he is not talking about the metaphysical meaning of *man*, which refers to God Himself. He says that being is like Paradise and contingency is like Hell. This is just metaphorical. He is talking here about *wujūd* and *imkān* of Ibn Sīnā. *Imkān* means possibility, that is, the world of contingency. Here I would translate it as, contingency, the contingent world, meaning everything other than God.

"Thy I (*man*) is in the middle like Purgatory" means that it can either enter Paradise or it can enter Hell.

چو برخیزد تورا این پرده از پیش
نماند نیز حکم مذهب و کیش

Once this veil is lifted from in front of thee,
There will not remain even the injunctions of the schools of law (*madhhab*)
and of religion (*kīsh*).

Kīsh here means religion in its ordinary sense and *madhhab* means a particular school of religious law that one follows. This verse does not mean that Shabistarī is against practicing the *Sharī'ah*. He is saying that the practices of the *Sharī'ah* are for us in order to lift the veil that separates us from God. Nor does Shabistarī claim that once the veil is lifted, one should not practice the injunctions of the religion. He followed the example of the Prophet. So he continues,

همه حکم شریعت از من توست
که آن بربستهٔ جان و تن توست

All the injunctions of the *Sharī'ah* are for thy I-ness (*man*);
For it is what is congealed in thy body and soul.

Man (I) refers here to the individual consciousness or spirit for which the injunctions of religious law are meant.

من تو چون نماند در میانه
چه کعبه چه کنشت چه دیرخانه؟

When thy I-ness is no longer in the middle,[3]
What difference is there between the Ka'bah, a synagogue (*kinisht*) or a
monastery (*dayr-khānah*)?

"When thy *man* is no longer in the middle," refers to when the ordinary I with which we identify ourselves is no longer there. The word *kinisht* in Persian and Arabic is similar to the word "Knesset" in Hebrew. *Dayr* means of course monastery. When this ego-center is removed, one goes beyond form to the essence which heavenly religions share. Concerning this "I" Ḥallāj writes:

بيني وبينك إنّي ينازعني
فارفع بلطفك إنّي من البيني

Between I and Thou, it is my I-ness that is in contention;
Through Thy grace lift this I-ness from between us.

تعیّن نقطهٔ وهمی است بر عین
چو صافی گشت عینت غین شد عین

Determination is an imaginary point placed upon the *'ayn*,
When thy *'ayn* is purified, the *ghayn* (otherness) becomes the *'ayn* itself.[4]

This verse again is enigmatic . Here, *'ayn* refers to the *'ayn thābit*, the archetype, but it is also the name of one of the letters of the Arabic alphabet. If you put a dot upon the letter *'ayn* (ع), it becomes *ghayn* (غ), which is another letter of the Arabic alphabet. Now, what does *ghayn* mean here? I consider it to be a reference to the word *ghayr*, which means otherness, separation from God. So, when "thy *'ayn* is purified," otherness is removed. *Ghayn* also means cloud and the verse could be read to mean, "When the cloud is removed."

دو خطوه بیش نبود راه سالک
اگر چه دارد او چندین مهالک

The path of the traveler has only two elements (*khaṭwah*),
Although he faces many life-threatening situations.

"The path of the traveler has only two elements" means that there are only two obstacles to overcome. *Khaṭwah* can also mean "step," so that the verse could be rendered as "two steps." But what are these two most important obstacles to overcome or steps to take?

یک از های هویت در گذشتن
دوم صحرای هستی در نوشتن

One is to go beyond the "i" of identity (*huwiyyat*);
The second, to traverse (*dar niwishtan*) the desert of existence.

This is a synthetic summary of the spiritual path. There are only two things one has to do: "One is to go beyond the 'i' of identity," to go beyond always being selfish, always wanting everything for oneself, to transcend ordinary self-identity, that is, to go beyond the boundaries of individual existence. The second is "to traverse the desert of existence." Note that in order for these lines to rhyme, *dar niwishtan* must be pronounced *dar nawashtan*. Today, in Khurāsān this pronunciation is still used, and the fact that Shaykh Maḥmūd Shabistarī lived in Azerbaijan, on the other side of Iran, means that this pronunciation must have been also used there also during his time.

در این مشهد یکی شد جمع و افراد
چو واحد ساری اندر عین اعداد

In this spiritual station of vision (*mashhad*), the one became collectivity (*jam'*) and many individuals,
Like the number one which runs through all of the numbers.

As mentioned above, *mashhad* is the place noun (*ism maḥall*) meaning place of witness, from both *shuhūd* and *shahādah*. The word *shuhūd* means vision, especially spiritual vision. *Shahādah* means both bearing witness and martyrdom. Arabic being such a synthetic language, these two concepts are also related, because you have to be a martyr (*shahīd*), meaning to undergo spiritual death, in order to have *shuhūd* in the spiritual sense. In a sense you have to martyr your *nafs*, you have to go beyond that state in order to be able to have *shuhūd*. Of course, the most famous *mashhad* is the city of Mashhad in Khurāsān, where Imam 'Alī al-Riḍā, the eighth Shi'ite Imam, was martyred and is buried and where still many go to beseech the Imam to help them find a spiritual path. So, there is a cluster of words that are all related to each other, and are related to the word *shāhid*, to be a witness, to be present. There is an awareness in Sufism of the significance of the cluster of meanings of these terms. When you are there in Mashhad, you should be aware of being present before God, of being *shāhid*, since you are now in Mashhad, and a *shāhid* as far as your *nafs* is concerned.

There are also in Iran other cities called the *mashhad* of this or that saint. When Shi'ism came to Iran, they identified these places with tombs of martyrs, but its deeper and earlier meaning is a place of vision, and that is how Shaykh Maḥmūd Shabistarī uses it.

"Like the number one which runs through all of the numbers" is related to the point mentioned above, that all numbers are repetitions of the number one, all multiplicity is the theophany of the One.

تو آن جمعی که عین وحدت آمد
تو آن واحد که عین کثرت آمد

Thou art that multiplicity (*jam'*) that came as identical to unity.
Thou art that unity that is identical to multiplicity.

Jam' means addition, multiplicity, assembly, and also both collectivity and collectedness. This verse means that, spiritually speaking, man is both unity in multiplicity and multiplicity in unity. You all know that during the day we have several moods, thinking different ideas about ourselves, and still we are one single person. We experience both multiplicity and unity within ourselves. We know that we are the same person at two o'clock in the afternoon as we were at ten o'clock in the morning, but at the same time, different thoughts and feelings have come into our minds at different times and we have had different states of consciousness. The sage, however, is always in the state of unity even when immersed outwardly in multiplicity.

کسی این سر شناسد کو گذر کرد
ز جزوی سوی کلّی یک سفر کرد

That person knoweth this mystery who has traveled,
And made a journey from the particular to the Universal.

Question [4]

مسافر چون بود رهرو کدام است؟
کەرا گویم که او مرد تمام است؟

Who is a traveler? Who is it who moves upon the path?
Who is it whom I can call the complete man (*mard-i tamām*)?

Rah-raw, like *musāfir*, means traveler, but refers here to the traveler upon the spiritual path; so, it can be translated here as the traveler upon the path, he who traverses the path.

In the second hemistich Shabistarī uses an expression that needs some explanation. Here, he is referring to the important term *insān-i kāmil* in Persian, meaning the perfect man or the universal man, but instead he uses the term *mard-i tamām*. *Tamām* in Arabic has many different meanings. It comes from the word *tāmma*, to end, to finish, and also means complete and perfect. In Sufism the phrase *mard-i tamām* is used only occasionally. So, it could be translated as the "complete man," whereas *insān-i kāmil* is the "perfect" or "universal" man. Titus Burckhardt used the term *l'homme universel* to translate the title of 'Abd al-Karīm Jīlī's famous work *al-Insān al-kāmil*, and I also prefer to translate it as universal man, although Nicholson used perfect man. The term itself was not invented by Jīlī, but was used already by Ibn 'Arabī. It is a very important term in *taṣawwuf*, where we also have 'Azīz al-Dīn Nasafī's famous book *Insān-i kāmil*, with the same title as Jīlī's work.

Some Sufi writers make a distinction between *insān-i tamām* and *insān-i kāmil*. For others, they connote the same meaning. Now, for those who make a distinction, such as 'Abd al-Karīm al-Jīlī in the beginning of his book *al-Insān al-kāmil*, they refer to a subtle metaphysical point. They say that *insān-i tamām* (the complete man) is a person who has realized all of the potentialities of the human state, and point to Adam as being the first example of *insān-i tamām*. Those who make the distinction, however, say that not only does the *insān-i kāmil* possess all the possibilities of the human state in an actualized manner, but he has also actualized within himself all the states of being. So *insān-i kāmil* refers to a station above *insān-i tamām*.

There is also an advantage of the term *insān-i kāmil* over *mard-i tamām* in that it is gender neutral. *Insān* can mean either man or woman. When in Persian we say *mard-i tamām*, for *mard* we think of its literal translation man, but this does not mean necessarily male. A woman could be a *mard-i tamām* in its traditional sense.

So, the questioner is asking, who is *mard-i tamām*? Who is the complete person? He is really asking a question about the nature and identity of *al-insān al-kāmil*. Having asked questions about God, and about the nature of the "I," Shabistarī now is asked about the Universal Man.

Answer

دگر گفتی مسافر کیست در راه؟
کسی کو شد ز اصل خویش آگاه

Then thou hast said, "Who is the traveler upon the path?"
The person who has become aware (*āgāh*) of his own root.

It is very important to understand the symbolism of traveling. We live at a time in human history in which you have the largest amount of traveling and also the least. You have the most people traveling physically because everybody is running around from Belgium to Russia, from San Francisco to New York, from Paris to Beijing and Delhi and so forth, all over the globe. But spiritual traveling has become much less common. And so the symbolism of wayfaring and traveling that was so universal in all religions has lost a great deal of its meaning for most ordinary people. In the old days most people did not travel very much physically, but they traveled a great deal spiritually. Now, the situation is reversed. We travel a great deal physically, but we do not travel very much spiritually. We go all over the globe, but at the end of the trip we are still the same person we were when the trip began. So, you have to understand the symbolism of traveling in the traditional sense and not compare it to the situation today.

There are so many great saints who never went anywhere geographically speaking but also went "everywhere" inwardly. Of course, some of them did also travel physically. Shaykh Abū'l-Ḥasan al-Shādhilī traveled from Morocco to Iraq, all the way across the Arab world. Ibn 'Arabī went from Spain also to Iraq and finally settled in Syria. I am not saying that no one among the Sufis traveled extensively in the ordinary sense of the term. But even that kind of traveling was always seen in its spiritual aspect, and here what Shabistarī is saying is that as soon as you become aware of the reality of things, you become a spiritual traveler, what in Sufism is called *sālik*.

If you know where you come from and where you should be going, you will start traveling. It is as simple as that. If only we all knew concretely that one day we shall die, we would live in such a way as to journey toward our ultimate goal and prepare ourselves for the only journey worthy of undertaking during the flow of our life, which itself is a journey. So, this awareness cannot come about without our becoming conscious of the need to prepare ourselves for the journey. Otherwise, we do not have a real awareness of who we are and where we should be going. There are many people who have read these matters, but they do not travel and do not do what is needful. They do not have real awareness of who they are and where they are. *Āgāh*, therefore, means to become spiritually and intellectually fully conscious, to become aware of the nature of reality and our state and role in the scheme of things.

مسافر آن بود کو بگذرد زود
ز خود صافی شود چون آتش از دود

The traveler is one who passes rapidly,
Who becomes purified from himself, like fire from smoke.

The debasing of language makes it difficult to translate this verse into English. The term "traveler" came even to mean a member of the Communist Party, "fellow traveler." Can you imagine what a debasing of language occurred when people who had sympathy toward the purely materialistic philosophy of Marxism were called "fellow travelers"? That is going from the apogee to the perigee of meaning of a cardinal term used so widely in spirituality.

سلوکش سیر کشفی دان ز امکان
سوی واجب به ترک شین و نقصان

Consider the journey of that person to be a journey of discovery of the world of contingency,
Towards Necessity through the abandonment of defects and faults.

Again, this verse refers to the passage from the world of contingency, of possibility (*imkān*), to the Necessary (*wājib*), towards God, the Necessary Being (*Wājib al-wujūd*) in the terminology of Islamic philosophy.

به عکس سیر اوّل در منازل
رود تا گردد او انسان کامل

Reversing the journey through the various states of being,
He will journey until he becomes the Universal Man.

Here, we come to the expression of the Universal Man. "The various states of being" refers to all the states that man has traversed as he has descended from God to this world and will traverse again in returning to God. The Quran says, *innā li'Llāh wa innā ilayhi rāji'ūn*, "Truly we are God's, and unto Him we return (or 'is our returning')," (Q. 2:156) reversing the states that he has traversed to get here to this lowly world.

Principle

بدان اوّل که تا چون گشت موجود
کز او انسان کامل گشت مولود

Know that the first (reality) that was brought into existence,
The Universal Man was born from it.[1]

Now, this is a very difficult concept to accept for people enmeshed in the worldview of modern philosophy and science, in which the traditional perspective is seen as just human wishful thinking. However, let me explain what this esoteric teaching means. There is an enigmatic *ḥadīth* of the Prophet—*'alayhi'l-ṣalātu wa'l-salām*—in which God addresses him and says, *law lāk mā khalaqtu'l-aflāk*, "If thou wert not, I would not have created the heavens." This dictum does not make any sense from a modern scientific point of view. However, it makes perfect sense from a traditional point of view.

If the Universe has a purpose, what is this purpose? The answer of Sufism is that the purpose of the creation of the Universe is that God wanted to know Himself in a sense "objectively." I have already mentioned the *ḥadīth*, "I was a Hidden Treasure; I loved to be known. Therefore, I created the world so that I would be known." God in fact loved to be known. So, the purpose of the Universe is knowledge of God. He Himself wanted to be known objectively, objective to Himself; so, He created the world and man. Since He is the creator of the world and "loved to be known," these two realities, creation and knowledge, must be related. What He did was to create a world with all different creatures in it, each manifesting an aspect of His Creative Power and also Nature. And He also created a creature to whom He gave the possibility of knowing Him actively, making that creature the full theophany of all of His Names and Qualities, which are contained in the Name *Allāh*.

Every creature in the Universe is a reflection of some Divine Name and Quality. But man, the human being, both male and female, is the *tajallī*, the theophany, of the name *Allāh*, which contains all the Divine Names. That is why the Prophet was called 'Abd Allāh, in addition to his other names. Therefore, the purpose of creation was to create such a creature who would follow the path of knowing God. The purpose of creation was *al-insān al-kāmil*, the Universal Man, who is, therefore, both the reality by which God created the world, and the *maqṣad*, the final aim of creation itself. Now, regarding this being who manifests himself finally as man Shabistarī says,

در اطوار جمادی گشت پیدا
پس از روح اضافی گشت دانا

He first became manifest in the mineral (*jamād*) states (*aṭwār*),
Then through the Spirit added to him became aware.

Jamād means mineral, stone, or inanimate object. The word *aṭwār* is a plural of the word *ṭawr*, which means stage, state, going from one condition to another, and so forth. In modern Arabic evolution is called *taṭawwur*, and in this sense it is a modern term invented in the nineteenth century, which entered also from Arabic into Persian. *Taṭawwur* means going from *ṭawr* to *ṭawr*, but now it connotes the Darwinian sense of evolution. This word was chosen by Shabistarī in its traditional sense, and it is important that it should not be confused with its modern meaning. Many mistakes have been made in interpreting this term by modern scholars, thinking that Sufis such as Shabistarī believed in Darwinian evolution. However, Shabistarī is really referring here to Quranic gynecology, according to which first there is a sperm, which belongs to the *jamādī* state, the mineral state. Then during the fourth month of pregnancy, God blows the spirit into the *nuṭfah*, the embryo, and a human being is born, traversing the mineral, vegetative, and animal realms. That is why it is not against Islamic Law to have an abortion during the first months of pregnancy if there is a cogent reason. It is discouraged, but it is not against Islamic Law. Only after a hundred days is it forbidden, because by then the fetus has a soul, whereas in traditional Christianity it is forbidden at all stages of pregnancy from the moment of conception, unless the fetus is impaired.

پس آنگه جنبشی کرد او ز قدرت
پس از وی شد ز حقّ صاحب ارادت

Then it began to move because of the power [given by God].
Then it gained will given by the Truth.

"Then" refers to having received the spirit from God while it is still in the mother's womb. "God gave it free will," as soon as the child was born. Of course, probably in the womb of the mother, the child has some degree of freedom. When he or she is kicking, does he or she choose to kick or is it determined? In any case it is only when it is born that it manifests its free will to the parents and others.

به طفلی کرد باز احساس عالم
در او بالفعل شد وسواس عالم

As a child felt again the world,
In it became actualized meticulousness about the world.

Waswās here means extra care or being meticulous about something. So, it is the Divine Gift that makes possible *waswās* by the child about the world surrounding him or her.

چو جزویّات شد در وی مرتّب
به کلّیّات ره برد از مرکّب

When particulars became orderly within him,
He found a path to universals from compounds.

It is interesting to note that when a child is born, you cannot teach him or her about universal concepts. The child lives in the concrete and also in the angelic state. One of the signs of growing up is that his or her consciousness gradually separates the universal and the particular, and we think it is a sign of growth, but in a sense it is not; rather, it is a falling away from the angelic state. In any case Shabistarī is saying that the child begins to know universals (*kulliyyāt*) as he or she matures.

غضب شد اندر او پیدا و شهوت
وز ایشان خاست بخل و حرص و نخوت

Anger began to appear in him and also passion,
And then from them arose miserliness, greed, and hatred.

This is in reference to a continuation of the stages of development of the human being.

به فعل آمد صفتهای ذمیمه
بتر شد از دد و دیو و بهیمه

Negative qualities became actualized [in that person].
He became worse than savage beasts, demons (*dīw*), and wild animals.

Dīw means negative forces or demons. It is related to the Sanskrit word *deva*, but in Sanskrit this word is mostly positive, whereas in Persian *dīw* has a totally negative connotation.

تنزّل‌را بود این نقطه اسفل
که شد با نقطهٔ وحدت مقابل

This point is the lowest in the process of descent,
For it became opposite of the point of Unity.

The lowest point of descent is reached in human beings not at birth, but when all these negative qualities become actualized in him as a grown up person. He then reaches a point opposite to that of Unity (*tawḥīd*).

شد از افعال کثرت بی‌نهایت
مقابل شد از این رو با بدایت

He became, because of multiple actions that are endless,
Opposite in this way to that which has no beginning.

When one is young, one thinks that one can do anything, one feels that one has infinite possibilities. In this sense in a way he or she confronts that reality that has no beginning and by implication no end.

اگر گردد مقیّد اندر این دام
به گمراهی بود کمتر ز انعام

If that person becomes constrained in this trap,
In his having lost his way, he becomes less than animals,

"In this trap" refers to the illusion of being able to do whatever he desires, the trap of passions and all the negative elements of the soul to which, if he surrenders, he falls to a grade below the animals which always remain true to their nature.

وگر نوری رسد از عالم جان
ز فیض جذبه یا از عکس برهان

But if a light comes to him from the world of the Spirit,
From the emanation of Divine attraction or from the reflection of demonstration.

The state cited above can be avoided if help comes from the world of the Spirit through God attracting the soul unto Himself or from the power of the intellect reflected in one's mind.

دلش با نور حقّ همراز گردد
وز آن راهی که آمد باز گردد

[If that happens] that person's heart comes to share the secret of the Light of the Truth,
And from the same path from which he came, he will return [to God].

Once our hearts are impregnated by the Light of the Truth, we realize who we are, where we are and where we should be going. And so, we begin to undertake the only journey ultimately worthy of being made, that is, the journey back to our original home, back to God.

ز جذبه یا ز برهان یقینی
رهی یابد به ایمان یقینی

Either through Divine attraction or demonstration based on certitude,
He will find a path to certitude-based faith.

"Demonstration based on certitude" (*burhān-i yaqīnī*) involves intellectual intuition and not reason or rationalism alone as some people say. *Burhān-i yaqīnī* is not possible without intellection in its traditional sense.

کند یک رجعت از سجّین فجّار
رخ آرد سوی علّیّین ابرار

He will make a return from the infernal state (*sijjīn-i fujjār*),
Pointing himself towards the highest Paradise (*'illiyyīn-i abrār*).

Sijjīn-i fujjār is a reference to Hell. The *abrār* are the select people of God, who are in the highest paradise, and *'Illiyyīn* means elevated. Thus, he will return from *sijjīn* which is infernal to the highest degrees of paradisal existence.

به توبه متّصف گردد در آن دم
شود در اصطفا ز اولاد آدم

He will become repentant in that moment,
Through this purification (*iṣṭifā*), he will become a child of Adam.

If man experiences what is mentioned in the above verse, he will repent that very moment. *Iṣṭifā* here means to become purified, from the term *ṣafā* (purity). Of course, this term contains also an allusion to the name of the Prophet, Muṣṭafā, *salawāt Allāh 'alayhi.*

از افعال نکوهیده شود پاک
چو ادریس نبی آید در افلاک

He will become purified from negative actions,
Like the Prophet Idrīs, he will come to the heavens.

"He will come to the heavens," as did Idrīs who, according to traditional teachings, was taken to Heaven alive. Having mentioned Idrīs (Enoch), Shabistarī continues by referring to the names of different prophets.

چو یابد از صفات بد نجاتی
شود چون نوح از آن صاحب ثباتی

Once he is saved from bad qualities,
He will become like Noah, a person of endurance.

The author is referring to the quality of the Prophet Noah, who endured through so many trials persistent in his faith in God.

نماند قدرت جزویش در کلّ
خلیل‌آسا شود صاحب توکّل

His particular power will not remain [once he is] in the Universal,
Like Abraham, he will become possessor of confidence in God.

"His particular power will not remain . . ." could have two meanings. It could mean either that his particular power will be integrated in the Universal, or that his particular power will disappear altogether. In either case he will have *tawakkūl*, confidence and reliance upon God, as did the Prophet Abraham.

ارادت با رضای حقّ شود ضمّ
رود چون موسی اندر باب اعظم

His will becomes combined with satisfaction of the Truth (*riḍā-yi Ḥaqq*),
Like Moses, he will go through the great gate.

"With satisfaction of the Truth" means that his will becomes surrendered to God's Will and His being satisfied with Him and He with God. "The great gate" refers to Mount Sinai.

ز علم خویشتن یابد رهائی
چو عیسای نبی گردد سمائی

He will become freed from his own knowledge.
Like the Prophet Jesus he will become Heavenly.

دهد یکباره هستی‌را به تاراج
درآید از پی احمد به معراج

At once he will give up all of his existence as if plundered.
He will try to follow Aḥmad on the nocturnal ascent.

Aḥmad here refers of course to the Prophet of Islam and the nocturnal ascent to his *mi'rāj* to the Divine Throne. Having mentioned various prophets, Shabistarī then ends this section with this verse:

رسد چون نقطهٔ آخر به اوّل
در آنجا نی ملک گنجد نه مرسَل

When the last point has reached the first,
There, neither an angel will fit nor a prophet.

This is a reference to the *ḥadīth* mentioned previously, "I have had a time with God which I do not share with any angel brought nigh, nor any prophet sent forth." This verse is also a reference to Quran 53:9, the *maqām* of *aw adnā*, "or nearer."

Illustration

نبی چون آفتاب آمد ولی ماه
مقابل گردد اندر «لی معالله»

The Prophet has come like the Sun, the saint like the Moon,
Who faces within "I have [a time] with God."

In comparison to the Prophet, a saint is like the Moon, which reflects the light of the Sun and faces the Sun within the reality of the above-cited *ḥadīth.*

نبوّت در کمال خویش صافی است
ولایت اندر او پیدا نه مخفی است

Prophecy in its perfection is purity.
Sanctity is manifest in it, not hidden.

This is a very powerful esoteric verse about the relation between prophecy (*nubuwwah*) and *walāyah/wilāyah*, which I have translated as sanctity but that also means initiation, the esoteric dimension, inner spiritual power. In the hemstitch, "Prophecy (*nubuwwat*) in its perfection is purity (*ṣāfī*)," *ṣāfī* means not only purity but also clarity. *Walāyah/wilāyah* is evident and manifest (*paydā*) in it but only for those who have eyes to see. For the spiritually blind it is hidden.

ولایت در ولی پوشیده باید
ولی اندر نبی پیدا نماید

Sanctity is veiled (*pūshīdah*) in the saint,
But in the Prophet appears as manifest.

Pūshīdah or veiled means literally covered or dressed, and also hidden. *Walāyah/ wilāyah* is veiled and hidden in the saint (*walī*); that is, the *awliyā'* do not manifest it outwardly. But in the case of the Prophet, his *walāyah/wilāyah* manifests itself within *nubuwwah.* The Prophet was both a *nabī* and a *walī.* He had both the power of *walāyah/wilāyah* and *nubuwwah*, not only the power of *nubuwwah*. His power of *walāyah/wilāyah* is the origin of Sufism and also all other esoteric teachings in Islam.

ولی از پیروی چون همدم آمد
نبی‌را در ولایت محرم آمد

> Since through following [the Prophet] the *walī*, has become intimate (*hamdam*),
> He has become in sanctity the intimate keeper of secrets (*maḥram*) [of the Prophet].

As mentioned above, the word *dam* means breath. *Hamdam* means literally "having the same breath," that is, being so close that two people can feel each other's breath. It, therefore, means intimacy as in this verse of Rūmī's *Mathnawī*: *Muṣṭafā āmad ki ārad hamdamī*, "The Prophet came in order to bring about intimacy," that is, spiritual intimacy.

ز «ان كنتم تُحبّون» يابد او راه
به خلوتخانهٔ «يحببكم الله»

> From "If you love [God]," he finds the path,
> To the spiritual retreat of "God will love you."

This verse contains two phrases from Quran 3:31, "Say, 'If you love (*in kuntum tuḥibbūn*) God, follow me, and God will love you (*yuḥbibkum Allāh*) and forgive you your sins. And "God is Forgiving, Merciful.'"

در آن خلوتسرا محبوب گردد
به حقّ یکبارگی مجذوب گردد

> In that place of spiritual retreat, he becomes the beloved [of God].
> All of a sudden, he becomes attracted to the Truth.

Making a spiritual retreat (*khalwah*) is a central Sufi practice in which one who undertakes it seriously realizes that he is God's beloved and is drawn to Him. One cannot make a *khalwah* without initiation whose chain goes back to the Prophet and, for both Sunnis and Shi'ite Sufis, through 'Alī, who received this aspect of the prophetic reality more than anyone else and disseminated it. That is why he is the head of all the Sufi orders, except the Naqshbandiyyah. But even for the Naqshbandiyyah Imam Ja'far al-Ṣādiq is a pole; so the Naqshbandīs consider that this truth also pertains to him considering the relation of Imam Ja'far to 'Alī.

In this context the following poem always comes to my mind because its author was a dear friend who was executed during the Iranian Revolution at the age of nearly one hundred. He was a senator and a very good poet, and once we made the pilgrimage to the Ka'bah together. He composed a poem for me concerning the Prophet in which he said,

> It was in thy light that 'Alī became a *walī*,
> He became the mirror, reflecting the Truth.[2]

The accusation often made that Shi'ites and therefore most Persians do not pay enough attention to the Prophet is not valid, because you cannot conceive of 'Alī, who is so important in Iran as in any other Shi'ite country, without the Prophet. Spiritually it is inconceivable to think of 'Alī as *walī* without the Prophet being the supreme *walī* who enabled 'Alī to become *walī*.

بود تابع ولی از روی معنی
بود عابد ولی در کوی معنی

He is obedient, but on the basis of [inner] meaning,
He is a worshipper, but in the quarter of meaning (*kū-yi ma'nā*).

The *walī* "is obedient but on the basis of [inner] meaning," means that his obedience is not what is called *ta'abbudī*, in Arabic, that is, just for external surrender. His obedience is based on understanding the inner meaning. *Kūy* means a quarter of the city, and *ma'nā*, although it means meaning could be translated here as spirit; so, this phrase means "in the world of the spirit."

ولی وقتی رسد کارش به اتمام
که تا آغاز گردد باز انجام

The spiritual work of the saint comes to an end,
When the beginning becomes again the end.

The spiritual path ends when the traveler realizes that the *alpha* has become *omega*. So, the whole of the spiritual life is that return to where we came from; that is what Shabistarī is saying in this whole section.

In the preceding lines Shabstarī has dealt with the inner reality of the Prophet and the saint, the *nabī* and the *walī* and the symbolism related to them, one of whom is compared to the Sun and the other to the Moon because the Moon receives its light from the Sun as does the saint from the Prophet. Now, he turns to a second response to the question that was asked earlier in the text.

کسی مرد تمام است کز تمامی
کند با خواجگی کار غلامی

A man (*mard*) is complete (*tamām*), who, because of his completeness,
Although being a master (*khwājah*), he will serve as a slave.

He says *mard*, which means literally man, but here, as before, it means also the *anthropos* and, therefore, could also mean a woman; that is, it means human being. Although a complete man is a *khwājah*, a master in this world, he will serve as a servant or slave of God. So, that is the meaning of being a real man.

پس آنگاهی که ببرید او مسافت
نهد حقّ بر سرش تاج خلافت

Then when he cuts the distance [of the journey],
The Truth will place upon his head the crown of vicegerency.

"When he cuts the distance [of the journey]" refers to the distance between himself and God. Then he will become the real *khalīfah* of God, which is part of man's primordial nature.

بقا می‌یابد او بعد از فنا باز
رود ز انجام ره دیگر به آغاز

He will regain subsistence after annihilation,
Having terminated the path, he will go to a new beginning.

The first hemistich refers to the two *maqāms* or stations of *fanā'* (annihilation in God) and *baqā'* (subsistence in and through God). One has to experience *fanā'* in order to reach *baqā'*. The second hemistich refers to a further journey even after *baqā'* in the Divine Reality Itself.

شریعت‌را شعار خویش سازد
طریقت‌را دثار خویش سازد

He will make the *Sharī'ah* his motto.
He will make the *Ṭarīqah* (the spiritual Path) his embellishment.

Such a person will continue to practice the *Sharī'ah*. Although Shabistarī is talking about pure esoterism, he wants to emphasize that throughout the process of spiritual realization one never abandons the *Sharī'ah*. Hence he says, "He will make the *Sharī'ah* his motto," that is, the *Sharī'ah* remains inseparable from him. Only in such a case can one practice the *Ṭarīqah* seriously and have it become the embellishment of one's soul.

حقیقت خود مقام ذات او دان
شده جامع میان کفر و ایمان

As for *Ḥaqīqah* (the Truth), consider it to be the station of his essence.
He is now the sum of faith (*īmān*) and infidelity (*kufr*).

In these verses Shabistarī is talking about the basic Sufi doctrine of the three levels of *Sharī'ah*, *Ṭarīqah* and *Ḥaqīqah*, and then the perfect man whose journey through the path has enabled him to attain all three stages. He will still follow and practice the *Sharī'ah*; he will make the *Ṭarīqah* his own path, his own life, his own embellishment; and the *Ḥaqīqah* becomes his real station. Furthermore, he is in a state of being *jāmi'*, that is, the sum bringing together faith and infidelity.

But what does this mean to possess both faith (*īmān*) and its opposite infidelity (*kufr*)?[3] There is an *īmān* beyond *kufr* and *īmān*, that is the paradox of it. So, it is not as many usually imagine that one goes simply beyond both *kufr* and *īmān*, no longer having faith or *īmān*. It means that one goes beyond the duality of *kufr* and *īmān* into a state of unity. To do so, one must still have *īmān* in the One, not that one loses one's faith in the Divine Principle. There has been a lot of iconoclastic misunderstanding of Sufism concerning this issue. Some people say, "We are gnostics (*'urafā'*), and are beyond faith and infidelity, beyond morality and good and evil." But beyond the duality of good and evil is the Supreme Good. *Kufr* and *īmān* comprise a duality, and the person who has reached the *Ḥaqīqah* has gone beyond all duality including this one. It does not mean, however, that the person who has reached the *Ḥaqīqah* is now a *kāfir* (infidel) in the ordinary sense. But he cannot be defined by this duality, by this division, that is, the opposition between *kufr* and *īmān*. He is above and beyond all dualities and opposition. That is the basic message of this doctrine.

به اخلاق حمیده گشته موصوف
به علم و زهد و تقوی بوده معروف

Such a person is qualified (*mawṣūf*) by positive virtues;
He has become known for having knowledge, asceticism (*zuhd*), and reverence (*taqwā*).

The word *mawṣūf* can mean both qualified by and described by. *Akhlāq* means ethics, and also mores, and of course virtue. *Ḥamīdah* (as opposed to *radhīlah*) in Arabic means "that which is good," here meaning good character or virtue. The second hemistich reiterates the basic characteristics of such a person.

همه با او ولی او از همه دور
به زیر قبه‌های ستر مستور

Everyone is close to him, but he is far away from everyone,
Under the domes of the hiddenness of the Hidden.[4]

"The Hidden" is in reference to the Divine Reality that is at once hidden and manifest in Its theophanies.

This verse, impregnated by so much meaning, indicates that everybody is drawn to and close to the gnostic and saint, but he is actually with God and so is not close to them in the same way that they are to him. This verse must not be misunderstood. It is not that he does not pay attention to those close to him, but that inwardly his heart is with God and God is always near (*fa-innī qarībun*). So, this verse is a description of a person, the *mard-i tamām* (complete man) to which the first verse of this section refers.

Now, Shabistarī provides an example that is very telling.

Illustration

تبه گردد سراسر مغز بادام
گرش از پوست بخراشی گه خام

The heart of an almond will be completely ruined,
If thou takest off its skin while it is still unripe.

As you may know, before they are ripe, almonds are green. In Iran, we eat them before they have ripened, and we call it *chughālah bādām*. It is tasty in itself, but it is not an almond. It does not look or taste like an almond. It is something else. But in order for it to become an almond, that green stage is necessary. On the tree almonds have a green skin. Then you have to remove the skin, and then there is the hard shell. Then you break the shell and inside is the actual almond only when the almond has ripened. Shabistarī is saying that if you remove that green protection which God has put there in order for the almond to grow, you are not going to get the almond. It will never ripen. He is stating this symbol in order to explain why it is important to have the outward protection of the *Sharī'ah*. In fact in our life itself, we need to have a skin on our body in order for our bodies to function.

ولی چون پخته شد بی پوست نیکوست
اگر مغزش بر آری بر کنی پوست

But once it ripens, it is good without the skin.
If thou wantest to reach the fruit, thou wilt remove the skin from it.

This daring saying is used to explain the religion of Islam, the religion itself.

شریعت پوست مغز آمد حقیقت
میان این و آن باشد طریقت

The *Sharī'ah* is the skin, the *Ḥaqīqah* the heart,
And the *Ṭarīqah* is what is in between.

This again is a very famous verse of Persian literature using the example of the almond. It is the *Ṭarīqah* that makes one to go from the outer green skin that one does not eat to the point where one breaks the shell and reaches the heart of the almond, which one consumes.

خلل در راه سالک نقص مغز است
چو مغزش پخته شد بی‌پوست نغز است

> Disorder (*khalal*) on the path of the traveler is [like] the imperfection of the kernel of the almond (*maghz*);
> But once the almond is ripe, it is pure (*naghz*) without the skin.

Khalal means disorder, imperfection, blemish or infirmity. The shell or skin is needed in order for the almond to ripen, but once it is ripened, no shell is needed. That is the whole point he is trying to make, but this assertion does not mean that once one reaches the *Ḥaqīqah* one no longer needs the *Sharī'ah.*

چو عارف با یقین خویش پیوست
رسیده گشت مغز و پوست بشکست

> When the gnostic (*'ārif*) has joined his certitude,
> He has reached the kernel and the shell is broken.

"When the gnostic (*'ārif*) has joined his certitude" means he has reached metaphysical certitude. "He has reached the kernel" points to the almond itself, and therefore the goal of the path beyond the outer shell.

وجودش اندر این عالم نپاید
برون رفت و دگر هرگز نیاید

> His existence does not persist in this world.
> He has gone and will never return.

That does not mean that he has died physically but spiritually. This is the inner meaning of the Prophetic *ḥadīth*, *mūtū qabla an tamūtū*, "Die before you die." In a sense he is here outwardly, but he is no longer here inwardly. He has gone to God and will not return.

وگر با پوست یابد تابش خور
در این نشأه کند یک دور دیگر

> But if the Sun shines upon it again,
> [The human soul] comes back to this state of being (*nash'ah*) another turn.

In the same way that the almond tree will give fruit the next spring, the human soul can return to this world, can remanifest itself in this world in order to gain further perfection. It can have another cycle (*dawr-i dīgar*). This does not, however, mean reincarnation, but refers rather to another cycle in this life, that is, after *mūtū qabla an tamūtū*, "Die before you die," God can have you come back into this world but in an altered state of being. "If the Sun shines upon it again," presumes in reality to "if God wills"; *tābish-i khur*, "the shining of the Sun," contains implicitly the meaning of the Will of God. Hence, this verse does not refer to the physical Sun except symbolically; it means that the Sun of Divine Manifestation, Divine Power. *Nash'ah* is a very important philosophical term meaning state of being. So, now this person has come back to manifestation, to this world, but in a new state by the Will of God.

درختی گردد او از آب و از خاک
که شاخش بگذرد از هفتم افلاک

He becomes a tree, [fed by] water and earth,
Whose branches will grow beyond the seven heavens.

The spiritual person becomes like a tree that, although rooted in the earth and fed by water, grows so high that its branches reach beyond the cosmos.

همان دانه برون آید دگر بار
یکی صد گشته از تقدیر جبّار

That same seed will come out again;
Through the Will of *al-Jabbār* (the Compeller), one becomes a hundred.

God has absolute Will and so is the Determiner or Compeller of things. In fact, one of the Names of God is *al-Jabbār* (the Compeller).

Now, let us turn to the symbolism of the tree, which has profound eschatological as well as ethical implications. First of all, you plant a seed in the earth; then you water it. A shoot comes out, and after a while it grows branches, has leaves and flowers, and in the middle of the flower is that very seed again. That is a clear example of the regeneration of life, and it is also symbolic of spiritual regeneration. Now, a healthy tree is such that the seed is multiplied. If the world were made in such a way that each seed would only produce one seed, we would all be dead. God has made it possible that if you plant one wheat seed in the earth, for example, you get a whole ear filled with numerous seeds.

This account has several levels of meaning. First of all, what we sow we reap, that is, whatever actions we perform, the consequences come back to us. Secondly, good acts and their consequences multiply. There is an allusion to this truth at the highest level in the sacred saying of the Prophet (*ḥadīth qudsī)* in which God says, "If my servant takes a single step towards Me, I take a hundred steps towards him." But if the seed is not good, it will not have the same power of regeneration and often it will die. This is also a fact. That is how nature protects itself. If bad seeds were also to multiply indefinitely there would be no harmony left in nature. Diseases do work like that, of course. Bad germs multiply, but that action is always limited in such a way that the total harmony of things is not destroyed. Nature preserves its balance in this manner.

This principle is also very important spiritually. One seed that you plant spiritually produces a hundred seeds and can have an effect beyond your ken. The effect of one good act that you perform can proliferate, increasing its effect both in your soul and beyond you. Test it for yourself sometime. If you do something bad, you usually feel unhappy and ask God's forgiveness and you might be unhappy for only a few hours, the unhappiness being in accord with the nature of the bad act that you performed. But if you do something good, its effect upon your soul is much greater. You feel good longer, and so, there is not a mathematical equality between the two. This truth is the consequence of God's Mercy. The good always bears more fruit, like a goodly tree as the Bible also says.[5]

چو سیر حبّه بر خطّ شجر شد
ز نقطه خط ز خط دوری دگر شد

When the journey of the seed turns to a line of the tree,
The point becomes a line, and the line becomes another cycle.

What does this difficult verse mean? It means that in the same way that that big tree up there is really nothing more than its seed actualized; everything is already contained in its seed, which has now grown into its full reality. In the same way all lines are really the point repeated, and everything in the world comes from a single point. Again, in the world of nature every plant comes from a single seed. That is what Shabistarī is trying to make us understand.

چو شد در دایره سالک مکمّل
رسد هم نقطهٔ آخر به اوّل

When in the circle the traveler on the spiritual path has reached perfection,
The last point also reaches the first.

Shabistarī is again referring to the circle of existence (*dā'irat al-kawn*), which has several different interpretations. In one of these interpretations, you begin with Adam, and then you have the whole cycle of prophets, ending with the Prophet of Islam who stands at the point exactly opposite Adam. This is called *dā'irat al-nubuwwah*, the cycle of prophecy. From there you have the cycle of return, that is, *dā'irat al-walāyah/wilāyah*. This is one understanding of this verse.

Another understanding of this verse, which is ontological rather than prophetological, is that we have the arc of descent and the arc of ascent for cosmic existence itself; that is, one begins from the Origin, and levels of existence descends step by step to the material realm and then creatures return to their Source. The Darwinians would say that life ascends, but existence and life actually descend from the Origin of all reality. There are, of course, minerals, plants, animals—all the levels of creation—until you reach supreme complexity, this process marking the point of return. It is interesting to note that the cycle goes from simplicity to complexity with man being the most complex. Man is not only created in the *ṣūrah* (form) of God, but he is also cast into the state of *asfala sāfilīn*, "the lowest of the low" as the Quran asserts (95:4–5). However, we are also the point of return back to God. We are very strange creatures; both farthest away from God and the closest to Him possible. That flower is closer to God than we are in a certain sense because it is beautiful and innocent. It does not do anything wrong. It is itself. We can be much worse than this flower, but we can also ascend, in a conscious way that the flower cannot, to the Presence of God. So, the second half of the circle is called the arc of ascent, the return back to God, and it is this second meaning of the circle of existence that Shaykh Maḥmūd Shabistarī has in mind in this verse.

"The last point reaches the first point." This refers to the famous Quranic verse that we always quote when somebody dies, *innā li'Llah wa innā ilayhi rāji'ūn* "Truly we are God's, and unto Him we return." (Q. 2:156) It is also a metaphysical and eschatological statement, that is, our origin is in God and our end is also bark to God. The intermediate journey that we are making is through the various levels of being back to the Source.

دگر باره شود مانند پرگار
بدان کاری که اوّل بود بر کار

Once again, he becomes like a protractor,
Returning to what he did at the beginning.

This verse might seem enigmatic. A protractor (*pargār*) usually has a tip, which is like a needle. You press it into the paper, and the other end has a pen or a pencil, and by turning the protractor around you draw a circle. "Once again, he becomes like a protractor" means that the spiritual man is like the center of existence and like the protractor he creates a circle around his central being. It is a space, a spiritual space created around himself.

Ḥāfiẓ has a famous verse in which he says,

> ʿāqilān *nuqṭa-yi pargār-i wujūdand walī,*
> *ʿishq dānad ki dar* īn *dā'yirah sargardānand.*
> "The people of intellect are the point of the protractor of existence [that is, the center of the circle of existence.] "But love knows that they are all meandering within that circle."

"Returning to what he did at the beginning" refers on the highest level to the following truth: The first being that was created was the Universal Man, the Muḥammadan Reality (*al-ḥaqīqah al-muḥammadiyyah*). Sufis believe that it was the Universal Man who through God's Will became the instrument for the creation of the whole circle of existence.

چو کرد او قطع یکباره مسافت
نهد حقّ بر سرش تاج خلافت

> When he traverses at once the distance,
> The Truth places upon his head the crown of vicegerency.

As a result of journeying through the states of being, man becomes God's vicegerent (*khalīfat Allāh*) in actuality as the Quran states and is crowned by Him as such.

تناسخ نبود این کز روی معنی
ظهوراتی است در عین تجلّی

> This is not meant as reincarnation, if its meaning is heeded;
> (Rather,) it points to manifestations through theophany.

As mentioned above, Shabistarī is not talking here about reincarnation, that one dies and then comes back to the same state of being.

و قد سألوا و قالوا ما النهاية
فقیل هی الرجوع الی البداية

> They asked and said, "What is the end?"
> It is said, "Returning to the beginning."

Here, Shabistarī is quoting a famous Arabic verse of poetry (which is probably by himself) referring to the fact that the human being's final end is none other than return to his beginning.

Principle

نبوّترا ظهور از آدم آمد
کمالش در وجود خاتم آمد

> Prophecy became manifested with Adam;
> Its perfection came in the being of the Seal of Prophecy (*Khātam*).

This again is one of the most famous verses of the Persian language. It points to the whole prophetic cycle from *Ādam* to *Khātam*, as we say in Arabic because they rhyme in that language, that is, from Adam to the Prophet of Islam—*'alayhimā'l-ṣalāṭu wa'l-salām*. So, first Shabistarī refers to the prophetic cycle, which covers the whole of sacred history, and then he turns to *walāyah/wilāyah*.

ولایت بود باقی تا سفر کرد
چو نقطه در جهان دور دگر کرد

Walāyah/wilāyah remained; so the journey was made,
Like a point making another round in this world.

Walāyah/wilāyah, as mentioned before, has many different meanings, including initiation and spiritual guidance. It has also a political meaning, that is, rule, but that is not what Shabistarī has in mind here. When *walāyah/wilāyah* is juxtaposed to *nubuwwah*, as one sees in Ismāʿīlī philosophy, in Twelve Imām (*Ithnā ʿasharī*) Shiʿite philosophy, and in Sufism such as in the works of in Ibn ʿArabī with its discussion of the seal of *walāyah/wilāyah*, it means the spiritual power that God gave to the Prophet for spiritual guidance. The Prophet was both *nabī* and *walī*, and one could in a sense analyze the whole of the spiritual and intellectual history of Islam on the basis of this one principle, that is, how each school relates *nabī* to *walī*. One can see doctrines all the way from the extreme Ismāʿīlīs who think that within the Prophet *walāyah/wilāyah* was more important than *nubuwwah*, to Ibn Taymiyyah who did not pay attention to *walāyah/wilāyah*, and the whole spectrum of its meaning. For example for the Wahhabis *walāyah/wilāyah* in its spiritual sense plays no role at all. In contrast in Iran, on top of the entrance of many houses is written *Walāyat-i ʿAlī ibn Abī Ṭālib*. Obviously *walāyah/wilāyah* plays a very important role in Persia and the Shiʿite world in general. Moreover, Twelve Imām Shiʿism has always tried to preserve a balance between *walāyah/wilāyah* and *nubuwwah*. It is Ismāʿīlī Shiʿism that considered *wilāyah* to be more important than *nubuwwah* even within the Prophet himself, but not *Ithnā ʿasharī* Shiʿism.

"*Walāyah/wilāyah* remained" means that it was not terminated with the death of the Prophet, the function of spiritual guidance continuing after him. "Like a point making another round in this world" refers to spiritual journeying.

ظهور کلّ او باشد به خاتم
بدو یابد تمامی هر دو عالم

The total manifestation of it (*ū*) occurs with the Seal [of prophets].
With him the whole cycle (*dawr*) of both worlds becomes complete.

Now, to what does *ū* ("it") refer? Is it *walāyah/wilāyah* or *nubuwwah*? It is really both. Shabistarī has left this issue ambiguous on purpose. So, this verse can mean that the total and universal manifestation of both functions of *nubuwwah* and *walāyah/wilāyah* is in the reality of the Prophet.

وجود اولیا اورا چو عضوند
که او کلّ است و ایشان همچو جزوند

The existence of saints is like the members of his body (*ʿuḍw*);
For he is the totality, and they are like the parts.

ʿUḍw can mean member and also employee, but here its primary meaning is the members of the body or organs of the Prophet, "for he is the totality." If we consider a universal such as evenness, every even number, 2, 4, 6, 8, 10, and so forth, belongs to that category by virtue of participating in that universal. This is a subtle philosophical idea. Universal is usually *kullī* in Arabic, not *kull*, but in poetry it can be *kull*. In philosophical texts in Persian as well as in Arabic the distinction between these two terms is very important, but in poetry, sometimes they are used as synonyms.

چو او از خواجه یابد نسبت تامّ
از او با ظاهر آمد رحمت عامّ

Since he [the saint] finds his complete genealogy through the Master,
General Divine Mercy is manifested through him.

What the verse means is that the saint is a channel of Mercy because of his relation to the Prophet. Mawlānā Jalāl al-Dīn Rūmī, Ḥāfiẓ or Abū'l-Ḥasan al-Shādhilī, and other great saints and Sufi poets of Islam are a source of *barakah*, a source of grace, even for us after so many centuries because of the Prophet who has made this reality possible. Mawlānā has a poem about this very point, saying, "Whatever I have, I have because of the Prophet."

These days many people look at things in just the reverse way. For example, people many who teach and study Islamic literature at universities think that spiritually Rūmī is more important than 'Alī ibn Abī Ṭālib or even the Prophet himself. This is because they study these great medieval saints, but cannot understand the inner dimension of sanctity of the Prophet or those around him. This kind of myopia is prevalent. How many books have we read saying that Sufism reached its peak in the twelfth century. You can say that in April for example there are more flowers in this garden than in the winter. But the seeds were already there in the winter; otherwise there would be no flowers in April. What was planted was through the Prophet.

شود او مقتدای هر دو عالم
خلیفه گردد از اولاد آدم

He [the Prophet] becomes the leader (*muqtadā*) of both worlds;
He becomes God's *khalīfah* among the children of Adam.

It is by virtue of his prophetic function and spiritual nature given by God that he is the supreme vicegerent of God among all of humanity.

Illustration

چو نور آفتاب از شب جدا شد
تورا صبح و طلوع و استوا شد

When the light of the Sun became separated from the night,
Thou hast the morning, the sunrise and noon (*istiwā*).

Istiwā means the time when the Sun is exactly above one's head, and that is why the equator is called *khaṭṭ al-istiwā'* in Arabic and Persian. Shabistarī is stating here that our day and light come out of the darkness of the night, and he then explains what that means metaphysically and from the perspective of prophetology.

دگر باره ز دور چرخ دوّار
زوال و عصر و مغرب شد پدیدار

Once again through the circular movement of the revolving wheel,
Sunset, afternoon and the evening appeared.

This verse follows the one before it to complete the twenty-four hour cycle of a complete day and night. These verses set the background for the symbolism of the cosmic and prophetic functions of the Prophetic Light.

بود نور نبی خورشید اعظم
گه از موسی پدید و گه ز آدم

The light of the Prophet is the great Sun;
Sometimes it appears in Moses and sometimes in Adam.

Here Shabistarī is comparing the appearance of the prophets in the prophetic cycle to the light of the Sun. Wherever there is natural light during the day, it is the light of the Sun. So it is with the Muḥammadan Light, which in Sufism is associated with the light of all the prophets. This same light appeared in Adam, Abraham, Moses, Christ and the other prophets and became fully manifested in the Prophet of Islam.

اگر تاریخ عالمرا بخوانی
مراتبرا یکایک باز دانی

If thou readest the history of the world,
Thou wilt be able to read about each step.

"The history of the world" alludes to sacred history that reveals the appearance of one prophet after another.

ز خور هر دم ظهور سایه‌ای شد
که آن معراج دین‌را پایه‌ای شد

Every moment from the Sun there appeared a shadow,
Which itself became the basis for the ascension (*mi'rāj*) of religion.

Each moment of the day the Sun casts a shadow except at noon. Each prophet casts a shadow except the Prophet of Islam who appeared at high noon symbolically speaking. It is to this truth that the following verse refers:

زمان خواجه وقت استوا بود
که از هر ظلّ و ظلمت مصطفی بود

The time of the Master was the time of high noon,
Which was pure of any shadow and darkness.

"Master" (*Khwājah*) refers of course to the Prophet of Islam. You may have heard this account that according to Islamic sources the Prophet of Islam cast no shadow and that he is called the shadowless Prophet. It is said that when he walked in the streets in Makkah, even when the Sun was shining, he never cast a shadow. This phenomenon was considered to be one of his miracles, and was recounted by many of the Companions. The Sufis understand this truth metaphysically: there is one place in the world where there is no shadow when the Sun shines right above your head, namely the equator (*khaṭṭ-i istiwā'*), and the Prophet stands metaphysically at the equator of existence and hence casts no shadow. It is to this truth that Shabistarī is alluding. There is even a biography of the Prophet in English called *The Shadowless Prophet of Islam*.[6]

به خطّ استوا بر قامت راست
ندارد سایه پیش و پس چپ و راست

When standing upright at the equator,
One casts no shadow behind and before, to the right or left.

This verse is simply the reconfirmation of this fact with a hidden allusion to its inner meaning.

چو کرد او بر صراط حقّ اقامت
به امر «فاستقم» می‌داشت قامت

Because he stayed upon the Path of the Truth (*ṣirāt-i Ḥaqq*),
Through the order [of God], "Stand up," he stood up. (Q. 11:112)

"Stand up" (*fa'staqim*) refers to the Quranic verse 11:112 which is taken here to mean standing on the Path of God in following His Command.

نبودش سایه کو دارد سیاهی
زهی نور خدا ظلّ الهی

He does not cast any shadow, but he has blackness.
This comes from the Light of God, the shadow of the Divine.

Shabistarī is referring here to *nūr-i siyāh*, the Black Light of the Divine Essence, that we have discussed above.

ورا قبله میان شرق و غرب است
ازینرو در میان نور غرق است

His direction of prayer (*qiblah*) is between East and West,
And so he is drowned in the middle of light.

Shabistarī is referring here to the Quranic verse "neither of the East nor of the West" (*lā sharqiyyah wa lā gharbiyyah*, Q. 24:35). Islam as a religion is "in the middle" in many ways, such as creating a balance between the inward and the outward. Even geographically, it came originally neither from Japan nor France but from Arabia in the middle of the Eurasian land mass, and it soon covered the middle belt of the world. Intellectually also it stands between Judaism and Christianity in the Abrahamic world, emphasizing both the Law and the Way, the exoteric and the esoteric.

"He is drowned in the middle of light" because both the light of the East and the light of the West shine upon him.

به دست او چو شیطان شد مسلمان
به زیر پای او شد سایه پنهان

Since in his hand Satan became a Muslim,
Darkness disappeared under his feet.

The Prophet revealed a truth that can bring even the satanic elements within the human soul into submission (*taslīm*) making them *muslim*.

مراتب جمله زیر پایهٔ اوست
وجود خاکیان از سایهٔ اوست

All the states of being are under his feet,
The existence of beings created from dust comes from his shadow.

As Universal Man, the Prophet contains within himself all levels of existence. In fact the creatures are the result of his shadow and in a sense *are* his shadow.

ز نورش شد ولايت سايه گستر
مشارق با مغارب شد برابر

Through his light, *walayah/wilayah* spread its shade;
The Easts and the Wests became equal.

Do not forget that in Arabia, and most of the rest of the Islamic world including Persia, the Sun is very strong, and so shade has a very positive connotation. It is not like in England where shade and shadow have mostly a negative sense. "The Easts and the Wests" is an enigmatic phrase. First of all, the Quran sometimes uses easts and wests in the plural, that is, not only *al-mashriq wa'l-maghrib* but also *al-mashāriq wa'l-maghārib*. (Q. 70:40) There has been much debate over what this plural usage means. Some of the metaphysicians, some of the Sufis, believe that it refers to the East and the West of all the different worlds, including the intermediate world. Some believe that it means different parts of the East and different parts of the West, and there are also other interpretations.

ز هر سايه كه اوّل گشت حاصل
در آخر شد يكى ديگر مقابل

Whatever shadow was cast at the beginning,
At the end, another appeared facing it.

Here "whatever shadow" refers to the Prophetic Reality which at the end of the cosmogonic and prophetological manifestation appears again.

كنون هر عالمى باشد ز امّت
رسولىرا مقابل در نبوّت

Now whichever scholar appears within the religious community,
He faces a messenger in the domain of prophecy.

This verse does not limit itself to Islam but concerns all authentic religions based on prophecy.

نبى چون در نبوّت بود اكمل
بود از هر ولى ناچار افضل

The prophet, since he was the most perfect in prophecy,
Is of necessity higher than any saint.[7]

Shabistarī comes to a very important theological point. A prophet is always higher than a saint, and no human being, no matter how perfect, can be above the rank of the prophets. In Islam the greatest saints such as Junayd, Ḥallāj, 'Abd al-Qādir Jīlānī, Ibn 'Arabī, Rūmī and so forth, cannot possess a higher spiritual rank than the Prophet. They are what they are by virtue of attachment to the Muḥammadan Reality. Now, in the history of Islam, we have had moments in which some have considered themselves as being in a state higher than that of a prophet, but these are always either spurious claims, not in the mainstream of Sufism, or their sayings belong to the category of theophanic locutions (*shaṭḥiyyāt*).

It is important to know this fact, because a lot of *awliyā'* do remarkable things. They seem to have displayed tremendous spiritual powers and also often the meaning of their writings is more accessible than the Quran and *Ḥadīth*. For example, some people might be more attracted to reading Rūmī than reading *aḥādīth* or the Quran. Sometimes that great fruit of the tree is so sweet that we forget the tree itself that bore the fruit. But this is short-sightedness on our part. It takes a long time to appreciate the spiritual reality of the Prophet or the Quran. Rūmī himself says the Quran is like a beautiful bride. She does not unveil her beauty to just anyone. You have to have intimacy and closeness before she reveals her beauty to you. This is a saying of Mawlānā Jalāl al-Dīn Rūmī, so it is not something unnatural or abnormal to fail to discover the inner meaning of Islam's sacred texts as easily as the expositions of a Rūmī, but such great masters Ibn 'Arabī and Rūmī have all said that everything they have comes from the inner reality of the Prophet and the Quran.

The prophet or avatar in every religion is above every saint in that religion, and one cannot find a saint to be seen as above a prophet in any religion, whether it be Islam, Christianity, Hinduism or Buddhism. The greatest Buddhist saints and sages, Bodhidharma, Nagarjuna, and people like that were not higher than the Buddha. There is one point, however, that must be added here, one that concerns another level of reality and its exposition. A man such as the great Shankaracharya in India was talking about Ātman, about the Supreme Reality above and beyond even the avatars such as Rama and Krishna; so, you might think that he was in a higher state than them. But no—by virtue of what reality did Shankara become Shankara? By virtue of that chain of the avatars and the grace and *barakah* of Hinduism that was provided for him. So, some people especially today make this great mistake. Look at Meister Eckhart, the remarkable German mystic. He said, "I am swimming in the ocean of Divinity and I have gone beyond the Trinity." Can you imagine that? A German, saying he is beyond the Father, the Son, and the Holy Ghost, but this same person did not miss one mass. He went to church three times a day to take the Eucharist. So, let us not be myopic when considering this important issue. What Shabistarī is saying is that the greatness of the saints and metaphysicians of various traditions should not confuse us and make us forget that the perfection of a prophet is greater than that of even the most exalted saints. Even a Shankara, the greatest metaphysician of Hinduism, was Shankara by virtue of Hinduism. These are important matters that must be remembered in reading this verse.

ولایت شد به خاتم جمله ظاهر
به اوّل نقطه هم ختم آمد آخر

> *Walāyah/wilāyah* became completely manifest with the appearance of the Seal [of prophets];
> The first point also became the last point.

The *walāyah/wilāyah Muḥammadiyyah* is the origin of Sufism and also the origin of the esoteric teachings of Shi'ism. But here I want to come back to another meaning of the circle we considered before, with half of the circle representing *dā'irat al-nubuwwah* (the cycle of prophecy) and the other half representing *dā'irat al-walāyah/wilāyah* (the cycle of *walāyah/wilāyah*). The point at the top of the circle represents the beginning and the point at the bottom of the circle, the end of the cycle of prophecy and the beginning of the cycle of *walāyah/wilāyah*, which is associated with Sayyidunā Muḥammad, *ṣalawāt Allāh 'alayh*. The prophet before him is Christ, the plenary manifestation of Abrahamic sanctity and the first *walī* after the Prophet is 'Alī. There is, therefore, a correspondence between 'Alī and Christ. There are also later saints who correspond to earlier prophets. For example, Imam Mūsā al-Kāẓim, who is the seventh Shi'i Imam and is also a pole of Sufism, corresponds to Moses in some Sufi writings.

The important point to note here is that the Prophet is also the first *walī* in Islam, and he is thus the ultimate founder of all the Sufi orders. He then transferred this sanctity and initiatic power to 'Alī, and so with 'Alī the Islamic esoteric teachings become manifest. Of course, 'Alī was not a prophet; but because he was such a great spiritual and religious figure, some have made this mistake of considering him a prophet; however, this view is rejected by both Sunnis and Shi'ites. 'Alī carried this treasure of *walāyah/wilāyah* within himself, and with him the cycle of *walāyah/wilāyah* began. There will be no more prophets, but *walāyah/wilāyah* continues. Spiritual guidance will always be present in the Islamic tradition until the end of the world. When the Mahdī appears at the end, he will unveil the reality of *walāyah/wilāyah* for everyone. Until then, *walāyah/wilāyah* is not public while *nubuwwah* is. The Mahdī will bring out the esoteric dimension of religion openly. That is one of his functions, and with him we shall reach the end of the cycle of *walāyah/wilāyah* and come back to the beginning, to the origin. These are very complicated matters, and this doctrine is one of the more difficult aspects of Sufi teachings. Corbin wrote a great deal on these matters, and if you want to read more about it, you can refer to some of his works.[8]

از او عالم شود پر امن و ایمان
جماد و جانور یابد از او جان

> From him the world will become full of security (*amn*) and faith (*īmān*);
> The inanimate and the animate will receive life from him.

Amn (security), and *īmān* (faith) come from the same root but have different meanings. To be *amn* is to be secured in peace and protected, and of course *īmān* means faith.

"The inanimate and the animate, will receive life from him" emphasizes that not only the human world but also the world of nature derives its life from the Muhammadan Reality. This verse is considered by some commentators to refer to the Prophet as well as the Mahdī, but pertains more directly to the latter.

نماند در جهان یک نفس کافر
شود عدل حقیقی جمله ظاهر

> There will not remain in the world a single infidel;
> Real justice will become completely manifest.

Like myself, many of those who have interpreted the *Gulshan-i rāz* believe that this verse, the two verses preceding it, and the verse that follows refer to the Mahdī, who will come at the end of the world, not to the Prophet. Do not forget that according to both Sunni and Shi'ite belief, the name of the Mahdī will be the same as the name of the Prophet. The Prophet said a descendant of mine, or a man of my community according to some, whose name will be the same as mine will come at the end of time. So his name will be Muḥammad.

These verses probably refer to the Mahdī, because after saying that with the Prophet of Islam *walāyah/wilāyah* became manifest, Shabistarī stated that the last point became the first. This is a reference to the end of the cycle of *walāyah/wilāyah* itself, which goes back to the first, with the coming of Muḥammad al-Mahdī. Shabistarī says that through the power of the Mahdī the world will become full of *amn*, security, peace, and *īmān*, faith. Certainly, after the Prophet of Islam the world has not become full of security, peace, and faith, and indeed has now become almost empty of these qualities in many places. So, this is a strong argument that this assertion must indeed be a reference to the Mahdī.

This interpretation also sheds light on the previous verse, "The inanimate and the animate, will receive life from him." In a sense the Mahdī will breathe new life into nature and revive it. This thesis contains, therefore, an environmental lesson, you might say. Many talk these days about the degradation of the environment, but few think that God could breathe one breath and all the trees of the world could be renewed. Understanding the rejuvenation of nature spiritually in this manner is beyond the vision of modern man. Traditionalists believe, however, that when the Mahdī comes, not only human society but also nature will be rejuvenated. Nature, including the fish in the sea, will become healthy again; it will be a period of return to the beginning of the earth when everything was still paradisal and beautiful. Some traditional authorities say that his reign will last forty years, some say seventy years, after which Christ will come, and the world will end. Anyway, these three verses are undoubtedly also eschatological verses. They deal with eschatological events and the Mahdī, or at least that is my interpretation of it. So according to this interpretation, not only will the human world become full of security and faith, but the natural world will regain a new spiritual elan, a new spiritual energy, a new spiritual life.

As for the verse "Real justice will become completely manifest," it points to the fact that one of the functions of the Mahdī is to reestablish justice. Where there is oppression, he will replace it with justice.

بود از سرّ وحدت واقف حقّ
در او پیدا نماید وجه مطلق

He will be through the mystery of Unity aware of the Truth (*wāqif-i Ḥaqq*);
In him will become manifest the Face of the Absolute (*wajh-i muṭlaq*).

Wāqif-i ḥaqq means to be truly aware or divinely aware. *Wāqif* means to be aware, but since it comes from the Arabic *waqafa*, meaning "to stop," some scholars have not understood it in its metaphysical sense. *Wāqif* here means in a sense to stop the mind from knowing the peripheral, so that one can become aware and knowledgeable of the Divine Truth. *Wajh* in Arabic and Persian can mean not only "face" but also "side," or "aspect."

Question [5]

که شد از سرّ وحدت واقف آخر؟
شناسای چه آمد عارف آخر؟

Who finally became aware (*wāqif*) of the mystery of unity?
Finally, what it is that the gnostic has come to know?

This is a very important question with several dimensions: What is the end of knowledge? What can one know? And what does one know? Where are we from the point of authentic knowledge?

There is one word here that I want to analyze for you from a linguistic point of view, that is, the Persian word *wāqif*, which comes from Arabic. This is a word whose meaning some people have mistaken, including scholars such as A. J. Arberry, who misread its meaning completely in his translation of the *Fīhi mā fīhi* of Rūmī. The word *wāqif* is also a technical mystical term, and that is why I am emphasizing it here. Of course, *wāqif* comes from the root *waqafa*, which has many meanings in Arabic, the first of which is to stop, to stay in one place. *Waqf* means endowment, that is, putting your money in one place so that it does not "move." For that very reason many understand *wāqif* as meaning stopping when it does not always mean that. In Persian it also means to become aware or conscious of something. In a sense our mind stops and looks at a particular reality when we gain awareness of it. For example, we have the phrase *wāqif shudam ki*, "I became aware that . . ." Words from the root *waqafa* have meanings all the way from *waqf* or religious endowment, to physically stopping (*tawaqquf*), to the idea of gaining awareness or knowledge (*wuqūf*).

Answer

کسی بر سرّ وحدت گشت واقف
که او واقف نشد اندر مواقف

He becomes aware (*wāqif*) of the mystery of Unity,
Who does not stop (*wāqif*) at stopping places (*mawāqif*).

Here Shabistarī has used terms derived from the root *waqafa* three times. In the first hemistich, *wāqif* means to become aware as discussed above, whereas in the second hemistich, the same word means to stop or to halt and then, at the end of the hemistich, "stopping places" (*mawāqif*) points to stations of the path. From this meaning comes the title of the famous treatise of al-Niffarī, *Kitāb al-mawāqif, The Book of Halting Places*, which refers to the stations on the journey toward God, *mawāqif* being the plural of *mawqif* (halting place).

دل عارف شناسای وجود است
وجود مطلق اورا در شهود است

The heart of the gnostic is the knower of Being,
Absolute Being is his in contemplation.

Here, the word *shuhūd* means contemplation implying spiritual union, that is, with the heart one can contemplate *wujūd*. Of course, here *wujūd* means God, Pure Being.

به جز هست حقیقی هست نشناخت
و یا هستی که هستی پاک در باخت

Except for real Being, he did not recognize any being;
Or a being who has lost his being completely.

The term *hastī* (being, *wujūd*) used here is related to the word "is" in English and is even close ,to the German word *ist*. In Indo-Iranian and Indo-European languages, words related to this root refer to "be," and in Persian, *hastī* is used as the equivalent of *wujūd*. As Mullā Ṣadrā has discussed, Persian has a certain advantage over Arabic when one discusses ontology, since when you talk about being in Arabic your only choice is a word that has to do with finding (*wajada*), hence *wujūd*. So, it is an action, an act of knowing that means "being" in Arabic. However, in Persian you have a choice between *hastī* and *wujūd*.

Now, to come to the first hemistich, "Except for real Being, he did not recognize any being": this statement refers to a basic initiatic reality. The gnostic, in whose heart he discovers *wujūd*, knows only the Real Being, not just being as existence or metaphorical being, which people usually identify with objects. Our knowledge is usually not of Being as such but rather of beings or existents, which exist only metaphorically. We call them "beings," but in reality "being" belongs to God alone. *Hast-i ḥaqīqī*, means "real Being," which he juxtaposes to *hast-i majāzī* or metaphorical being—ordinary things that we associate with existence.

The second hemistich of the verse means that one has to throw one's own existence away or to transcend it in order to reach God. This hemistich is a somewhat ambivalent phrase. It can mean either that the gnostic only knows the real Being, or that he knows he has no real being without throwing his own metaphorical being away. *Dar bākhtan* means losing or throwing away the metaphorical existence at the center of one's being.

وجود تو همه خار است و خاشاک
برون انداز از خود جملهرا پاک

Thy existence is all thorn and brush;
Throw completely all of that away from thyself.

Thorn and brush (*khār-u khāshāk*) are part of a proverb in Persian referring to something without value. *Khār* and *khāshāk* often go together. *Khāshāk* means little bits of dried vegetation you find in the desert, bushes and leaves and so forth, almost like the dirt that you sweep, and *khār* means thorn. So, Shabistarī says that thy ordinary and separative existence is nothing of value; it is like thorn and brush to be thrown away. One should purify oneself, casting away one's limited and separative existence.

برو تو خانهٔ دلرا فرو روب
مهیّا کن مقام و جای محبوب

Go and sweep the house of thy heart clean.
Prepare it for the station and place of the Beloved.

Even if you are going to have ordinary guests, you still clean the house, preparing it for their arrival. And if the heart is where God resides, you first have to clean that house before this Supreme Guest comes to reside in it.

چو تو بیرون شوی او اندر آید
به تو بی تو جمال خود نماید

If thou goest out, She will come in.
She will show Her Beauty to thee without thee.

Once we empty our heart of our ego, God will come into it. Our duty is to cleanse the "house" of our heart. The rest is accomplished by the real owner of the "house."

کسی کو از نوافل گشت محبوب
به لای نفی کرد او خانه جاروب

The person who through performing the supererogatory acts (*nawāfil*) has become beloved [of God],
With the "*lā*" of negation, he has swept his house clean.

This verse is not easy to decipher without knowing its background in traditional Islamic thought. We have the following two words in Arabic that first we have to learn. Religious acts are of two kinds: *farā'iḍ* are obligatory acts and *nawāfil* are those that are recommended or supererogatory. For example, when a Muslim gets up in the morning he should perform two *rak'āhs* (*rak'tayn*) (cycles) of prayer. This is what is *farḍ* (obligatory). If he performs two extra *rak'āhs* of prayer, it is considered to be *nawāfil*. In the early Islamic period, *nawāfil* prayers played a very important role in the daily life of the members of the community, and they still do so for many Muslims, especially the Sufis. In a certain sense much of what the Sufis do, such as invoking the Name of God (*dhikr*), is *nawāfil*. It is not obligatory from the *Sharī'ite* point of view, but it is what enables one to reach God. There is a famous *ḥadīth qudsī*, called *ḥadīth al-nawāfil*, which states, "My servant ceases not to draw nigh unto me until I become the eye with which He sees and the ear with which he hears and the feet with which he walks." Ibn 'Arabī and certain other Sufis have in fact spoken of the unity achieved through both the *nawāfil* and the *farā'iḍ*. Ibn 'Arabī says that there is a *ḥadīth al-farā'iḍ* which is as follows: "My servant ceases not to draw nigh unto Me, until he becomes the eye with which I see, the ear with which I hear, and the feet with which I walk." This is implied but does not appear in Shabistarī's text, but it is, nevertheless, a very important Sufi lesson.

"With the "*lā*" of negation, he has swept his house clean" refers to *lā ilāha illa'Llāh*. Metaphysically and spiritually that is what Sufis understand when they utter *lā ilāha illa'Llāh*. In a sense with *lā ilāha* they sweep away into nonexistence all that is *siwā'Llāh*, all that is other than God, so that all that remains will be Allāh.

درون جای محمود او مکان یافت
ز «بی یسمع و بی یبصر» نشان یافت

He found a place in the praised position;
He received a sign upon him of "Through Me he hears and through Me he sees."

The praised position is called *maqām maḥmūd* and is mentioned in the Quran (Q. 17:79). It is a very exalted spiritual state. The word *ḥamd* in Arabic is usually translated as praise, as in *al-ḥamdu li'Llāh*. *Maḥmūd*, along with many other Arabic words, comes from this root as do many proper names, such as Aḥmad, Muḥammad, Ḥamīd, Ḥāmid, Ḥamīdah, and of course Maḥmūd itself. Here the *maqām maḥmūd* indicates a very exalted place in Heaven.

"Through Me he hears and through Me he sees" is part of the *ḥadīth al-nawāfil* mentioned above. In the praised position or station one hears through God and one sees through Him.

ز هستی تا بود باقی بر او شین
نیابد علم عارف صورت عین

As long as [separative] existence (*hastī*) remains as a mark (*shayn*) upon him,
The knowledge of the gnostic will not attain the form (*ṣūrat*) of the essence (*'ayn*).

Here, *hastī* does not mean God's Being; it means man's "separative existence." In this verse, Shabistarī is using the term *'ayn* to rhyme with *shayn*. *'Ayn* is said to have seventy-two meanings in Arabic, and it also corresponds to one of the letters of the Arabic alphabet. There is no word in Arabic that has as many meanings as *'ayn*, meanings that include "spring," "eye," "essence," "source," etc. But here *ṣūrat-i 'ayn* is most likely in reference to the essence of things. The *'ayn* refers to the pure essence.

موانع تا نگردانی ز خود دور
درون خانهٔ دل نایدت نور

As long as thou dost not remove obstacles from thyself,
Inside the house of thy heart, the light will not shine.

So, first of all, one has to open the windows and remove the obstacles within the soul before the light of the Truth shines into one's heart.

موانع چون در این عالم چهار است
طهارت کردن از وی هم چهار است

Since in this world, the obstacles are four,
Purification (*ṭahārat*) from them is also four.

Now, Shabistarī goes into specifics. *Ṭahārat* means "purification," or more specifically "ritual purification." *Ṭahārah* is part of Islamic Law concerned with bodily purification but also means "purification" in the general sense. The word *muṭahhar* means "pure" and comes from the same root as *ṭahārah*. Since there are four obstacles there are also four purifications to prevent those obstacles from confronting us and to remove them. These four purifications are described in the verses that follow:

نخستین پاکی از احداث و انجاس
دوم از معصیت وز شرّ وسواس

The first is purity (*pākī*) from excrements and impurities (*aḥdāth-u anjās*).
The second is from sin and the evil of the Tempter [the Devil] (*waswās*).

These are, again, remarkable verses. What are these four obstacles in the spiritual life? The first is that you have to purify yourself from filth, from all that is unclean. This verse refers not only to the body, and not only to not taking a shower, but also to the soul and its purification. *Anjās* is the plural of *najis*, which refers to impure substances according to Islamic Law. For example, if you touch something impure such as the cadaver of a pig, then you have to make an ablution. So, this verse refers to avoiding things that destroy one's purity (*pākī*), both corporeally and inwardly. This verse does not just concern keeping one's body and one's clothing clean physically, but it also refers to what is religious, moral, and psychological.

In the stanza, "The second is from sin and the evil (*sharr*) of the Tempter," *waswās* is a difficult word to translate. It actually has two meanings: One is temptation and suspicion, coming from the use of it in the Quran (Q. 114:4), which refers to the Devil whispering into the ears of human beings, tempting them and making them suspicious. Another common meaning of *waswās*, which is used often in the Islamic world, also has a religious origin, but it has become exaggerated. It implies having scruples, but often excessively and not positively. But here *sharr-i waswās* refers to the evil of temptation that is created in us by demonic forces, which the Quran identifies as *Shayṭān*.

سیم پاکی ز اخلاق ذمیمه است
که او با آدمی همچون بهیمه است

The third is purification from negative traits (*akhlāq-i dhamīmah*)
Which are within man like a wild beast.[1]

As noted before, *akhlāq* usually means "ethics" in Arabic and Persian. It also can refer to behavior or traits of one's character or even character itself. Most of the time it has a positive connotation. The Prophet—*'alayhi 'l-ṣalātu wa 'l-salām*—said, *bu'ithtu li-utimma makārim al-akhlāq*, "I was sent [by God] to perfect for you the *makārim* or virtues of *akhlāq*." Here, *akhlāq* has a purely positive meaning. But, as mentioned, *akhlāq* can also mean "character," and so in Persian *khush-akhlāq* refers to someone who has a pleasant character and smiles all the time, and *bad-akhlāq* refers to someone who is unpleasant and often angry. In these cases the term *akhlāq* is in itself neutral. *Akhlāq-i dhamīmah* means negative or evil traits or characteristics, and *akhlāq-i ḥamīdah* positive and good traits or characteristics.

There have been many Sufi texts written about *akhlāq-i dhamīmah*, the origin of which is forgetfulness of God but also includes lying, deceit, forgetfulness, indifference, lack of kindness to others, and so forth. As I said, the opposite of these negative traits is found in *akhlāq-i ḥamīdah*, positive characteristics, which come from the same root as *ḥamd*, another Arabic word meaning praise and related to the term *maḥmūd*.

The negative character traits are within man "like a wild beast." We all carry this wild beast within us. We have to tame it, but often no matter what we do, it raises its head again somewhere else in our soul. The Sufis insist that we all need to learn this lesson. Talking about it is not enough. We have to act upon this very important matter.

چهارم پاکی سرّ است از غیر
که اینجا منتهی می‌گرددت سیر

Fourth, is purification of the inner secret (*sirr*) from otherness,
For here thy whole journey reaches its end.

The word *sirr* of course means secret, and Sufism is often called *maktab al-asrār*, the School of Divine Secrets. *Sirr* in Arabic and Persian does not have to refer to something Divine, but in Sufism it usually means Divine Secret, not just a personal and human secret. But *sirr* also has a second meaning. Many Sufis consider that our heart has different levels of interiority, and sometimes they use words such as *qalb*, *fu'ād*, *sirr*, and *sirr al-sirr* for these levels. Here, *sirr* refers to an inner reality within the heart. Shabistarī is using it in that sense, referring to the very center of one's heart (*qalb*, *fu'ād*), which is called *lubb al-lubāb* in Arabic. So, this verse means to purify the center of our heart from all otherness, that is, only God should be present at the center of our heart. Hāfiẓ says, "There is only the *alif* of the stature of the Friend [that is, of *Allāh*] on the tablet of my heart. What can I do when the Master only taught me that?'[2]

This is the description of the spiritual journey. Spiritual realization is not only reading books. It is not just learning complicated cosmological, metaphysical ideas. It is also and above all realization of the Truth through self-purification. That is really a very direct lesson for us all, especially when a group of highly intellectual people who constantly live on the mental plane are involved. Such people can think a lot about metaphysical matters, but what they have come to know theoretically is not always integrated into the rest of their being as they neglect spiritual practice. If all of us were simple peasants digging the earth in Hamadan or Aleppo, it would be a very different situation. If, however, we have read extensively the writings of Ibn Sīnā or Ibn ʻArabī and have understood them well, and say "I can read the *Fuṣūṣ* of Ibn ʻArabī with my eyes closed and need nothing more," the response from the Sufi point of view would be, "So what? You can get a tape recorder to repeat his words." Gaining doctrinal knowledge is important, but it is only one half of the matter. The other half is to become what one has learned theoretically when it comes to the truths of religion. A person would not be considered a good Muslim if he knew the daily prayers by heart but did not perform them. This truth also holds for esoterism. These verses have to do with this truth. The same *Gulshan-i rāz* that discussed pure metaphysics earlier is now telling us what to do. So, this is a very important lesson for all those who are seriously interested in spirituality.

هر آن کو کرد حاصل این طهارات
شود بی شک سزاوار مناجات

Whoever has performed these purifications (*ṭahārāt*)
Without doubt becomes worthy of Divine supplications (*munājāt*).

The word *munājāt* is, of course, of Arabic origin and comes from the word *najwā* (intimate discourse) and the root *najawa*. It is also used often in Persian. The most famous usage of this term in the Persian-speaking world is in the *Munājāt* of Khwājah ʻAbd Allāh Anṣārī, a masterpiece of Sufi literature written in the fifth Islamic century in Herat. He was one of the great masters of Persian literature, and this text takes the form of direct prayer to God, *munājāt*. The canonical prayers are not called *munājāt*; they are called *ṣalāh* or *namāz*, but afterward many sit down and pray to God. That personal prayer is called *du'ā'*, but is sometimes also called *munājāt*. It means an intimate discourse with God. *Najwā* in Arabic refers to a close discourse, that is, a discourse in which the participant is close to the Divine Being. So, *munājāt* contains the idea of close proximity to and intimacy with God.

تو تا خودرا بکلّی در نبازی
نمازت کی شود هرگز نمازی؟

Until thou losest thyself completely,
When will thy prayers ever become [real] prayers?

This verse is addressed to all Muslims. When Muslims start the canonical prayer, they recite the *iqāmah*[3] and then put their hands behind their ears. This is a symbol of forgetting the world completely, because they are going beyond what came before and forgetting what is behind them. The Reality that is in front of them is God. Their world, their parents, their work, their wealth, and everything else earthly is behind them. So, when a Muslim raises his or her hands at the beginning of *ṣalāh* or *namāz*, that Muslim should remember that he or she is standing before God and putting everything else away. He or she is looking only toward God and Him alone when he or she is performing the canonical prayer (*namāz*, *ṣalāh*).

Dar nabāzī in Persian comes from *bākhtan*, to lose, which includes losing in gambling or any kind of game or contest. *Khud* means the individual self though in certain cases it can also mean the Divine Self. The word for God in Persian is *khudā*, which is etymologically the same word as God in English and *Gott* in German, and related to *khud* or self in Persian.

So, "Until thou losest thyself completely," means until thou transcendeth the ego with which thou usually identifieth thyself, thy prayers will never be real prayers. That is why we, as forgetful beings, have to repeat the prayers all the time so that we remember this truth. For many, two seconds after starting the canonical prayers they think of themselves, what problems are facing them, this and that thought and image. They become just like a parrot repeating something. It is very difficult to be present even in the daily prayers because to be present before God one has to go beyond oneself.

چو ذاتت پاک گردد از همه شین
نمازت گردد آنگه قرّة العین

Once thy essence becomes purified of all imperfection,
Thy prayer becomes *qurrat al-'ayn* (coolness of the eyes).

Qurrat al-'ayn means the cold tears that come out of the eye. Usually when we weep, the tears are warm, but you can also weep with cold tears when you are crying with joy. That is called *qurrat al-'ayn*, or "the coolness of the eyes." In Arabic and Persian it implies happiness and something very precious. The closest phrase in English is "the light of the eyes," as when one says, "my grandchild is the light of my eyes." This is not a literal equivalent, but this is the real meaning of it, something that brings one joy because when we weep in joy cold teardrops are a mark of it. As I said, when we are sad, our tears are warm. Have you thought of that experience? It is only when you cry because of happiness that the eye changes the temperature of the tears, and you get cold teardrops coming down your cheek. This is really one of the remarkable features of the human body in its relation to the state of the soul. A psychological state transforms the physical temperature of something that is material, namely tears. If you really think about this fact alone, the purely materialistic explanation of things reveals its inadequacy, that is, the idea that it is only material causes that can bring about physical changes.

You might ask why such importance is placed on weeping. It is said that in the distant past, generally people used to weep more, both from joy and sorrow. This is, of course, different in different cultures. The Persians cry much in religious rites associated with Muḥarram when Imam Ḥusayn was martyred. Egyptians do not cry as much as Persians do, even in similar religious rites. The Japanese are hardly ever seen to cry. There are emotional, cultural, social, and ethnic factors involved. In any case, the important point to remember here is the meaning of the expression *qurrat al-'ayn*, literally "the coolness of the eye" that corresponds in some ways to "the light of one's eyes" in English.

نماند در میانه هیچ تمییز
شود معروف و عارف جمله یک چیز

There remains in the middle no distinction (*tamyīz*).
The known and the knower (*ma'rūf-u 'ārif*) become one reality.

Now, one gets to the heart of the matter. When one reaches such a state, nothing distinct remains. One cannot discern separate realities; every defining limit is gone. This verse also expresses the idea of *ittiḥād al-'āqil wa'l-ma'qūl*, the unification of the intellector and the intelligible in Islamic philosophy, which Mullā Ṣadrā discussed so extensively, just as Sufis talk about the unity of the knower and the known (*ma'rūf-u 'ārif*).

Question [6]

اگر معروف و عارف ذات پاک است
چه سودا بر سر این مشت خاک است؟

If the Pure Essence is both the known and the knower,
What is the passion (*sawdā*) behind this fistful of dust?

Shabistarī is indirectly asking the question, Why are we here? What are we doing here? At the beginning of the second hemistich, he asks *chi sawdā*? *Sawdā* (*sawdā'* in Arabic) means, first of all, one of the four humors in classical medicine, called "black bile." The word *sawdā* is also related to *sud* "profit." But it also means "love," ambition," "madness," and "concupiscence." *Sawdā'ī dar sar dāshtam* means to have a passionate thought or idea in one's mind. "What is the passion behind this fistful of dust?" implies "What are we who are made of a fistful of dust doing here? Why are we here? What is the significance of our being?" That is what he is asking.

Answer

مکن بر نعمت حقّ ناسپاسی
که تو حقّ‌را به نور حقّ شناسی

Do not be ungrateful for the bounty of the Truth,
For thou knoweth the Truth through the Light of the Truth.

He is reminding us not to be ungrateful for the bounties of God, since with us God has created a being who is able to know God through God. Be aware then, that one can know God only through His Light. So, why does He need us to know Himself? That is a basic question to which Sufism has provided the deepest answer, which we have already discussed above.

God wanted to have a kind of witness to His knowing Himself, and He knows Himself, in a sense, through us. Whoever knows God, it does not mean that it is he or she who knows God, but rather it is God within who knows Himself through that woman or man. They are a way by which God sees Himself or knows Himself. This is the metaphysical key to this verse.

جز او معروف و عارف نیست دریاب
ولیکن خاک می‌یابد ز خور تاب

Come to know (*dar yāb*) that other than He there is no Known and Knower,
Rather, the dust finds through the Sun the shining of light.

Dar yāb means understand, discover, come to know, come to possess and also pull out someone or something from a precarious situation.

The second hemistich implies indirectly that if there were no Earth, there would be no reflection of the light of the Sun, and directly that it is the reflection of the Sun itself that allows the world of dust to shine. Shabistarī is, of course, using the Sun as symbol of Divine Light.

عجب نبود که ذرّه دارد امید
هوای تاب مهر و نور خورشید

> It is no wonder that an atom has the hope,
> Of the "atmosphere" of the shining of the Moon and the light of the Sun.

Even the lowliest creature in the cosmos thirsts for the Light of Being.

به یاد آور مقام حال فطرت
کز آنجا باز دانی اصل فکرت

> Remember the station of the condition of the primordial state (*fiṭrat*),
> Because it is from there that thou canst rediscover the root of thy thinking (*fikrat*).

The term *fiṭrat* in Persian, or *fiṭrah* in Arabic, is found in the Quran (Q. 30:30) and in the *Ḥadīth*, such as, *wulida 'l-insān 'alā 'l-fiṭrah*, "Man is born in the primordial state." So, Shabsitarī is saying, "Remember that primordial condition into which thou wert born." As we have mentioned above, *fikrat* can mean both "thinking" and "meditation," or sometimes even "consciousness."

Some time in our lives many of us have tried to go back to the origin of our thinking and consciousness. None of us can do it, however, because consciousness has no temporal origin. You may be able to remember when you were four years old, three years old, even two years old, but you finally reach a stage in which you do not remember anything farther back. You do not remember where it all began. This is because consciousness has no beginning. It is not that you were in your mother's womb and one morning, God decided to originate consciousness in you and suddenly you became conscious. What He did was to allow consciousness to become actualized in a particular human being, but the reality of consciousness has no temporal beginning. In its essential reality consciousness is above time. So, return to the primordial state before the fall, to the primordial state that is still carried within thyself, in order to understand the root of thy thinking (*fikrat*), to the *fiṭrah*, that is, the root of thy consciousness.

«الست بربّکم» ایزد چرا گفت؟
که بود آخر که آن ساعت «بلی» گفت؟

> Why did God say, 'Am I not your Lord?'[1]
> What was then that time when He said, "Yea" (*balā*)?

This stanza is, of course, a reference to a Quranic verse, when before the creation of Adam and descending him to Earth, God addressed Adam and all his progeny, asking, *Alastu bi-rabbikum?* "Am I not your Lord?" (Q. 7:172). He did not address Adam in the singular. He did not say *Alastu bi-rabbik? Alastu bi-rabbikum* uses the second person plural pronoun; so, the Islamic commentators believe that it addresses the whole progeny of Adam, that is, all human beings. At that moment, which is beyond time, we all said, "Yea, verily we bear witness" (*balā, shahidnā*). So, our being is molded by that "Yea." We ourselves accepted to be God's creature and to worship Him, and that is why when we do not, we fall away from our real selves. We fall away from the promise that we made to God and to ourselves, or to that inner reality that we carry within the depth of our own being. We carry the *asrār-i alast*, the mysteries of *alast*, within us, and this reality contains the secret of all beauty and the mystery of all existence. In the *Mathnawī* Mawlānā Rūmī says,

> The musician began performing before the drunken Turk,
> Behind the veil of music, the secrets of *Alast*.[2]

This poem refers, of course, to the same Quranic verse. In Arabic and Persian we often speak about *yawm al-alast* or *rūz-i alast* (the Day of *Alast*). The *a* is the question, and *lastu* is a negation in the first person singular, so *a lastu* means "Am I not?" Here, Shabistarī is alluding to two very important questions: Why did God say, "Am I not your Lord?" and why and when did we say, "Yea"?

در آن روزی که گلها می‌سرشتند
به دل در قصهٔ ایمان نوشتند

On the day when they were kneading the clay [of Adam],
In the heart, [the angels] wrote the story of faith.

Shabistarī answers the question posed above in this beautiful way. From the very beginning faith in God is inscribed in our hearts. It is part of our very nature.

اگر آن نامه‌را یک ره بخوانی
هر آن چیزی که می‌خواهی بدانی

If thou readest that letter once,
Whatever thou wantest, thou shalt know.

"If thou readest that letter once" refers to the reality of what God wrote on the tablet of our heart. Everything essential that we can ever know is already contained within ourselves. Socrates was right when he said that knowledge is remembrance, *anamnesis* in Greek, *tidhkār* in Arabic. So, what can a teacher do for us? A teacher, as Socrates said, is like a midwife who delivers babies. The "baby" is already in our own being. A teacher can only deliver it, that is, actualize it. So, every human being contains potentially all essential knowledge within himself or herself. When it comes to principial knowledge, all the education we have—I do not mean only going to school, or learning lessons in the street, or from your friends and family—all the different channels through which we learn in life are really means of actualizing what is already within us. All of us become ultimately only what we are potentially. Frithjof Schuon once said something extremely profound and beautiful: "Man is what he becomes, and becomes what he is,"[3] that is, we gain a state of being as a result of our becoming, and also what we become is the actualization of what we are already.

تو بستی عقد عهد بندگی دوش
ولی کردی به نادانی فراموش

Thou madest the pact of being in the state of servitude [to God],
But because of ignorance, thou hast forgotten.

On the *Day of Alast* we accepted our servitude or slavehood to God. We accepted God's *rubūbiyyah*, His Lordship, but because of our ignorance we have forgotten the pact we made. It is as if this verse is addressed especially to modern man, to all those agnostics and atheists who, of course, deny this whole way of seeing man having broken his pact with God.

کلام حقّ بدان گشته است منزل
که تا یادت دهد آن عهد اوّل

The Word of the Truth (*kalām-i Ḥaqq*) has become revealed (*munzal*) so that,
It will remind thee of that original pact.

Munzal here comes, of course, from the verb *nazala* with the root meaning of descent. As for *inzāl*, it means revelation, and *munzal* means revealed. *Kalām-i Ḥaqq*, the Word of God, refers to the Quran and by extension to the other sacred scriptures.

"It will remind thee of that original pact" refers to the pact that all human beings made with God on the *Day of Alast*. All revelation is to remind us of that original pact with God, which reveals on the deepest level who we are. If we had never had any previous relation with God, no revelation would have any meaning for us. Why should anyone bother with the prophet—*'alayhi 'l-ṣalātu wa 'l-salām*—or Moses, or Christ, or Lao Tzu, or any other prophet? A prophet always reminds us of something that is already in us but that we have forgotten, something that is broken and that needs to be mended. That is why the prophet is able to gain adherents. If we had never had any relation to God, if somebody were to come to say something about Him, he would not attract our attention. So, Shabistarī is saying that all prophets come for that reason.

اگر تو دیده‌ای حقّرا در آغاز
در اینجا هم توانی دیدنش باز

If thou hast seen the Truth at the beginning,
Thou canst also see It here again.

"If thou hast seen the Truth [or God] at the beginning" refers again to the "event" in preeternity when God asked, "Am I not your Lord?" and we said, "Yea." We were there standing before God, "seeing Him," and we can do so again.

صفاتش‌را ببین امروز اینجا
که تا ذاتش توانی دید فردا

Today, here, see His Qualities,
So that tomorrow thou shalt be able to see His Essence.

This world is the theophany of God's Names and Qualities, His Essence being above all manifestation. "Tomorrow," which he mentions here, does not refer to a temporal future but to the "time" and state beyond manifestation.

وگرنه رنج خود ضایع مگردان
برو بنیوش «لا تهدی» ز قرآن

Otherwise, do not waste your pain.
Go and hear from the Quran about those who are not guided (*lā tahdī*).

The phrase *lā tahdī* is a reference to Q. 28:56, "Surely thou dost not guide (*lā tahdī*) whomsoever thou lovest, but God guides whomsoever He will. And He knows best those who are rightly guided."

Illustration

ندارد باورت اکمه ز الوان
وگر صد سال گوئی نقل و برهان

A blind person does not believe thee about colors,
If for a hundred years, thou talkest about it and giveth demonstration.

If one speaks at length and with demonstration about the reality of colors, a blind person will not believe or understand it. Such is also the case of those who are spiritually and intellectually blind.

سفید و سرخ و زرد و سبز و کاهی
به نزد وی نباشد جز سیاهی

> Whiteness, redness, yellowness, greenness and creamy color,
> Are for that person nothing but blackness.

As the Quran says, those who are bereft of *īmān* and spiritual understanding are deaf and blind.

نگر تا کور مادرزاد بدحال
کجا بینا شود از کحل کحّال

> Look, a person born blind, in a bad state,
> How can he become able to see through the collyrium (*kuḥl*) of the ophthalmologist (*kaḥḥāl*).

Collyrium (*kuḥl*) is a black substance that is put around the eyes, and many Oriental women still use it to enhance the beauty of their eyes. A *kaḥḥāl* is an ophthalmologist, a physician of the eye. In the old days *kuḥl* would be used also to increase vision, but now it is used mostly for enhancing the beauty of the eyes.

خرد از دیدن احوال عقبا
بود چون کور مادرزاد دنیا

> Human reason (*khirad*), in trying to see the conditions of the other world (*'uqbā*),
> Is like a person born blind into this world.

This verse means that a rationalist is like a person born blind who cannot, therefore, see the spiritual realities, which are associated here with the realities and condition of the other world, or the world of the Spirit.

ورای عقل طوری دارد انسان
که بشناسد بدان اسرار پنهان

> Beyond reason (*'aql*), man possesses a state (*ṭawr*)
> Through which he will be able to know the hidden mysteries.

Here *'aql* means "reason" not "intellect," as does *khirad* in the previous verse. *Ṭawr* means "state," "stage," or "condition." Even in colloquial Persian this word is used often. When we want to say, "How are you?" we say *chiṭawr-ī*. This uses the same word, *ṭawr* and means "what condition are you in?" But *ṭawr* has also a philosophical significance. Some philosophers use it to refer to the levels of being (*marātib al-wujūd*), referring to *al-ṭawr al-awwal* (the first stage of being), *al-ṭawr al-thānī* (the second stage of being), and so forth.

Beyond reason, man possesses a *ṭawr*, a state of being or a condition, through which he is able to know the hidden mysteries or secrets (*asrār-i pinhān*) of existence. By using only our everyday reason, we cannot understand the inner meaning of things, but we do have that possibility within ourselves if we have recourse to our intellectual and spiritual faculties.

بسان آتش اندر سنگ و آهن
نهاده است ایزد اندر جان و در تن

Just like fire within stone and iron,
God has placed [it] within the soul and the body.

What does this mean? It means that if you take a piece of flint or a stone and a piece of iron you can hit one against the other, which produces sparks. This means that the fire is, as it were, hidden within the stone and the iron. In the same way between the soul and the body there is hidden that fire, like the spark that one can see physically, by which one is able to understand the Divine Mysteries.

از آن مجموع پیدا گردد این راز
تو بشنیدی برو خودرا برانداز

From this assembly becomes revealed that secret;
Thou hast heard it; go and overcome (*bar andāz*) thyself.[4]

Shabistarī's choice of verb here is notable: *bar andāz* comes from *bar andākhtan* meaning to overthrow. For example, if you have a coup d'état and a government is overthrown, the verb used is *bar andākhtan*. So, he says, go and overthrow thy lower self; that is, overcome thy *nafs*, overcome thy carnal soul.

چو بر هم اوفتاد این سنگ و آهن
ز نورش هر دو عالم گشت روشن

Once that stone and iron hit against each other (*bar ham uftād*),
Then from the light, the two worlds can became illuminated.

The verse above means that man can create a fire within himself that illuminates everything.

توئی تو نسخهٔ نقش الهی
بجو از خویش هر چیزی که خواهی

Thou art, thou, the copy of the Divine Pattern.
Go and ask thyself (*khwīsh*) whatever thou wantest.

"Ask thyself" is a major theme of the *Gulshan-i rāz*. As I have mentioned several times above, of all the texts of Sufism I have seen, this work is one of the closest to the view of Advaita Vedanta, in the sense of placing the Divine as the subjective Pole (rather than the objective Pole), pointing to the Supreme Self. This verse is again a reference to that truth, not to one's own individual self, but *khwīsh* or the real Self, the spiritual Self, the spiritual heart.

Question [7]

کدامین نقطه‌را نطق است «انا الحقّ»؟
چه گوئی هرزه بود آن رمز مطلق؟

Which point can say "I am the Truth?"
What do you say [to those who say] that that Absolute Secret is frivolous (*harzah*)?

"Which point can say, 'I am the Truth?'" refers to the famous *ana'l-Ḥaqq* of Ḥallāj. *Nuṭq* can also mean "intellect" here or thought but *nuṭq* usually means "speech." *Harzah* means "frivolous," "futile," and also "nonsensical."

Answer

انا الحقّ کشف اسرار است مطلق
به جز حقّ کیست تا گوید انا الحقّ

"I am the Truth" is the discovery of the Absolute Mysteries;
Who is there besides the Truth who can say "I am the Truth"?

This is one of the most powerful verses of metaphysical poetry in Persian. It implies that ultimately only God can say *ana'l-Ḥaqq*, "I am the Truth." As I have written elsewhere, it is God in Ḥallāj who said *ana'l-Ḥaqq*, not Ḥallāj himself. In fact one is in a sense a *kāfir* (infidel) if one does not say *ana'l-Ḥaqq* because not to do so is to deny the *anā'iyyah*, the I-ness, of God within us at the center of our being. Let us recall *qalb al-mu'min 'arsh al-Raḥmān* ("The heart of the believer is the Throne of the All-Merciful") and "The Kingdom of God is within you."[1]

همه ذرّات عالم همچو منصور
تو خواهی مست گیر و خواه مخمور

All the particles of the world are like Manṣūr [al-Ḥallāj];
Whether you want to consider the drunken (*mast*) or the inebriated (*makhmūr*).

Metaphysically all creatures in the world by virtue of existing are saying *ana'l-Ḥaqq*.

در این تسبیح و تهلیلند دائم
بدین معنی همه باشند قائم

[All creatures of the world] are in praise and in "there is no god but God" (*tahlīl*);
It is through this meaning that they all persist.

Tahlīl means *lā ilāha illa'Llāh* and its recitation. The very reality, subsistence, and existence of all beings is through their invocation of it.

اگر خواهی که بر تو گردد آسان
«و ان من شیء» را یک ره فرو خوان

If thou wantest this [meaning] to become easy for thee,
Go and read the verse "there is nothing. . ."

The last phrase is a reference to the Quranic verse, *wa in min shay'in illā yusabbiḥu bi-ḥamdihi*, "And there is no thing, save that it hymns His praise" (Q. 17:44).

چو کردی خویشتن‌را پنبه‌کاری
تو هم حلّاج‌وار این دم برآری

If thou makest thyself the carder of wool,
Then thou becomest like Ḥallāj at this moment.

First of all, *ḥallāj* in Arabic means "carder of wool," that is, someone who deals with wool and things like that. A carder has a long instrument with which to beat the wool to make it fluffy and then make threads and strings out of it to make a dress or something similar. The second hemistich refers to the example of Ḥallāj and *ana'l-Ḥaqq*.

برآور پنبهٔ پندارت از گوش
ندای «واحد قهّار» بنیوش

Go pull out the cotton of thine own thoughts from thy ear;
Listen to the call of "the One, the Victorious (*Wāḥid-i Qahhār*)."

Al-Wāḥid and *al-Qahhār* (the One, the Victorious) are two of the Names of God mentioned in the Quran one after another (Q. 14:48, 40:16, 12:39, 13:16, 38:65, 39:4). They go together because when you mention *al-Wāḥid*, the One, it obliterates multiplicity (*kathrah*) and so has dominion over it. *Qahhār* in Arabic and Persian can also mean someone who is very dominant or strong, but in relation to God it means completely Victorious.

ندا می‌آید از حقّ بر دوامت
چرا گشتی تو موقوف قیامت

There comes a voice from the Truth concerning thy lastingness,
Why did you have to wait for the Day of Judgment?

Say and realize *ana'l-Ḥaqq* now. Why art thou waiting for the Day of Judgment?

درآ در وادی ایمن که ناگاه
درختی گویدت «انّی انا الله»

Come into the Valley of the Right when suddenly,
A tree will say to thee, "Verily, I am God."

This is in reference to the Quranic story about Moses. When Moses was going to the Presence of God, he came to the Sacred Valley where he had to take off his sandals (*khal' al-na'layn*), about whose symbolism many treatises have been written. Then, as he was ascending, a tree said *innī ana'Llāh,* "Truly, I am God." (Q. 28:30) It was God who made the tree to speak, and so Shabistarī adds:

روا باشد انا الحقّ از درختی
چرا نبود روا از نیکبختی

It is becoming for a tree [to say] "I am the Truth" (*ana 'l-Ḥaqq*);
Why should it not be becoming for one fortunate?

If God makes a tree say *ana 'l-Ḥaqq*, why then should the man or woman who is fortunate enough to realize this principial truth not be able to do the same?

هر آن کس‌را که اندر دل شکی نیست
یقین داند که هستی جز یکی نیست

Whoever doth not have doubt in his heart,
Knoweth with certitude that Being is but one.

On the highest level, *lā ilāha illā 'Llāh* asserts that Being in its most universal sense can only be one. There cannot be two ultimate Origins for being. This belief in the ultimate oneness of the Divine Principle is emphasized even in the Trinitarian theology of Christianity and is stated in the Latin liturgy: *credo in unum Deum* (I believe in one God).

انانیّت بود حقّ‌را سزاوار
که هو غیب است و غایب وهم و پندار

I-ness is worthy [only] of the Truth (*al-Ḥaqq*),
For He is the Absent, and apprehension (*wahm*) and thought (*pindār*) are absent.

We come now to the very important issue of *anāniyyat* in Persian, or *anā'iyyah* in Arabic, which means I-ness. As Shabistarī says, "I-ness is worthy only of the Truth." On the deepest level, only God can say "I." As mentioned previously, in polite Persian we never say *man* (I); we say "we." Likewise, in Sanskrit, Arabic and many other classical languages, we try to avoid saying "I" because it can lead to mistaking the ego for the real "I." In Persian one should try to avoid this error, which is called *man man kardan*. To say "I, I" is to be avoided, and traditional parents teach their children not to say it. We have all kinds of formulas to avoid this error, even using the third person in referring to oneself as *bandah* (servant). When I write a polite letter using flowery Persian, I never write *chunān ki man guftam* ("as I said"). Instead, I write *chunān ki īn bandah guft* ("as this servant said"), *chunān ki ḥaqīr guft* ("as this humble one said"), *chunān ki nivīsandah guft* ("as this author said"), using the third person. This is a remnant of the metaphysical impact on traditional languages. In the deepest sense only God can say "I." "I" is capitalized in English for the same reason. In French *je* is not capitalized, nor is *io* in Italian, but in English something of that traditional truth remains, the truth that only God as the pure and ultimate Subject is worthy of I-ness.

"For He is the Absent, and apprehension and thought are absent" means that He is hidden from them, but what is really hidden and not real is our own *wahm* (apprehension), and *pindār*, which means thinking, everyday thinking. But what is it that hides God from us? Our thinking, our ordinary thinking, the fact that we have a kind of *ḥijāb* or veil in our mind that is always busy with creating concepts and images as veils, and that prevents us from realizing God in ourselves. We are always thinking about the future and the past but are absent from the present where and when God is Present. It is that daydreaming all the time that hides God from us.

جناب حضرت حقّ‌را دوئی نیست
در آن حضرت من و ما و توئی نیست

The Exalted Divine Presence (*jināb-i ḥaḍrat-i Ḥaqq*) has no duality;
In that Presence, there is no I, we or thou.

Jināb here means Exalted, and *ḥaḍrat* means, of course, Presence, from the Arabic root *ḥaḍarah*, but it is also used as an honorific term for human beings in Arabic and Persian.

In one of his treatises Suhrawardī says that you can say *lā ilāha illā'Llāh*, but you can also substitute each of the pronouns for the word *ilāha*, and each will have a particular metaphysical meaning related to Divine Unity: *lā anā illā'Llāh* (there is no I but God), *lā anta illā'Llāh* (there is no Thou but God), *lā huwa illā'Llāh* (there is no He but God), *lā naḥnu illā'Llāh* (there is no We but God), *lā antum illā'Llāh* (there is no You but God), *lā hum illā'Llāh* (there is no They but God), and so forth. One could also say *lā anā illā Anā,* etc.[2] Once you realize what God is, however, you realize that ultimately God is beyond all the pronouns. This truth ties up our mind like a Zen koan, because everything in our mind is associated with either I, thou, he, she, it, we, you, or they. Suhrawardī says that God is That which is beyond all of these categories. It is, therefore, impossible to think in the ordinary sense about His Reality using everyday pronouns.

Of course, we usually refer to God as He, or in Sufism as She when referring to the Divine Essence. The Quran sometimes also uses for God the first person plural We (*naḥnu*), and sometimes Thou but not They. This pronoun is not used in Islam, but is, of course, used in polytheistic religions. But the fact is that on the highest level God is beyond all the pronouns, a concept that is one of the most difficult to conceive, although it is at the same time so easy because you go through the pronouns and realize that God is beyond all of them while being at the same time associated with some of them. That is to what Shabistarī is alluding.

من و ما و تو و او هست یک چیز
که در وحدت نباشد هیچ تمییز

I, we, thou and he [or she] are a single thing,
For in Unity there is no distinction.

This verse refers to the same truth pointing especially to the nature of oneness.

هر آن کس خالی از خود چون خلا شد
انا الحقّ اندر او صوت و صدا شد

Whoever has become empty of himself like a vacuum,
Anā'l-Ḥaqq in him has become sound and voice.

All you have to do is just empty yourself. Then the reality of "I am the Truth" resonates in you.

شود با وجه باقی غیر هالک
یکی گردد سلوک و سیر و سالک

With the ever-persistent Face [of God] otherness is obliterated;
Journeying, the traveling, and the journeyer all become one.

In Islamic metaphysics on the highest level, *fi'l*, *fā'il* and *maf'ūl* (action, actor, and recipient of action) become one, as do *'aql*, *'āqil*, and *ma'qūl* (intellect, intellector, and intelligible). Also, *sulūk*, *sayr*, and *sālik* (journeying, traveling, and the journeyer) become one. All of the relations that we have with God are ultimately the same in their depth: *'ishq*, *'āshiq* and *ma'shūq*, *ḥubb*, *muḥibb*, *maḥbūb* (love, lover, and beloved) become the same.

حلول و اتّحاد اینجا محال است
که در وحدت دوئی عین ضلال است

Here, incarnation and unification are impossible.
For in Unity duality is the same as deviation (*ḍalāl*).

Here, Shabistarī is denying the Christian view, the incarnationist position, and the usual idea of man becoming united with God, which is only metaphorical because how can the finite become united with the Infinite? That is metaphysically absurd, because, if the Infinite is devoid of the finite, it is not the Infinite to start with.

"For in Unity duality is the same as deviation," for there cannot be duality in Unity. In God's Essence there is only oneness.

تعیّن بود کز هستی جدا شد
نه حقّ شد بنده نه بنده خدا شد

It was determination that became separated from Being.
The Truth did not become servant, and the servant did not become God.

"It was self-determination that became separated from Being," like ice that is still water but at the same time is not water. As for, "The Truth did not become servant, and the servant did not become God," it implies that to consider the matter otherwise as the truth is a great mistake. So, Shabistarī is denying the idea of union the way that it is described in so many books on mysticism.

وجود خلق و کثرت درنمود است
نه هرچه آن می‌نماید عین بود است

The existence of creatures and multiplicity is in appearance (*namūd*).
Not all that appears to be is exactly like Being.

The Persian word *namūd* or *nimūd* is difficult to translate. First of all, the verb *namūdan* or *nimūdan* is sometimes used wrongly by some modern Iranians as an auxiliary verb, as in the phrase *kār-ī namūd*, which is used to mean "he did something," but it is incorrect, although to many it sounds eloquent. The real meaning of *namūdan* is to manifest, to make to appear, and that is how this verb should be used. So, the word *namūd* has also something to do with the word *namād*, which is used sometimes as symbol in Persian and is an elegant term.

In the present context *namūd* means precisely manifestation or appearance, just as the related word *namāyish* is used in the theater for "play" or "putting on a show," which is precisely the manifestation or bringing out of something for display.

"The existence of creatures and multiplicity is in appearance" means that the apparent existence of things is not *būd* (being); it is *namūd* (appearance) of a reality that transcends appearance. There is a book by Owen Barfield, the famous British philosopher, titled *Saving the Appearances*, which was translated into Persian as *Būd-u namūd*.

Illustration

بنه آئینه‌ای اندر برابر
در او بنگر ببین آن شخص دیگر

Place a mirror before thyself,
Look into it to see the other person.

That is, see your own reflection in the mirror.

یکی ره باز بین تا چیست آن عکس؟
نه این است و نه آن پس کیست آن عکس؟

Go ahead and ask thyself, what is that reflection?
It is neither this nor that. Then who is it?

When thou lookest at thyself in the mirror, it is thou and yet it is not thou. Then, what is that image? Who is then reflected in the mirror?

چو من هستم به ذات خود معیّن
ندانم تا چه باشد سایهٔ من

Since I am determined through my own essence,
I know not what my shadow is.

This is again a subtle verse. "Since I am determined through my own essence" means that I have direct contact with the reality of my own being, which determines who I am. As for, "I know not what my shadow is," we really have no direct knowledge of our own shadow, except through our own selves. I mean that we can imagine and also see our shadow when we are walking in the street but do not determine it. We have no power to existentiate it or control it. So, Shabistarī is asserting this important point concerning existential knowledge of one's own shadow, which is "nothing" yet reflects the reality of one's body.

عدم با هستی آخر چون شود ضم؟
نباشد نور و ظلمت هر دو با هم

How can then non-being and being become combined?
Light and darkness cannot both exist together.

The verse emphasizes the truth that something cannot exist and not exist at the same time in the same way, that something cannot be at the same time luminous and dark. The message of this stanza must not be confused with the doctrine of black light (*nūr-i siyāh*), which is discussed elsewhere in the *Gulshan-i rāz*.

چو ماضی نیست مستقبل مه و سال
چه باشد غیر از آن یک نقطهٔ حال؟

Since the past is not the future, then month and year,
What are they, but one single point of the present?

Here, Shabistarī extends the difficult point that he set forth in the previous verse: if being and nonbeing, or light and darkness, cannot exist together, then what should one do with the elusive subject of time? When we divide time into past, present, future (*māḍī*, *ḥāl*, *mustaqbal* in both Persian and Arabic), we do so knowing that the past has already gone; we have no access to it. The future has not yet come, and again we have no access to it. We only have access to and can be in the present. However, most of us are daydreaming all the time, trying not to be present in the "now." We live in the irreality either of past memories or of future dreams. And so Shabistarī says, when you really examine it, since the past is already gone and the future has not come, what can the reality of time be except the single point of the present?

یکی نقطه است وهمی گشته ساری
تو آنرا نام کرده نهر جاری

There is a single point, which through the power of apprehension (*wahm*) becomes flowing,
It is thou who hast given it the name "running stream" (*nahr-i jārī*).

This is another version of Shabistarī's famous verse on the idea that in the world of becoming we conceive of things moving (*jārī*) but do not realize that really it is ultimately the same immutable Reality. It is through apprehension (*wahm*) that we identify Divine Reality with motion and change, with past, present and future, whereas in fact It is beyond all these categories.

Wahm in Arabic means the faculty of apprehension in the classical philosophical sense, and is contrasted with intellection, but it can also mean "imagination," "fantasy," and "irreality" in both Arabic and Persian.

I want to add a side note here. We have two classical positions concerning time and becoming in Greek philosophy, identified with the pre-Socratic philosophers Parmenides and Heraclitus. Parmenides believed that there was no such thing as change, only immutability and permanence, while Heraclitus held the opposite view and uttered the famous phrase that you can never put your finger in the same water of a running stream twice, that is, the whole world is a constant flow. Some later philosophers have tried to juxtapose these views, while others have claimed that is not necessarily so, as Empedocles has pointed out. What Heraclitus is trying to say indirectly is to distinguish becoming from the Divine Reality, whereas Parmenides is trying to show that the Divine Reality is the only Ultimate Reality. These two positions are not really contradictory. In the Islamic philosophical tradition many were aware of this truth, and Mullā Ṣadrā especially deals with this matter extensively.

The pre-Socratics were seen in a very different way by Islamic philosophers than by the German scholars of the nineteenth century who first assembled and published the fragments of the writings of the pre-Socratics. What do I mean by this? The Muslim philosophers saw the pre-Socratics as sages, almost prophet-philosophers, who were inspired by Heaven, and they had a lot more respect for them than for the later philosophers. Here Shabistarī is bringing out the juxtaposition between these classical positions. He knew a lot about the history of philosophy in addition to Sufism. Of course, he does not mention the names of Heraclitus or Parmenides, but these are the figures associated with each of these positions in the history of Western thought.

به جز من اندر این صحرا دگر نیست
بگو با من که تا صوت و صدا چیست؟

There is no one in this desert except I.
Tell me what is this sound (*ṣawt*) and its echo (*ṣadā*)?

There is a break here in the ideas that are being expressed. The previous verse talks about becoming and being. Now, Shabistarī says something that Shankara would have said. "There is no one in this desert except I," that is, the *Ātman*, the Supreme I.

"Tell me what is this sound and its echo?" This is a beautiful verse if you really understand it. *Ṣidā* means "sound" or "noise," but *ṣadā* means the "reflection" of sound, or "echo." A lot of people confuse these two since they are written the same way in Arabic script, which is usually written without the short vowels being indicated. So, if I am the only person in this desert, what is the sound and what is this echo that I hear?

To what is he referring? Let me speak in Hindu terms. You might say that the world, as Hindu metaphysics says, was created through OM (AUM), the supreme sacred sound, and that all of the Universe is the *ṣadā*, the echo, of AUM. God said "AUM" and all the reflections or echoes of that sound is what constitutes the world. Are you not surprised that you have such an expression in Islamic writings? It is quite amazing.

عرض فانی است جوهر زو مرکّب
بگو کی بود یا خود کو مرکّب؟

The accident is transient (*fānī*); substance is compounded with it,
Tell me, when was or how it became compounded?

Now, again after making this remarkable statement, Shabistarī turns to the structure of the Universe. Here, he is using the terms "accident" and "substance" again in the philosophical sense, which Sufis also used sometimes. So, the accident "is transient" (*fānī*). Accidents become annihilated. But how about substances, which are compounded with them? How are they distinguished from each other? So, he is asking this question about the Universe, composed of substances and accidents, and then in the following verse he tries to answer it.

The philosophical definition of substance (*jawhar*) is *wujūd idhā wujida fī'l-khārij lā huwa fī'l-mawḍū'*, that is, "a being that if it exists externally, it does not need a substratum or subject in which to subsist." And "accident" is defined as *idhā wujida fī'l-khārij fa-huwa fī'l-mawḍū'*, that is, "if it is found externally, it exists in a substratum or substance (other than itself)." For example consider this wall. The yellow color cannot stand by itself, nor can the black of your jacket. You cannot have the color black walking down the street. It has to be a black cat, a black dog or your black coat. So, black is an accident. But the wall itself, or the wood in the wall, or the material of the jacket, is a substance. This goes back, of course, to the categories of Aristotle, in which he says you can understand all of reality through ten categories. One is substance and the other nine are accidents. The word category is originally Greek, a word that entered also into Arabic as *qāṭīghūriyās*. The book called *Qāṭīghūriyās*, *The Categories* of Aristotle, was criticized by Suhrawardī who argued that there are only four accidents, not nine. This is a very important turning point in the history of philosophy, because in Western philosophy it was not until much later with Kant that the Aristotelian categories were criticized and reduced in number. Strangely enough, Kant believed in the same four categories of Suhrawardī. It is difficult to believe that this is only an accident, though it might be so.

Another example of these correspondences between Islamic and Western philosophy is seen in the work of the Scottish philosopher David Hume. He wanted to disprove causality and gave the famous example, which we also have in Ghazzālī's writings, that if you take a piece of cotton and put it in a fire, the cotton catches fire. As a result of this, we say that the fire is the cause of the cotton burning, but the Ash'arites believe that these are two different events united together by God, since they deny causality between created entities. There are innumerable examples that one could give to illustrate this point, but both Ghazzālī and Hume give the same one. The probability of this happening by coincidence is miniscule. So, there must have been some influences about which we do not have precise knowledge.

ز طول و عرض و از عمق است اجسام
وجودی چون پدید آمد ز اعدام؟

Bodies consist of length, width and depth.
How is it that an existent like this appeared from nothingness?

In the external world bodies have these dimensions. But how could such an existing object become manifest out of nothing?

از این جنس است اصل جمله عالم
چو دانستی بیار ایمان و فالزم

The whole world is of this genus (*jins*).
Once thou knowest this, it is necessary that thou gaineth faith.

The word "genus" in Latin most likely comes from the word *jins* in Arabic, used in logic, though many Western scholars do not accept this derivation. *Falzam* in Arabic means "it is necessary."

جز از حقّ نیست دیگر هستی الحقّ
هوالحقّ گوی و گر خواهی انا الحقّ

There is verily no being except from the Being of the Truth.
Say "He is the Truth" (*huwa'l-Ḥaqq*) or if thou likest, "I am the Truth" (*ana'l-Ḥaqq*).

Both *huwa'l-Ḥaqq* ("He is the Truth") and *ana'l-Ḥaqq*, are famous Sufi sayings. Here, Shabsitarī is going from the third person pronoun to the first person pronoun. So, I have to come back here to the doctrine that with God you can use nearly all the pronouns, that is, God can be "I," "We," "Thou," "He," "She," or "It" in different circumstances. In Islam "She" was used for God only by Sufis symbolically, since the word for the Divine Essence is *al-Dhāt*, which is feminine in Arabic. Of course, we do not use the third person plural in monotheism where one cannot refer to God as "they," while in the Quran the first-person plural, We (*naḥnu*), is often used by God. It is interesting to note that in the Quran, the pronouns used in reference to God go from one form to another. As I already said, sometimes the pronoun is "He," sometimes it is "I," sometimes it is "We," and sometimes it is "Thou." All these different pronouns are used. So, when Ḥallāj said *ana'l-Ḥaqq,* it was not the individual ego of the sage making such an assertion, but God within his heart. I repeat that from the metaphysical point of view only God can say "I" (*anā*).

And so Shabistarī says, "Go and say *huwa'l-Ḥaqq*," which is a very common epithet and often used at the beginning of a letter or a book. *Ana'l-Ḥaqq* is seen rarely, of course, except in esoteric Sufi circles.

نمود وهمی از هستی جدا کن
نه‌ای بیگانه خودرا آشنا کن
Separate this apparent apprehension from Being.
Thou art not a stranger, familiarize thyself.

The apprehension of things as they appear in their outwardness, in their appearance, should be distinguished from Being that belongs only to God. Separate that apparent reality from Pure Being and become familiar with the Real and thyself. Come and know thyself in Light of the Divine Truth which is also the Self within.

Question [8]

چرا مخلوق‌را گویند واصل؟
سلوک و سیر او چون گشت حاصل؟

Why do they call a creature one who has arrived (*wāṣil*)?
How did his spiritual journey (*sayr-u sulūk*) take place?

Of course, *chirā* in Persian at the beginning of the first hemistich means "why?," but here it also implies under what condition. "One who has arrived" (*wāṣil*) is used here in the technical Sufi sense. In English we might say "the one who has attained union," but Shabistarī and many other Sufis usually do not use the word "union" (*ittiḥād*). *Wāṣil* means one who "has arrived" or "reached the end of the path," or literally one has become connected (*waṣl*) to the Source.

The words *sulūk* and *sayr* from Arabic both mean journeying. So, *sayr-u sulūk* means the spiritual journey.

Answer

وصال حقّ ز خلقیّت جدائیست
ز خود بیگانه گشتن آشنائیست

To reach (*wiṣāl*) the Truth is to become separated from creaturliness;
To become a stranger to oneself is familiarity.

Wiṣāl here means not only to reach but also to embrace, but in a deeper sense, *wiṣāl* means to have arrived at the desired goal. The root *w-ṣ-l* in Arabic means simply to connect two things together. To reach God is to become separated from creation, from the creatures. "To become a stranger to oneself is familiarity" with one's real Self.

چو ممکن گرد امکان برفشاند
به جز واجب دگر چیزی نماند

When the contingent (*mumkin*) removes the dust of contingency from itself,
There remains nothing but the Necessary (Being).

The word *mumkin* that he is using here is the well-known Avicennan expression meaning contingent, and the way Ibn Sīnā used this term is considered by many to be one of his most important contributions to Islamic thought. Contingency is what distinguishes all existence or creation from God, Who is the Necessary Being. In Sufism this term is used for all that is other than God. This term is very important to understand in both its philosophical and Sufi sense. So, when Shabistarī says *mumkin* here, it means everything other than God (*mā siwā'Llāh*).

وجود هر دو عالم چون خیال است
که در وقت بقا عین زوال است

The existence of both worlds is like imagination,
Which at the moment of subsistence is identical to non-existence.

We think usually that the world exists as a simple material reality, but that is not the case. Now, in this verse he is using the word *khayāl*, imagination, in the ordinary sense of the term, not in the Suhrawardian or Ṣadrian sense, which considers the imaginal world to possess an ontological reality higher than the physical.

نه مخلوق است آن کو گشت واصل
نگوید این سخن‌را مرد کامل

> The creature is not "the one who has arrived" (*wāṣil*).
> The perfect man does not make such an utterance.

The creature as creature is never "the one who has arrived" (*wāṣil*), that is, to have become one with the Divinity. Ibn ʿArabī says the same thing: "The servant remains the servant and the Lord remains the Lord." Union is of God within with God as Objective Reality. The process of spiritual realization involves removing our selves from in between. As Ḥāfiẓ has said, "Thou art o Ḥāfiẓ thine own veil; lift thyself from in between."

عدم کی راه یابد اندر این باب؟
چه نسبت خاکرا با ربّ ارباب؟

> When can non-existence ever find a path to this door?
> What relation exists between the earth (*khāk*) and the Lord of lords (*rabb-i arbāb*)?

This is also a famous verse. "To this door?" means the gate to the Being of God.

This stanza is very similar to another verse that states, "What relation is there between *khāk* (that is, dust or earth) and *ʿālam-i pāk* (the world of purity)?"

عدم چبود که با حقّ واصل آید؟
وز او سیر و سلوکی حاصل آید؟

> What is non-existence that it should become unified with the Truth,
> That a journeying should result from it.

Obviously, that which has no existence cannot undertake a journey. The question asked wants us to become aware of this truth.

تو معدوم و عدم پیوسته ساکن
به واجب کی رسد معدوم ممکن

> Thou art nonexistent and non-existence is always immobile.
> When can the contingent nonexistent reach the Necessary (Being)?

Nonexistence is always immobile because since it does not exist, there is no subject that can move. Here, Shabistarī is reminding us of the error that is often made: How is it possible for that which does not even exist to reach God?

اگر جانت شود زین معنی آگاه
بگوئی در زمان استغفرالله

> If thy soul becometh aware of this meaning,
> In time thou wilt say, "I ask pardon of God (*astaghfiru'Llāh*)."

We should ask God to pardon us for wanting to have, as an individual, union with Him. If we do so, we should ask Him for forgiveness. In fact *astaghfiru 'Llāh* itself is based precisely on the realization that God is the one and only Reality who can pardon our transgressions and sins. *Istighfār* (asking forgiveness) is not only for our sins in the ordinary sense but esoterically from the highest sin, which is our apparent separative existence: *Wujūduka dhanbun lā yuqāsu bihi dhanb*, "Thy existence is a sin to which no sin can be compared."[1] We must, therefore, perform *istighfār* for that sin (*dhanb*) of separation from the One. *Astaghfiru 'Llāh* is, thus, a kind of allusion to *fanā'* (annihilation), and that is why the expression begins with *a*, indicating the first person in Arabic, and ends with *Allāh*.

ندارد هیچ جوهر بی‌عرض عین
عرض چبود چه؟ لا یبقی زمانین

No substance can become objectively manifested without accident.
What is an accident, what is it? It does not last for two moments (*lā yabqā zamānayn*)?

Let us consider a wall, which is a substance, and the color of the wall, which is an accident. You cannot have a wall without any color. It has to have some color. Even if you say that something is colorless, this is only metaphorical. You cannot have a substance as an objective reality without accidents. He asks, "What is accident?" And he answers by saying that which "does not last for two moments," because it is transient. It comes and goes, but has no abiding reality.

حکیمی کاندر این فن کرد تصنیف
به طول و عرض و عمقش کرد تعریف

The philosopher who composed a work on this field,
Defined [material substance] as one having length, width and depth.

This is simply the reassertion of the standard definition of a material body in Islamic philosophy.

هیولی چیست جز معدوم مطلق
که می‌گردد بدو صورت محقّق؟

What is *materia prima* (*hayūlā*) but absolute non-existence,
Through which the form becomes realized (*muḥaqqaq*)?

Here we come to another difficult issue. We have previously mentioned the Aristotelian distinction between form and matter. The matter is not to be confused with the wood that makes up this table or this door, since the wood itself is composed of form and matter. So, the *materia* in Latin, which in Greek is *hylé*, and came from Greek into Arabic as *hayūlā'*, is a substratum that receives the form, and Aristotle says that there is no existent in this world without form and matter. Through prime matter, the form becomes *muḥaqqaq*, which means "realized" or "reified." Again, you cannot have pure form existing by itself in this world. You have never sat on the form of a chair. Rather, a carpenter has imposed the form of a chair upon the wood, and then you are able to sit on it.

چو صورت بی‌هیولی در قدم نیست
هیولی نیز بی او جز عدم نیست

Since there is no form without *material prima* in eternity,
Without form also *materia prima* is nothing but non-existence.

Here, Shabistarī is explaining the point discussed above. Prime matter is just pure receptivity. It has no existence, no actuality, by itself. By themselves both form and matter are nonexistent.

شده اجسام عالم زین دو معدوم
که جز معدوم از ایشان نیست معلوم

The bodies of this world are made from these two non-existents.
For the only thing we know about them is their non-existence.

The great mystery is that "The bodies of this world are made from these two non-existents" and yet appear to exist.

ببین ماهیتترا بی کم و بیش
نه معدوم و نه موجود است در خویش

Look at thy own quiddity, no more nor less.
It is neither non-existent nor existent in itself.

It is clear from this verse and also so many other verses that Shabistarī knew a great deal about Islamic philosophy. Here, he is pointing to the word *māhiyyah* or "quiddity," which is an Avicennan term. Ibn Sīnā modified Aristotle's approach using this term, which is purely Arabic to complement *wujūd*, although sometimes this term is translated as "essence" in works in English dealing with Avicennan ontology. Quiddity is not to be confused with substance (*jawhar*) as one sees occasionally. The word "quiddity" in English comes from the phrase *quid est* (hence *quidditas*) in Latin, which is the direct translation of *mā huwa* or *mā hiya* in Arabic. The term *māhiyyah* means the essence of something, that which answers the question, "What is it?" irrespective of whether it exists or not. It is not the same thing as *dhāt* (also meaning essence but in a different sense) in Sufism and also in Islamic philosophy. Simply put, *māhiyyah* is that by which a thing is what it is, as Ibn Sīnā says. Therefore, when you conceive of a *māhiyyah*, it is irrelevant whether it exists or not objectively. Ibn Sīnā gives very extensive reasoning for the usage of this term and its meaning in the *Shifā'* and also in the *Najāh*.[2] You can conceive right now of even a two-headed pink cow in your imaginal faculty. Whether it exists outside your mind or not is another matter. The mind has the power of conceiving *māhiyyāt*, or quiddities, irrespective of whether they exist externally or not.

نظر کن در حقیقت سوی امکان
که او بی‌هستی آمد عین نقصان

Glance truthfully upon [the world of] contingency,
That without existence is identical with imperfection.

Existence (or being) comes ultimately from God and without it, there is nothing "but imperfection," that is, there is in reality "nothing."

وجود اندر کمال خویش ساری است
تعیّن‌ها امور اعتباری است

Being flows in its own perfection.
Determinations (*ta'ayyun-hā*) do not possess a reality of their own (*umūr-i i'tibārī*).

These are all highly metaphysical stanzas. "Being flows in its own perfection" means that it flows, as a consequence of its perfection, through everything. Now, the word *ta'ayyun* here, which I have translated as "determination," is related to one of the many meanings of the word *'ayn*. If you have water and it freezes and becomes ice, that is like a determination of water into another state. *Ta'ayyun* is in a sense *wujūd* becoming "congealed."

Shabistarī adds that all determinations are *umūr-i i'tibārī*. In Arabic *i'tibār* usually means to have positive value, but in Islamic philosophy it means the opposite. *Amr-i i'tibārī* means that which does not possess a reality of its own. We can, therefore, call it a contingent matter. *I'tibārī* in philosophy has just the opposite meaning to its ordinary sense in Arabic and Persian.

امور اعتباری نیست موجود
عدد بسیار و یک چیز است معدود

Contingent matters are not existent.
Numbers are many, but the number one is limited [to one] (*ma'dūd*).

جهان‌را نیست هستی جز مجازی
سراسر کار او لهو است و بازی

The world is nothing but a metaphorical reality.
All it does from beginning to end is dissipation and play (*bāzī*).

Play (*bāzī*) could of course be interpreted in the sense of *līlā*, or "Divine Play" in Hinduism, but it does not mean that here. It means that the world is frivolous, not to be taken seriously as an independent order of reality as it appears to be for fallen man. The world is not to be taken seriously in this sense, not as a preparation for the other world (*al-ākhirah*). The Prophet has said, *al-dunyā mazra'at al-ākhirah*, "This world is the planting field for the Hereafter."

Illustration

The verses of this section are closely connected together, and give us an account of how the creation of the world was seen in traditional science and cosmology. Shabistarī describes the stages, one might say, of the life of the Three Kingdoms, *al-mawālīd al-thalāth* in Arabic.

بخاری مرتفع گردد ز دریا
به امر حقّ فرو بارد به صحرا

Vapor rises from the sea;
By the order of the Truth, it pours down [as rain] in the desert.

He begins with not earth but water, which in Islamic cosmology is identified with the sustenance of life, as the Quran states, *wa ja'alnā min al-mā'i kulla shay'in ḥayy,* "And We made every living thing from water" (Q. 21:30).

شعاع آفتاب از چرخ چارم
بر او افتد شود ترکیب با هم

The ray (*shu'ā'*) of the Sun from the fourth sphere (*charkh-i chahārum*),
Casts upon it and becomes compounded with it.

As mentioned already, in traditional cosmology the fourth of seven spheres is the sphere of the Sun, which is therefore central in the seven heavens.

کند گرمی دگر ره عزم بالا
در آویزد بدو آن آب دریا

Again the heat is determined to ascend,
The water in the sea hangs from it.

This completes the cycle of evaporation and precipitation.

چو با ایشان شود خاک و هوا ضمّ
برون آید نبات سبز و خرّم

When earth and air become combined with them,
Green and pleasant vegetation grows.

At the next stage the elements earth and air come into play and the result is the appearance of the Second Kingdom, the vegetative, which is thus based on the First Kingdom.

غذای جانور گردد ز تبدیل
خورد انسان و یابد باز تحلیل

It becomes the food of the animal through transformation,
Man eats it and it again becomes digested.

To summarize again traditional astronomy, we have seven planets above the earth and below the heaven of the fixed stars, starting with the Moon and ending with Saturn. There are three planets above the Sun, namely Mars, Jupiter, and Saturn, and three below the Sun, namely Venus, Mercury, and the Moon. The Earth is the center of the spheres of these planets. Yet, interestingly enough, in traditional cosmology (which is geocentric) the Sun nevertheless occupies a central position in the planetary system. It is true that the Earth is at the center, but the Sun is nevertheless also central in its own way. So Venus, Mercury and the Moon can be called subsolar in this system, and Mars, Jupiter and Saturn can be called suprasolar. It is to this scheme that Shabistarī is referring when he says "the fourth sphere" (*charkh-i chahārum*), that is, the fourth of the astronomical spheres of traditional astronomy.

The Sun creates heat, which then seeks to move upward, because it is lighter than cold air, and that heat affects the water of the sea causing evaporation and clouds. And when the rain that is created out of this process becomes combined with earth and air, gradually green and pleasant (*khurram*) plants emerge. The plants in turn become the food for animals, and man, in turn, eats the plants and animals, and what is eaten dissolves and is transformed.

شود یک نطفه و گردد در اطوار
وز آن انسان شود پیدا دگر بار

It becomes a sperm and journeys through stages [of existence] (*aṭwār*),
And again man appears from it.

So, we have a summary treatment of the cycles of the Three Kingdoms, and the fact they are hierarchical and feed upon each other. Man is the crowning terrestrial reality and hence is at the top of the food chain. He eats the flesh of animals, the animals eat the plants, and the plants are nourished by minerals.

چو نور نفس گویا در تن آمد
یکی جسم لطیف روشن آمد

When the light of the rational soul came into the body,
A subtle body (*jism-i laṭīf*) that is illuminated appeared.

We have here the appearance of a very important technical term. What is *jism-i laṭīf*? This matter needs some discussion. In Islamic thought the ordinary body is called *jism-i kathīf. Kathīf* in modern Persian means usually dirty, but in philosophy and Sufism it means weighty, heavy. *Laṭīf* has just the reverse meaning. It means subtle or delicate and is also a Divine Name (the Subtle). If someone has *rūḥ-i laṭīf* that means he or she has a very delicate soul. But also *jism-i laṭīf* refers to a higher body that we also possess above our ordinary corruptible corporeal bodies. And so, Shabistarī is alluding to the fact that man by virtue of what he is in his totality stands at the highest point of the stages of gradation of creatures, mineral, plant, and animal, with levels of reality that stand beyond them. He feeds upon them, but he is not only physical; he has a subtle body (*jism-i laṭīf*) as well along with soul and spirit.

شود طفل و جوان و کهل و گمپیر
بداند علم و عقل و رای و تدبیر

He becomes a child, then a young person, then an older person, then a very old person.
He comes to gain knowledge, the intellect, correct opinion, and wise experience (*tadbīr*).

Tadbīr means to have experiential knowledge, combining both knowledge and experience and so acting wisely. The verse implies that he becomes someone who has knowledge that is combined with experience and not just theoretical knowledge.

رسد آنگه اجل از حضرت پاک
رود پاکی به پاکی خاک با خاک

Then comes the event of death (*ajal*) from the Pure Divine Presence (*ḥaḍrat-i pāk*)
Purity goes unto purity, dust unto dust.

The word *ajal* means the event of death. There is a famous Arabic saying, *al-'ajal min al-shayṭān wa'l-ajal min al-Raḥmān*, "Haste comes from Satan and thee event of death comes from God." The last part of the verse "Purity goes unto purity, dust unto dust," is similar to the saying in English when someone dies one says, "dust to dust."

همه اجزای عالم چون نباتند
که یک قطره ز دریای حیاتند

All the parts of the world are like plants,
For they are a single drop from the ocean of life.

It is a very important traditional belief that the whole world is alive, *al-arḍu ḥayy*; as the Islamic philosophers say, "The earth (itself) is alive." This is not only an Islamic idea. In Latin you have the phrase *anima mundi*, the world soul, going back to Stoic teachings, and the idea that the Earth itself is a living animal. It is this idea that is being revived these days by the Gaia hypothesis.

Many of the proponents of this idea are agnostics or even atheists, but the concept itself is taken from the traditional idea that the earth is a living being, as we see here in the *Gulshan-i rāz*.

زمان چون بگذرد بر وی شود باز
همه انجام ایشان همچو آغاز

When time passes, everything in it opens up.
The end of all of them is like their beginning,

This verse is another confirmation that everything comes from God and returns to Him.

رود هر یک از ایشان سوی مرکز
که نگذارد طبیعت خوی مرکز

Each of them will journey towards the Center,
For nature does not have the quality of the Center.

Each being goes back ultimately to the Center or God, and nature does not possess the quality of the Center of Reality to which all things return. This ontological truth must not be confused with the natural cycles of generation and corruption.

چو دریائی است وحدت لیک پر خون
کز او خیزد هزاران موج مجنون

Since Unity is like an ocean, but filled with blood,
From which arise thousands of crazy (*majnūn*) waves.

Reference is to waves that seem to be without rhyme or reason of which are aware, the waves themselves being like the state of Majnūn as understood by the Sufis, a person crazed by Divine Love.

نگر تا قطرهٔ باران ز دریا
چگونه یافت چندین شکل و اسما

Look at a drop of rain from the sea,
How it came to have different shapes and names,

This verse refers again to the rain cycle mentioned above.

بخار و ابر و باران و نم و گل
نبات و جانور انسان کامل

[That very drop] becoming vapor, cloud, rain, dew and mud,
Plant and animal, Universal Man.

All the states of being (or existence) are in gradation and are related leading to the Universal Man who contains all the degrees of being or existence within himself leading to Pure Being that resides at his Center.

همه یک قطره بود آخر در اوّل
کز او شد این همه اشیا مُمثّل

It was all a drop at the end that was at the beginning,
From which all of these different things took form (*mumaththal*).

This is similar in many ways to the idea of the World Egg (*Hiranyagarbha*) in Hindu cosmology. *Mumaththal* in the second hemistich means having taken shape or form.

جهان از عقل و نفس و چرخ و اجرام
چو آن یک قطره دان ز آغاز و انجام

The cosmos, from intellect, soul, spheres and bodies,
Consider as that one single drop from beginning to end.

All the stages of cosmic existence exist in that original drop.

اجل چون در رسد در چرخ و انجم
شود هستی همه در نیستی گم

When the time of death arrives for the spheres and the stars,
Existence will become all lost in nonexistence.

This is an eschatological reference, that is, everything will finally perish except "the Face of God." As the Quran states, *Kullu man 'alayhā fān, wa yabqā wajhu rabbika dhū'l-jalāli wa'l-ikrām*, "All that is upon it passes away. And there remains the Face of thy Lord, Possessed of Majesty and Bounty" (Q. 55:26–27).

چو موجی بر زند گردد جهان طمس
یقین گردد «کإن لم تغن بالأمس»

When a wave comes the whole world will perish,
It will become certain, "as if it had not flourished the day before!" (Q. 10:24)

The world exists through God's Will and the emanation of existents from His Being. When He wills for it to cease to exist, it will be as if it had not existed before.

خیال از پیش برخیزد به یک بار
نماند غیر حقّ در دار دیّار

The power of imagination will be lifted at one time;
There will remain not in the house (*dār*) other than the Truth, the Possessor of the House (*dayyār*).

In Persian and Arabic *dār* means "abode" or "place," as for example in the name of the famous publisher in Cairo, *Dār al-Kutub al-Miṣriyyah*. *Dayyār* is the person who lives in the *dār* or possesses the *dār*. There is a famous Sufi phrase, in Arabic *laysa fi'l-dār ghayrahu dayyār*, that is, "There is no one in the house except the real owner of the house" (i.e., God). Knock at the door, only God appears, only God is there. And so, "There will remain not in the house other than the Truth, the Possessor of the House" This verse also alludes to the doctrine of *waḥdat al-wujūd* (the Unity of Being).

ترا قربی شود آن لحظه حاصل
شوی تو بی توئی با دوست واصل

At that point a proximity (*qurbī*) will come to thee.
Without thy thou-ness (*tu'ī*), thou wilt become connected to the Friend.

"At that point" refers to both spiritual realization and eschatological realities. And "without thy thou-ness" refers to the truth that one can only be God's friend if one casts aside his or her he-ness or she-ness.

وصال این جایگه رفع خیال است
چو غیر از پیش برخیزد وصال است

To arrive at this station (*jāygah*) is to transcend imagination (*khayāl*)
When otherness is lifted from in-between, there is arrival (*wiṣāl*).

Here, imagination (*khayāl*) is again used in the ordinary sense, not the technical sense used by Ibn 'Arabī and others referring to creative imagination (*khayāl-i fa''āl*), but they are related. Imagination is seen here as the intermediate state between *'aql* (intellect) and *jism* (body). We reside in this intermediate world most of the time. Most of the day we do not live in and have consciousness in relation to our physical bodies. It is the reflection of our body in the imagination in which we "live." So, in a sense, we live in our *khayāl* most of the time. That is what Shabistarī is talking about here.

مگو ممکن ز حدّ خویش بگذشت
نه او واجب شد و نه واجب او گشت

Do not say that the contingent has gone beyond its limit.
Neither the contingent has become necessary, nor has the necessary become contingent.

This verse means that the *mumkin* (contingent) can never become *wājib* (necessary), and *wājib* can never become *mumkin*. This is a very important point that, although usually accepted theoretically, is not always realized existentially.

هر آن کو در معانی گشت فائق
نگوید کین بود قلب حقائق

Whoever has succeeded in knowing the meaning of things,
Will never say such a thing, for this is the distortion of truths.

Shabistarī is saying that the idea that human beings qua contingent human beings have union with God, the Necessary Being, qua God is incorrect.

هزاران نشأه داری خواجه در پیش
برو آمد شد خودرا بیندیش

Thou hast thousands of states of being (*nash'ah*), O *Khwājah*, before thee.
Go and think about thine own coming and going.

He means go and think about all the states of existence that thou must traverse to reach God. The idea of this world and the next is a summary of the wider reality, which in the Abrahamic traditions is treated more fully only in esoteric teachings.

ز بحث جزو و کلّ نشئات انسان
بگویم یک به یک پیدا و پنهان

In discussing the particular and the universal of the stages of man,
I shall recount for thee one by one openly and in a hidden manner.

Shabistarī announces here what he will discuss in the long section that is to come.

Question [9]

وصال ممکن و واجب به هم چیست؟
حدیث قرب و بُعد و بیش و کم چیست؟

What does it mean for the contingent to reach the Necessary Being?
What is the meaning of the utterance of Proximity and Distance, more and less?

In these two questions Shabistarī has been asked about man's relation to God in the process of spiritual realization. How can a contingent being have *wiṣāl* with God, the Necessary Being? Why does the spiritual journey involve not only increasing proximity but also sometimes distancing, not only receiving more and more during the journey but also sometimes receiving less and less?

Answer

ز من بشنو حدیث بی کم و بیش
ز نزدیکی تو دور افتادی از خویش

Hear from me the saying, neither less nor more;
Through nearness thou hast become distanced from thyself.

Shabistarī wants to emphasize in the first hemistich the importance of the message of the verse that comes in the second hemistich. The message is that by drawing near to God man overcomes and transcends his self as *nafs*, not, of course, the Divine Self, which resides at the center of his being.

چو هستی‌را ظهوری در عدم شد
از آنجا قرب و بعد و بیش و کم شد

Since existence appeared in [the realm of] non-existence,
From there came proximity and distance, the more and the less.

Creation itself is separation from Pure Being, but also existentiation is the presence of the light of Being in the mirror of nothingness. Nearness and distance (more and less) are the consequence of separative existence that issues from Being and consequently reflects such qualities and states. Had there been no existentiation, there would be nothing to reflect nearness and distance from the Source nor the "greater" or "lesser" traits. That is why, from the perspective of Pure Being, none of these characteristics even exist.

قریب آن هست کورا رشّ نور است
بعید آن نیستی کز هست دور است

Near is one on whom the Light is shed,
Far that non-existent which is distant from Being.

Spiritually our position in the hierarchy of being is dependent upon the light shed upon us from the Source of all light. The nearness and farness of a being are determined by the degree of the light of Being that shines upon it, and in fact it is nothing but that light.

اگر نوری ز خود بر تو رساند
تورا از هستی خود وا رهاند

If [the Divine] causes thee to receive a light from Itself,
It frees thee from thine own existence.

If God casts His Light upon us, this Light frees us from the illusion of taking our separative existence as reality and bestows upon us the knowledge that all reality belongs ultimately to God. Nothing exists or can exist without the Light of the Divine.

چه حاصل مر تورا زین بود نابود
کز او گاهیت خوف و گه رجا بود

What benefit is there for thee from the existence of this non-existent?[1]
For from it there comes sometimes fear, sometimes hope.

What good comes to us from knowing nonexistents parading as existence and resulting in our soul oscillating between fear and hope without being anchored in the Divine Reality?

نترسد زو کسی کورا شناسد
که طفل از سایهٔ خود می‌هراسد

He who knows Him fears Him not,
For the child fears its own shadow.

This verse should not be considered as a rejection of the three well-known stages of fear, love, and knowledge, or the overlooking of the *ḥadīth*, "The beginning of wisdom is the fear of God." Here, Shabistarī is concerned with the gnostic who has already traversed the stages of fear and love.

نماند خوف اگر گردی روانه
نخواهد اسب تازی تازیانه

Fear remains not if thou starteth moving;
The Arabian horse needs no whip.

Although there should be no fear as long as one is journeying steadily upward toward the Source, like the case of a fast-moving Arabian horse, there should always remain the fear of dangers lurking on the path. The virtue of vigilance should always be present. The steed of the soul may be galloping right now, but the disciple must make sure that it continues to do so until it reaches the Goal.

تورا از آتش دوزخ چه باک است
که از هستی تن وجان تو پاک است

What fear dost though have of hell-fire,
If thy body and soul are cleansed of existence?

Heaven and hell are conditions pertaining to the human soul in its individual state. When the soul reaches the Divine Reality, it attains a realm beyond the infernal and even paradisal states, unless it be *jannat al-Dhāt*, the Paradise of the Essence. Existence in the second hemistich refers not to *wujūd* in general, but to separative existence.

ز آتش زرّ خالص برفروزد
چو غشّی نبود اندر وی چه سوزد؟

From fire pure gold glows forth.
If there be no alloy in it, what will burn?

If gold is put in a fire, it does not burn out but glows. If it is pure gold and not an alloy, there is nothing there to burn.

تورا غیر از تو چیزی نیست در پیش
ولیکن از وجود خود بیندیش

There is nothing before thee but thyself,
And so, reflect upon thine own existence.

The main obstacle on the spiritual path is not the world seen objectively, but worldliness and attachment to it in the soul. So, Shabistarī advises us to reflect upon our own soul and its imperfections to realize that our own *nafs* and not God's creation is the greatest obstacle upon the path to Him.

اگر در خویشتن گردی گرفتار
حجاب تو شود عالم به یک بار

If thou becomest entangled in thyself,
The world becomes at once thy veil.

The world becomes a veil in relation to God on the spiritual path only if we become imprisoned in our own ego, the term thyself in the first hemistich referring to our concupiscent self or ego, not to the *nafs* in its higher meaning.

توئی در دور هستی جزو اسفل
توئی با نقطهٔ وحدت مقابل

Thou art in the circle of existence the lowest part.
Thou are in opposition to the point of Unity.

Certain Sufi texts have used the accompanying diagram to elucidate this matter. God is at the pinnacle of reality. From Him issues forth the arc of descent moving to ever greater complexity through the angelic world and the Three Kingdoms until one reaches man. Man occupies the lowest point in the circle, which is also the beginning of ascent back to God. From Unity is generated multiplicity, which then ascends back to Unity.

تعیّن‌های عالم بر تو طاری است
از آن گوئی چو شیطان همچو من کیست؟

The determinations of the world are obscure over thee.
That is why thou sayest, like Satan, "Who is there like unto me?"

The arcs of ascent and descent.

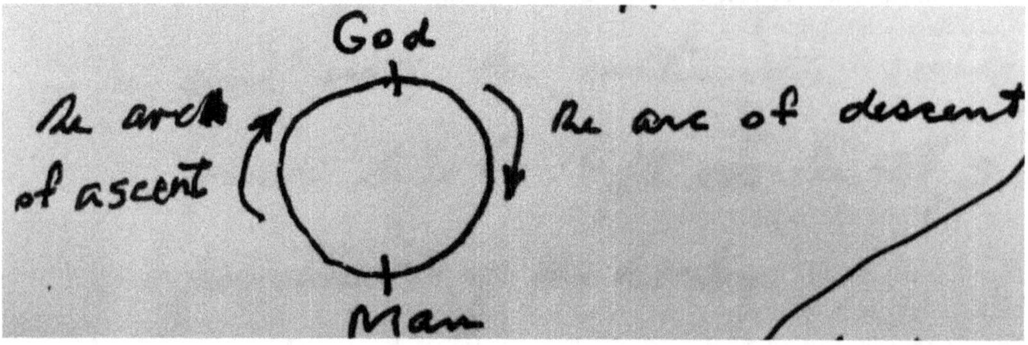

The world itself consists of dterminiations (*ta 'ayyunat*) of *wujūd*, a truth that is not realized by most ordinary people and, therefore, appears obscure. Although the verse says *bar tu* or over thee, it means in thee, diciating that it is so as long as one does not realize that these realities are determinations of *wujūd* and not independent existents. Being in this state of ignorance, one becomes proud like Satan.

Concerning Free Will He Says

از آن گوئی مرا خود اختیار است
تن من مرکب و جانم سوار است

Therefore, thou sayeth "I myself possess free will,
My body is the steed and my soul the rider."

This false attribution of independent existence to oneself leads one to a false sense of freedom of the will independent of God's Will. Consequently, one thinks of one's *nafs* as being the rider and the body as the steed, which the *nafs* is able to lead to wherever it wants to go.

زمام تن به دست جان نهادند
همه تکلیف بر من زان نهادند

They left the reins of the body in the hand of the soul.
They placed all obligations upon me because of it.

The spiritual and psychological battles of life take place within the soul. The body in itself is innocent and not the ultimate source of evil. Therefore, all responsibilities in human life are left to the mind and soul of man, even those that are related to the functions of the body.

ندانی کین ره آتش‌پرستی است
همه این آفت و شومی ز هستی است

Thou knowest not that this is the way of fire-worship.
All this corruption and deceptive evil comes from [separative] existence.

"This" in the first stanza refers to the whole gamut of dualism in which most people live. Only a true believer in Unity (*muwaḥḥid*) lives fully in the Light of Unity.

کدامین اختیار ای مرد جاهل
کسی‌را کو بود بالذات باطل؟

What free will, O ignorant man,
For one who is in his essence false?

We have freedom on our level of relative existence, but the spiritual reason for having been given this freedom is to submit our free will and our being to God. To realize our "nothingness" before God is to become free of that sense of freedom to move away from Him. The purpose of human freedom is to transcend that freedom and surrender our will to God. Let us recall the famous saying of Bāyazīd Basṭāmī. When he was asked "What dost thou will?" he answered *urīdu an lā urīd*, "I will not to will" (because then God wills for me).

چو بود توست یک سر جمله نابود
نگوئی کاختیارت از کجا بود

Since thy existence is through and through non-existence,
Sayest thou not from where does thy free will come?

Once we realize that what we take to be our existence is not in reality existence but nonexistence "parading in the guise of existence," to quote Rūmī, then surely we must ask ourselves how we can have free will.[2] How can the ordinary "I" (the *nafs*) that has no existence metaphysically speaking even have a will that is free?

کسی کورا وجود از خود نباشد
به ذات خویش نیک و بد نباشد

One whose existence is not from himself,
In his essence is neither good nor evil.

This verse is not meant to negate the categories of good and evil on the level of relative existence, but to refer to the state of the realized person who has become aware that his existence is not his own but belongs to God. Such a person has gone beyond the moral duality of good and evil. The Being of God is beyond this duality; yet He is the Supreme Good.

کرا دیدی تو اندر جمله عالم
که یک دم شادمانی یافت بی‌غم؟

Whom hast thou seen in the whole world,
Who found for a moment joy without sorrow?

In our ordinary human world joy and sorrow are combined and intertwined precisely because of the relativity of separative existence. Only in the embrace of the Divine Beloved and the illumination of the Light of the One is there pure joy and peace.

کرا شد حاصل آخر جمله امید؟
که ماند اندر کمالی تا به جاوید؟

Who did then ever realize all his hopes?
Who did ever remain in a perfection unto eternity?

In asking these questions Shabistarī is inviting the reader to ponder and answer the above question with, "Only the person who has realized God."

مراتب باقی و اهل مراتب
به زیر امر حقّ والله غالب

The stages [of the path] remain, and the people of the stages
Are under the Command of the Truth, and God is victorious.

Having posed various questions in the above verses, Shabistarī now turns to realities concerning those who are marching through the various stages (*marātib*) of the path to God and the conditions for such a transformation. So, he emphasizes that the stages of the path remain and those who journey through those stages do so under Divine Command, which also means only through His Will. This truth is emphasized by the phrase at the end that it is God, implying only God, Who is victorious.

مؤثّر حقّ شناس اندر همه جای
ز حدّ خویشتن بیرون منه پای

Know the Truth as being effective everywhere;
Never set foot beyond thy limit.

One should recognize the Truth as being effective in all domains of reality, being the Ultimate Cause of all effects. This fact means that one should realize one's own limitations and never venture beyond them.

ز حال خویشتن پرس این قدر چیست؟
وز آنجا باز دان کاهل قدر کیست.

Ask thine own state what is this predestination (*qadar*)?
And through it know who is the follower of predetermination.

This verse is a return to the question of predestination and free will, and it emphasizes that we should be certain that we know its real significance and recognize those who understand and follow it.

هر آن کس‌را که مذهب غیر جبر است
نبی فرمود کو مانند گبر است

Whoever whose religious school is other than predestination (*jabr*);
The Prophet said, he is like a Zoroastrian.

Madhhab, which I have translated here as "religious school," can also mean "religion" in general, but in Islamic thought it is usually identified more particularly with the school of Divine Law, of *Sharī'ah* that a Muslim follows, and sometimes with the theological school of a person. In Islamic thought, the Mazdeans or Zoroastrians were considered to be against *jabr*.[3]

چنان کان گبر یزدان و اهرمن گفت
همین نادان احمق ما و من گفت

As that Zoroastrian spoke of Yazdān and Ahrīman,
This ignorant person spoke of we and I.

Here, Shabistarī identifies the Zoroastrian dualism of Ahūrāmazda or Yazdān and Ahrīman with the dualism that permeates the mind and soul of the ignorant person who is unaware of the Unity that both permeates and transcends all duality.

به ما افعال‌را نسبت مجازی است
نسب خود در حقیقت لهو و بازی است

To attribute actions to ourselves is metaphorical.
In truth attribution itself is a play and a game.

To attribute actions to ourselves and our own will is not the truth but a metaphorical way of speaking. God Himself is alone the ultimate Actor. To think otherwise is simply a play of the mind of fallen man. The sage realizes that "there is no one in the house except its owner" (*laysa fi'l-dār ghayrahu dayyār*).

نبودی تو که فعلت آفریدند
تورا از بهر کاری برگزیدند

Thou didst not exist when thy action was created.
Thou wert chosen for a particular task.

God had already created our actions before He cast us into this lowly world and had chosen for us the task that we are to follow in this life.

به قدرت بی‌سبب دانای بر حقّ
به علم خویش کاری کرده مطلق

The knower of Truth [is aware] that through His Power without cause,
He has through His Knowledge performed an absolute action.

He who knows the Truth knows that through His Absolute Power and without any intermediate cause God through His Knowledge has performed acts that have an absolute character. God has created the apple tree, which cannot be anything but an apple tree. It cannot bear pears or plums as its fruit. There is something absolute in its nature that comes from the Absolute Who created it.

مقدّر گشته پیش از جان و از تن
برای هر یکی کاری معیّن

Before soul and body, it has been predestined,
For each person a determined action.

This verse again refers to our primordial nature that precedes our body and soul ontologically, and wherein God has already determined our destiny that we are to perform in this life. This verse must, of course, be understood in light of the doctrine of free will and determinism discussed above.

یکی چندین هزاران ساله طاعت
به جا آورد و کردش طوق لعنت

One person a thousand years of obedience,
Performed, yet he made it a collar of curse.

We can spend a whole lifetime thinking that we are obeying God whereas we are really obeying the inclinations of our own ego, which is, therefore, not surrender to the Divine Will but a curse.[4]

دگر از معصیّت نور و صفا دید
چو توبه کرد نور «اصطفی» دید

Another saw through sinfulness light and purity.
Since he repented, he saw the light of "being chosen" (*iṣṭafā*).

Then there are those who, having sinned and rebelled against God's Will, realize their error, see the Light of God, and become purified. Once they repent, they experience the light related to those chosen by God, *iṣṭafā* being a term drawn from the Quran (Q. 3:33).[5]

عجب‌تر آنکه این از ترک مأمور
شد از الطاف حقّ مرحوم و مغفور

Stranger still (*'ajabtar*) is the person who through abandoning what is ordered,
Through the grace of the Truth become the object of Mercy and Forgiveness.

There are also those who do not follow what is Divinely ordained, yet through the Grace of God receive His Mercy and are forgiven. These cases display the imponderable aspects of Divine Mercy. Since such matters seem to stand beyond the exoteric teachings of religion, Shabistarī begins the verse with *'ajabtar*, "Stranger still."

مر آن دیگر ز منهی گشته ملعون
زهی فعل تو بی چند و چه و چون

Yet, another through the forbidden became cursed.
Many of thy acts are without how much, what and because.

The reverse of what is mentioned in the above verse can also take place, a person becoming cursed not by abandoning what is ordained by religion, but as a result of doing what is forbidden. Shabistarī concludes that man performs many acts without inquiring fully about their nature and the consequences of performing them. The second hemistich could also be taken to refer to God.

جناب کبریائی لاابالی است
منزّه از قیاسات خیالی است

Majestic Magnificence (*janāb-i kibriyā'ī*) is licentious (*lā ubālī*),
Free from imaginary conjecture (*qiyāsāt*).

Usually, the word *janāb* is used in Persian to mean "excellency" by which people of high rank such as ministers and ambassadors are often addressed. This term is not used for kings and queens in the same way that in English one refers to a monarch as Your Majesty and not Your Excellency. But in Persian poetry it is also used for God, who is the supreme Majesty, the King of the Universe. As for *lā ubālī*, it is often used for people who are insolent, petulant, or licentious. But when used for God, it means being above all ordinary norms, rules, and manners. As for *qiyās*, it is also a term in logic meaning "reasoning" and "logical judgment," and also sometimes logic itself.

چه بود اندر ازل ای مرد نااهل؟
که این یک شد محمّد و آن ابوجهل؟

What was there in pre-eternity, O unfit man?
That one [person] became Muḥammad, and the other Abū Jahl?

A basic question is brought forth in this verse. We were all in the state of preeternity before coming into this world. The essential question is this: Why did one being come into this world and become the Messenger of God and another became Abū Jahl who, although a relative of the Messenger, was so ignorant that he rejected the Quranic revelation and thus gained the title of Abū Jahl (literally "the father of ignorance")?

کسی کو با خدا چون و چرا گفت
چو مشرک حضرتش‌را ناسزا گفت

The person who wrangled with God,
Like a polytheist uttered what is impertinent concerning His Presence.

For a mind cut off from the intellect and a soul uprooted from its spiritual foundation, to argue with God causes that person to become deprived of the grace of *tawḥīd* and say words that are impudent concerning God, therefore committing the major sin of taking a partner unto God or *shirk*, which is usually translated as polytheism.

ورا زیبد که پرسد از چه و چون
نباشد اعتراض از بنده موزون

It is becoming of him to ask what and how,
[But] protest is not harmonious with [the nature of] the servant.

God has given us a mind and the power of thinking. Therefore, it is natural for us to inquire into the nature of things and seek knowledge of the what and the how of His creation, but that does not mean that we should protest what God has willed. If we do so, we are no longer living in harmony with our own nature, for we were created as His servants to obey His Will.

خداوندی همه در کبریائی است
نه علّت لایق فعل خدائی است

The Nature of God is all in [His] Magnificence.
Cause is not worthy of [being considered as] Divine Action.

We live in a world of cause and effect, but the truth of the matter is that God is "the Cause of all causes" (*'illat al-'ilal*), as it is said in Islamic philosophical parlance. He is the ultimate Cause of everything, and there is no secondary cause independent of the Supreme Cause Who is thereby called "the Cause of all causes."

سزاوار خدائی لطف و قهر است
ولیکن بندگی در فقر و جبر است

Worthy of God are grace and victory;
And as for servanthood, it is in poverty (*faqr*) and determination (*jabr*).

God is at once grace and love combined with victorial dominion and power. What is worthy of us corresponding to these Divine Qualities is accepting the determination that comes from God's will and poverty, which means the awareness that all we have, and all that we are, is owned by God, and that we are *ontologically* "nothing" if considered independent of Him.

کرامت آدمی‌را اضطرار است
نه آن کورا نصیبی ز اختیار است

The beneficence of man is in necessity,
Not in one who shares [the idea of] free will.

In light of what he had said before about predestination and necessity, Shabistarī repeats that a person's goodness, generosity, and beneficence depend on his acceptance of *jabr* and the fact that God's Will is all dominant. Such qualities in man, if he accepts free will and tries to use his will independent of God's Will, deprive him of God's Mercy and Guidance.

نبوده هیچ چیزش هرگز از خود
پس آنگه پرسدش از نیک و از بد

Never has there been anything of his from himself,
But then he is asked about good and evil.

Again Shabistarī refers to a theological enigma. All that man has and is comes from God, but then on the Day of Judgment God asks him about his good and evil actions and judges him according to the nature of the acts he has performed in this world. This is a major question that those who accept *jabr* must answer, and there is much in Islamic theological works about this enigma of determination and free will.

ندارد اختیار و گشته مقهور
زهی مسکین که شد مختار مجبور

He has no free will and has become vanquished.
There is many an indigent person who was coerced to become free.

Man has no free will of his own but has become vanquished by God's Will. Our only real freedom is the surrender of our will to God so that our will becomes His Will.

نه ظلم است این که عین علم و عدل است
نه جور است این که محض لطف و فضل است

This is not oppression, but is the essence of knowledge and justice.
It is not iniquity, but pure mercy and grace.

To the skeptic the condition mentioned in the above verse appears as oppression whereas it is the manifestation of God's Knowledge and Justice. The person of true knowledge and faith realizes that whatever God wills for him is in its inner reality mercy and grace no matter how it might appear to him as injustice and iniquity.

به شرعت زان سبب تکلیف کردند
که از ذات خودت تعریف کردند

They made the Divine Law (*shar'*) obligatory for thee because,
They made known thine own essence.

God has made the following of His Law as codified in the *Sharī'ah* obligatory for us, because He knows our nature and what is good for us better than we ourselves do.

چو از تکلیف حقّ عاجز شوی تو
به یک بار از میان بیرون روی تو

If thou becometh helpless (*'ājiz*) [to carry out] the Divinely ordained
obligations,
At once thou wilt be removed from in between.

If we fail to follow the obligations ordained for us by God, we fall away from our real human nature as the agent in this life commanded by God to follow the straight path. When in our daily prayers we ask God to lead us upon the straight path, we are also asking Him not to make us helpless (*'ājiz*) in doing so. This verse contains also another meaning that I shall discuss in the commentary on the verse that follows.

به کلّیه رهائی یابی از خویش
غنی گردی به حقّ ای مرد درویش

Altogether thou shalt become free of thy self,
Thou shalt become rich through the Truth, o darvish!

The first hemistich of the previous verse can also be understood as reaching a state in which one's will becomes united with God's Will so that what God has ordained as obligation becomes one's own nature, the following of which is no longer an obligation imposed from the outside. To reach this state makes one rich through God, although in oneself one remains poor, or *faqīr*. As stated before, darvish, whom Shabistarī addresses here, means the same as *faqīr* in Sufism.

برو جان پدر تن در قضا ده
به تقدیرات یزدانی رضا ده

Go o "soul of thy father," yield to God's Will;
Become satisfied with Divine Fore-ordinance.

"Soul of thy father" (*jān-i pidar*) is a Persian expression of endearment. In endearing language Shabistarī advises us to surrender our will to God and be content with what He has ordained for us.

Question [10]

چه بحر است آنکه نطقش ساحل آمد؟
ز قعر او چه گوهر حاصل آمد؟

What is the Sea whose shore is speech?
What pearl is formed in its depths?

In this question Hirawī asks Shabistarī to explain the symbolism of that Sea whose word or speech is the shore of existence and the nature of the pearl of wisdom that is hidden in the Sea's depths. The Sea here is obviously reference to the Divine and word or speech to both creation and revelation.

Answer

یکی دریاست هستی نطق ساحل
صدف حرف و جواهر دانش دل

Being is a Sea of which speech is the shore;
The shell is the word and the pearls heart knowledge.

In the very first verse of his response, Shabistarī asserts that indeed Being, which here means, of course, the Divine Being, is the "Sea" whose shore is the "Word" in the metaphysical sense as mentioned also at the beginning of the Gospel of John in the New Testament to which I referred earlier in this commentary. The shell that lies at the bottom of the sea symbolizes the external form of the Divine Word and the pearls within it quintessential knowledge and gnosis that are identified in Sufi literature with heart-knowledge.

به هر موجی هزاران درّ شهوار
برون ریزد ز نقل و نصّ اخبار

In every wave are a thousand royal pearls,
There pour out from the transmission and in texts of prophetic sayings.

The waves of this "Sea" cast forth the many words and teachings of the revelation, which include by extension the *Sunnah* and *Ḥadīth*.

هزاران موج خیزد هر دم از وی
نگردد قطره‌ای هرگز کم از وی

Thousands of waves arise from It at every moment;
Yet, not a drop ever diminishes from It.

The waves from the Divine "Sea" continue to flow from the "Sea," as the power and fruits of *walāyah/wilāyah* even after the temporal end of *nubuwwah* (prophecy) with the death of the Prophet, and the "Sea" or the Divine remains Absolute and Infinite and Its Nature does not diminish in any way through the continuous flow of cosmic existence from it.

وجود علم از آن دریای ژرف است
غلاف درّ او از صوت و حرف است

The existence of knowledge comes from that deep Sea.
The sheath of its pearl is made of sound and word.

God is *al-'Alīm*, the Knower, and all knowledge flows from this Quality and Attribute. Sounds and words with which that knowledge is made manifest to us are in their external form like the shell containing the pearl of authentic knowledge within itself.

معانی چون کند اینجا تنزّل
ضرورت باشد آنرا از تمثّل

Since meanings descend here,
Symbolism becomes necessary for it.

The spiritual realities of beings descend at this point, that is, their explanation becomes necessary. Hence, Shabistarī asserts that he must take recourse to the language of symbolism (*tamaththul*) with which he can explain the inner truths involved in this issue.

Illustration

شنیدم من که اندر ماه نیسان
صدف بالا رود از قعر عمّان

I have heard that during the month of Naysān,
The shell that contains the pearl rises from the bottom of the Sea of Oman.

According to the Syriac calendar, Naysān is the second month of the spring season. The Sea of Oman refers to the Persian Gulf.

ز شیب قعر بحر آید برافراز
به روی بحر بنشیند دهن باز

From the deep bottom of the sea it comes to the surface;
It sits on [the surface of] the sea with its mouth open.

Shabistarī points to the fact that the shell is open toward the sky, ready to receive from above what will become a pearl.

بخاری مرتفع گردد ز دریا
فرو بارد به امر حقّ تعالی

Vapor rises from the sea,
Then descends through the Command of the Transcendent Truth.

The text goes back to the meteorological cycle of water rising from the sea as vapor and again descending on earth as rain through God's Command.

چکد اندر دهانش قطره‌ای چند
شود بسته دهان او به صد بند

A few of the drops fall into its mouth,
Its mouth [then] becomes firmly closed.

The verse refers, of course, to the shell and the process of the formation of a pearl within it.

رود در قعر دریا با دل پر
شود آن قطرهٔ باران یکی درّ

It sinks into the bottom of the sea, but with a heart that is full;
That drop of the rain becomes a pearl.

This verse continues the description of how a pearl is formed.

به قعر اندر رود غوّاص دریا
برآرد از صدف لؤلؤ لالا

The pearl-diver (*ghawwāṣ*) dives deep into the sea;
He brings out from within the shell, the incomparable jewel.

Ghawwāṣ means deep sea diver, but especially in the Persian Gulf it connotes especially a pearl diver.

Now, having given this example, Shabistarī turns to its metaphysical significance when it is understood symbolically.

تن تو ساحل و هستی چو دریاست
بخارش فیض و باران علم اسماست

Thy body is the coastline, and existence like the sea,
The vapor that rises from it is Divine Grace, and the rain [that pours down]
knowledge of the Divine Names.

The symbolism is explained by pointing to the sea as a symbol of *wujūd* Itself, but here he excludes from it the existence of the body, the lowest level of man's *wujūd*, which he compares to the shore of the sea. The vapor that rises from the sea is not only through the Grace of God, but symbolizes Grace itself, which results in rain that here symbolizes principial knowledge, which we could not attain without Divine Grace.

خرد غوّاص آن بحر عظیم است
که اورا صد جواهر در گلیم است

Wisdom (*khirad*) is the deep-sea diver of that stupendous sea,
Which contains a hundred precious stones within its mat.

Khirad, wisdom, can also mean "intelligence," which is the faculty within man that has the ability to dive into the deep sea of *wujūd* to fetch the spiritual realities hidden therein beneath its surface, to which the poem refers as its mat.

دل آمد علمرا مانند یک ظرف
صدف بر علم دل صوت است با حرف

The heart is like a container for knowledge,
The shell for the knowledge of the heart is sound with word.

The knowledge about which Shabistarī is speaking is, of course, not mental knowledge but spiritual knowledge that is known by the heart and is contained therein. The shell or external form of this knowledge is the spoken or written word, which although a phenomenon, contains within itself the noumenon, as the physical shell hides and also nurtures the pearl within.

نفس گردد روان چون برق لامع
رسد زو حرفها در گوش سامع

The breath becomes fluent like striking lightning;
From it words reach the ear of the hearer.

When heart-knowledge is expressed, the breath of an authentic expositor of it becomes like lightning that strikes and for a moment illuminates everything around it. The hearer has to possess, however, sound eyes and ears. Otherwise, he could not see or hear the light and sound of that illuminating lightning. But if he does have sound ears, he will hear the transforming sound of lightning, and the same is true of the eye and vision of lightning.

صدف بشکن برون کن درّ شهوار
بیفکن پوست مغز نغز بردار

Break the shell and bring out the precious pearl.
Cast the skin aside and choose the beautiful pith.

To reach the fruit of a nut, one has to break the shell. This image is used widely in Sufism as a symbol of going beyond the outward aspect of things to reach their inner reality.

لغت با اشتقاق و نحو با صرف
همی‌گردد همه پیرامن حرف

Language with its derivation, and syntax with grammar,
Constantly all revolve around the word.

This verse summarizes the main concerns of those who are engaged in the study of the linguistic aspects of speech, both written and oral. There are many scholars whose only concern, even in studying the Quran, involves only these elements. Shabistarī is also insinuating indirectly that such scholars are not concerned with the inner meaning of the messages that the words are meant to convey.

هر آن کو جمله عمر خود در این کرد
به هرزه صرف عمر نازنین کرد

Whoever spends his life in this matter,
Has spent his precious life in frivolity.

Although studying the outward aspect of language has its value, for the spiritual person to confine himself only to such outward sciences is a frivolous pursuit.

ز جوزش قشر خشک افتاد در دست
نیابد مغز هر کس پوست نشکست

The dry skin of the nut (*jawz*) falls into his hand,
But whoever does not break the skin will not reach the fruit.

Jawz means any kind of nut, whether it be pistachio, walnut, hazelnut, or any other kind. The heart of a religion is, of course, its inner teachings. There is no other way to reach it except to remove the outer skin or shell that, however, is necessary on its own level. One cannot go beyond the outer meaning of the Divine Law without practicing the Law. One cannot remove the outer skin of a fruit that one does not possess.

بلی بی پوست ناپخته است هر مغز
ز علم ظاهر آمد علم دین نغز

Yea, without the shell the kernel is never ripe.
From external knowledge cometh pure knowledge of religion.

This is a very important point. As I mentioned above, the outward is necessary to reach the inward. Shabistarī emphasizes in the second hemistich the importance of external knowledge, by which he means traditional exoteric knowledge and not profane knowledge, exoteric knowledge as the ground that leads to the esoteric knowledge of religion.

ز من جان برادر پند بنیوش
به جان و دل برو در علم دین کوش

O dear brother, listen to my advice.
Go with thy soul and heart and use effort in [learning] the science of religion.

While reiterating the message of the above verse, he advises the reader to try—with the fullest use of his intelligence and will to strive—to master *'ilm-i dīn* (the science of religion), which includes both exoteric and esoteric knowledge.

که عالم در دو عالم سروری یافت
اگر کهتر بد از وی مهتری یافت

For the knowledgeable person (*'ālim*) has become distinguished (*sarvar*) in both worlds,
Even if he were to be less, he becomes greater through it.

Sarvar means a "leader" or someone who is distinguished. "It" at the end of the verse refers to the knowledge mentioned in the verse above.

عمل کان از سر احوال باشد
بسی بهتر ز علم قال باشد

Action that is based on states,
Is much better than a knowledge that is based simply on words (*'ilm-i qāl*).

'Ilm-i qāl at the end of the second hemistich refers to *qīl-u qāl,* literally "it was said and he said," which is a reference to simply external knowledge of words cut off from their inner meaning. It is used in Sufism in a denigrating sense. In Arabic when you used to have discussions in the *madrasah*, it would be called *qīl-u qāl*, that is, somebody says something, and then somebody else answers him. The student asks a question, and the teacher answers him; the teacher asks a question, and the student answers him. *Qīl-u qāl* means a purely mental discourse. *'Ilm-i qāl* or *'ilm-i qīl-u qāl* means, therefore, mental knowledge cut off from heart-knowledge. What one learns in ordinary schools is nothing but knowledge on the level of *qīl-u qāl.*

ولی کاری که از آب و گل آید
نه چون علمی‌است کان کار دل آید

But a work that results from water and clay,
Is not like the knowledge that comes from the working of the heart.

"A work that results from water and clay" relates to the physical aspect of human existence, the body of Adam before God breathed His Spirit into it. The heart is the center of the human being, which received the Divine Breath and therefore the seat of a knowledge that differs from what comes from water and clay.

میان جسم و جان بنگر چه فرق است
که اینرا غرب گیری و آن چو شرق است

Look, what difference there is between body and soul.
If you consider the one to be the West, the other is like the East.

This means that they are opposite to each other, and one is therefore associated with the West and the setting of the Sun and the other with the East and the Sun's rising.

از اینجا باز دان احوال اعمال
به نسبت با علوم قال با حال

From here learn the states of actions,
In relation to the sciences of words and [those of] spiritual states.

"From here learn the states of actions" refers to the spiritual states related to human actions. The second hemistich points to their relation to both exoteric and esoteric knowledge, both of which have a relation to human actions.

نه علم است آنکه دارد میل دنیا
که صورت دارد اما نیست معنا

It is not knowledge if one has worldly inclinations;
For it possesses the external form, but is deprived of meaning.

If you seek knowledge only for worldly ends, you only gain the external forms, not the inner meaning of things.

نگردد علم هرگز جمع با آز
ملک خواهی سگ از خود دور انداز

Knowledge can never be combined with worldly desire (*āz*).
If thou wantest an angel, distance the dog from thyself.

Āz means actually wanting to have more, to amass wealth and belongings; so it means greed, or you can call it material greed. In Islamic Law the dog is considered a ritually impure animal. So, it generally has a negative significance in Islamic literature, although there are many Sufis who refer to the positive aspect of dogs, but here it is the former that is intended.

علوم دین ز اخلاق فرشته است
نیاید در دلی کو سگ سرشت است

The sciences of religion issue from the ethics of the angel.
They do not penetrate a heart that has the nature of a dog.

Expressing things in this manner must be understood in its traditional context. In reality dogs are closer to God than those human beings who have rebelled against Him.

حدیث مصطفی آخر همین است
نکو بشنو که البته چنین است

The saying of the Prophet is verily this;
Listen to it carefully, for definitely it is so.

This verse must also be understood in light of what I said above.

درون خانه‌ای چون هست صورت
فرشته ناید اندر وی ضرورت

In a house in which there is an image (*ṣūrat*),
Of necessity, the angel does not enter into it.

This is a reference to one of the famous and important *ḥadīth*s that define the status of the plastic arts in Islam, in which the Prophet says that the angels do not enter a house in which there are figures or images of a naturalistic nature of living creatures. There has been a great deal of debate about what this saying means as far as Islamic art is concerned. Of course, it does not mean a geometric form on a wall or something like that. It means primarily naturalistic painting, particularly of the human form.

The *ḥadīth* in question, from Bukhārī and Muslim, is as follows: *lā tadkhul al-malā'ikah baytan fīhi kalbun wa lā ṣūrah*, "The angels do not enter a house in which there is a dog or a figure (image)."

برو بزدای روی تختهٔ دل
که تا سازد ملک پیش تو منزل

Go and purify the tablet of the heart,
So that the angel will make his abode with thee.

Shabistarī now turns to the highest sense of this saying that involves the heart itself, which must be purified of all worldly forms in order for the angelic presence and by extension the Divine Presence to descend upon it and make it its abode.

از او تحصیل کن علم وراثت
ز بهر آخرت می‌کن حراثت

Learn (*taḥṣīl*) from him inherited knowledge (*'ilm-i wirāthat*);
Guard thyself for the sake of the Other World.

'Ilm-i wirāthat belongs to one of several categories or divisions of the sciences in Islam, such as *ma'qūl* (intellectual) and *manqūl* (transmitted). One of these divisions is between *al-'ilm al-kasbī* and *al-'ilm al-mawrūthī* in Arabic, or *'ilm-i kasbī* and *'ilm-i mawrūthī* in Persian. *'Ilm-i kasbī* means acquired knowledge, and indicates that which you gain through studying and reading, through formal learning from teachers. *'Ilm-i mawrūthī* (or *'ilm-i wirāthat*) is the science that you inherit. Now, it is important to add that there is a big debate about the exact meaning of these terms. For example, the Sufi sciences, the esoteric sciences, are called *mawrūthī*, but we do not automatically possess them as inherited in an actualized manner. It is something we have to gain, but it is said that gaining it is a reminder of what is within us potentially already. So, this is a somewhat complicated affair philosophically.

The way this is phrased is very interesting. *Taḥṣīl* means to learn or to acquire. But one is supposed to inherit *'ilm-i wirāthat*; so, this seems contradictory. However, what it really means, is "Go and become aware." *Taḥṣīl* here means to gain something, and not just to learn.

Principle

This principle or *qā'idah* deals mostly with ethical questions, the matter of virtues that are essential for those seeking to follow the spiritual path.

کتاب حقّ بخوان از نفس و آفاق
مزیّن شو به اصل جمله اخلاق

> Read the book of the Truth within the soul and upon the horizons.
> Gain the ornament (*muzayyan shaw*) of the principles of all ethics.

Of course, the first hemistich is a reference to the famous verse of the Quran (41:53), *sanurīhim āyātinā fī'l-āfāq wa fī anfusihim ḥattā yatabayyana lahum annahu'l-ḥaqq*, "We shall show them Our signs upon the horizons and within themselves till it becomes clear to them that it is the truth." So, *nafs* (the soul) and *āfāq* (the horizons) in the language of the Sufis, are a syzygy. They go together because of this Quranic verse.

Muzayyan shudan means to become ornamented from *zīnah* meaning ornament. Ethical virtue is a precious ornament of the soul.

اصول خلق نیک آمد عدالت
پس از وی حکمت و عفّت شجاعت

> The principles of good character are justice,
> Thereafter wisdom, temperance (*'iffat*) and courage.

'Iffah in Arabic, or *'iffat* in Persian, means "temperance" but also "shyness," a kind of calm and inward shyness that is opposed to egoistic display. It can also mean "chastity," but it is more than that since chastity in English is associated usually only with sexuality. The Arabic term really means not only shyness but also keeping to oneself and not violating any norms. All of these meanings are there. We even say *'iffat-i kalām* in Persian, which means to use speech that is polite, endearing, not abrasive, and does not abuse a person or break someone's heart. So chastity is part of the meaning of *'iffat*, but is not a complete translation. *'Iffat* is a key virtue and it is difficult to find an exact synonym for it in English.

حکیمی راست گفتار است و کردار
کسی کو متّصف گردد بدین چار

> To become a wise person (*ḥakīm*) is to have correct speech and action,
> The person who gains the quality of these four:

This verse indicates the main virtues that must be attained as indicated in the verses that follow.

ز حکمت باشدش جان و دل آگه
نه گربز باشد و نه نیز ابله

> The heart of such a person through wisdom (*ḥikmat*) will be conscious and aware.

He will not be cunning (*gurbuz*) and will not be a simpleton.

Gurbuz means excessively clever and cunning, that is, clever in a negative way. Many people fall into one of two categories of people: Some act stupidly; others are cunning. Both are to be avoided by one who wishes to follow the spiritual path.

به عفّت شهوت خود کرده مستور
شره همچون خمود از وی شده دور

Through temperance he has hidden his passions,
The fire [of passions] has abated and has been removed from him.

This verse emphasizes the importance of the virtue of temperance that once attained removes negative passions from the soul.

شجاع و صافی از ذلّ و تکبّر
مبرّا ذاتش از جبن و تهوّر

Courageous and pure from baseness and haughtiness,
His essence divorced from fear and impetuosity (*tahawwur*).

Tahawwur refers to heedless courage that causes man to do things without considering the consequences. The virtues mentioned in this verse result from the virtue of temperance mentioned in the verse above.

عدالت چون شعار ذات او شد
ندارد ظلم از آن خلقش نکو شد

When justice becomes the motto of his essence,
There will be no injustice coming from him, since his nature thereby becomes good.

Goodness of character requires the virtue of justice that is so often mentioned in Sufi texts in its universal and not only legal sense.

همه اخلاق نیکو در میانه است
که از افراط و تفریطش کرانه است

All good ethical norms come from equity,
Excess from one side or the other (*ifrāṭ-u tafrīṭ*) is marginal.

This verse needs some explanation; otherwise, it can cause problems for those who interpret it only outwardly. In the *Nicomachean Ethics*, Aristotle has a theory that virtue is a happy medium between extremes. Platonic ethics, however, does not see the matter in the same way. Aristotelian ethics had a lot of effect upon the West also, and St. Thomas Aquinas has written about it. Islam, totally independent of Aristotle whose ethical works were well known by Muslims, likewise emphasizes the happy medium, or the mean between two extremes in human action. The Quran calls the Islamic *ummah*, *ummatan wasaṭan*, “the middle community” (Q. 2:143).

This verse has many meanings. It could mean “middle” geographically, it could mean intellectually, it could be in regard to the relation between the Law and the Way, or it could be in relation to legal injunctions. Moreover, in the Abrahamic religions, Judaism emphasizes the Law above everything else. Christianity, especially early Christianity not the Christianity that is practiced now by most people, emphasized love mysticism as the Way. Islam came as a balance between the two, and sees itself as the *wasaṭ*, as the happy medium between two extremes, avoiding both reducing religion to simply law and externality, or overlooking externality and only looking at the inner aspect of religion. I could go on to mention many instances of this reality, for example, the question of marriage and sexuality. Islam on the one hand does not have monasticism, banning totally all forms of it as institution, but at the same time it curtailed the pre-Islamic Arabic practice of having just any number of wives and concubines and so forth, by putting limits upon it and regulating it.

The question arises as to whether Sufi ethics is like Aristotelian ethics, just trying to promulgate a happy medium in ethical matters and religious matters or not. The answer is yes and no. It is not completely one or the other. For example, is there a happy medium between loving and knowing God and not loving and knowing Him? No. On the level of the *Sharī'ah*, however, the Sufis like other Muslims try to balance things out; yet, some Sufis would fast for a hundred days and only drink warm water in the Mesopotamian desert. They were considered to be extremists, but they were doing such acts in order to awaken the consciousness of the ordinary people, to wake them up to spiritual realities. But that type of action is not the ordinary Islamic practice. This kind of action is comparable to the Hindu yogis, sitting on nails and things like that, or in early Christianity the extreme ascetic practices of the Eastern monks. I am not saying that Islam did not ever see that phenomenon within itself. There were occasionally people like the early Sufis of Mesopotamia, who were very ascetic, some of whom through fasting and not speaking went through extreme ascetic practices, but that is not the norm in exoteric Islam or in Sufism. In India where Islam and Hinduism both exist, many great yogis are very good friends of Sufis, and they exchange and share much together, but among the Muslims of India you rarely see the phenomena that you see among some Hindus. I am referring to phenomena such as, for example, walking nude in nature, sitting on nails and winding up their body, putting their legs around their head and so on. Muslims are not seen to do such things. So, from one point of view, yes, Islam including Sufism are based on a balance in all domains of life.

However, from another point of view, a *faqīr* is like an arrow that is shot toward Heaven. There is not a cancellation of forces between the movement of the arrow toward Heaven and gravity toward the earth that would prevent the arrow from moving at all. The movement of the arrow is unidirectional.

Moreover, there is no limit to how much we should remember God. Practitioners of Sufism do not try to balance *dhikr* with enjoying worldly pleasures. The goal is for the *dhikr* to become central, total, and all-embracing in one's life. Even if one is enjoying worldly things, the *dhikr* should be present. There is no limit to goodness, humility, and all the other virtues, and there should be no effort to balance them in the soul with their opposite.

So, this is a sensitive issue, and Shaykh Maḥmūd Shabistarī is trying to bring out the spiritual significance of *i'tidāl*, of *'idālah*. *I'tidāl* means balance, which comes from the word *'adl* in Arabic, which means justice. *I'tidāl* means balance in deeds and thoughts. Among all the great mysticisms that we see, Sufism is one of the most balanced as far as the outward and inward are concerned. Look at these Taoist masters in China living on top of mountains and other nearly inaccessible places. Again, I am not saying that we did not have *qalandar*s in Islam who sometimes did the same, but mainstream Sufism has always tried to strike a balance between inner and outward life. Many Western Christian monks and contemplatives have been disconcerted by the fact that Sufis have wives and children. On a personal note, when I was twenty-four years old and already a *faqīr*, I visited Morocco. It was there that, for the first time, I met a German nun. We were traveling with two or three other nuns there, and we sat down for a meeting together. The German nun was very beautiful, but she had become a nun, and I was only twenty-four years old.

She looked at me and said, "Are you married?"

I said, "No, I am still studying."

She said, "You should never marry. You should become a monk."

She saw something of an affinity in me with her own spirituality. I did not say anything but pondered her reaction. Many Westerners, especially Catholics, even today have this problem with Sufism. In this matter Protestants are, of course, more like Muslims because their pastors and ministers marry, but in Catholicism where the celibacy of Christ is held as the ideal, the priests and monks do not marry. It is not, however, correct to equate spirituality with celibacy. In Hinduism, where one has the period in one's life of being a householder, that is distinct from becoming a *sanyasin*. After having gone through that period in which one has wives and children, one leaves them all and becomes a *sanyasin* if that person wants to follow a strict spiritual path. But even in Hinduism some of the great saints have been and have remained married. So, Islam strikes a balance here, and Shabistarī is trying to bring out the importance of preserving this balance.

I think that this question should not be looked upon only superficially. Let us remember that there are ethical treatises in Islam such as *Akhlāq-i nāṣirī* of Ṭūsī, or the *Tahdhīb al-akhlāq* of Miskawayh, and other classical works that always talk about this balance, following Aristotle, particularly the *Nicomachean Ethics*, which is probably his most important work on ethics. However, they place greater emphasis than does the Stagirite on the spiritual dimension. So, in the Islamic tradition, keeping the happy mean—the *wasaṭ*, the medium of things—is emphasized. But Sufi ethics is not only that balance. It is not a question of simply being balanced in society because if you are only a balanced social being, you cannot really be a saint. A saint from a social point of view is "imbalanced," an exception. From the point of view of an ordinary Muslim, the Sufi is too much involved with otherworldliness, with the Divine and the Spirit. The extreme example of this kind of person is the *majnūn*, a person crazed for God, having a Divine madness, which you also have in Christianity and Judaism, and in all religions in fact. In all these cases such a person breaks the social norm. Such a phenomenon, however, is also necessary, and without him or her, spirituality cannot survive as a living reality in a society. This reality is an important matter; the disappearance of such people is a spiritual tragedy for the social order.

میانه چون صراط مستقیم است
ز هر دو جانبش قعر جحیم است

The medium is like the straight path (*ṣirāt-i mustaqīm*),
On both sides of which are the depths of hell.

Al-ṣirāt al-mustaqīm, is of course mentioned in *Ṣūrat al-Fātiḥah*, *Ihdinā'l-ṣirāṭ al-mustaqīm*, "Guide us upon the straight path" (Q. 1:6) referring to following the correct path toward salvation while in this world. But according to Islamic eschatology, it is also the actual bridge (*ṣirāṭ*) that we have to cross after death. There are many traditions about this path. For good people it becomes wider and wider until they reach Paradise, but for evil people it becomes narrower and narrower until they fall off it into the infernal states. Anyway, on the two sides of the bridge are the fires of Hell, and we have to cross it in order to reach Paradise. In this verse, Shabistarī is referring to this traditional teaching.

به باریکی و تیزی موی و شمشیر
نه روی گشتن و بودن بر او دیر

In thinness and in sharpness it is like a hair and a sword,
There is no way of turning back nor standing on it long.

The bridge to Heaven is as thin as a hair and as sharp as the blade of a sword. It is also a one-way road that one has to keep traversing. One cannot turn back once one begins to cross it nor even stay stationary on it for long.

عدالت چون یکی دارد ز اضداد
همین هفت آمد این اضداد ز اعداد

Since justice has but one opposite,
Opposites became this same seven in number.

The number seven, so prevalent in esoteric teachings and in religion in general, is mentioned here as the number of different forms of opposition to justice.

به زیر هر عدد سرّی نهفت است
از آن درهای دوزخ نیز هفت است

Under each of these numbers there is a mystery.
For that reason, the gates of Hell are also seven.

Some people say there are nineteen gates of Hell; some say there are seven.

چنان کز ظلم شد دوزخ مهیّا
بهشت آمد همیشه عدل‌را جا

In the same way that Hell was prepared for [those who have committed] oppression,
Paradise is always the place of those who are just.

Although the first hemistich in Persian mentions only oppression, it also refers indirectly to those who have been oppressive. He then asserts again that Paradise is for the just.

جزای عدل نور و رحمت آمد
سزای ظلم لعن و ظلمت آمد

The reward of justice is light and mercy,
The punishment of oppression is condemnation and darkness.

This is simply a poetic rendition of the Quranic teaching concerning the reward or punishment of the just and the unjust.

ظهور نیکوئی در اعتدال است
عدالت جسم‌را اقصی الکمال است

The appearance of goodness is in equilibrium, (*i'tidāl*),
Justice is the closest perfection for the body.

The root of the term *i'tidāl*, which I have translated here as "equilibrium," and that could also be translated as "balance," is, perhaps needless to repeat, related to the root for the term "justice" or *'adl*. "The appearance of goodness" is in avoiding excesses, in having equilibrium. Furthermore, if we are just, it is easier even for our body to gain its highest perfection and not only our soul. The *Sharī'ah* is based on the practice of *i'tidāl* in one's everyday life. Of course, our obedience to God or our love for Him and Knowledge of the Truth are not bound by the limits set by *i'tidāl*.

مرکّب چون شود مانند یک چیز
ز اجزا دور گردد فعل و تمییز

When a compound (*murakkab*) becomes like a single thing,
Action and distinction become distanced from its parts.

When two things are compounded into a single thing, the identity of each part fades away as does the separate actions of each. When cream is put into a cup of coffee, the result has a color different from both white cream and black coffee and the coffee has a different taste from both if taken separately.

بسیط الذات‌را مانند گردد
میان این و آن پیوند گردد

It becomes like something simple (*basīṭ*) in [its] essence.
It becomes a connection between that and this.

Basīṭ (simple) used at the beginning of the verse is a technical philosophical term juxtaposed to *murakkab* (compound). Something becoming *basīṭ* in its essence means becoming like a new single substance, a single reality. And becoming like a new single reality, it "creates a connection between this and that," that is, it integrates both substances of which it is composed within itself into one thing, into a simple reality.

نه پیوندی که از ترکیب اجزاست
که روح از وصف جسمیّت مبرّاست

Not a connection that results from the mixture of parts,
For the spirit is beyond the description of corporality.

This connection is not simply the connection of parts considered physically. Do not think that we have pieces of the spirit put together like pieces of the body, for the spirit is a unified whole. This verse also implies that everything, including bodies, has an idea in the Platonic sense or form in the Aristotelian one and is not simply *materia*.

چو آب و گل شود یکباره صافی
رسد از حقّ بدو روح اضافی

When water and clay become at once pure,
From the Truth, an added spirit reaches it.

Shabistarī is now going back to the creation of the human being and refers to when God kneaded man from water and clay, as mentioned in the Quran (Q. 23:12). The Sufis always add that when water and clay came into perfect equilibrium, that is when the creation of the human body was completed and ready to receive the spirit from God.

چو یابد تسویت اجزای ارکان
در او گیرد فروغ عالم جان

When the parts of the four natures (*arkān*) become separated (*taswiyat*) from each other,
The Light of the world of the Spirit begins to shine upon them.

Taswiyah in Arabic and *taswiyat* in Persian are related to the root word *sawā*, which means "to be separated," to "smooth out" or "to make equal or level." The four *arkān*, which constitute the foundations of the world, can refer here to either the four natures (cold, hot, dry, and wet) or the four elements (fire, air, water, and earth). *Arkān* can refer to both. *Taswiyat* means the condition of the body that must exist in order for the Spirit to descend upon it.

شعاع جان سوی تن وقت تعدیل
چو خورشید و زمین آمد به تمثیل

The Ray of the Spirit that comes towards the body when equilibrium is established,
Can be compared to the Sun and the Earth.

"When equilibrium is established" refers to the corporeal equilibrium between the *arkān*, between the elements. God has created the body from water and clay, from the elements in such a way as to reach equilibrium. That is the goal of the whole discussion about equilibrium between the four *arkān*. When that equilibrium was complete, then God breathed the Spirit unto it: *nafakhtu fīhi min rūḥī* "I… breathed into him of My Spirit" (Q. 15:29, 38:72). Even our bodily health is based on maintaining equilibrium. In Persian one refers to *sardī-u garmī* (cold and hot natures) in various foods, an idea fully developed in Islamic medicine. For example, in certain cases one should eat dates because they are hot in nature—or cucumbers because they are cold. Islamic medicine as well as traditional diet are based on this principle of balance as is much else. The seasons are related to the four elements and the four natures and the food you eat in different seasons; the whole of the cuisine, the architecture, everything is related to the four natures and elements. This issue is a profound matter, which has applications in numerous aspects of life in many traditional societies, especially Islamic societies.

Shaykh Maḥmūd Shabistarī continues by giving some examples of the principles cited in the above verses.

Illustration

اگرچه خور به چرخ چارمین است
شعاعش نور تدبیر زمین است

Although the Sun is in the fourth sphere,
The ray of its light governs the Earth.

To reiterate, according to traditional astronomy, the solar system is geocentric. So, we have the Earth in the middle and the first sphere, above it is the Moon, and then there are Venus, Mercury, and then the Sun. The Sun is in the fourth sphere. Then above it are Mars, Jupiter, and Saturn. We thus have three planets below the Sun and three planets above the Sun; the Sun is always in the fourth heaven at the central sphere in the seven planetary heavens of traditional cosmology. Now, this schema is based on observation of the speed of the planets from the Earth visually. The one that goes the fastest is the Moon, circling the earth once every lunar month, which is a bit shorter than the solar month. And then we go from there, step by step, until we get to Saturn, which is the last of the visible planets. There are seven visible planets, and the Sun is the middle one. So, when they say "the fourth heaven" in traditional texts, it is in reference to the orbit of the Sun in the geocentric system. Counting either from above down or from down up, the Sun is in the middle of the seven heavens.

طبیعتهای عنصر نزد خور نیست
کواکب گرم و خشک و سرد و تر نیست

The natures of the elements do not exist in the Sun.
The stars are not hot, dry, cold or wet.

According to Aristotelian cosmology, which Muslims and Christians adopted, we have a sublunar section of the cosmos, the sublunar region being where there is generation and corruption associated with the four elements and natures in their various combinations, from the Moon down to the Earth. And then we have the region above the Moon, which includes all the planets where there is no generation and corruption. This view was rejected and modified by Suhrawardī, and later on all of modern astronomy comes from the rejection of this view. When Galileo observed the moons of Jupiter, which were waxing and waning, he presented what he considered to be the astronomical proof of the falsity of this distinction between the sublunar and the planetary because according to Aristotelian cosmology, the part of the Universe above the Moon is constituted of another substance than the sublunar and does not undergo any change save circular movement. In this verse Shabistarī is simply reiterating the tenets of traditional *mashshā'ī* cosmology according to which the sublunar region is constituted of the four elements: fire, air, water, and earth, with the four natures that were just mentioned in this poem, whereas the supralunar region is beyond such the four elements and nature and their changes.

Most of the Islamic philosophers and astronomers believed that the astronomical heavens were made of ether, the *quintessentia*, the fifth nature, the fifth element, the Latin word from which comes "quintessence" in English, which also means the very "root" or "heart" of something. They believed that all four elements have their root in the fifth element. Most Muslim cosmologists believed that this fifth element was *athīr*, ether, a concept that has survived into modern times. So, the idea of ether did not disappear with Galileo and Newton but continued in Newtonian physics. There is the Michelson–Morley experiment, which was carried out in 1887 to try to show that the speed of light in one direction—and at ninety degrees perpendicular to it—is always the same. So, they concluded that there cannot be ether that would be an obstacle to the speed of light.

Now, however, the idea of ether has come back. Though this issue is not a subject that we need to pursue here, it is worth adding that Wolfgang Smith, who has written some remarkable works on the philosophy of quantum mechanics, says that in fact the stars should not be considered to consist of earthly substances and that traditional cosmologists were right—in other words, to reject the whole of traditional cosmology is mistaken.[1]

This issue is a complicated matter that I cannot discuss in detail here, but I need to mention that what they do in modern astronomy is to apply terrestrial physics to celestial physics. In the history of science, the physics of motion came from the movement of the planets studied by Kepler and applied to the Earth, hence Kepler's three laws of motion. In modern times they speak of astrophysics, but it is really terrestrial physics extrapolated for the rest of the cosmos for all these billions of years, which does not really mean anything metaphysically speaking and is not based on firm scientific proof. All these incredible pictures of galaxies and so forth show that, of course, there are remarkable phenomena going on out there. But what are we seeing? We really do not know because of this extrapolation, and it is an incredible extrapolation. It is like drawing a line from A to B here on Earth and then extrapolating it for the next millions of light years to the heavens, but we have no guarantee that the line is not going to "curve" or do something else far away from where we make our observations.

Coming back to our text, "The natures of the elements do not exist in the Sun" means that because the Sun is not in the sublunar region, it is not constituted of the four natures and the four elements. You might know that the word for element that is used in classical Arabic is *'unṣur*, and we still use this term with the same meaning in modern Arabic and also in Persian. But we also use the word *'unṣur* for many other meanings such as the constituting elements (*'anāṣir*, pl. of *'unṣur*) of this problem are such and such.

عناصر جمله از وی گرم و سرد است
سپید و سرخ و سبز و آل و زرد است

The four elements are all hot or cold because of it,
They are white, red, green, reddish-yellow and yellow.

"The four elements are all hot or cold" because of the Sun, although the Sun itself is not constituted of these elements or these natures. And all the various colors come from the light of the Sun, but the Sun has no color itself.

بود حکمش روان چون شاه عادل
که نه خارج توان گفتن نه داخل

The order of the Sun flows like (that of) a just king,
That one cannot say that it is outside or inside.

Like the rule of a just king that dominates all of society, the rays of the Sun are everywhere and not confined to only the outside or the inside.

چو از تعدیل شد ارکان موافق
ز حسنش نفس گویا گشت عاشق

When the elements (*arkān*) became harmonious through equilibrium,
The rational soul became its lover because of its beauty.

This verse is a beautiful account of a central truth. One can begin by asking how the soul became trapped in the body. There are all kinds of stories about this question. Some talk about the music that it had heard, or the beauty of the body and matters like that, and there are many poetic and philosophical ideas associated with this question. But the question was always asked, "What ensnared the soul?" I was once traveling in the East and heard a person beautifully playing an old instrument that we also have in Iran, especially in Kurdistān, called *dutār*, that is a *tār* (stringed instrument) with only two strings. And he said that one string that I pluck ensnares the soul as a prisoner into the body, and the second frees the soul from the prison of the body. So Shabistarī is referring to this truth of the attraction of the Spirit to the body because of the equilibrium that was created by the four elements and the four natures, which causes the Spirit to fall in love with the body.

The word equilibrium or *ta'dīl* is related to the word *'adl*, which again means justice. *Ta'dīl* means the happy mean, avoiding excesses, equilibrium, being in the middle, and related concepts.

As for "When the elements" that constitute the world "became harmonious through equilibrium, the rational soul became its lover because of its beauty" also implies that our imprisonment in this world begins paradoxically with a form of love, which itself can act as the springboard to the Love of the Source of all love.

نکاح معنوی افتاد در دین
جهان‌را نفس کلّی داد کابین

A spiritual marriage took place in religion,
The world was given, by the Universal Soul, this wedding.

Within religion a spiritual wedding took place between the outward and the inward, the formal and the spiritual, this event taking place through the agency of the Universal Soul (*nafs-i kullī*), not human agency.

از ایشان می‌پدید آمد فصاحت
علوم و نطق و اخلاق و صباحت

From them there appeared eloquence,
The sciences, speech, ethics and perspicacity (*ṣibāḥat*).

From the wedding to which reference is made above various positive features that human beings possess saw the light of day. *Ṣibāḥat* is a rarely used word meaning to be sharp, perspicacious, to see things clearly, and so forth.

ملاحت از جهان بی‌مثالی
درآمد همچو رند لاابالی

Delicateness (*milāḥat*) from the world without comparison,
Came out like an unprincipled rogue (*rind-i lā ubālī*).

Once this wedding takes place, from it issues what is most delicate, appearing suddenly like a careless rogue. *Milāḥat* means literally "delicateness," which we usually associate with a woman. In Arabic, of course, you can use *malīḥ* also for a man, but it is usually used for a woman especially in Persian. *Milāḥat* is a kind of delicate female beauty. A man can also have, for example, *milāḥat* of speech, but one rarely says that a man's face is *malīḥ*. However, for speech or song (*āwāz*), the sound of a voice, one can refer to it being *malīḥ* for both a male and a female speaker or singer. Both men and women can also be said to have a *malīḥ* nature.

In the phrase, "Delicateness from the world without comparison," the incomparable world refers to the world above, the spiritual world. As for the hemistich, "Came out like an unprincipled rogue (*rind-i lā ubālī*)," it needs some explanation. Now, *rind* is a difficult word to translate. It means a kind of freewheeling clever person and also an unscrupulous person or something like that. It can thus be translated as rogue, but rogue is very negative in English, whereas in Persian *rind* also has its positive meaning. It must be understood that in fact some Sufis are called *rind*, which not only means being indifferent to external norms but also includes cleverness. In everyday Persian, a *rind* is someone who is clever and fools people. But in Sufism it usually means someone who is clever enough to love the Divine Reality and is not bound by externals. This is the meaning of *rind* used by Ḥāfiẓ, who employs this word in its mystical sense a great deal. A *rind* might be compared to a man who says *lā ilāha* in a loud voice and utters *illa'Llāh* silently.

به شهرستان نیکوئی علم زد
همه ترتیب عالمرا به هم زد

He hoisted the flag in the province of goodness;
He [thus] turned upside down the order of the world.

The spiritual person lives according to the principles of goodness and virtue, and so his very existence transforms worldly life and uproots it.

گهی بر رخش حسن او سوار است
گهی با نطق تیغ آبدار است

Sometimes, his beauty is riding [the horse] *Rakhsh,*
Sometimes, with speech he is a cutting sword.

Rakhsh is the name of a mythical horse in Persian literature. Here, it means his *ḥusn*, that is, virtue and beauty mounted on this mythical steed. Yet, he also uses trenchant words when it comes to the expression of the truth like Shabistarī himself in this book.

چو در شخص است خوانندش ملاحت
چو در نطق است گویندش فصاحت

When [this quality] appears in a person, it is called delicateness.
When it appears in speech, it is called eloquence (*faṣāḥat*).

This quality is called delicateness when it is manifested in a person, and it is the same quality, called "eloquence," when it appears in human speech.

ولی و شاه و درویش و توانگر
همه در تحت حکم او مسخّر

The saint and the king and the darvish and the rich person,
All are dominated under his order.

All orders of human beings—from a king to a mystic to a rich merchant—become dominated by the person who has spiritual realization, as one sees in a living Sufi order. In speaking of such a person, Shabistarī is really referring to the realized person, to the Universal Man, and to one who has realized the Adamic state.

درون حسن روی نیکوان چیست؟
نه آن حسن است تنها گویی آن چیست؟

What is the inner reality of the beauty of the face of good people?
It is not that goodness alone. Tell me, what is it?

The inner beauty of the realized person is not only external. So, Shabistarī asks, what is it then?

جز از حقّ می‌نیاید دلربائی
که شرکت نیست کس‌را در خدائی

The stealing of hearts (*dilrubā'ī*) doth not come but from the Truth,
For no one can share in [God's] Divinity.

This is indeed a remarkable answer as it refers particularly to a feminine quality. *Dilrubā* is also the name given to women in many Islamic languages, and it means the "stealer of hearts." It is a beautiful Persian name also used in Pakistan and India, and is, furthermore, popular in Turkey. *Rubūdan* in Persian means "to steal" and *dil* means "heart." *Dilrubā* is someone who is so beautiful that she steals your heart.

Only the Divine Truth can steal the heart of the spiritual person, the heart that is the seat of Divine Presence in us. No one else should steal our heart. That is why Shabistarī is saying, "For no one can share in [God's] Divinity."

کجا شهوت دل مردم رباید؟
که حقّ گه گه ز باطل می‌نماید

From where is it that passion steals the hearts of people?
For sometimes the Truth manifests Itself in falsehood.

This is a subtle point related to the Hindu concept of *māyā*, or "cosmic play" or "illusion." Sometimes we are fooled because the Truth, the Beauty of God, manifests Itself in what is not God or from God, but in what, if viewed only outwardly, appears as falsehood.

مؤثّر حقّ شناس اندر همه جای
ز حدّ خویشتن بیرون منه پای

[Know] the Truth as being effective everywhere;
Never set foot beyond thy limit.

"Never set foot beyond thy limit" means one should know one's own limits and never try to be more than one is. This is the opposite of the person who has *'aql-i fuḍūlī*, the intrusive mind, the type of mind that is always putting itself everywhere without knowing where it is going and without realizing its own limits.

حقّ اندر کسوت حقّ دین حقّ دان
حقّ اندر باطل آمد کار شیطان

Know the Truth in the dress of the Truth as the religion of the Truth.
To present the Truth in falsehood is the work of Satan.

True religion (*dīn-i Ḥaqq*) presents "the Truth in the dress of the Truth." This hemistich must not be confused with the earlier verse, "For sometimes the Truth manifests Itself in falsehood." I do not think there is a contradiction here. It is a question of manifestations of *wujūd. Wujūd* comes only from God; so, in anything that has existence, there is some element of truth, reality, and goodness that is present. However, sometimes evil prevails and here in this verse, Shabistarī refers directly to Satan, who subverts truth into falsehood and thereby ensnares human beings.

Question [11]

چه جزو است آنکه او از کلّ فزون است؟
طریق جستن آن جزو چون است؟

What particular (*juzw*) is there that is greater than the universal (*kull*)?
What is the path for finding this particular?

This is an enigmatic question that needs some explanation. I want to distinguish here between two terms that are very important in Sufism as well as in both Islamic and Western philosophy, and that is the technical terms for "universal" and "particular," *kull* and *juz'*. Usually in Arabic universal is *kullī*, and *kull* means "totality," but sometimes in poetry *kull* can mean also "universal" as well as "totality." The same may be said *mutatis mutandis* of *juz'* and *juz'ī*. Now, what is the philosophical definition of these terms? Any concept that can pertain to many particulars is universal. A concept that can pertain to only one particular is particular. So, if you say "tree," that is a universal concept because it pertains to more than one object out there called "tree." But if you say, for example, "my cousin Sulaymān," you use the term to refer to one particular person, Sulaymān; so, it is called *juz'ī*, or *ism-i juz'ī* in Persian, particular name. Also, in the realm of mathematics the number two is particular but even number is universal.

Let us start with the question, "What particular is there that is greater than the universal?" The question is significant because in our everyday life it seems to often be the other way around, if *kull* be understood as "total" and *juz'* as "part." How then can a part of a thing be greater than the whole?

It is necessary to explain a subtle metaphysical point here, to which Shabistarī is in fact alluding. Is God universal or particular? This is a very important metaphysical and philosophical question. From one point of view, God is the most universal reality; we say "Universal Being" in metaphysics in referring to Him, Universal with a capital U, and the phrase means that the Divinity, the Reality is the Source of everything, that contains the reality of everything, and that *is* ultimately the reality of everything. But if you just say, "O my God!" or "O God, help me!" in that sense, God is a particular Person Whom you are addressing. This is a very important theological, religious, mystical, and metaphysical issue discussed extensively in theological and philosophical writings of various traditions. And in nearly every religion, taken in its totality, God is seen as both universal in the metaphysical sense and particular. In theological terms, you might say that God is both a Person and beyond personhood. In Christian theology, you have the terms *ousia* in Greek and *esse* in Latin. *Ousia* is used for God primarily to refer to the Divine Essence (*al-Dhāt*) above and beyond Divine Attributes (*al-asmā' wa'l-ṣifāt*).

Now, the Divine Essence in metaphysics is not a person. One of the major issues of debate in Christianity, between the Catholics and the Orthodox and other schools in the East, concerns this very question. What is the relation between God as the three Persons and the Divine Essence? *Ab*, *Ibn*, and *Rūḥ al-quddus*, Father, Son, and the Holy Ghost, being Persons. God, as the Father is a Person, God as the Son is a Person. But is God in His totality, that is, including the Godhead only a Person? If you answer affirmatively, you have limited the Godhead metaphysically speaking. So, this debate went on in Christianity for centuries on end. When Meister Eckhart, for example, who was Catholic, spoke about *Gottheit*, the Godhead; he said that It is beyond personhood. Ordinary Catholic theology does not accept that view. Formal Catholic theology believes that Father, Son and Holy Ghost are all God, and the Divine Essence does not have any reality outside of these *hypostases*. From the Islamic point of view, in a sense, however, this Christian manner of understanding the issue "relativizes" the Divine Reality to the level of the Trinity, whereas Catholics think that we do not understand that the Trinity is the inner reality of God. I do not want to get into issues of comparative Christian and Islamic theology here; but I want you to learn the very important concepts of universal and particular, religiously, philosophically, and metaphysically, even in the case of God.

Now, Shabistarī is asked a very strange question. Usually if you say "tree" and you have this one tree, obviously this object is one instance of the universal tree. But the question here asks, "What is it that is the reverse?"; that is, what particular is there that is greater than the universal? "What part is greater than the whole?" you might say. And how can one seek it? This means that the one asking is not concerned with just a tree. Rather, that person is concerned with a philosophical, metaphysical understanding of this issue that pertains above all to God.

Answer

وجود آن جزو دان کز کلّ فزون است
که موجود است کلّ وین باژگون است

Consider Being to be that particular which is greater than the universal,
For the universal exists but in an inverted manner.

This verse is one of the most difficult in the *Gulshan-i rāz*. It seems to mean the particular in the case of God exists universally while the universal is manifested in particular things. Since God is God, His Particularity is His Universality and His Universality His Particularity, while the existence of ordinary universals is limited, to be found only in their manifestation in the particular.

بود موجودرا کثرت برونی
که از وحدت ندارد جز درونی

The existent is in the world of multiplicity (*kithrat*) outwardly,
For it does not possess unity except inwardly.

If there are ten different trees outwardly, we have *kithrat* or multiplicity, but the inward is the one single reality of the tree, in contrast to the Particularity and Universality of God, Who is Universal and Particular at the same time.

وجود کلّ ز کثرت گشت ظاهر
که او در وحدت جزو است سائر

The being of the Universal became manifested through multiplicity,
For it runs through the unity of the particular.

This verse again is an enigmatic one. The first hemistich means that if a world out there did not exist, the Universal Reality would not itself become manifest. There would just be the universal tree in itself as archetype or "idea" in the Platonic sense, but there would be no material garden with trees in it. The universal would not have a *ẓāhir* (an outward aspect); it would not manifest itself outwardly. What exists out there in the world that surrounds us is the manifestation of the universal in the realm of multiplicity. As for the second hemistich, it means that the universal flows within or is within the unity that we find in everything and provides for each being its unity.

We have this tree here and another tree out there. Within both *wujūd-i kull*, the Universal Being manifests Itself and that is why each tree possesses unity and each tree is a tree.

چو کلّ از روی ظاهر هست بسیار
بود از جزو خود کمتر به مقدار

Since the Universal became outwardly many,
It is less in quantity than its own particular.

This verse might at first seem to be illogical. However, what it means is that outwardly (and only outwardly) the universal seems to be many realities, although it is only one reality, and so it is less in quantity than all the realities in which it is manifested. Each particular *ḥaṣṣah* or each particular mode of being, like this tree or that tree, is an existent, which also has a quiddity or *māhiyyat* and all the qualities that pertain to that quiddity as a tree. Whereas *wujūd-i kull*, when it is manifested in multiplicity, in a sense flows through all the members of that set or species. So, in a sense, it is less. We do not see the *wujūd-i kull* here and there, but we see this tree and that tree as particular existents. So, the universal is not less metaphysically but less only in the quantitative and outward sense.

نه آخر واجب آمد جزو هستی
که هستی کرده اورا زیردستی

It is not to say that in the end the Necessary Being came as part of existence,
And existence has made it subservient.

No, one should avoid such a blatant error. The source of all existents is the Necessary Being.

ندارد کلّ وجودی در حقیقت
که او چون عارضی شد بر حقیقت

The Universal does not possess being, in [external] truth,
For it is like an accident of the truth.

The universal as a mental concept, philosophically speaking, or as a logical concept (not as Platonic Idea) does not possess being; in truth, it is objective reality that does. The reality of the universal is mental. You do not have a universal dog walking around the streets. Any time you see a dog, you see a particular dog manifesting the reality of the universal dog but not that universal itself, although the particular dog manifests its universal archetype.

In the hemistich, "For it is like an accident of the truth (*ḥaqīqat*)," *ḥaqīqat* refers to the reality of a thing. When you consider the reality of things externally, the universal appears as an accident. There was a great debate that took place between Suhrawardī and Ibn Sīnā on this issue, regarding whether *wujūd* is an accident or not. This is also an issue regarding which Mullā Ṣadrā criticizes Ibn Sīnā, but I shall not get into this issue now because it is a major question that concerns ontology and cannot be treated briefly. I shall only add that if we examine our ordinary experience, we say "the tree is green," "the sky is blue." We think that there is a tree, and then existence is added to it. So, existence seems to have been an accident added to the quiddity of the tree, which has a reality of its own. Of course, as you know, Mullā Ṣadrā opposes this view completely. He says that it is *māhiyyah*, the quiddity, that is really an accident; so, when you say "the tree exists" it means the *wujūd* that alone is real appears in the limited form of the tree. Reality belongs to *wujūd* and not *māhiyyah*, a view that is known as *aṣālat al-wujūd* or principiality of being in later Islamic philosophy.

وجود کلّ کثیر واحد آمد
کثیر از روی کثرت می‌نماید

The being of the Universal came as the multiplicity of the one.
The many appears as such when there is multiplicity.

"The being of the Universal appears in the multiplicity of the one" means that we can only perceive the universal in the world of multiplicity within each particular that manifests that universal but not the universal in itself, although the universal is a single reality manifesting itself in many particulars. We have to remember again that this statement does not negate the possibility of the vision of the archetypal world through intellection and spiritual realization. In our ordinary experience, however, we do not see the universal horse, for example, but we see this horse or that horse. The one universal horse manifests itself in the world of manyness, appearing as multiplicity while remaining one.

عرض شد هستیی کان اجتماعی است
عرض سوی عدم بالذات ساعی است

The accident (*'araḍ*) became the existence that is multitudinous.
In its essence accident rushes to nonexistence.

As mentioned previously, in philosophy we distinguish between accident and substance, from Aristotle's categories, which included substance (*jawhar*) and nine accidents (*a'rāḍ*) such as quality, quantity, action, reception, and so forth. As for, "The accidents gain existence that is multitudinous," consider the accident of whiteness. We never see whiteness walking in the street. You have a white wall, or a white door. You have to have something, a substance, that is white. It is, therefore, obvious that you cannot have an *'araḍ* existing on its own without a substance it pertains to. You can have a tall man or a tall tree, but you cannot have "tallness" out there in the street. You cannot have red, as a quality, which is one of the nine accidents, on its own. You have a red apple, a red flag—a red this, a red that. So, an accident always has to have a substance in order to exist or to be experienced. It has to be in something. By itself the accident "rushes to non-existence," that is, it does not exist, and you cannot have an accident that exists by itself. Whether you study Western philosophy or Eastern philosophy, this truth is a very important point to realize.

به هر جزوی ز کلّ کان نیست گردد
کلّ اندر دم ز امکان نیست گردد

For every particular of the universal that ceases to exist,
At that very moment, the universal disappears from contingency.

The moment the particular of a universal disappears, the universal ceases to exist in the world of contingency or possibility because it ceases to be manifested.

جهان کلّ است و در هر طرفة العین
عدم گردد و لا یبقی زمانین

The world is total, and [yet] with the blinking of an eye (*ṭurfat al-'ayn*),
It becomes non-existent, and does not endure for two moments.

The first hemistich begins with the idea of the totality of the world but quickly turns to its non-existence. This verse is also related to the idea of the re-creation of the world at very moment (*tajdīd al-khalq fī kulli 'l-ānāt*), which I discussed earlier. The blinking of an eye (*ṭurfat al-'ayn*) is a common Arabic expression that indicates a very short moment and has become proverbial for expressing the idea of in a moment or suddenly.

The enigma of the verse "With the blinking of an eye, it becomes non-existent, and does not endure for two moments" is evident. As we discussed before, our ordinary experience of the world is that it has a continuity that our consciousness experiences with the flow of the world about us in time. We feel that there is a continuity of time, of the duration of the existence of the world around us, whereas the Sufis claim that God creates and re-creates the world at every instant. He creates and then withdraws the world unto Himself and then re-creates it. This process is instantaneous; therefore, we are not able to experience it. In the same way if you have a light that goes on and off quickly and repeatedly, if it goes fast enough, you do not know it is going on and off. Or, if you take a burning coal and spin it very fast, as we do in Iran when preparing coal for the *shīshah* (*qalyān*) or the samovar to make tea for instance, you will only see one light. When the burning coal is whirled around fast enough, you just see a circle of light, whereas actually it is particular moments of our perception of light that become continuous. In the same way we have an experience of the continuity of the world and of time, while the Sufis believe that there is the destruction and re-creation of it at every moment. The following verse refers directly to this doctrine.

دگر باره شود پیدا جهانی
به هر لحظه زمین و آسمانی

Once again there appears a world,
In every moment, an Earth and a Sky.

Earth and sky are the only realities mentioned, but here they imply the whole world, not only the sky and earth but also everything in between. The central practice of Sufism is *dhikr*. Why is it that we have to invoke the *dhikr* more than once? It is precisely because of the rejuvenation of ourselves at every moment that results in our experiencing time as a continuous flow. We are not the same person that we were a minute ago, but we think that we are by virtue of God remanifesting our reality in this world. God "absorbs us" and brings us back. If we could remember God with the same rapidity as God's re-creation of us, we would be saints. To remember God all the time requires remembering Him in the instantaneous now.

In ordinary life if we work and put $10,000 in the bank, we do not repeat it again tomorrow. We have money in the bank and so now can do something else. But the *dhikr* has to do with this rejuvenation or re-creation of our being by God at every instant, and it is a lifetime affair. When Sa'dī at the beginning of the *Gulistān* (*The Rose Garden*) says, *har nafasī . . . mumidd-i ḥayāt ast*, that is, "Each breath . . . allows life to continue" and therefore requires thankfulness to God, he is alluding to the *dhikr*.[1] There would be no other way we can thank God at every moment except by our breathing becoming combined with remembrance so that it becomes identified with His Name. So, there is also an esoteric meaning in this famous saying to which I wanted to allude.

به هر ساعت جوان کهنه پیر است
به هر دم اندر او حشر و نشیر است

Every hour that which is young becomes old,
At every moment there is in it a resurrection (*ḥashr-u nashīr*).

Yawm al-ḥashr means the Day of Resurrection, and *nashīr* means rebirth in Arabic, but it also means resurrection.

در او چیزی دو ساعت می‌نپاید
در آن لحظه که می‌میرد بزاید

In it nothing endures for two hours.
At the very moment that it dies, it gives birth.

"In it" means in God's creation, which is not static but in its existential reality dynamic, being re-existentiated constantly. Here, Shabistarī is repeating the same idea mentioned in the above verses.

ولیکن طامّة الکبری نه این است
که این یوم عمل وآن یوم دین است

However, the *ṭāmmat al-kubrā* (the Great Calamity) is not this.
For today is the day of action and that day is the day of religion.

Shabistarī wants to warn us to avoid confusion and reminds us not to confuse this constant regeneration of creation with the eschatological event, *al-ṭāmmat al-kubrā*, the Great Calamity (Q. 79:34), which refers actually to the resurrection of bodies and judgment before God in the life after death on "the day of religion." "Today" means our life in this world, which is a life filled with action, while "that day" is the day in which we shall receive retribution for our action in accordance with the principles of religion.

از آن تا این بسی فرق است زنهار
به نادانی مکن خودرا گرفتار

There is a very big difference between that and this, beware.
Through ignorance do not entangle thyself.

Do not think that since the world is renewed at every moment there is no such thing as judgment, Paradise, and Hell, or there is no such thing as facing the consequences of our actions. Do not get these two truths mixed up with each other.

نظر بگشای در تفصیل و اجمال
نگر در ساعت و روز و مه و سال

Open thy eyes to both the analyzed (*tafṣīl*) and the synthesized (*ijmāl*).
Take a look at the hour, the day, the month and the year.

Tafṣīl means to analyze something, to bring out the details. *Ijmāl* means the whole, the synthesis or summary. They are often juxtaposed in Arabic and Persian. "Take a look at the hour, the day, the month and the year" means learning from the passage of time, from every moment of life.

همه اقوال وافعال مدخّر
هویدا گردد اندر روز محشر

All sayings and action that have been accrued,
Become manifest on the Day of Resurrection.

The first stanza refers to all that had been performed before in this world by us; they all "become manifest on the Day of Resurrection," on *yawm al-qiyāmah*, the day of the revealing of all our actions, thoughts, and words in this world. All that is inside us here will become externalized there in the other world.

همه پیدا شود آنجا ضمائر
فرو خوان آیهٔ «تبلی السرائر»

All that is within human souls (*ḍamā'ir*) becomes revealed there.
Go and read the verse of "the Day when secrets are tested" (*tublā'l-sarā'ir*).

Here, Shabistarī is again speaking about the Day of Resurrection. *Ḍamīr* (pl. *ḍamā'ir*) means "inner being." The inner being of all things will become manifest on the Day of Judgment. Then he suggests that we go and read the Quranic verse, *tublā'l-sarā'ir* (Q. 86:9), in which the Quran says, "On the Day when secrets are tested," the day when everything within us becomes manifested externally and tested.

Illustration

اگر خواهی که این معنی بدانی
ترا هم هست مرگ و زندگانی

If thou wantest to know the [inner] meaning of this,
Thou hast both death and life.

To know the truth mentioned above we must be aware that we experience both death and life. External life is attained with th going through the experience of death.

ز هرچه از جهان از زیر و بالاست
مثالش در تن و جان تو پیداست

From whatever exists in this world from below and above,
A sample (*mithāl*) of it is found in thy body and soul.

Mithāl has many meanings, but here it can be said to mean "sample." Now, this is another way of speaking about the microcosm-macrocosm correspondence. In the human being all elements of the macrocosm are, in fact, present in some way, and this verse is another way of stating this truth.

جهان چون توست یک شخص معیّن
تو اورا گشته چون جان او تورا تن

The Universe like thee is a distinct person (*shakhṣ-i mu'ayyan*);
Thou art for it like soul and it thy body.

This verse refers to a very important truth that is now totally rejected by modern science. Modern man has lost the idea that the cosmos is a "person." Modern science destroyed that way of looking at things completely. All kinds of pejorative terms are used for people who believe in this doctrine, and they are called "animists" or "totem worshippers," etc. But from the spiritual point of view, the cosmos itself *is* a person, *al-insān al-kabīr* (the great man) in Islamic thought. It has consciousness, and there are psychic and spiritual elements as well as physical ones in it just as there are in us. *Shakhṣ* here means person in the philosophical sense. *Shakhṣ-i mu'ayyan* means a distinct or particular person.

سه گونه نوع انسان‌را ممات است
یکی هر لحظه آن بر حسب ذات است

There are three kinds of death for human beings,
One every moment, according to the essence of man.

This kind of death is what was mentioned above. We die and are resurrected at every moment by God, as is the cosmos.

دویم زآنها ممات اختیاری است
سیم مردن مراورا اضطراری است

The second among them is "willed-death" (*mamāt-i ikhtiyārī*),
The third kind of death is what is necessary (*iḍṭirārī*) death.

The second kind of death is what the Sufis call "willed-death," *mawt-i ikhtiyārī*. This well-known "mystical death" means the death of one's carnal soul (*al-nafs al-ammārah*). That is what Sufis try to do when they meditate and invoke the Divine Name saying *Allāh*, *Allāh*, *Allāh* or another Divine Name. They are trying, while biologically alive, to die to the ordinary *nafs* and reach the higher levels of the soul.

The third kind of death is *mawt-i iḍṭirārī* (necessary death). This is when the Angel of Deal (*Malak al-Mawt*) comes to take the soul and someone dies in the ordinary sense of death. In English when you indicate "death" as referring to an individual, it is only usually in reference to the third kind, although the second meaning is also prevalent in Christian spirituality.

So, there are then three kinds of death: One is *iḍṭirārī*, which you cannot do anything about: it is necessary death that God has willed. The question of suicide is another matter I cannot deal with here. Number two is willed or spiritual death, *mawt-i ikhtiyārī*, which is central in Sufism and means to surrender one's will completely to God and die to the world. The canonical origin of this kind of death in Islam is the famous *ḥadīth* of the Prophet—*'alayhi 'l-ṣalātu wa 'l-salām*—*mūtū qabla an tamūtū* . . ." "Die before you die so that when the time of death comes thou shalt not die." And the first one has to do with this rejuvenation of creation at every moment, the metaphysical idea of absorption back into the Origin of creation and its remanifestation.

چو مرگ و زندگی باشد مقابل
سه نوع آمد حیاتش در سه منزل

Since death and life face each other (*muqābil*),
There are three kinds of one's life in three stages.

"Since death and life face each other (*muqābil*)" means that they are opposites of each other, or confront and also complement each other. Shabistarī adds that since there are three forms of death, likewise there are three stages (*manzil*) of life. The word *manzil* of course means literally "the place of descent." It is the *ism maḥall*, the place noun, for the verb *nazala*, to descend, and it was used also for the place where caravans would settle in the evening on their journey. And then of course it came to mean a home where you could seek refuge and spend the night. In Persian and Arabic you say, "Come to our *manzil*," which means, "Come to our home." But originally it meant *maḥall al-nuzūl*, the "place of descent." So, he is using that term instead of such terms as *maqām* (station), and here we have translated it as "stage."

جهان‌را نیست مرگ اختیاری
که آن‌را در همه عالم تو داری

The Universe does not have [power of] willed death.
Thou art the only one in the whole Universe who possesses it.

This is one of the most important points Shabistarī makes in this section. Let me put this in another language. None of the creatures of the world can reach *fanā'* (annihilation) in the spiritual sense except man. That is what distinguishes us from everything else. Everything that exists in the Universe has done so with all kinds of qualities and characteristics, whether it likes it or not. But we as human beings can even will not to exist, spiritually speaking. There is a Sufi prayer in Persian, *khudāyā ni'mat-i 'adam-i hastī 'aṭā farmā*, "O God, give us the blessing of nonexistence."

ولی هر لحظه می‌گردد مبدّل
در آخر هم شود مانند اوّل

But every moment it is transformed.
At the end it also becomes as it was in the beginning.

"It" in the first stanza refers to the cosmos. So, the first kind of change, the rejuvenation at every moment, is also undergone by the cosmos. It is not only us. And through this kind of change it becomes what it was before from the point of view of our perception of it, and therefore we experience a continuity in the world about us, although it is annihilated and re-created at every moment.

هر آنچه گردد اندر حشر پیدا
ز تو در نزع می‌گردد هویدا

Whatever will become manifest on the Day of Resurrection,
Becomes manifested in thee when thou hast the agony of death.

In the Sufi context, *naz'*, translated here as "the agony of death," means going beyond yourself and being in your inner spiritual reality. So, the agony of death should be understood in its spiritual sense. *Naz'* can also refer to a certain psychological disease, but here it means a kind of state that manifests what is within us. Having said that, Shabistarī now gives an example of the microcosm-macrocosm correspondence and says:

تن تو چون زمین سر آسمان است
حواست انجم و خورشید جان است

Thy body is like the earth, thy head [like] the sky;
Thy five senses are the stars, and the Sun thy soul.

These verses continue the microcosm-macrocosm comparison.

چو کوه است استخوان‌هائی که سخت است
نباتت موی و اطرافت درخت است

Thy bones, which are hard, are like mountains;
Thy hair is the plant and that which is around thee trees.

The mountain is hard like bones and yet vegetation grows on it, just as our bones are covered with flesh from which grows hair similar to vegetation on a mountain.

تنت در وقت مردن از ندامت
بلرزد چون زمین روز قیامت

Thy body, at the moment of death because of regret (*nidāmat*)
Shakes like the Earth on the Day of Resurrection.

This is in reference to the fact that usually when one dies, one's body shakes as the *Malak al-Mawt*, the Angel of Death, takes the soul away. This event must also be understood in its symbolic and esoteric sense. And now he turns to what happens when one dies.

دماغ آشفته و جان تیره گردد
حواست هم چو انجم خیره گردد

The mind (*damāgh*) becomes confused and the soul becomes darkened,
Thy senses, like the stars, become dazzled (*khīrah gardad*).

Damāgh usually means "the brain" but by extension also "the mind." This word also means "nose" in Persian. It might appear strange that in Persian two different organs of the body should have the same name. Moreover, *damāgh* also can indirectly mean "the power of thinking," since thinking is associated with the activity of the brain. So, while this verse literally says that your brain becomes mixed up and confused, it is, of course, referring to your mind. Thy senses, like the stars, become dazzled (*khīrah gardad*), meaning that they no longer function in the ordinary sense and like the stars that stand still cannot experience life that changes and is in a state of becoming.

مسامت گردد از خو هم چو دریا
چو در وی غرقه گشته بی سر و پا

The pores of thy body, from habit (*khū*) become like a sea,
In which thou hast drowned from head to foot (*bī sar-u pā*).

In the first hemistich Shabistarī uses the word *khū*, which usually means "nature" or "habit." *Bī sar-u pā* literally means without head and foot, but here it implies the idea of "completely" or "totally."

شود از جان‌کنش ای مرد مسکین
ز سستی استخوان‌ها پشم رنگین

O poor man, through the soul leaving the body,
The bones become weakened like colored wool.

That verse means that the bones that were hard during life suddenly become completely weakened and lose their solidity.

به هم پیچیده گردد ساق با ساق
همه جفتی شود از جفت خود طاق

Shank (*sāq*) becomes intertwined with shank;
Everything that was coupled (*juft*) becomes uncoupled from its complement.

The *sāq* of a person refers to his or her shank in the middle of the leg. The phrase *al-sāq bi'l-sāq* is mentioned in the Quran, 75:29. The second hemistich points to the disconnection of the parts of the body at death.

چو روح از تن به کلّیت جدا شد
زمینت «قاع صفصف لاتری» شد

Once the soul has left thy body,
[The body that remains is like] "a barren ground in which one does not see
anything" (*qā'-i ṣafṣaf la tarā*).

This verse refers to the Quranic verses, "They ask thee about the mountains. Say, 'My Lord shall scatter them as ashes. And He will leave it a barren plain. You will see no crookedness or curvature therein'" (Q. 20:105–7).

بدین منوال باشد حال عالم
که تو در خویش می‌بینی در آن دم

Such is the condition of the world,
That thou thyself seeth at that moment.

"That moment" refers to the time of one's death. As for the first hemistich, it refers to the end of the world that results in its condition being like that of human beings at the moment of death.

بقا حقّ‌راست باقی جمله فانی است
بیانش جمله در «سبع المثانی» است

Subsistence (*baqā*) belongs to the Truth. Everything else perisheth (*fānī*).
The explanation of it all is in "the Seven Oft-Repeated Verses" (*sab' al-mathānī*).

The first hemistich refers to the Quranic verses, *kullu man 'alayhā fān, wa yabqā wajhu Rabbika dhū'l-jalāli wa'l-ikrām*, "All that is upon it passes away. And there remains the Face of thy Lord, Possessed of Majesty and Bounty" (Q. 55:26–27).

The phrase "The Seven Oft-Repeated Verses" (*sab' al-mathānī*) usually is considered to refer to the seven verses of *Sūrat al-Fātiḥah*. It is worthwhile to consider for a moment why this truth is explained in "the Seven Oft-Repeated Verses." If you consider the seven verses of the *Fātiḥah* you can see that the first three are about God. The last three are about man. And the middle one concerns man's relation with God. Many works have been written just on this one *sūrah*. For example Ṣadr al-Dīn Qūnawī has a four-hundred-page book on the commentary upon the *Sūrat al-Fātiḥah*,[2] and many others have also written lengthy commentaries on it. There is a sacred symbolism in the number seven, which also appears in the musical scale. So, it also has a symbolic musical aspect to it. To understand the reference to *al-Fātiḥah* in this context requires remembering the esoteric meaning of it, which points to the fact that reality belongs to God alone. And being led upon the Straight Path means the realization of this truth, and therefore awareness of our own "nothingness" before the Absolute Reality.

به «کلّ من علیها فان» بیان کرد
«لفی خلق جدید» هم عیان کرد

He explained it in, "All that is upon it passes away." (Q. 55:26)
He made manifest, "You shall be in a new creation?" (Q. 34:7, 13:5)

All things perish save the Face of God, but also God, being eternally the Creator, brings about a new creation.

بود ایجاد و اعدام دو عالم
چو خلق و بعث نفس ابن آدم

The creation and the destruction of the two worlds is,
Like the creation and the resurrection (*ba'th*) of the soul of the descendants of Adam. (*banī Ādam*)

Ba'th is an Arabic word, which has become famous these days because of the Ba'th Party in Iraq and Syria, but it is originally a Quranic term and means "resurrection" and also means being "chosen as a prophet." The Prophet was *mab'ūth*, which is the passive form of *ba'th*, and the day in the lunar Islamic calendar in which the Prophet was chosen as a prophet is called *'īd al-mab'ath* and is celebrated annually in much of the Islamic world. The word *ba'th* in Arabic also means to cause something to occur. So, it is a very rich root. But here, the word *ba'th* is used in the sense of resurrection.

همیشه خلق در خلق جدید است
و گرچه مدّت عمرش مدید است

Creation is always in a new creation,
Although the duration of its life is long.

Again, there is a spiritual lesson that can be drawn from this doctrine of the renewal of creation, which we discussed in a general sense already. Every morning you get up is a new day of God and of your soul; also during the day, every moment is one of rejuvenation. Practically speaking, suppose you received a bad letter yesterday from your friend, your father, or your employer that made you angry or unhappy. Learn not to drag the negative effect along. That event belonged to that particular moment, which has now passed. The next moment is a new one, and in that moment, something good may happen. Have *tawakkul* (trust in God) and pray for the best. The tendency of the soul is to continue to drag its pains along with it, because it does not realize that every moment is a new moment in which God re-creates and renews the world. Maybe the next moment something wonderful will happen. God's Help, God's Succor, is always there. If you have a problem, of course, it is natural that you become anxious or sad, but do not drag that state of your soul along. The next moment belongs to God. We think that we are sitting here controlling the next moments and days of our lives, but we could all be dead in the next fifteen minutes, *astaghfiru'Llāh*.[3] So, this idea that every moment belongs to God is very important spiritually. In addition to its metaphysical significance, its practical aspect is extremely significant.

همیشه فیض و فضل حقّ تعالی
بود از شأن خود اندر تجلّی

Always the Emanation (*fayḍ*) and Bounty (*faḍl*) of the Transcendent Truth,
Is manifesting (*tajallī*) Itself through Its State (*sha'n*).

The Emanation (*fayḍ*) and Bounty (*faḍl*) of God never cease and continue to caste their theophanies in each particular *sha'n* or state. The Quran says *kulla yawmin huwa fī sha'n*, "Every day He is upon a task" (Q. 55:29). At every moment God Himself manifests His Names and Qualities as a different *sha'n*. God might have been angry with us yesterday, and He might be pleased with us and kind to us today. He might forgive us in a way that we could not imagine. This is a very important point to remember in every moment of life. We have a saying in Persian *bārī bi-har jihat* (performing something incompletely), which usually refers to careless people, but spiritually it has a positive meaning in the sense of always relying on God and not calculating everything as if one were in a bank or a factory—leave matters open to God, carrying with patience and gratitude the weight He has put on our shoulders and do not be lackadaisical. One should be *bārī bi har jihat* in the sense of being open always to Divine Grace and His Command, but not in the ordinary sense of the term.

از آن جانب بود ایجاد و تکمیل
وز این جانب شود هر لحظه تبدیل

From that side there is existentiation and perfection;
From this side, transformation at every moment.

What comes from the side of God is continuous creation and re-creation and all the perfection that characterizes His creation, but from the human side there is continuous renewal and transformation existentially even if we are unaware of it. In the philosophical sense, the world is dynamic and yet also reflects in its reality the immutable archetypes like the abiding reflection of the Moon in a running stream.

ولیکن چون گذشت این طور دنیا
بقای کلّ بود در دار عقبی

When, however, the state of the world passeth,
The subsistence of the universal is in the World to Come (*dār-i 'uqbā*).

In Persian in everyday language, and also in Arabic, *ṭawr*—translated here as "state"—means "kind" or "way," but *ṭawr* in Islamic philosophy, *'irfān*, and Sufism means also "state of being" or a particular level of manifestation of God's Names and Qualities. Many Arabs and Persians who use the word *ṭawr* all the time are not aware of its philosophical meaning. Here, when Shabistarī mentions *ṭawr-i dunyā*, he means "the state of being of this world," not how the world works. *Dār-i 'uqbā* means the other world, *al-ākhirah*, *dunyā* and *'uqbā* being opposites of each other.

که هر چیزی که بینی بالضرورت
دو عالم دارد از معنی و صورت

For whatever thou seest, of necessity,
Belongs to two worlds, that of meaning (*ma'nā*) and that of form (*ṣūrat*).

Meaning and form in Sufism also signify the internal and the external. *Ma'nā* (meaning) here means "inwardness," the "esoteric," and *ṣūrat* form, the "outward" and the "exoteric." As mentioned previously, *ṣūrat* in Sufi writings is not to be confused with Aristotelian form. In Sufism *ṣūrat*, as used often by Mawlānā and others, concerns outward form, not *morphos* or *forma* that we find in philosophical texts. In philosophical discourse the word form, *ṣūrat* in Persian and *ṣūrah* in Arabic, is juxtaposed to *māddah*, *hylé*, *materia*, and is what gives reality to things. In Sufi parlance, however, its meaning is just the reverse, for what gives reality to things is not the form but the *ma'nā*, the inner meaning. This term is ubiquitous in Persian Sufi literature, and also in Arabic, though perhaps not used as often as in Persian.

وصال اوّلین عین فراق است
مر آن دیگر ز «عند الله باق» است

In the first case, every union is the same as separation.
But the other is from "What is with God (*'inda'Llāh*) always subsists (*bāq*)."

"In the first case," that is, what has to do with the world, "every union is the same as separation." In this world everything united is also combined with the possibility of separation that results from the very nature of the world. The word *bāq*, rarely used in modern Persian, comes from the Arabic word *bāqī*, and is the active noun of the root *b-q-y*. This verse is a reference to the verse of the Quran, "That which is with you comes to an end, but that which is with God subsists" (Q. 16:96).

بقا اسم وجود آمد ولیکن
به جائی کان بود سائر چو ساکن

Subsistence (*baqā*) has been used as a name for Being, and yet,
In a place that is in movement but also stationary.

The soul possesses a permanent aspect and an aspect that is in the state of becoming. This enigmatic reality is a key for understanding the process of spiritual realization. As Frithjof Schuon has said, "Man becomes what he is, and also is what he becomes."[4]

مظاهر چون بود بر وفق ظاهر
در اوّل می‌نماید عین آخر

Since the places of manifestations (*maẓāhir*) are in harmony with the outward reality of things,
In the beginning there is manifested that which comes last.

The first hemistich says that the realities of things are manifested outwardly in harmony with the conditions in which they are manifested. For example, if someone is sitting opposite us, we can only see him or her really because that person's outward countenance is a true reflection of who he or she is. We see in the end the face that was there from the beginning.

هر آنچه هست بالقوّه در این دار
به فعل آید در آن عالم به یک بار

Whatever exists in this world potentially,
Will in the other world become at once actualized.

There is no potentiality in the usual sense of the word of permanence but only actuality. That is why there is no movement in the completely actualized world. To exist motion and change need potentiality, as Aristotle said.

ز تو هر فعل که اوّل گشت صادر
بر آن گردی به باری چند قادر

Whatever action that issued from thee first,
After a few times, thou shalt become powerfull over it.

Through the repetition of an act we become more and more competent in performing it. This general truth applies also to the spiritual practices of the Sufi path.

به عادت حالها با خوی گردد
به مدّت میوه‌ها خوشبوی گردد

Through habit, the states of the soul become habituated (*bā khūy*) [to it].
Through time, fruits gain a sweet smell.

The first hemistich refers to temporary states becoming permanent character traits through repetition, the passage of time spent in spiritual practice ripening the soul that then becomes sweet and fragrant like ripened fruit. When you have an unripe pear on the tree, at the beginning it smells like the rest of the tree, but once it has ripened it produces a sweet fragrance.

از آن آموخت انسان پیشه‌ها را
وز آن ترکیب کرد اندیشه‌ها را

Man learned various professions through it,
And through it he combined his thoughts together.

In fact man has learned various professions by the gaining of good habits modeled upon the maturing of fruits, from the growing of things. Consequently, he is able to combine and integrate his mind, thoughts and inner states.

همه افعال و اقوال مدخّر
هویدا گردد اندر روز محشر

All actions and sayings that have been accrued,
Become manifest on the Day of Resurrection.[5]

This verse is simply the re-assertion of the doctrine that all the actions and words of man in this life become externalized and manifested on the Day of Judgment.

چو عریان گردی از پیراهن تن
شود عیب و هنر یکباره روشن

When thou becomest bare (*'uryān*) from the shirt on the body,
Both [thy] infirmities and virtues (*hunar*) become suddenly clear.

'Uryān means nude both literally and symbolically. When you become nude as a result of removing your clothing from your body, your usually hidden body becomes apparent. Shabistarī is using this image symbolically to point to the fact that once man's outer veil is removed, his inner character is revealed. "Both [thy] infirmities" or weaknesses or imperfections, and thy *hunar*, which usually means art, but really refers to virtues, perfections, positive gifts, good elements, become suddenly clear, that is, once you are out of the prison of the body, your soul and inner nature become manifest.

تنت باشد ولیکن بی‌کدورت
که بنماید از او چون آب صورت

Thy body will remain, but without opacity (*kudūrat*),
Which will be shown like water on the face.

Again, this is a cryptic but important verse that many people might not understand immediately. Thy body will be without *kudūrat*, which here means not without dirt, but rather without a dark veil because it is reflecting directly your inner nature without opacity. Here, without doubt Shabistarī is also referring to *jism-i laṭīf*, the subtle body. This doctrine exists in all traditions, and in the Islamic tradition it was expounded extensively, especially by 'Alā' al-Dawlah Simnānī and the whole Central Asian School of Sufism, including Najm al-Dīn Kubrā and masters like him, who dealt with subtle bodies, and the seven *laṭā'if*. Corbin has written about that subject as far as Simnānī is concerned.[6]

This doctrine is not found in all the schools of Sufism in such detail, but it is nevertheless a very important doctrine. We do not only have a physical body, not even only one subtle body, but we have several subtle bodies. The most extensive treatment of this subject is to be found in Mullā Ṣadrā, who says that we have seven bodies in a hierarchy stretching from the physical body to "the Divine Body." Of course, this doctrine refers to the seven states of being. That is why, even though in a sense it sounds like *kufr*, one could even speak of the Body of God, the Divine Body. This way of looking at things is very different from the form and matter or the body and soul models, where the two are juxtaposed against each other. Here, we have levels of the "body" itself. In the West this idea also existed in certain mystical schools in the Middle Ages and even during the Renaissance. The discussion of the whole issue of the subtle body was popular in some Renaissance writings in Italy as well as in other places in Europe, especially in Germany.

همه پیدا شود آنجا ضمائر
فرو خوان آیهٔ «تبلی السرائر»

All that is within souls (*ḍamā'ir*) becomes manifest.
Go and read the verse of "the Day when secrets are tested." (Q. 86:9)[7]

On the Day of Judgment what is within the souls of man becomes externalized, and they are tested and judged accordingly. There will be no way to hide oneself from the Presence of God.

دگر باره به وفق عالم خاصّ
شود اخلاق تو اجسام و اشخاص

Once again according to the particular world,
Thy ethical characteristics will become bodies and persons.

"Particular world" refers to the next world where one's hidden actions and nature become exposed. It is said traditionally that on the Day of Judgment as we stand before God, all the *jawāriḥ,* the limbs of our body, independent of our will, will testify depending on the condition of each of us, either for or against us, regarding for example what our ears have heard, what our eyes have seen, and so forth. Here, Shabistarī says that the characteristics that we have themselves become *ajsām-u ashkhāṣ* (bodies and persons), that is, there will be in the Hereafter corporealization in the sense of externalization of what is noncorporeal in this world. Let us not forget that the Abrahamic religions emphasize corporeal resurrection, which is against the views of Greek philosophy and also much of postmedieval Western theology and philosophy. This issue has been debated a great deal also in Islamic philosophy. The spiritual significance of the body has been deemphasized in the West for other reasons also, and many have forgotten or neglected the fact that the body participates in the resurrection according to both traditional Catholic and Orthodox eschatological doctrines.

چنان کز قوّت عنصر در اینجا
موالید سه‌گانه گشت پیدا

In the same way that from the power of the four elements (*'unṣur*) here,
The Three Kingdoms appeared.

The three kingdoms, as already mentioned, are the mineral, plant and animal realms, and they all are said to consist of various combinations of the four elements, fire, air, water and earth, the four traditional elements.

همه اخلاق تو در عالم جان
گهی انوار گردد گاه نیران

All of thy ethical character (*akhlāq*) in the world of the soul,
Becomes sometimes lights (*anwār*), sometimes fire (*nayrān*).

Anwār (lights) and *nayrān* (fire) are a reference to the light of Paradise and the fire of Hell that also exist within the human being. The words *nūr* (light) and *nār* (fire) are derived from the same root in Arabic. One could say that the reason for this is that *nār* has *nūr*, and *nūr* does not exist without *nār*. They are in a sense two theological and cosmological opposites of the same reality, although they have different connotations in ordinary language. Cosmologically and metaphysically, however, they are related, and one is often manifested as the opposite of the other. That is why, for example, in Islamic and Christian eschatology these terms represent Heaven and Hell.

For example, Dante sees fire in Hell and light in Heaven. They are both lit; the fire in Hell is also lit, but it has a negative aspect that burns and destroys, whereas light in Heaven illuminates and is the source of knowledge and also ecstasy.

تعیّن مرتفع گردد ز هستی
نماند درنظر بالا و پستی

> Determination (*ta'ayyun*) will be removed from the world of existence,
> There will not remain in view up or down.

Again, Shabistarī is referring here to the other world. *Ta'ayyun* is determination, and in philosophical language the world itself consists of stages of determination of the Divine Reality. Sometimes this world is called *'ālam al-ta'ayyunāt* (the world of determinations) in Arabic. The *ta'ayyun* of something is like taking water and putting it in the refrigerator to make ice so that it becomes different cubes. The ice is a *ta'ayyun* of water in a sense, speaking philosophically.

نماند مرگ تن در دار حیوان
به یک رنگی برآید قالب و جان

> Death of the body does not remain in the World of Life (*dār-i ḥaywān*),
> The corpus (*qālib*) and the soul become of the same color.

Now, *ḥayawān* in Arabic and Persian means "animal," coming from the word *ḥayy*, which means life, just as the word "animal" itself in English comes from the Latin word *anima*, which means to be alive or have life. So, *dār-i ḥayawān* does not mean "Animal House" or something like that. *Dār-i ḥaywān* means the living world and therefore the other world, which is always living and does not die. *Dār-i ḥayawān* is the world above.

"The corpus (*qālib*) and the soul become of the same color" also refers to the doctrine of the subtle body mentioned above. There is a very famous saying by one of the Shi'ite Imams: *arwāḥunā ajsādunā wa ajsādunā arwāḥunā*, "Our spirits are our bodies, and our bodies are our spirits." Much has been written on this subject, philosophically and metaphysically, by sages such as Mullā Ṣadrâ. Corbin has also treated this subject in several of his works especially *Terre céleste et corps de la résurrection.*[8]

بود پا و سر و چشم تو چون دل
شود صافی ز ظلمت صورت گل

> Thy foot, head and eye will become like the heart.
> The form of the clay will become cleared of darkness.

کند از نور حقّ بر تو تجلّی
ببینی بی‌جهت حقّ‌را تعالی

> The Light of the Truth will cast Its theophany upon thee,
> Without direction (*bī-jihat*), thou wilt be able to see the Truth, Transcendent.

"The light of the Truth will cast Its theophany upon thee" refers to God's direct emanation. *Bī-jihat* often means "without any reason" in Persian, but here it also means "without direction," that is, wherever, as in the Quranic statement, *fa-aynamā tuwallū fa-thamma wajhu'Llāh* "Wheresoever you turn, there is the Face of God' (Q. 2:115). You will be able to see God everywhere.

دو عالمرا همه بر هم زنی تو
ندانم تا چه مستی‌ها کنی تو

Thou wilt embroil the two worlds.
I do not know in what kinds of states of drunkenness thou wilt be.

"Thou shalt embroil the two worlds" means that thou wilt cause a commotion in the two worlds. "I do not know in what kinds of states of drunkenness thou shalt be" is of course symbolic, referring to the person's spiritual state.

«سقاهم ربّهم» چبود؟ بیندیش
«طهورا» چیست؟ صافی گشتن از خویش

What is [the verse], "Their Lord shall give them to drink"? Ponder.
What is purity (*ṭahūrā*)? It is to become pure from oneself.

This verse is in reference to Quran 76:21, *saqāhum rabbuhum sharāban ṭahūran*, "Their Lord shall give them to drink of a drink most pure." *Ṭahūr* means clean and pure here in reference to the pure wine, *sharāban ṭahūran* that the people of Paradise will drink. "What is purity?" It is to become pure from oneself, that is, from one's ego. This is the foundation of the process of spiritual realization.

زهی شربت زهی لذّت زهی ذوق
زهی حیرت زهی دولت زهی شوق

Hail the wine, hail the enjoyment, hail the tasting!
Hail wonder (*ḥayrat*), hail dominion (*dawlat*), hail ardent desire (*shawq*)!

All of these phrases use the word *zahī*, which means "hail" or "long live."

The verse in Persian is very musical and rhythmic, and has an ecstatic quality.

خوشا آن دم که ما بی‌خویش باشیم
غنیّ مطلق و درویش باشیم

How wonderful that moment when we shall be without our selves,
Be the absolutely rich, and at the same time poor (*darwīsh*).

"How wonderful that moment, when we shall be without our selves" means freed from the ego, independent of the ego. The second hemistich is in reference to the Quranic verse, *wa'Llāhu'l-ghaniyy wa antum al-fuqarā*, "God is the Rich, and you are the poor" (Q. 47:38). *Ghaniyy* is a Divine Name and Quality. So, if we follow the life of the Spirit, we shall both reflect this Divine Quality and at the same time be *darwīsh*, *faqīr*, poor in the spiritual sense.

نه دین نه عقل نه تقوی نه ادراک
فتاده مست و حیران بر سر خاک

No religion, no intelligence, no asceticism, no perception,
Fallen down, drunk and in wonder, upon the earth.

This again is a very ecstatic verse with powerful rhythm describing the state of the realized soul.

بهشت و حور و خلد اینجا چه سنجد؟
که بیگانه در آن خلوت نگنجد

Paradise, the houris, perpetual realities (*khuld*), what will they be worth here?
For no stranger can fit in the spiritual retreat.

Only when we are shorn of our ego and individual self can we be in intimate proximity to God. Intimacy with God excludes the person who is a stranger in His Presence. There is only God and the soul there, no otherness.

چو رویت دیدم و خوردم از آن می
ندانم تا چه خواهد شد پس از وی

When I saw Thy Face and drank that wine,
I do not know what is going to happen after that.

We cannot grasp with our mind the consequences of the flight and meeting of the alone with the Alone.

پی هر مستیی باشد خماری
در این اندیشه دل خون گشت باری

After every drunkenness comes stupor (*khumārī*),
So, in this thought the heart has become blood (*khūn gasht*).

After one has this spiritual experience, one enters into a mystical state, like the stupor that comes after drunkenness, this stupor or *khumārī* referring to that mystical condition of the soul. The heart becoming blood (*khūn gasht*) means becoming wounded by the presence of the Truth, "wounded" here having a completely positive connotation. To reach the Truth, the shell of our hardened heart has to melt with the heart becoming wounded so that the Truth can penetrate it.[9]

Question [12]

قدیم و محدث از هم چون جدا شد
که این عالم شد آن دیگر خدا شد؟

How did the Eternal and the created become separated,
So that this became the world and the other God?

The discussion of Eternal (*qadīm*) and created (*muḥdath*) and their relation has a long history in Islamic philosophy and theology and involves also the question of the eternity of the world. We see extensive discussions of it in the works of Mīr Dāmād, Mullā Ṣadrā, and many others. Here, however, Shabistarī, like most Sufis, identified *qidam* solely with God, the absolutely Eternal.

Answer

قدیم و محدث از هم خود جدا نیست
که از هستی است باقی دائما نیست

The Eternal and the created are not separated from each other;
For they come from Being, the rest exists not perpetually.

The *muḥdath* itself comes from God, the *qadīm* Who alone possesses abiding Reality, Who alone Is. The *muḥdath* possesses only transient existence that is not permanent and abiding.

همه آن است و این مانند عنقاست
جز ازحقّ جمله اسم بی‌مسمّاست

All is That, and this is like the Griffin (*'Anqā*).
Except for the Truth, all is a name without the named.

"That" refers to the Divine and "this" to the world that is compared here to the mythical bird, the *Sīmurgh* or *'Anqā',* taken here not in its symbolic reality but as just a name that does not possess external existence. From the metaphysical point of view, only the Name of God refers to reality. Other names are only names without a reality of their own since all reality belongs ultimately to God. This verse is also another formulation of the doctrine of *waḥdat al-wujūd.*

عدم موجود گردد؟ این محال است
وجود از روی هستی لایزال است

Non-existence becoming existent? That is impossible.
Being, because of being, is ceaseless.

That which is nonexistent cannot become existent in the sense of having its own independent *wujūd*, whereas Pure Being, the Being of God, is and never ceases to be.

نه آن این گردد و نه این شود آن
همه اشکال گردد بر تو آسان

Neither That becomes this; nor does this become That.
All difficulties become [therefore] easy for thee.

If one could only understand that God is not the world and that the world is not God—although it issues from Him and returns to Him—usual cosmological and metaphysical difficulties would be easily removed.

جهان خود جمله امر اعتباری است
چو آن یک نقطه کاندر دور ساری است

The world itself is all a contingent (*i'tibārī*) order,
Like that single point that runs in a circle.

The world is like a circle generated by a single point moving circularly. Only the point is real; the circle is contingent upon the movement of that single point.

برو یک نقطهٔ آتش بگردان
که بینی دایره از سرعت آن

Go and rotate a fiery point.
So that thou seest a circle because of [the point's] speed.

This verse is again a reference to the *ātashgardān* used in Persia to turn coal into fire by putting a piece of lit coal along with unlit pieces in a small metallic container with a metallic string attached to it; then the hand is rotated in such a way that the piece of unlit coal in the container catches fire which is then taken out to put in a samovar to make tea or for other purposes.

یکی گر در شمار آید به ناچار
نگردد واحد از اعداد بسیار

If of necessity one is counted,
One does not become many through numbers.

We can count one, two, three, etc., but the number one, whose repetition generates other numbers, remains, nevertheless, the same number one.

حدیث «ما سوی الله»را رها کن
به عقل خویش این‌را ز آن جدا کن

Let go of the saying, "What is other than God";
Through thy intellect separate this from That.

"What is other than God" (*mā siwa'Llāh*) refers to all of creation as distinguished from the Creator, *Allāh*. Here, to let go means to realize that Reality belongs to God alone. Man can know this truth through the correct use of his intellect and intelligence.

چه شک داری در آن کین چون خیال است
که با وحدت دوئی عین محال است

What doubt dost thou have in that, for this is like imagination;
For with Unity duality is exactly impossibility.

There should be no doubt in this matter; and if one does have doubt, one should know that it comes from one's imagination and not the intellect, which knows that in the light of Divine Unity there can be no duality. Here, imagination (*khayāl*) is used in its ordinary sense and not in the sense used by Suhrawardī, Ibn 'Arabī, Mullā Ṣadrā, and other later Islamic metaphysicians.

عدم مانند هستی بود یکتا
همه کثرت ز نسبت گشت پیدا

Nonbeing is, like Being, unique.
All multiplicity appears from relationality.

It is said in Islamic philosophy, *lā tamyīz fi'l-a'dām,* "There is no distinction in non-existents," so that there is only one *'adam* (nonexistence) as there is metaphysically only one *wujūd.*

ظهور اختلاف و کثرت شأن
شده پیدا ز بوقلمون امکان

The manifestation of difference and the multiplicity of states,
Have appeared through the chameleon of contingency.

It is in the nature of the world of multiplicity to change, appearing differently at different moments like the chameleon that changes color.

وجود هر یکی چون بود واحد
به وحدانیّت حقّ گشت شاهد

Since the being of each thing is one,
It is witness to the Oneness of the Truth.

Because multiplicity comes from Unity, it reflects something of that Unity, and that is being a single thing, like a tree or a bird, each one being distinct as a particular existent. In this trait, as in other ways, each existent is witness to God's Oneness. As a well-known Arabic poem asserts:

And in everything there exists a portent,
Bearing proof that He is One.[1]

Question [13]

One of the most effective, central, and positive ways in which metaphysical realities have been conveyed in Sufism is through the symbolism of the beauty of a woman's features. Now, I must clear the ground first of all because of the kind of world in which we live. Many modern people today would say that if this book were written by a woman, it would be the beauty of a man that would be described, but that is not true. Female beauty and male beauty both exist but are not the same. Each has its own kind of beauty, each comes from God—for we are all created by God—but female beauty symbolizes the inner and interiorized aspect of the Divine Reality and male beauty the manifested and outward aspect. Both *Jamāl* (Beauty) and *Jalāl* (Majesty), which are Divine Qualities, are reflected in both the male and the female but in different ways. It is not that the male has no *jamāl* and the female no *jalāl*. This is another complicated issue—the complementarity between *jalāl* (majesty) and *jamāl* (beauty) in the male and female—and I will not go into now. But the fact that Sufis chose to write about the beauty of the female as a manifestation or theophany of Divine Realities needs to be explained. Why and how did they do this? The verses of this section of the *Gulshan-i rāz* provide the answer.

We have the supreme example of the symbolic significance of female beauty in the *Tarjumān al-ashwāq* (*The Interpreter of Desires*) of Muḥyī al-Dīn Ibn ʿArabī, who, while making circumambulation around the Kaʿbah, saw a beautiful Persian woman from Isfahan circumambulating on the other side. As soon as he saw her, he writes, the entire knowledge of Divine Reality was revealed to him in such a way that every part of her being that he saw was the occasion for God revealing to him an aspect of His Mysteries. As a result, he wrote this powerful work, *Tarjumān al-ashwāq,* which is one of the great masterpieces of Arabic Sufi poetry. It is a difficult work, and he wrote a commentary upon it himself because some accused him of praising the beauty of women erotically. The critics did not understand what he was saying, and then he wrote a gloss upon his own commentary. The three parts of the *Tarjumān al-ashwāq* were translated by the famous English orientalist R. A. Nicholson in 1911,[1] and the work became well known in the West, being later translated into French and Italian. This work is a kind of epitome of the teachings of *taṣawwuf* concerning this subject. In the realm of Persian literature of course there are a great many references to this subject by Ḥāfiẓ, Rūmī, and many other Sufi poets, but there is no work in the Persian language, as far as I know, that speaks with such eloquence and completeness on this issue as the last part of the *Gulshan-i rāz*. So, this section is very important from the point of view of Persian literature as a whole as well as of Sufism.

The section begins with two questions:

چه خواهد مرد معنی ز آن عبارت
که دارد سوی چشم و لب اشارت؟
چه جوید از رخ و زلف و خط و خال
کسی کاندر مقامات است و أحوال؟

What does a person of inner meaning (*mard-i maʿnā*) imply by the phrase:
Which indicates the eye and the lip?
What is he seeking from the face, the hair (*zulf*), the line [of the face] (*khaṭṭ*)
and the mole (*khāl*),
A person who is in spiritual stations and states?

The phrase "a person of inner meaning" (*mard-i maʿnā*) is used by Shabistarī to connote a person of spiritual attainment who understands the inner reality of things, a person who is attracted to the world of meaning. We explained previously the difference between *ṣūrat* (external form) and *ma'nā* (inner reality) as used by Mawlānā and others in Sufism. Ordinarily, the word *ma'nā* in Arabic and Persian means meaning, but, as stated before, in Sufism it means the inner reality of something.

A mole used to be a sign of great beauty in the old days. Now, many women have it removed. "For a person who is in spiritual stations and states" points to a spiritual person, and the verse asks, what do such terms mean to him when he confronts them?

Answer

هر آن چیزی که در عالم عیان است
چو عکسی ز آفتاب آن جهان است

Whatever is evident (*'ayān*) in this world
Is like a reflection (*'aks*) of the Sun of the other world.

'Aks means both reflection and picture. It can also mean reversed, but here the first meaning is more applicable. Everything that exists in this world—including us, the trees, the sky—is a reflection of a reality that resides in the archetypal world. This one sentence summarizes the nature of the cosmos understood traditionally. Whatever is *'ayān*—visible, objective, manifested in this world—is like an image, a picture of the Sun or the light of the other world.

جهان چون زلف و خطّ و خال و ابروست
که هر چیزی به جای خویش نیکوست

The world is like hair, line of the face, mole and eyebrow,
For everything is beautiful in its own place.

This is again one of the most famous verses of Persian poetry, and the second hemistich has become a proverb in the Persian language. If everything were in its place, everything would be good; everything would be beautiful. The problem is that things are often out of place in the human soul. From the point of view of Sufism, we cannot destroy our soul, for God created it. What we have to do is to rearrange the "furniture" within the inner space of our being. Everything has to be put in its proper place. In place of fear we need love. In place of love of the world we have to substitute awareness of and disdain for it. In place of hatred we have to have compassion and forgiveness. In place of attraction to the world we need detachment and so forth.

Beauty is in everything being in its proper place as we see in the beauty of the human face and especially the beauty of a woman. If she has big eyes, we think that it is very beautiful, but if she has a big nose, we would not think it to be beautiful. In a beautiful face everything is in its proper place in correct proportion.

تجلّی گه جمال و گه جلال است
رخ و زلف آن معانی‌را مثال است

Theophany is sometimes Beauty, sometimes Majesty.
The face and the hair are examples of those meanings.

"Theophany," that is, of the Divine Names and Qualities, "is sometimes Beauty, sometimes Majesty." How is it that "the face and the hair are examples of those meanings"? The face represents Divine Beauty (*jamāl*), but the hair not only covers the face but also complements it and is thus a symbol of the aspect of Majesty (*jalāl*). Of course, the hair is also beautiful, and the face has an aspect of majesty, but these are on another level of understanding. So the face reveals the Beauty of God, whereas the hair hides it; so, in that sense they correspond to *jalāl* and *jamāl*.

صفات حقّ تعالی لطف و قهر است
رخ و زلف بتان‌را زآن دو بهر است

> The Qualities of the Transcendent Truth are Gentleness (*luṭf*) and Rigor (*qahr*),
> The face and the hair of the idols (*butān*) benefit from both.

Luṭf is one of the Qualities of God associated with *Jamāl*, and connotes kindness, gentleness, mercy. *Qahr,* also a Divine Quality, means dominion, power, punishment and is associated with *Jalāl*. *But* means literally "idol," but in Persian Sufi poetry it can also mean a beautiful woman and is the highest symbol of female beauty. In Sufism it symbolizes Divine Beauty. Of course, idol worship is forbidden in the Islamic tradition, but for that very reason in Sufism, *but* is used in a very positive sense as the reflection of Divine Beauty. It is like speaking about Divine Wine: even though on the *Sharī'ite* level wine is forbidden, on the spiritual level it has another meaning, which is positive. As we shall discuss below, Shabistarī also writes,

> If the Muslim were only to know what the idol is,
> He would know that religion is idol-worship.

This is one of the most daring verses in the Persian language, which uses the word *but* in the positive sense of central *tajallī*, that is, theophany or manifestation of Divine Qualities. To know esoterically what an idol (*but*) is means to see it not as idol but as theophany of a Divine Name and Quality.

چو محسوس آمد این الفاظ مسموع
نخست از بهر محسوس اند موضوع

> Because these expressions, which have been heard, have been expressed in sensible forms,
> (Our) subject begins with that which can be sensed.

Shabistarī is seeking to explain in this verse why the subject begins with a reality that can be grasped by the senses.

ندارد عالم معنی نهایت
کجا بیند مراورا چشم غایت

> The world of meaning has no end.
> How can the eye, which is made only to see limits, see it?

The spiritual world has no end. As the Catholics say, "World without end, amen." Our eyes are able to see limited forms: the form of a face, of a plate on the wall, of the wall itself. It is finite forms that we see. So, Shabistarī is asking how the eye can see that which has no finite boundary.

هر آن معنی که شد از ذوق پیدا
کجا تعبیر لفظی یابد اورا

> Whichever inner meaning (*ma'nā*) has appeared [in our soul] through spiritual intuition (*dhawq*),
> How can interpretation in words be found for it?

Dhawq means literally "tasting," but in Islamic languages (and especially in Sufism and later Islamic philosophy), it means "spiritual intuition" and "capacity to comprehend sapiential knowledge." Sapience, from *sapere* in Latin meaning "to taste," is not commonly used in English, but it does exist and corresponds exactly to *dhawq*. It is through *dhawq* that one can understand the real and inward meaning of things. *Dhawq* is also often used in the domain of various arts.

چو اهل دل کند تفسیر معنی
به مانندی کند تعبیر معنی

When the "person of the heart" interprets inner meaning,
He does so through something like it in order to explain it.

"People of the heart" is in reference to Sufis. "Something like it" indicates an appropriate symbol that can be used to bring out and explain that inner meaning.

که محسوسات از آن عالم چو سایه است
که این چون طفل و آن مانند دایه است

For sensible things are like the shadow of that world,
For this world is like a child and the other [world] like the wet nurse (*dāyah*).

The closest translation of *dāyah* in English is wet nurse, but it can also mean someone who takes care of the baby like a mother without breastfeeding it.

به نزد من خود الفاظ مأوّل
بر آن معنی فتاد از وضع اوّل

For me, expressions that are to be hermeneutically interpreted (*mu'awwal*),
From the very beginning they contained that meaning within them.

In spiritual hermeneutics you discover a meaning that is already within a term and do not add an external meaning to it. The word *mu'awwal* is from the word *awwal*, and hence means literally "taking back to the origin" or "beginning." Hence, I have translated it as spiritual hermeneutics for which term *ta'wīl* is usually used in Persian and Arabic.

به محسوسات خاصّ از عرف عامّ است
چه داند عامّ کاین معنی کدام است؟

Dealing with the objects of the senses is the specialty of the habit (*'urf*) of
common people;
How will such common people know what the inner meaning is?

'Āmm means (or *'awāmm*) common people, or ordinary people, and in Arabic and Persian is contrasted with *khawāṣṣ*, the elite. When ordinary people look at things, such as a tree, a mountain, the sky and so forth, they do not look at the inner meaning of these realities.

نظر چون در جهان عقل کردند
از آنجا لفظهارا نقل کردند

When [the sages] looked into the intelligible world,
They transmitted expressions from there.

Why do we say *dirakht* (tree)? Why do we say *mū* (hair)? What is the origin of the basic words of human language? This is a major question discussed in linguistics both traditional and modern. Some people say there were early men and also some animals making sounds, and gradually these sounds became words; while in various traditions it is believed that language was originally revealed. Even Heidegger, the modern German philosopher, believed the origin of language is "divine" in his understanding of this term. It did not come from simply animal sounds that have been adopted. by man Shabistarī is presenting here the Sufi understanding of this issue, namely that words originally come from the higher world, and so there is a relationship between the expressions that we use in language and the realities of the world of existence, to which these expressions refer.

تناسبرا رعایت کرد عاقل
چو سوی لفظ معنی گشت نازل

> The person of intelligence has always paid attention to harmonious (*tanāsub*)
> relationships,
> When the inner meaning descended upon the external expression.[2]

This verse emphasizes again the inner ink between inner meaning and external form.

ولی تشبیه کلّی نیست ممکن
ز جست و جوی او می‌باش ساکن

> But it is impossible to have complete similitude;
> Be stationary in looking for it.

There are some things in the higher world that you cannot explain in terms of the realities of this world. There is not even a proper term in ordinary language for them. Therefore, do not go looking for them.

در این معنی کسی‌را بر تو دقّ نیست
که صاحب مذهب اینجا غیر حقّ نیست

> No one is expecting of thee any more questioning,
> For the owner of this school (*madhhab*) is none other than the Truth.

This word *daqq* comes from the Persian word *dakk*, which means "to beg" or "to question," but it can also mean to knock, to gain awareness, or to look at or pay attention to something with precision. *Madhhab* usually means "religion" or "school of law," but one can also have a philosophical *madhhab*, which connotes either a school of thought or a particular way of thinking. "The owner of this school (*madhhab*)" is ultimately God Himself. Hence, only God Himself can make us aware of this reality.

ولی تا با خودی زنهار زنهار
عبارات شریعت‌را نگه‌دار

> But as long as thou art still with thyself, take care, take care;
> Preserve the forms (*'ibārāt*) of the *Sharī'ah*,

The first hemistich means as long as thou identifieth thyself with thy *nafs*, as long as thou art still entrapped in thy lower self. "Preserve the forms (*'ibārāt*)" or the words of the *Sharī'ah*, that is, do not destroy their meaning and, by implication, act on them. Do not abandon the *Sharī'ah* while thou art still in the world of forms.

که رخصت اهل دلرا در سه حال است
فنا و سکر پس دیگر دلال است

The people of the heart can take leave (*rukhṣat*) under three conditions:
If they are in a state of annihilation in God (*fanā'*), drunkenness (*sukr*) or a state of inspired spiritual vision (*dalāl*).

Dalāl is a technical term that refers to being totally absorbed in a spiritual vision so that one is not in one's normal conscious state, as if one were in drunken stupor.

The people of the heart can go beyond the *Sharī'ah* under three conditions that are mentioned in the second hemistich. In the states of annihilation and intoxication, men are no longer their normal selves. According to Islamic Law, a drunken person should not perform his canonical prayers. It is in fact *ḥarām* to perform the canonical prayers when one is in a state of *sukr*. Those who have faith in God, who accept religion, who are people of the spirit, would not make excuses for not saying their prayers, except under the three conditions mentioned in this verse.

هر آن کس کو شناسد این سه حالت
بداند وضع الفاظ و دلالت

Whoever recognizeth these three conditions,
Knoweth the creation of these expressions and their signification.

This verse asserts simply that to know these three conditions enables one to become aware of what they signify for oneself.

ترا گر نیست احوال مواجید
مشو کافر ز نادانی به تقلید

If thou dost not possess the spiritual states of thee who are in a state of ecstasy (*mawājīd*),
Do not become an infidel (*kāfir*) through ignorance, [simply] imitating them.

Mawājīd comes from *wujūd* and means here that which possesses a reality, that which brings one to reality. The hemistich stanza implies that if one does not possess the necessary spiritual states, one should not imitate simply outwardly those who do. If one makes such a mistake, one becomes in a sense an infidel.

مجازی نیست احوال حقیقت
نه هر کس یابد اسرار طریقت

The states of the Truth are not metaphorical.
Not everyone discovers the mysteries of the spiritual path.

The states in which the Truth manifests Itself are not simply metaphorical but are real. Consequently, not everyone is capable of reaching the mysteries of the *Ṭarīqah.*

گزاف ای دوست ناید ز اهل تحقیق
مراینرا کشف باید یا که تصدیق

O friend, exaggeration comes not from the people of verification (*taḥqīq*),

It is discovered by intuition (*kashf*) or by affirmation [through intellectual
judgment] (*taṣdīq*).

Ahl-i taḥqīq, "the people of verification," refers to the people who are able to confirm the truth of the spiritual path—people who are really serious concerning the spiritual path. *Ahl al-taḥqīq* is an expression used in particular by Ibn 'Arabī. *Kashf* means spiritual discovery or vision. In logic *taṣdīq* means "judgment," but in metaphysics it means the "accord of the soul with the truth."

بگفتم وضع الفاظ و معانی
ترا سربسته گر خواهی بدانی

I have told thee how expressions and their meanings are established,
This in a hidden way (*sarbastah*), if thou wantest to know.

Shabistarī is emphasizing here that he has only alluded to or mentioned these important truths in passing.

نظر کن در معانی سوی غایت
لوازمرا یکایک کن رعایت

Look at the meanings of things with an eye towards their end (*ghāyat*);
Take into consideration, one by one, all the necessary conditions.

"Look at the meanings of things with an eye towards their end (*ghāyat*)" refers to the *telos*, the teleology or the purpose of things. "Take into consideration, one by one, all the necessary conditions" is to consider every step and all the conditions that are necessary for this realization.

به وجه خاصّ از آن تشبیه می‌کن
ز دیگر وجه‌ها تنزیه می‌کن

Compare those truths in a particular way (*wajh-i khāṣṣ*),
Become purified from all the other ways [of trying to understand these
meanings].

"In a particular way (*wajh-i khāṣṣ*)" means in a serious spiritual and metaphysical way.

چو شد این قاعده یک سر مقرّر
نمایم زان مثالی چند دیگر

Now that this principle has become completely established,
I shall reveal to thee a few more examples.

The section ends with this verse alluding to what is to come in the form of other examples.

An Indication of the Eyes and Lips

نگر کز چشم شاهد چیست پیدا
رعایت کن لوازمرا بدانجا

See what is visible from the eye of the witness (*shāhid*),
Consider all the necessary conditions therein.

The word *shāhid* is a key Arabic philosophical and mystical term from the root *shahada,* which means to "bear witness" as in the Islamic testification of faith (*shahādah*), *ashhadu an lā ilāha illa'Llāh.* As mentioned before, this term is related to the word *mashhad* (a place of spiritual vision), which also indicates the place of burial of a *shahīd* or martyr. There are also other concepts in Sufism related to this root. The word *shāhid* is also used in a special and subtle way in Sufism. In some Sufi gatherings they would have a handsome young boy, called a *shāhid*, be present specifically to teach more self-control to all the *fuqarā'* so that they could learn to concentrate on the *dhikr* even with the presence of distractions. This practice has sometimes been interpreted as pedophilia, but that is a mistaken interpretation. The term *shāhid* can mean, moreover, the kind of angelic presence that comes to the *faqīr* and is both witness to his esoteric knowledge and also a source of that knowledge. It must be remembered that a base meaning of *shuhūd* (in the Sufi and philosophical sense) is vision.

"Consider all the necessary conditions" refers to the spiritual path and what one must do as a *sālik* (journeyer) upon the path. Having said that, Shabistarī now turns to the description of the *shāhid* who here is not a male *shāhid* but rather a female *shāhid*, to whose *rukh* (face), *zulf* (tresses) and so forth he makes reference. These are symbolic and erotic verses, and I translate the pronouns, which are without gender in the original Persian, using the feminine forms "she" and "her."

ز چشمش خاست بیماری و مستی
ز لعلش گشت پیدا عین هستی

From Her Eyes have arisen illness and drunkenness,[3]
From Her ruby [Lips] there became manifest the Essence of Being (*'ayn-i hastī*).

In the hemistich, "From Her Eyes arise illness and drunkenness," illness does not of course mean physical illness but rather going beyond one's ordinary state; thus, he adds the term "drunkenness." The kiss implies proximity and union, and so the ruby Lips of the Divine Beloved refer to intimacy with the source of Being as well as Its very Essence.

ز چشم اوست دلها مست و مخمور
ز لعل اوست جانها جمله مستور

From Her Eyes all the hearts are drunken and inebriated,
From her ruby [Lips] all souls have become hidden.

The eye looks at objects even distant from it, but those who catch a glance of the Eye of the Beloved become drunken through that very vision. But to touch Her Lips is only for the spiritual elite. Others have no possibility of experiencing those Lips.

ز چشم او همه دلها جگرخوار
لب لعلش شفای جان بیمار

From Her Eyes all of the hearts suffer deeply (*jigar-khwār*),
Her ruby Lips are cure for the sickness of the ill person.

Hearts of those who love the Beloved and long for Her suffer from beholding Her Eye but being removed from Her. The cure for their suffering is union with Her by kissing Her Lips. *Jigar-khwār* in Persian means literally "eating one's liver" but means deep suffering.

به چشمش گرچه عالم در نیاید
لبش هر ساعتی لطفی نماید

Although by looking at Her Eyes the world is not discovered,
Her Lips manifest a blessing every hour.

The glance of the Eye of the Beloved also employs distance and separation whereas the Lips touched in a kiss indicate proximity, intimacy, and union.

دمی از مردمی دلها نوازد
دمی بیچارگان‌را چاره سازد

Sometimes She caresses the heart of people,
Sometimes She provides help to those who are destitute.

This verse refers to modes of blessing that come from the Beloved. There is no boundary to God's Grace.

به شوخی جان دهد در آب و در خاک
به دم دادن زند آتش بر افلاک

Through humor, She gives life to water and earth;
Through breathing, She sets fire to the heavens.

The term *shūkhī*, which has been translated here as "humor," can also mean "joy" and "happiness." The Beloved created life in joy and not in sorrow, but Her Breath can also consume the heavens in fire, that is, return the cosmos to its Source by removing from it separative existence.

از او هر غمزه دام و دانه‌ای شد
وز او هر گوشه‌ای میخانه‌ای شد

From Her, every coquettish move became a trap and a seed,
From Her, every corner became a tavern.

Here, the word "seed" refers to the bait in the trap. As for the second hemistich, it points to the reality that every Sufi center, which proliferated everywhere in the traditional Islamic world, is established as a result of God's Will.

ز غمزه می‌دهد هستی به غارت
به بوسه می‌کند بازش عمارت

Through Her coquettish move, She plunders the world of existence,
But with Her kiss She builds it again.

It is through the Power of the Divine that all of existence is "plundered" by sacred Presence. Yet, it is Her kiss that re-creates all that has been "plundered." The world emanates from Pure Being and returns to It.

چو از چشم و لبش جوئی کناری
مر این گوید که نه آن گوید آری

If thou tryest to separate thyself from Her Eyes and Lips,
One will say "nay"; the other will say "yea."

The Eyes refer to distance and separation (*bu'd*) and the Lips to intimacy and union (*qurb*); so, one says no keep thy distance and the other yes, come near and remove the separation.

ز غمزه عالمی‌را کار سازد
به بوسه هر زمان جان می‌نوازد

Through Her coquettish moves She makes a whole world operate;
With Her kiss She caresses the soul at every moment.

It is the theophanies of the Beloved that make possible the operation of the world of existence, while with Her ever-continuing intimacy She caresses the soul of those who seek Her.

از او یک غمزه و جان دادن از ما
ازو یک بوسه و استادن از ما

One coquettish move from Her, and it is for us to give our life.
One kiss from Her, and it is for us to become totally stationary.

A spiritual person would give his or her life for a single coquettish move from Her, and a single kiss from Her would make one be done with becoming and reach the state of Being beyond movement and change.

ز «لمح بالبصر» شد حشر عالم
ز نفخ روح پیدا گشت آدم

From "the blinking of an eye" (*lamḥun bi'l-baṣar*) came the resurrection of the world;
From the breathing of the Spirit (*nafkh-i rūḥ*) appeared Adam.

The first hemistich cites the Quranic verse 16:77, and the second the Quranic verses 15:29 and 38:72. The verse as a whole refers to both eschatological events at the end of the world and the appearance of man in the world, and therefore, also the beginning of the world. The full Quranic verse mentioned partially in the first hemistich is: "Unto God belongs the Unseen of the heavens and the earth. The matter of the Hour is as the blinking of an eye, or nearer still. Truly, God is Powerful over all things" (Q. 16:77).

چو از چشم و لبش اندیشه کردند
جهانی می‌پرستی پیشه کردند

When they thought of Her Eye and Lip,
A world began to make its task the worship of wine.

Those able to think of and meditate upon the Eye and Lip of the Beloved become "worshippers of wine," that is, Sufis devoted to the invocation of Her Blessed Name.

به چشمش در نیاید جمله هستی
در او چون آید آخر خواب و مستی؟

From Her Eye the whole of existence does not take leave.
How then can sleep and drunkenness exist in Her?

If the whole world of existence remains in Her and does not emanate beyond Her, how can one say that the state of sleep and drunkenness exists in Her?

وجود ما همه مستی است یا خواب
چه نسبت خاک‌را با ربّ ارباب

Our whole existence is all drunkenness or sleep;
What relation is there between the dust and the Lord of lords (*Rabb-i arbāb*)?

This verse is again a very famous one, especially the second hemistich. The idea that, even though we think we are awake in our ordinary earthly state, we are in fact asleep—and when we die we awaken—goes back to the famous *ḥadīth* of the Prophet, "People are asleep, and when they die they awaken" (*al-nāsu niyām wa idhā mātū intabahū*). Another way of expressing this truth is that ordinary people are not sober in the sense of being awake in this world; they are really drunk or unconscious. We are not in our real state of awareness, just as someone who is drunk is not in an ordinary state of consciousness and cannot control their thoughts. This means that our real consciousness is not the ordinary consciousness that we have in this world. Our ordinary way of thinking when we get up every morning is like that of a drunk person who is not completely himself or herself.

خرد دارد در این صد گونه اشگفت
«ولتُصنع علی عینی» چرا گفت

The intellect wonders a hundred ways about this;
Why did He say, "That thou mightest be formed under my Eye"?

This is a reference to the Quranic verse 20:39, concerning the story of Moses and the Pharaoh.

Indication of the Hair (*zulf*)

حدیث زلف جانان بس دراز است
چه شاید گفت از آن کاین جای راز است

The story of the Hair of the Beloved (*jānān*) is a long one;
What should be said of it that it is the place of mystery.

The hair of the female head plays a major role in many Sufi poems, especially those of Hāfiẓ. The Hair both hides and reveals the beauty of the Beloved, and its curls entrap the soul.

مپرس از من حدیث زلف پرچین
مجنبانید زنجیر مجانین

Do not ask me about the story of the Hair full of curls.
Do not shake the chain of those who are mad.

In the old days when people went mad they were put in an asylum and were often chained. Shabistarī is combining in this verse the image of curls of the Beloved, Divine madness, and being consequently chained as a result of beholding the beauty of the curls.

ز قدّش راستی گفتم سخن دوش
سر زلفش مرا گفتا فروپوش

Concerning Her Height, last night I said something about it, in truth,
The tip of Her Hair told me, "Keep quiet!"

A reference is made here to Her vertical Stature in accordance with the truth, but not much is said for the end of Her curly Hair, which ordered the poet not to proceed and keep quiet. Not all the esoteric significance of these symbols has, therefore, been revealed.

کجی بر راستی زو گشت غالب
وز او در پیچش آمد راه طالب

When the curve became dominant over the straight,
This winding itself became the path of the seeker.

Since Her Hair is curled, the road to reach Her is a sinuous one, full of twists and turns and ups and downs.

همه دلها از او گشته مسلسل
همه جانها از او بوده مقلقل

All hearts have become attached in a series (*musalsal*) to Her;
All souls have been in excitement (*muqalqal*) through Her.

Musalsal comes from the word *silsilah*, meaning also initiatic chain in Sufism, and implies a series. *Muqalqal*, means "boiling up" and hence excited.

معلّق صد هزاران دل ز هر سو
نشد یک دل برون از حلقهٔ او

Hundreds of thousands of hearts are suspended in every direction,
[Yet], not a single heart was outside of Her Curl.

Souls are in different states and move in different directions. Yet, there is no soul that stands beyond Her dominion. There is no domain of reality beyond the reach of God's Reality. There is no extra-territoriality in religion.

اگر زلفین خودرا برفشاند
به عالم در یکی کافر نماند

If She were to reveal all Her Hair,
There would not be a single infidel in the world.

If the Divine Beloved were to show us Her Beauty, there would be no one in the world who would deny Her Reality. In the deepest sense, even God's hiding of Himself from us is proof of His infinite Power and Reality. He is both the Outward (*al-Ẓāhir*) and the Inward (*al-Bāṭin*).

وگر بگذاردش پیوسته ساکن
نماند در جهان یک نفس مؤمن

And if She leaves everything in rest (*sākin*)
There would not be left in the world a single man of faith (*mu'min*).

Rest here means "without movement" in a positive sense, that is, manifesting Herself and causing man to move toward Her. If God did not manifest Himself, not only would there be no *mu'min* in the world, but there would not even be any existent, whether *mu'min* or *kāfir*. Even the faithless are created by God and their existence is sustained by Him.

چو دام فتنه می‌شد چنبر او
به شوخی باز کرد از تن سر او

Since Her necklace (*chanbar*) was the trap of temptation to ensnare,
In humor, She separated Her head from Her body.

She first ensnared Her lover through the beauty of Her necklace and then opened Her Reality to that lover, to the seeker of God. *Chanbar*, translated here as necklace can also mean "Her Curl."

اگر ببریده شد زلفش چه غم بود؟
که شب گر کم شد اندر روز افزود

If Her Hair were to be cut, what sorrow would result?
For if the night were to be shortened, the day would increase.

If Her Hair, which is dark like the night, were to be shortened, the light of Her Face would be increased by being revealed more.

چو او بر کاروان عقل ره زد
به دست خویشتن بر وی گره زد

When She plundered the caravan of reason,
With Her own Hand, She tied it up in knots.

When the light of the Divine Intellect and the Presence of God conquer our ordinary mind and reason, the rational faculty is cast aside and "tied up in knots" by being integrated into higher levels of the intellect, which are not irrational but beyond the rational.

نیابد زلف او یک لحظه آرام
گهی بام آورد گاهی کند شام

Not for one moment is Her Hair still;
Sometimes She brings the morning, sometimes the evening.

There is no disruption in the manifestation of Her theophanies. It is this constant manifestation that makes possible the flow of becoming and temporality, the day and the night.

ز روی و زلف خود صد روز و شب کرد
بسی بازیچه‌های بوالعجب کرد

Through Her Face and Hair, She passed a hundred days and nights,
She played many games that were of wonder (*bū'l-'ajab*).

Bū'l-'ajab means "resulting in wonder." Her games, Her manifestations day in and day out are all sources of wonder. We live in a world of wonder if only we could wake up and realize it.

گل آدم در آن دم شد مخمّر
که دادش بوی آن زلف معطّر

The clay of Adam became mixed with wine at that moment,
When She cast upon it the sweet smell of Her Hair.

A drop of the Divine Wine was poured into the clay of Adam from the moment of his creation when She, the Divine Reality, cast the perfume of Her Curl upon it. The perfume of the world of the Spirit existed from the beginning in the heart of man.

دل امّا دارد از زلفش نشانی
که خود ساکن نمی‌گردد زمانی

> But the heart has a sign from Her Hair;
> Therefore, not for one moment does it remain still.

"Not for one moment does it remain still" means that it is always beating because it is imprinted by Her theophany and so is seeking Her constantly, the heart beating with life in order to reach the Source of that theophany.

از او هر لحظه کار از سر گرفتیم
ز جان خویشتن دل برگرفتیم

> Through Her every moment we have started anew,
> With our life, we have become impatient (*dil bar giriftīm*).

Because of God's constant manifestation of His theophanies, every moment of our life begins anew, and the spiritual person becomes ever more anxious and impatient to embrace the Beloved, the source of all theophanies. Spiritually speaking, our heart continues to beat in order to reach that Center where the Beloved resides.

از آن گردد دل از زلفش مشوّش
که از رویش دلی دارد بر آتش

> The heart becomes excited (*mushawwash*) because of Her Hair, because,
> As the result of Her face [man] has a heart that is on fire.

Mushawwash can mean "excited" and "mixed up," but here it connotes a positive reality: that the heart goes beyond the ordinary state of *sukūn* (rest) and calm and is set on fire because of the excitement of proximity to Her.

An Indication of the Face

رخ اینجا مظهر حسن خدائی است
مراد از خط جناب کبریائی است

> The Face (*rukh*) here is symbol of Divine Beauty.
> The Line (*khaṭṭ*) is in reference to the Majestic Exaltation (*kibriyā*).

Rukh or Face is the symbol of the aspect of Divinity turned toward creation, and since God is beautiful, it means that the Face manifests Divine Beauty. The Line is in reference to the marks of beauty of the face, which in the case of the Beloved are majestic and exalted.

رخش خطّی کشید اندر نکوئی
که بیرون نیست از ما خوبروئی

> Her Face drew a line through goodness,

[Saying], "There is no beautiful face outside of Us."

The Beloved underlined that there is no beautiful face outside the beauty and presence of Her Face.

خط آمد سبزه‌زار عالم جان
از آن کردند نامش دار حیوان

The Line [of the Divine Face] became the green pasture of the world of the soul,
That is why they have named it "the living world" (*dār-i ḥaywān*).[4]

The Line of Her Face refers to Divine manifestation. As for *dār-i ḥaywān*, here it does not mean the animal world that is its usual meaning, but rather the animated or living world.

ز تاریکی زلفش روز شب کن
ز خطّش چشمهٔ حیوان طلب کن

Through the blackness of Her Hair, pass thy day into night,[5]
From Her Line (*khaṭṭ*), seek the fountain of life (*chishmah-yi ḥaywān*).

"Through the blackness of Her Hair, pass thy day into night" means "remember during day and night the blackness of the Divine Essence." The Line of Her Face can lead the seeker to the Fountain of Life itself.

خضروار از مقام بی‌نشانی
بخور چون خطّش آب زندگانی

Khiḍr-like, from the station that has no indication (*maqam-i bī-nishānī*)
Drink the Water of Life following Her line.

"The station that has no indication" could be a reference to the station of no station (*maqām lā maqām*) to which Ibn 'Arabī refers. According to Islamic prophetology, Khaḍir or Khiḍr drank from the Fountain of Life. The spiritual seeker is advised to do the same following his example.

اگر روی و خطش بینی تو بی‌شک
بدانی کثرت از وحدت یکایک

If thou seest Her Face and the Line, without any doubt,
Thou wilt be able to know multiplicity in distinction from Unity, one by one.

To behold the Divine Face is to "see" Divine Unity and consequently be able to distinguish all forms and realms of multiplicity from Unity.

ز زلفش باز دانی کار عالم
ز خطّش باز خوانی سرّ مبهم

From Her Hair, thou wilt know the workings of the world;
From Her Line thou wilt be able to read the hidden secret.

It is knowledge of the Divine that allows us to know the world of creation, not simply in itself but in relation to Her, and also realize the mysteries of existence.

کسی گر خطّش از روی نکو دید
دل من روی او در خطّ او دید

If a person would be able to see Her Line on that beautiful Face,
My heart would be able to see Her face in Her Line.

The person who has had a vision of Her will bear a reflection, an emanation of Her Face in his or her being; so, the heart of the spiritual person will be able to see Her Face in Her Line. The face of those who have realized the Divine Reality bears a reflection of that Reality.

مگر رخسار او سبع المثانی است
که هر حرفی از او بحر معانی است؟

Is Her Face the "Seven Oft-Repeated Verses,"
Which has a sea of meaning in every single letter?

The "Seven Oft-Repeated Verses" (*sab' al-mathānī*) mentioned in the first hemistich is usually considered to be a reference to *Sūrat al-Fātiḥah*, which has seven verses and is believed to "contain" the essence of the whole of the Quran. Every letter of that *sūrah* contains a world of meaning.

نهفته زیر هر موئی از او باز
هزاران بحر علم از عالم راز

There is hidden under every Hair of Hers an opening
To a thousand seas of knowledge from the world of Divine Secrets (*rāz*).

Every manifestation of the Divine contains boundless knowledge of Divine Mysteries. *Rāz* in Persian is the same as *sirr*, which exists in both Arabic and Persian.

ببین بر آب قلبت عرش رحمان
ز خطّ عارض زیبای جانان

See upon the water of thy heart the Throne of the Compassionate,
From the Line inscribed [on the Face] of the Beautiful One of sweethearts.

The first hemistich is a reference to the *ḥadīth*, *qalb al-mu'min 'arsh al-Raḥmān*, "The heart of the person of faith is the Throne of the Compassionate," that is, God as the Compassionate (*al-Raḥmān*), which is of course a Divine Name. In the second hemistich, Shabistarī uses the term *jānān*, which I have translated as "sweethearts," here referring to God's lovers who are loved by Him.

An Indication of the Mole

بر آن رخ نقطهٔ خالش بسیط است
که اصل مرکز دور محیط است

On that Face, the point of Her mole is pure simplicity,
For it is the principle of the center of the encompassing circle.

"The point of Her mole is pure simplicity" should be taken in the metaphysical sense. The mole of a woman's face is a symbol of the center of the circle of existence, the mark of *tawḥīd*, in Sufism. In the old days even women who did not have moles would put a mole on their face as a sign of beauty. But this central reality, being the mole of the Face of the Beloved, also embraces all of existence. God is both the Center and Origin of existence and encompasses and embraces all existence.

از او شد خطّ دور هر دو عالم
وز او شد خطّ نفس و قلب آدم

From Her, the line that encircles both worlds came into existence,
And from Her, the line of the soul and heart of man came to be.

The Divine Reality encompasses both this world and the next. Moreover, what existentiates and defines man's soul and heart, the center of his being, comes from Her.

از آن حال دل پرخون تباه است
که عکس نقطهٔ خال سیاه است

It is for that reason that the heart full of blood (*dil-i pur-khūn*) is ruined,
For it is the opposite of the point of the Black Mole.

The heart full of blood (*dil-i pur-khūn*) here means a heart that is in anguish yearning for God, Whom it has not as yet reached. It is contrasted here to the darkened or Black Mole of the Beloved for which the heart yearns.

ز خالش حال دل جز خون شدن نیست
کز آن منزل ره بیرون شدن نیست

Because of Her Mole, the condition of the heart is nothing but becoming blood,
For there is no way to enable it to come out of that state.

Here also becoming blood is not negative but refers to the anguish of separation from the Beloved. The second hemistich means that there is no way to escape from that station.

به وحدت در نباشد هیچ کثرت
دو نقطه نبود اندر اصل وحدت

In Unity there is no multiplicity;
There are not two points in the principle of Unity.

This verse is a reassertion of the truth that while all multiplicity issues from Unity, Unity itself is beyond all duality and by implication multiplicity.

ندانم خال او عکس دل ماست
و یا دل عکس خال روی زیباست

I know not whether Her Mole is the image of our heart,
Or that our heart is the image of Her Mole.

The Presence of God resides in our hearts, and so Shabistarī asks in order to refer in a provocative manner to the relation between the Divine in our heart and Her Mole. He does so in order to awaken us to the awareness of this reciprocity.

ز عکس خال او دل گشت پیدا
و یا عکس دل آنجا شد هویدا

From the image of Her Mole the heart became apparent,
Or the image of the heart became manifest there.

This verse continues the reciprocity mentioned in the verse above and complements it.

دل اندر روی او یا اوست در دل؟
به من پوشیده شد این امر مشکل

Is the heart within Her Face or is She within the heart?
This difficult matter became hidden for me.

This verse is again composed of questions pertaining to the reciprocity mentioned in the above verses.

اگر هست این دل ما عکس آن خال
چرا می‌باشد آخر مختلف حال؟

If this heart of ours is the image of that Mole,
Why is it that it keeps going from state to state?

This verse poses a major metaphysical query. The Mole of the Beloved is still and unchanging while the heart beats and is in movement constantly. In Arabic and Persian, the root of the term for heart, that is, *qalb*, is related to change and transformation. In some Islamic prayers, God is addressed as *Muqallib al-qulūb*, the Transformer or Changer of Hearts.

گهی چون چشم مخمورش خراب است
گهی چون زلف او در اضطراب است

Sometimes, it is like Her drunken Eye in ruin (*kharāb*);
Sometimes, like Her Hair it is in distress.

"In ruin" in the first stanza is the translation of *kharāb*, which in Sufism often means beyond the ordinary human state in a state of spiritual exaltation and ecstasy. Sufis are sometimes called *kharābātī* (person of ruins). "It" at the beginning of the verse refers, of course, to the heart.

گهی روشن چو آن روی چو ماه است
گهی تاریک چون خال سیاه است

Sometimes, it is illuminated like Her moon-like Face;
Sometimes, it is dark like the black Mole.

Again the author points to this paradox that if there is the reciprocity mentioned above, why is the heart of man sometimes full of light like Her moonlike (that is, beautiful) Face and sometimes dark, which is here again compared to a feature of Her, that is, Her Mole?

گهی مسجد بود گاهی کنشت است

گهی دوزخ بود گاهی بهشت است

Sometimes, it is a mosque, sometimes a synagogue;
Sometimes, it is Hell, sometimes, Paradise.

Kinisht means "synagogue," as does the word *kanīsah*, which is, moreover, related to the word *kilīsā* (church), which also exists in Persian. The word "Knesset," name of the Israeli parliament, is also related to this word.

گهی برتر شود از هفتم افلاک
گهی افتد به زیر تودهٔ خاک

Sometimes it goes beyond the seven heavens,
Sometimes it falls below the mass of dust.

All these allusions are to the ever-changing states of the ordinary human heart.

پس از زهد و ورع گردد دگر بار
شراب و شمع و شاهدرا طلبکار

After undergoing asceticism and scrupulousness it comes again,
Demanding wine, candle, and witness.

Asceticism (*zuhd*) and scrupulousness (*wara'*) are stages of the Sufi path mentioned in many classical Sufi texts. These states then lead to higher ones that include the stages described symbolically in the second hemistich. This whole section deals with clarifying certain basic questions concerning the spiritual path without providing answers. The author's purpose here is to make the reader aware of these basic questions that arise once one seeks to undertake the spiritual journey.

Question [14]

شراب و شمع و شاهدرا چه معنی است؟
خراباتی شدن آخر چه دعوی است؟

> What is the meaning of wine (*sharāb*), of candle (*sham'*), of witness (*shāhid*)?
> What kind of claim is it to belong to the Tavern of Ruins (*kharābāt*)?

I have already mentioned the Sufi meaning of *kharābāt* used in a previous verse. It should be recalled here that the word *kharāb* is Arabic and is also found in Persian. The word usually refers to something that does not work, is in ruins, or is spoiled—it usually has a very negative connotation. *Kharābah* in Persian refers to a town or house that has fallen into ruin. Sufism, however, uses this term symbolically to allude to its reality being independent from the exoteric understanding of religion. Sufism is not derived from the *Sharī'ah* (the Law), but rather is derived from the *Ḥaqīqah* (the Truth) of the Islamic revelation, which is the source of both the *Sharī'ah* and the *Ṭarīqah* (the Way). At the same time Sufism respects the *Sharī'ah*, and serious Sufis practice the *Sharī'ah* meticulously; yet, Sufism does is not derived from the *Sharī'ah*. Its authority comes directly from the *Ḥaqīqah*. In order to point to that truth, Sufis make purposeful use of such symbols as "wine," "candle," and "witness," as well as *kharābāt*, the Tavern of Ruins, which Ḥāfiẓ often employs, as in the verse:

> In the Tavern of Ruins of the Magi I see the Light of God.
> See how strange it is that I see such a Light in such a place.[1]

"Tavern of Ruins of the Magi" (*Kharābāt-i mughān*) is actually a symbol of the Sufi center. So, the word *kharābāt* bears this symbolic significance and is deliberately used to show the independence of Sufism from the exoteric Law. That is why the Sufis also use the language of wine so much more than other forms of mysticism. One does see some verses in Jewish mysticism dealing with wine—as in the wine of knowledge—and there are even a few examples in Latin poetry, but it is used much more frequently in mystical works in Arabic, Persian, and other Islamic languages.[2]

Answer

شراب و شمع و شاهد عین معنی است
که در هر صورتی اورا تجلّی است

> Wine, candle, and witness are the essence of meaning.
> For there is Her theophany in every form.

What Shabistarī is saying is that God manifests Himself in all these three realities. In fact He is Present in every manifested as well as nonmanifested form.

شراب و شمع سکر و نور عرفان
ببین شاهد که از کس نیست پنهان

Wine and candle, drunkenness and the light of gnosis.[3]
Look at the witness, who is not hidden from anyone.

Wine is of course related to spiritual drunkenness while the candle that emanates light symbolizes the light of gnosis and realized knowledge. "Look at the witness" refers to one who witnesses the light of *ma'rifah* and who can be seen by everyone, even if that light within his heart can be detected only by those qualified to see it. This phrase also refers to *shahid* that has been discussed already.

شراب اینجا زجاجه شمع مصباح
بود شاهد فروغ نور ارواح

The wine here is the glass (*zujājah*), and the candle the lamp (*miṣbāḥ*),
The witness is the ray of the light of spirits.

In the first hemistich reference is, of course, to the Light Verse (*āyat al-Nūr*) (Q. 24:35), which mentions both the glass and the lamp. In this hemistich, Shabistarī compares wine with the glass that reflects the light of the candle within it. In the second hemistich, the witness is a direct reference to the light that shines forth from the spiritual world into the realm of temporal existence.

ز شاهد بر دل موسی شرر شد
شرابش آتش و شمعش شجر شد

Through the witness sparks (*sharar*) came to the heart of Moses.
Its wine became fire, and the candle, tree.

The witness or *shāhid* here refers to one who bears witness to the Divine Truth. This verse is in reference to the fire and the tree in the Quranic story of Moses going to al-Wadī al-Ayman, the Valley of the Right. The Quranic account reflects the experience of the burning bush mentioned in the Old Testament.

شراب و شمع و شاهد جمله حاضر
مشو غافل ز شاهدبازی آخر

Wine, candle and witness being all present,
Do not then become negligent of "playing with the witness."

One can find wine, candle, and witness on the Sufi path. So, Shabistarī advises us not to neglect them but rather to take advantage of the great blessings offered to man through them. *Shāhid-bāzī* means literally "playing with the witness," to which reference has been made before.

شراب و شمع، جام و نور اسری است
ولی شاهد همان آیات کبری است

The wine and the candle are the cup and the light of the Night Journey (*isrā*),
While the witness is those great signs (*āyāt-i kubrā*).

The first hemistich is in reference to the first part of the Night Journey of the Prophet, the *isrā'*, from Makkah to Jerusalem followed by the *mi'rāj* (or Nocturnal Ascent) from there through the heavens to the Divine Presence. The great signs are all those signs of God that the Prophet saw during that journey. One may add that there are two references for the Quranic expression *āyāt-i kubrā.* One is Q. 20:23, " . . . that We may show thee some of Our greatest signs" which refers to the signs given to Moses; and Q. 53:18, "Indeed, he saw the greatest of the signs of his Lord," which some commentators take to refer to the *mi'rāj*.

شراب بیخودی در کش زمانی
مگر از دست خود یابی امانی

On some occasion drink the wine that makes thee go beyond thyself
(*bī-khudī*),
Perhaps then thou wilt be able to free thyself from thyself.[4]

People drink usually to forget themselves and their sorrows for a while. But one can only drink the real wine, that is, the spiritual wine, after one rejects the self or ego, yet from another point of view one also gets rid of the ego by drinking the spiritual wine.

بخور می تا ز خویشت وارهاند
وجود قطره با دریا رساند

Drink wine so that it will free thee from thyself,
[And] make the drop of water reach the sea.

All of the reasons that people get drunk, even half-drunk, in a sense results from the fact that they are trying to run away from themselves, to forget themselves—that is their ego. So, Shabistarī tells us to drink the real wine of gnosis, which frees us from our ego and makes it possible for us to have our limited existence join the boundless ocean or sea of Being.

شرابی خور که جامش روی یار است
پیاله چشم مست بادەخوار است

Drink a wine whose cup is the Face of the Beloved.
The cup is the drunken eye of the drinker of wine.

This verse exalts the symbolic meaning of the cup in which the wine of *ma'rifah* is poured to the level of the Face of God (*wajh Allāh*) Whose gaze would then be the wine itself. Moreover, the verse identifies this cup with the eye of the person in the process of spiritual realization.

شرابی می‌طلب بی‌ساغر و جام
شراب بادەخوار و ساقی آشام

Seek a wine without the pourer of wine and without cup,
A wine that devours the drinker of wine and the pourer of wine.

Seek that pure wine that can be drunk without the power of wine or even the cup in which the wine is normally contained. This is a wine, the Divine Presence, that is beyond I-ness and It-ness, that devours everything including wine itself as well as its pourer, in the station or *maqām* of pure Unity (*tawḥīd*).

شرابی خور ز جام وجه باقی
«سقاهم ربّهم» او راست ساقی

Drink wine from the cup of the everlasting Face;
In "Their Lord shall give them to drink," the Saki is He.

God says in the Quran, "Their Lord shall give them to drink of a drink most pure" (Q. 76:21). God is, therefore, the real Pourer of that pure wine of paradise. God is the Saki, but this assertion is both rare and audacious. We usually interpret the saki in Persian literature as the spiritual master, who pours the Divine wine into the souls of disciples, but on the highest level it is God Himself who does so, as Shabistarī asserts here.

طهور آن می بود کز لوث هستی
تورا پاکی دهد در وقت مستی

Pure is that wine which, from the filth of existence,
Purifies thee at the time of drunkenness.

Only the wine of gnosis removes from our being the blemish of separation from the Source of all being, purifying our soul through that spiritual drunkenness that symbolizes the transcending of our ordinary consciousness.

بخور می وارهان خودرا ز سردی
که بد مستی به است از نیک مردی

Drink wine and free thyself from coldness,
For being badly drunk is better than being a good man.

Coldness (*sardī*) in the first hemistich can also be translated as indifference. This verse is again enigmatic, but what Shabistarī means in the second hemistich is the self-righteousness and the pretension of being good found so often in human beings. As I have mentioned before, there is a saying in Latin, *in vino veritas*, and we have in Persian *mastī-u rāstī,* which has the same meaning, that is, "in drunkenness is to be found truth." A drunkard does not lie if he or she is really drunk. And this state is really a reflection of spiritual *mastī*, to be drunk in the Reality of God. A drunkard can do all kinds of bad things, but he or she does not lie, and so we have the Persian proverb similar to the Latin adage.

کسی کو افتد از درگاه حقّ دور
حجاب ظلمت اورا بهتر از نور

He who has fallen away from the threshold of the Truth,
The veil of darkness is better for him than light.

An intelligence divorced from the Divine Truth becomes cleverness and cunning, which are worse than having no intelligence at all.

که آدمرا ز ظلمت صد مدد شد
ز نور ابلیس ملعون ابد شد

For a hundred forms of help come to man from darkness,
While the Devil became eternally cursed through light.

In the hemistich, "For a hundred forms of help come to man from darkness," darkness refers to such negative experiences as loss, pain, suffering and all the calamities that one bears throughout life. Yet, the darkness of such experiences can be followed by God's Help, which allows us to overcome that darkness, whereas Satan rebelled against God by asserting that he was made of fire or light, while man was molded of clay.

اگر آئینهٔ دل‌را زدوده است
چو خودرا بیند اندر وی چه سود است؟

If one has polished the mirror of his heart,
Yet he only sees himself in it, what benefit is there?

To polish the mirror of the heart, which according to a *ḥadīth* of the Prophet can only be achieved through *dhikr*, has for its purpose seeing the reflection of the Divine in it. If, however, one sees only one's own image in that mirror, then Shabistarī asks what benefit or good results from that polishing, which is obviously not the polishing to which Sufis refer.

ز رویش پرتوئی چون در می افتاد
بسی شکل حبابی بر وی افتاد

Since from Her Face there fell a ray of light (*partaw*) upon the wine,
Many forms of [veil-like] bubble (*ḥubāb*) were cast upon it.

Her Face is, of course, in reference to the Face of the Divine Beloved. By virtue of receiving that ray from Her Face, the wine of gnosis and forms of Divine Knowledge emanate unto the soul of the gnostic and the realized soul takes the shape of a *ḥubāb* [bubble].

جهان جان در او شکل حباب است
حبابش اولیائی‌را قباب است

The world of the Spirit in him is in the form of a bubble (*ḥubāb*),[5]
His bubble is, for the Friends of God, the dome.

The verse echoes the sacred prophetic tradition (*ḥadīth qudsī*): *Awliyā'ī taḥta qubābī, lā ya'ri-fuhum ghayrī*, "My friends are under my domes, no one knows them but Me." In light of this tradition one could consider the verse as referring either to *al-Ḥaqīqat al-muḥammadiyyah* (the Muḥammadan Reality), the Universal Man, or the Divine Beloved. In the verses that follow I have chosen the latter, but the former should also be kept in mind as a possibility.

شده زو عقل کلّ حیران و مدهوش
فتاده نفس کلّ‌را حلقه در گوش

Through Her, the Universal Intellect has come into a state of wonder and has fainted.
It has caused the Universal Soul to wear a ring in the ear (*ḥalqah dar-gūsh*).

In the Islamic metaphysical hierarchy, below the Divine Being comes the Universal Intellect and below it the Universal Soul. This verse reflects this hierarchy in a gnostic manner. In Persian, to have a ring in the ear refers to the state of a slave who receives orders from his master and is completely subservient to him.

همه عالم چو یک خمخانهٔ اوست
دل هر ذرّه‌ای پیمانهٔ اوست

All the world is like a tavern of Hers,
The heart of every atom is Her cup of wine.

Here, Shabistarī identifies the mystical wine with existence itself. Hence, every existent is Her cup of wine, that is, receives the gift of existence from the Beloved.

خرد مست و ملائک مست و جان مست
هوا مست و زمین مست آسمان مست

The Intellect drunk, the Angels drunk, and the soul drunk;
The air drunk, and the earth drunk, the sky drunk.

This is again a famous verse of Persian poetry because it repeats over and over the word *mast*, meaning "drunk." Since all existence comes from Her Being, everything is spiritually drunk as a result of the fact that it exists. To fully understand this verse causes the reader himself or herself to become spiritually drunk.

فلک سرگشته از وی در تکاپوی
هوا در دل به امّید یکی بوی

Heavens wandering, searching for Her with effort,
Desire in the heart with the hope of smelling [Her perfume].

This verse reasserts the truth of creatures moving in search of the Creator and the human heart yearning for Her Presence, expressed poetically as the sweet smell that emanates from the perfume of Her Being.

ملائک خورده صاف از کوزهٔ پاک
به جرعه ریخته دردی در این خاک

The angels have drunk directly (*ṣāf*) from the clean jug,
From that gulp, a dreg has fallen in this earth.

Pure or *ṣāf* refers to the Divine Wine from which dregs have dropped into the world of terrestrial existence. "Drunk directly" could also be rendered as "in a pure way."

عناصر گشته زان یک جرعه سرخوش
فتاده گه در آب و گه در آتش

The elements have become merry from that single gulp,
Sometimes, falling into water, sometimes fire.

The elements constituting this world have themselves become joyous from the single gulp of that wine that has fallen upon them, becoming sometimes the element water and other times its opposite, fire.

ز بوی جرعه‌ای کافتاد بر خاک
برآمد آدمی تا شد بر افلاک

From the aroma of that gulp that fell upon the Earth,
Man arose until he reached the heavens.

Much has been written in Sufi literature, including by Rūmī, about the drop of the Divine Wine that fell upon the Earth. Shabistarī follows this long tradition in this verse.

ز عکس او تن پژمرده جان یافت
ز تابش جان افسرده روان یافت

From Her Image, the decrepit body found life.

From the casting of Her Light, the sad soul began to flow.[6]

The body comes to life through Her, through emanation from the Source of all Life. And it is through and by means of the emanation of the Divine Light that the soul begins to flow toward its Source.

جهانی خلق از او سرگشته دائم
ز خان و مان خود برگشته دائم

A whole created world is constantly bewildered by Her,
It has turned away from its household and family [towards Her].

The verse turns again to the attraction of beings to the Beloved and the spiritual person's leaving worldly life for Her.

یکی از بوی دردش ناقل آمد
یکی از نیم جرعه عاقل آمد

One person, simply smelling the dregs, became a conveyor [of the truth] (*nāqil*),
Another from half a gulp, became wise (*'āqil*).[7]

Authentic spirituality is combined with truthfulness and wisdom. The Divine Wine brings about both drunkenness and wisdom. *'Āqil* which I have translated here as "wise" means literally possessing *'aql*, or intellect.

یکی از جرعه‌ای گردیده صادق
یکی از یک صراحی گشته عاشق

One person through one gulp has become truthful (*ṣādiq*),
Another from one container has become a lover.

The Divine Wine makes one a knower of the Truth as well as Its lover. It is the source of both sapiential knowledge and spiritual love. That is why Sufis speak of love and knowledge, *maḥabbah* and *ma'rifah* as the two paths and means available to man to reach God.

یکی دیگر فرو برده به یک بار
می و میخانه و ساقی و میخوار

Another person has gulped down all at once,
The wine, the tavern, the pourer of wine, and the drinker of wine.[8]

The verse is again a reference to the final goal of spiritual realization in which all that is other than God is transcended.

کشیده جمله و مانده دهن باز
زهی دریا دل رند سرافراز

He has drunk everything and remains open-mouthed.
Long live the exalted *rind* who has the heart of an ocean.[9]

The term *rind* is very difficult to translate into a single English term; so I have kept the original Persian. In Persian *rind* means a person who does not obey social norms outwardly but is chivalrous on the inside. In everyday language *rind* means "clever" or "cunning," but in Sufism it also refers to a person who lives for the inner meaning of life and its experiences and so seems not to superficially conform to regulations and norms.

در آشامیده هستی‌را به یک بار
فراغت یافته ز اقرار و انکار

He has drunk existence all at once;
He has become free from having to affirm or deny.

Having gone beyond the realm of separative existence, such a person transcends duality that characterizes the created order, including the duality of affirmation and/or negation that belong to the phenomenal world.

شده فارغ ز زهد خشک و طامات
گرفته دامن پیر خرابات

He has become free from dry asceticism and vainglorious speech (*ṭāmāt*),
He has grabbed the skirt of the spiritual master of the Tavern of Ruins.

Having gone beyond asceticism, which is the first stage of the spiritual path, such a person attaches himself and holds firmly to the Sufi master.

The States of the People of the Tavern of Ruins (*Kharābātī*)

خراباتی شدن از خود رهائیست
خودی کفر است اگر خود پارسائیست

To become a person of the Tavern of Ruins is to become free from oneself.
To be ensnared in oneself is infidelity even if it be the purity of the self.

The heart of the Sufi message is contained in this verse. To become free from oneself requires initiation and spiritual practice, which alone can free man from his lower self—the part that is not as yet purified but makes pious claims about itself. Only initiation allows one to enter the *kharābāt.*

نشانی داده‌اند اهل خرابات
که «التوحید اسقاط الاضافات»

The people of the Tavern of Ruins have indicated,
That "Unity (*tawḥīd*) is the casting away of [all] additions."

Those who have become Sufis know that to reach Unity one has to go beyond all otherness. The Arabic phrase, "Unity is the casting away of all additions" is a famous Sufi adage.

خرابات از جهان بی‌مثالی است
مقام عاشقان لاابالی است

The Tavern of Ruins comes from the world that has no similitude;
It is the spiritual station of lovers who are carefree (*lā-ubālī*).

"The world that has no similitude" refers to the upper or spiritual world. "Lovers who are carefree" means those who have broken all attachments to the world. They are detached from the world and its formalities but are attached to the spiritual path and, of course, ultimately to God.

خرابات آشیان مرغ جان است
خرابات آستان لامکان است

The Tavern of Ruins is the nest of the bird of the soul;
The Tavern of Ruins is the threshold of the Spaceless.

The real home of the soul is not this earthly abode but the Sufi "center," whose reality itself opens unto that Reality that is beyond the earthly, beyond space and by implication time.

خراباتی خراب اندر خراب است
که در صحرای او عالم سراب است

The dweller of the Tavern of Ruins is ruin within ruin,
For in his desert, the whole world is but a mirage.

The spiritual person has torn down his or her ego and even ruined that ruin. In the spiritual desert he reaches a state in which he or she realizes the irreality of this world, seeing it as it really is, that is, a mirage.

خراباتی است بی حدّ و نهایت
نه آغازش کسی دیده نه غایت

The dweller of the Tavern of Ruins is without limit and end.
No one has ever seen his beginning, or end.

The Sufi traveler on the spiritual path has gone beyond the confines of the ego to a state of being that has no boundary and opens unto the Reality of the Boundless. Hence, one sees in the soul of such a person nether an origin nor an end.

اگر صد سال در وی می‌شتابی
نه خودرا و نه کس‌را بازیابی

If for a hundred years thou hastenest in pursuit of him,
Thou wilt find neither thyself nor someone else in him.

The pursuit of authentic spirituality requires possessing the necessary qualifications for such a task. Without them, if one were to hasten a hundred years in search of the inner reality in oneself, one would not discover oneself nor anyone else.

گروهی اندر او بی پا و بی سر
همه نی مؤمن و نه نیز کافر

There is a group among them who have no feet and no head;
All are neither faithful nor infidel.

Among those who seek, however, there are those who have given up everything in their search and have gone beyond the dichotomy of faith and infidelity.

شراب بیخودی در سر گرفته
به ترک جمله خیر و شر گرفته

They have drunk the wine of selflessness;
They have left all good and evil.

"They have left all good and evil" means going beyond all duality. They have done so by drinking the Divine Wine that has enabled them to go beyond their selves, beyond their egos, and beyond otherness.

شرابی خورده هر یک بی‌لب و کام
فراغت یافته از ننگ و از نام

They have drunk wine without lips and without joy (*kām*),
Having become freed from all blemish and all name.

Kām means to benefit from the joy of doing something. "Without joy" here refers to the ordinary pleasure of drinking wine. The spiritual Wine is drunk without using one's lips or deriving ordinary pleasure from it. Thereby the drinkers of this Wine have overcome their shortcomings and even their ordinary consciousness of their own identity.

حدیث و ماجرای شطح و طامات
خیال خلوت و نور کرامات

The story and event of ecstatic locutions and great claims;
Imagination of the spiritual retreat and the light of miracles.

Shaṭḥ-u tāmāt is a reference to the extreme states in which the soul undergoes extraordinary experiences and utters ecstatic sayings that do not make sense if viewed only outwardly (*shaṭḥ*), as well as extraordinary claims of miraculous powers. The soul thus turns to the states attained in the Sufi spiritual retreat and the light that emanates from the miracles of saints and prophets.

به بوی دردئی از دست داده
ز ذوق نیستی مست اوفتاده

Smelling the dregs of the Wine which they have lost;
Falling drunk as a result of the taste of non-existence.

The aroma of the Divine Wine still persists even if the Wine is no longer there. The person who experiences it becomes drunk from the "tasting" of the state of nonexistence in the sense of the Sufi *fanā'*.

عصا و رکوه و تسبیح و مسواک
گرو کرده به دردی جمله‌را پاک

The cane, the prayer mat, the rosary and toothbrush,
They have exchanged them all purely for that dreg of Wine.

The first hemistich refers to different elements used by Muslims for purification and prayer. They are all given up for even the dregs of the Divine Wine. "Given up" here does not mean simply that they are neglected but also that they are transcended. One cannot give up what one does not possess.

میان آب و گل افتان و خیزان
به جای اشک خون از دیده ریزان

Between water and clay, he fell and got up,

In place of tears, blood flows from their eyes.

The spiritual seeker, like all men, is between "water and clay," which refers to the creation of all men. He still stumbles on the path, but each time he gets up and continues on the path to the One. The path presents many obstacles, and so he is in a state even beyond tears, shedding blood instead. The "they" in the above verses includes both men and women.

گهی از سرخوشی در عالم ناز
شده چون شاطران گردن افراز

Sometimes, from joy in the world of caress (*'ālam-i nāz*),
Having become like the bakers (*shāṭirān*) who hold up their necks.

"In the world of caress" (*'ālam-i nāz*), means in the spiritual world. *Shāṭir* means baker, but it is usually a symbol of a person who is very sure of himself, dominant, positive, and so forth. "Who hold up their necks" means they are proud of what they do.

گهی از روسیاهی رو به دیوار
گهی از سرخروئی بر سر دار

Sometimes, from the face becoming darkened, the head is turned towards the wall;
Sometimes, because of his the face, the head is upon the gibbet.

"His face becoming darkened" refers to the state resulting from loss of spirituality or loss of the way. While red face indicates spiritual intensity, which leads symbolically to the end faced by Ḥallāj. These verses are all references to both events in the history of *taṣawwuf* and different realities of the Sufi path. What Shabistarī is trying to do in this section is to show the vast variety and diversity of spiritual experiences of the men and women who walk upon the Sufi path.

گهی اندر سماع شوق جانان
شده بی پا و سر چون چرخ گردان

Sometimes in a state of spiritual concert (*samā'*) from the ardent desire (*shawq*) for the Beloved,
Having become without foot and head (*bī pā-wu sar*) like a turning wheel.

As mentioned already, *samā',* which means hearing, has a technical connotation in Sufism. It means the spiritual concert and spiritual dance developed so fully in the Mawlawiyyah Order. "Without foot and head" means losing one's ordinary balance and composure.

به هر نغمه که از مطرب شنیده
بدو وجدی از آن عالم رسیده

From every melody that he has heard from the troubadour,
From that other world, ecstasy has reached him.

Troubadour (*muṭrib* in Arabic and Persian, from which the English word is derived) refers here to the spiritual teacher, the bringer of the Divine Wine that is also celestial music. And so, each melody heard creates in him ecstasy.

سماع جان نه آخر صوت و حرف است
که در هر پرده‌ای سرّی شگرف است

The music (*samā'*) of the soul, finally, is not sound and words,
For in each mode (*pardah*) there exists a remarkable mystery.

The inner reality of *samā'* is beyond the world of sound and words. It is inaudible to the external ear. Yet, each mode of it reveals a Divine Mystery.

ز سر بیرون کشیده دلق دهتوی
مجرّد گشته از هر رنگ و هر بوی

He has taken off the ten-layered dress from his head,
And he has become freed (*mujarrad*) from every color and every smell.

The first hemistich refers symbolically to the layers or states of separative consciousness. In ordinary language, *mujarrad* means to be "single" or unmarried. Philosophically, it means to be in a state of catharsis, but in Sufism (and in some schools of Islamic philosophy) it means to pull the roots of the soul from the material world, to be cut off from all materiality and potentiality—and so, *mujarradāt* means "purely intelligible" beings.

فرو شسته بدان صاف مروّق
همه رنگ سیاه و سبز و ازرق

Through it, he has washed off that pure Wine,
[And] all black, green, and blue colors.

Through spiritual realization the manifested order is transcended.

یکی پیمانه خورده از میی صاف
شده زآن صوفی صافی ز اوصاف

Drinking one cup of that pure Wine, [becoming] purified from I-ness
He has become through it a Sufi pure from descriptions.

To become a Sufi one has to drink that pure Wine that enables one to become free of limitation, becoming a: *ṣūfi-yi ṣāfī zi awṣāf* (a Sufi pure from descriptions). In this second hemistich, Shabistarī plays in a clever manner with the letter *ṣād*, which is repeated consecutively three times.

به مژگان خاک مزبل پاک رفته
ز هرچه آن دیده از صد یک نگفته

With the eyelashes, he has swept clean the earth full of dirt,
From whatever he has seen, from a hundred he has not [even] revealed one.

The Sufi disciple cleans off the dust with the most delicate part of his face. Truths are then revealed to him about which he remains primarily silent, exposing outwardly even less than one percent of it.

گرفته دامن رندان خمّار
ز شیخی و مریدی گشته بیزار

He has grasped the skirt of the drunken *rinds*,
He has become alienated from the state of master and disciple.

Continuing to describe the state of one who has arrived spiritually, Shabistarī speaks of such a person grasping the dress of *rinds*, a term that has been explained already. In this state such a person goes even beyond the duality of master/disciple.

چه شیخی و مریدی این چه قید است؟
چه جای زهد و تقوی این چه شید است؟

What spiritual direction? What spiritual discipleship? What kind of restriction is this?
Where is the place here for asceticism and reverence? What kind of hypocrisy is this?

This verse follows the above, again breaking the ordinary mold of Sufi teachings in an iconoclastic manner.

اگر روی تو باشد در که و مه
بت و زنّار و ترسائی تورا به

If thy face be towards the great and the small,
The idol, the belt (*zunnār*) and being a Christian is better for thee.

"If thy face be toward the great and the small" means if thou art involved with all kinds of people, if thou art worldly, if thy soul is always immersed in the social ambiance around thee, and thou canst not tear thyself away to pay attention to God, it is better just to remain a Christian and not to become a Sufi.

Question [15]

بت و زنّار و ترسائی در این کوی
همه کفر است ورنه چیست بر گوی؟

The idol, the belt (*zunnār*) and Christianity in this domain,
Is it all infidelity? If not, then tell me, what is it?

Having spoken of elements of the traditional dress and its accompaniments of Christian monks, the question is then asked about its inner meaning.

Answer

بت اینجا مظهر عشق است و وحدت
بود زنّار بستن عقد خدمت

Here, idol is the manifestation of love and Divine Unity.
The belt is to tie the knot of service.

In contrast to the verse above, here Christian elements are explained positively in light of their symbolic meaning. Idol here, of course, means a Christian figure or form.

چو کفر و دین بود قائم به هستی
شود توحید عین بت‌پرستی

Since infidelity and religion subsist through Being,
Unity becomes the same as idol worship.

This is again one of the most famous verses of Persian poetry, being also a very daring verse. "Since infidelity and religion subsist through Being," they both confirm the primal reality of Being. If one were to turn to the reality of the being of even an idol, one would see therein the reality of Being Itself and therefore realize Unity. This verse reiterates to some extent the verses that will soon follow:

If the Muslim were to know what an idol is,
He would know that religion is idol-worship.[1]

چو اشیا هست هستی‌را مظاهر
از آن جمله یکی بت باشد آخر

Since objects are loci of manifestation (*maẓāhir*) of Being
Among them then one is the idol.

Maẓāhir is the plural of *maẓhar*, which can mean "reflection," "theophany," or "symbol," but literally it means the place of *ẓuhūr* (appearance) or locus of manifestation. The idol by the very fact that it exists is a *maẓhar* that reflects God.

نکو اندیشه کن ای مرد عاقل
که بت از روی هستی نیست باطل

Think clearly, o wise man,
That the idol is not false (*bāṭil*) because of its being.

The wise person, or literally "the person of intellect," realizes that the idol is not false because it exists but because of the false attribution that the ordinary idolator gives to it.

بدان کایزد تعالی خالق اوست
ز نیکو هر چه صادر گشت نیکوست

Realize that the Transcendent Divinity is its creator,
[And] whatever issues from the Good is good.

This verse brings up the question of evil and its origin, and therefore concerns a very subtle and difficult matter. Since all that exists comes from God, Who is good, and in fact *the* Good as Plato says, does that mean that there is no evil? The verse seems to imply that assertion and therefore leads to the whole question of good and evil. Where does evil come from? First of all, God is the source of all being. Secondly, God is good. Third, that which is good cannot but create that which is good, and the Quran points directly to the goodness of God's creation, a truth that is central to Islam. Islam is not like Manicheism or a popular interpretation of Christianity, where the world is seen as evil or in a fallen state. The Quran says, *rabbanā mā khalaqta hādhā bāṭilan*, "Our Lord, Thou hast not created this in vain" (Q. 3:191), which includes the word *bāṭil* (false, in vain) that was mentioned in the previous verse of the *Gulshan-i rāz*. So, the Islamic point of view, especially its metaphysical dimension, is that in Being and its manifestations there is no evil. Evil is really the "crystallization" and consequence of separation from God. One can compare it to light as it separates from a lamp and shines toward the other side of a room. In doing so the light grows weaker and weaker and shadows begin to appear. The shadows, however, do not possess a positive reality of their own although they seem to be real. Shadow is the result of the weakening or lack of light. Our eyes experience that lack as something, as if it had positive existence. You can say, "It is dark here," but that verb "is" that you are using is really metaphorical, because darkness has no being of its own. What has being is light, whose lack is experienced as darkness. It is to this reality that Shabistarī is referring.

Otherwise, to just say there is no evil and you can do whatever you like, as the Sufis are sometimes accused of believing, is a kind of New Age interpretation of traditional metaphysics. In modern times this kind of interpretation has become prevalent especially since Neo-Vedanta became popular in the United States and Britain after the Second World War. Many books were written by Neo-Vedantists, especially in California, based on the idea that since Vedantic nonduality is true, that there is no evil, and consequently "everything goes," you might say that this idea of evil so commonly used is a traditional Christian invention. This assertion is, however, false. There is evil on the level of relativity. Otherwise, the Quran would not speak so much about it. In Hinduism, and indeed in every orthodox religion, the issue of evil is discussed as a reality on the human plane, while the Absolute is both good and beyond the relativity of good and evil. That truth is not to be confused with what Shabistarī is saying here.

وجود آنجا که باشد محض خیر است
وگر شرّیست در وی آن ز غیر است

Wherever there is being, there is the pure Good.
If there is evil, it comes from something else.

If you see an evil or something bad, it is not from the Being of that thing or event. It is from the lack of and separation from being you might say. Evil is *'adam* (nonexistence), parading as existence or being.

مسلمان گر بدانستی که بت چیست
بدانستی که دین در بت‌پرستی است

If the Muslim were to know what an idol is,
He would know that religion is idol-worship.[2]

Considering all the Quranic verses about the sin of idolatry, this verse is certainly a very daring one, in fact perhaps the most daring verse of classical Sufi literature. Can you imagine this verse being written by a Muslim? The Prophet had 'Alī and Bilāl go on top of the Ka'bah and break all the idols of the *Jāhiliyyah*, and the Quran rejects idol worship so directly. This verse is, therefore, a very daring formulation but at the same time a very profound and beautiful verse.

To add a personal note, my father, who was a well-known authority in Persian literature and Islamic thought and a devout Muslim, always used to say this verse was his favorite poem in the Persian language, and I knew it already when I was just a child. It is incomprehensible to understand how a Muslim could say something like that unless one turns to its esoteric meaning. Ordinary people thought that what Shaykh Maḥmūd Shabistarī was saying was a terrible error, but what he says is that all that exists, by virtue of its very existence, is a *tajallī*, a manifestation of Divine Names and Qualities. That is why this daring verse is so important.

وگر مشرک ز بت آگاه گشتی
کجا در دین خود گمراه گشتی؟

If a polytheist (*mushrik*) were to become aware of what an idol is,
How could he go astray in his religion?

Mushrik means someone who takes a partner unto God, from the word *shirk* in Arabic that means "taking a partner unto God." It is a theological term in Arabic that goes back to Quranic Arabic and also exists in various forms in other Islamic languages. If one were to become aware of what an idol really *is*, how could one be lost and lose one's way in his religion?

ندید او از بت الّا خلق ظاهر
بدین علّت شد اندر شرع کافر

He did not see in the idol save the external creation of it.
It is for this reason that he became an infidel from the point of view of Divine Law.

To become limited in one's understanding of an idol by confining it to its external form is to be considered an infidel from the *Sharī'ite* point of view, not from seeing it in its very existence.

تو هم گر زو نبینی حقّ پنهان
به شرع اندر نخوانندت مسلمان

Thou also, if thou seest not the hidden truth in it,
According to the Divine Law, they will not call thee a Muslim.

Here, Shabistarī is talking about the importance of the esoteric meaning. If viewed only outwardly, one would not be called a Muslim from the point of view of the *Sharī'ah*.

ز اسلام مجازی گشته بیزار
که‌را کفر حقیقی شد پدیدار

Of this metaphorical Islam a person becomes disdainful,
He in whom the real *kufr* has become manifest.[3]

The meaning of this verse would be clearer if the order of the hemistiches were to be reversed. Real *kufr* here has an esoteric connotation and is positive. He who has realized the inner truth of the idol wishes to go beyond the outer meaning of Islam to reach its essence.

The term "metaphorical Islam" here connotes the superficial understanding of Islam.

درون هر بتی جانیست پنهان
به زیر کفر ایمانیست پنهان

Within every idol, there is a hidden soul;
Under every infidelity, there is a hidden faith.

These verses have meaning and application on many different levels, one of which is the world of nature. There are many people today who do not believe in God, but they have love for God's creation in the forms of the natural world. Many people who deal with the natural environment these days are agnostics or atheists, that is, they think they are so, but actually they are seeing God's Signs in His creation without realizing that they are *His* signs.

همیشه کفر در تسبیح حقّ است
«و ان من شیء» گفت اینجا چه دقّ است؟

Infidelity is always in praise of the Truth.
He said, "There is nothing [that does not praise God]." What is to question here?

In this verse Shabistarī is quoting the verse of the Quran, *wa in min shay'in illā yusabbiḥu bi-ḥamdihi*, "And there is no thing, save that it hymns His praise" (Q. 17:44). There is, therefore, nothing that does not praise God. So, the existence of infidelity qua existence can be no exception. False assertion is opposed to the truth, but the being of everything including the infidel cannot but praise the Source of all that exists, of all being.

چه می‌گویم که دور افتادم از راه
«فذرهم» بعد ما جائت «قل الله»

What can I say for I have fallen away from the path,
"So leave them" has come after "Say, *Allāh*."

This verse is a reference to the Quran, "Say, '*Allāh*,' (*qul Allāh*) then leave them (*thumma dharhum*) to play at their vain discourse" (Q. 6:91).[4]

بدان خوبی رخ بت‌را که آراست
که گشتی بت‌پرست ار حقّ نمی‌خواست؟

Who has embellished the face of the idol so well,
That a person becomes an idol worshipper, if the Truth did not will it so.

In such traditions as Hinduism and Christianity, the icon would not play such a major religious role if God had not willed it.

هم او کرد و هم او گفت و هم او بود
نکو کرد و نکو گفت و نکو بود

It was He who acted, He who said, He who was,
He did goodness (*nikū*), He uttered goodness, He was goodness.

God, to whom He refers in this verse, is ultimately the only Agent, the only Source of the Word, the only Reality or Being. He is the Source of all goodness.

Nikū like *ḥusn* combines the meanings of goodness and beauty.

یکی بین و یکی گوی و یکی دان
بدین ختم آمد اصل و فرع ایمان

See one, say one, know one,
Through this are sealed the root and branches of faith.

The first hemistich can also be translated as "See the One, Utter the One, Know the One" because in Persian there is no article to correspond to "the." Both meanings are there. "Through this, the root and branches of faith are sealed" means that all religious truth is contained in the first hemistich. This verse is again one of the most famous verses in Sufi literature.

نه من می‌گویم این بشنو ز قرآن
تفاوت نیست اندر خلق رحمن

It is not I who say this. Listen to the Quran.
There is no flaw (*tafāwut*) in the creation of the Compassionate.[5]

Tafāwut, translated here as "flaw," can also be rendered as "difference." If so, the hemistich would mean that all of God's creation participates in the goodness that God has bestowed upon the created order.

نظر کردم بدیدم اصل هر کار
نشان خدمت آمد عقد زنّار

I observed, I saw the principle of everything;
The tying of the belt was a sign of service.

Having observed and seen the principle or inner meaning of things, one is able to understand the purpose of what exists in the created order. One sees that even the special belt worn by Christian monks is a sign of service to God and man.

نباشد اهل دانش‌را مؤوّل
ز هر چیزی مگر بر وضع اوّل

The people of knowledge do not possess [the need for] something to be
interpreted,
Among all things, except [by returning it] to what it was at the beginning.

The person of real knowledge does not simply interpret things but understands them by returning them to their Origin or Source, which determine their true nature.

میان در بند چون مردان به مردی
درآ در زمرهٔ «اوفوا بعهدی»

Tie a sash around thy belt in a manly manner like men;
Become among those [about whom God has said], "Fulfill My covenant."

"Tie a sash around thy belt" (*miyān dar band*), which could also be translated "gird thy loins," was what the warriors or *pahlavāns* used to do when they went to battle, as Firdawsī often describes in the *Shāhnāmah* (*The Book of Kings*), and this was also a sign of chivalry. The second hemistich contains a quotation from the Quran (Q. 2:40).

به رخش علم و چوگان عبادت
ز میدان در ربا گوی سعادت

[Riding] on the horse (*rakhsh*) of knowledge with the polo stick of worship,
Steal the ball of happiness from the field.

The whole verse uses the symbolism of polo, which has always been a major traditional sport in Persia. *Rakhsh* is actually the name of the horse of Rustam, the hero of the *Shāhnāmah* of Firdawsī, but is used here symbolically as an exemplary power that carries one to spiritual realization. Field symbolizes life itself, especially intellectual and spiritual life.

تورا از بهر این کار آفریدند
اگر چه خلق بسیار آفریدند

Thou hast been created for this task,
Although numerous creatures have been created.

Shabistarī is addressing actually those who are interested in the spiritual path. "Thou hast" refers to the person who is a seeker and who is now reading the *Gulshan-i rāz*. Not everybody reads the *Gulshan-i rāz*, and among those who do, not everyone understands its deeper meaning. So, he is addressing people who have in their heart the desire to read this text and gain an understanding of it in depth.

پدر چون علم و مادر هست اعمال
به سان قرة العین است احوال

The father is like knowledge and the mother is actions.
The states of the soul are like the coolness of the eyes.

Qurrat al-'ayn, literally the coolness of the eyes, refers to someone who is very close to you, and it comes from the cold tears that flow from the eye when one is happy and radiant. In English it could be also translated as the light of one's eyes. Spiritual attainment needs both true knowledge and correct action, the two together being necessary to make possible spiritual realization.

نباشد بی‌پدر انسان شکی نیست
مسیح اندر جهان بیش از یکی نیست

No doubt, there is no person without a father.
In the world there is only one Messiah.

Islam does not accept the filial relation between God and Christ that one finds in Christianity, but Islam does believe in the miraculous birth of Christ, the Messiah (*Masīḥ*), who had no biological father.

رها کن ترّهات و شطح و طامات
خیال نور و اسباب کرامات

Let go of trifles, theophanic locutions (*shaṭḥ*), and raving nonsense,
Imagining light and causes of miracles (*karāmāt*).

Turrahāt, shaṭḥ and *ṭāmāt* are all elements that have to do with the practice of *taṣawwuf. Turrahāt*, meaning trifles, can also mean the expression of spiritual states in a form that is difficult to understand. *Shaṭḥ* means a profound saying that makes no sense outwardly, and *ṭāmāt* can mean vainglorious speech, raving nonsense, or an utterance that appears to be nonsensical.

In this verse Shabistarī is not denigrating such realities, but he wants to emphasize that the goal of the Sufi path is God and that one should not become stuck in spiritual states and stages in such a way as not to be able to advance further to the Abode of the One.

کرامات تو اندر حقّ‌پرستی است
جز این کبر و ریا و عجب و هستی است

Thy miracle is in worshipping the Truth.
Everything else is haughtiness, ostentation, pride and (assertion of thine own) existence.

The biggest miracle that you can perform is not to walk on water but to reach God. Everything below that goal can stultify the soul and lead to the negative states he mentions in the second hemistich.

در این هر چیز کان جز باب فقر است
همه اسباب استدراج و مکر است

In this matter, everything that is other than spiritual poverty (*faqr*)
Is all cause for gradual withdrawal (*istidrāj*) and machination.

The first hemistich is a powerful assertion of the centrality of *faqr* in Sufism. The term *istidrāj* can also be read as a reference to Q. 68:44, *sa-nastadrijuhum min ḥaythu lā ya'lamūn*, "We shall lead them on little by little, whence they know not."

ز ابلیس لعین بی‌سعادت
شود صادر هزاران خرق عادت

From the cursed Devil (Iblīs), without happiness,
Issue a thousand miracles (*kharq-i 'ādat*).[6]

Iblīs is related etymologically to the words *diabolos* and *diable*, the Devil. *Kharq-i 'ādat*, which is usually translated as miracle means literally breaking of habit. We are all used to various habits not only in ourselves but also in the world of nature where we identify habit with laws of nature. If suddenly a flower comes out of the ground, we think it is a miracle because it breaks our habitual experience of such phenomena.

گه از دیوارت آید گاه از بام
گهی در دل نشیند گه در اندام

Sometimes, it appears from the walls, sometimes, from the roof;
Sometimes, it suddenly settles in thy heart, sometimes, in thy body.

The word "it" in the first hemistich refers to the duplicitous machinations of the Devil, which can affect both body and soul.

همی‌داند ز تو احوال پنهان
در آرد در تو کفر و فسق و عصیان

He knows always thy hidden states;
He brings out in thee infidelity, immorality (*fisq*) and rebellion (*'iṣyān*).

The Devil knows man's soul and its weaknesses of which he takes advantage to lead man to various forms of evil and immoral actions and thoughts.

شد ابلیست امام و در پسی تو
بدو لیکن بدین‌ها کی رسی تو

Thy Iblis has now become thy imam and thou are behind,
Then with him when art thou ever going to reach them?

If the Devil becomes our imam, leaving our souls behind and without true guidance, how are we going to reach spiritual realities?

کرامات تو گر در خودنمائی است
تو فرعونی و این دعوی خدائی است

If thy "miracles" (*karāmāt*) are self-display,
Thou art a Pharaoh, and this the claim of Divinity.

The claim of divinity on the part of the Pharaoh is often used in Sufi literature as an example of supreme self-aggrandizement and is therefore highly criticized. This understanding of the Pharaoh is also seen in some Sufi writings as having a metaphysical significance concerning the very nature of duality and opposition—and not only a moral one.

کسی کوراست با حقّ آشنائی
نیاید هرگز از وی خودنمائی

He who has familiarity with the Truth,
There never appears from him self-display (*khudnamā'ī*).

Khudnamā'ī also means to be proud or to show off. Anyone who is familiar with the Divine never displays any form of self-aggrandizement because he or she is in the state of spiritual poverty or *faqr*. His pride is *faqr* itself. The Prophet has said, *al-Faqru fakhrī* (Poverty is my pride).

همه روی تو در خلق است زنهار
مکن خودرا بدین علّت گرفتار

Thy face is all turned to creation, beware;
Do not entangle thyself because of this cause.

If our only concern is with the world and worldliness, we become deprived of the possibility of reaching God. So, Shabistarī warns the reader not to become entangled in such a state.

چو با عامه نشینی مسخ گردی
چه جای مسخ یک سر نسخ گردی

If thou sittest with ordinary people (*'āmmah*) thou wilt become
metamorphosed (*maskh*),
Not only metamorphosed, thou wilt become superceded (*naskh*).

'Āmmah, translated here as "ordinary people," is used in Arabic and Persian to refer to the majority of people in society in contrast to the *khawāṣṣ* who are the elite in a positive traditional sense and not the pejorative modern one. To be deprived of the company of the intellectual and spiritual elite is to be left behind on the road to human perfection.

مبادا هیچ با عامت سر و کار
که از فطرت شوی ناگه نگونسار

Do not under any condition have association with ordinary people,
For suddenly thou wilt depart from thy primordial nature (*fiṭrat*).

The first hemistich does not mean ordinary association concerning daily life, a condition that is not practical or even possible anyway, but in what concerns one's spiritual life. If one does not heed this advice, one will become ever more removed from the primordial nature in which God created us.

تلف کردی به هرزه نازنین عمر
نگوئی در چه کاریست اینچنین عمر

Thou hast wasted this precious life through what is futile (*harzah*),
Thou sayest not what is it that thou hast done with this kind of life.

Not seeking to return to one's *fiṭrah* is a futile way of living. It is to be disdained. A person who does so does not stop to ask himself what he has done with life that is precious and not to be squandered.

به جمعیّت لقب کردند تشویش
خری‌را پیشوا کردی زهی ریش

The crowd has been given the title "unsettled" (*tashwīsh*).
Thou hast chosen a donkey as thy leader, what a sore.

To choose to follow the crowd as one's guide is like choosing an ass as one's leader. The first hemistich refers to the condition of an ordinary crowd, which is in an unsettled state deprived of the certitude of principial knowledge.

فتاده سروری اکنون به جهّال
از آن گشتند مردم جمله بدحال

Now, leadership has fallen upon the ignorant,
That is why everyone is in such a bad state.

Even in traditional societies, sages complained of leadership having fallen into the hands of those who lacked true knowledge and were therefore not qualified.

نگر دجّال اعور تا چگونه
فرستاده است در عالم نمونه

Look at how the one-eyed Antichrist,
Has sent into this world samples.

In the traditional description of the Antichrist, he is depicted as having only one eye. Before appearing, he has sent into this world his representatives who not only deny the truth but also propagate error as truth. Guénon refers to those two stages of the destruction of tradition as anti-tradition and countertradition.[7]

نمونه باز بین ای مرد حسّاس
خر اورا که نامش هست جسّاس

O man who has some sensitivity, look at this example,
At his donkey whose name is *Jassās*.

The proper name of the donkey of the Antichrist in traditional accounts is *Jassās*.

خران‌را بین همه در تنگ آن خر
شده از جهل پیش‌آهنگ آن خر

Look at those donkeys who are all assembled around that donkey,
Who through ignorance have become those who march in front of that donkey.[8]

"Donkey" here is used in this verse metaphorically to refer to those who deny tradition and even rebel against it and so are marching in front of the donkey of Antichrist.

چو خواجه قصهٔ آخر زمان کرد
به چندین جا از این معنی بیان کرد

When the Prophet (*Khwājah*) recounted the story of the end of the world,
In several places he explained this meaning.

Khwājah has many meanings in Persian, such as "master" or "learned person," but when it is used in this and also in much of Sufi literature, it is a title of the Prophet—*'alayhi'l-ṣalātu wa'l-salām*. In many Persian works the Prophet is called Khwājah-yi kā'ināt, or "the Master of creation." When the term *khwājah* is used alone in works of Sufi poetry it is often in reference to Ḥāfiẓ, while in Islamic philosophy it is in reference to Naṣīr al-Dīn Ṭūsī.

ببین اکنون که کور و کر شبان شد
علوم دین همه بر آسمان شد

Look how now the deaf and the blind have become shepherds.
The sciences of religion have gone up in the air.

It is as if this verse were written for our times, but this reality also existed to a lesser degree in Shabistarī's time and in fact here and there in earlier Islamic history. The second hemistich means that when those who are deaf and blind spiritually and intellectually become guides of the people who need real guidance, authentic sciences of religion disappear from the world.

نماند اندر میانه رفق و آزرم
نمی‌دارد کسی از جاهلی شرم

There does not remain any longer friendship and solidarity (*āzarm*).
No one is ashamed of being ignorant.

Āzarm means not only "solidarity" but also "amity" and "closeness." When this virtue disappears, the shame of being ignorant also disappears, and some even take pride in denying the truth and ignorance of it.

همه احوال عالم بازگونه است
اگر تو عاقلی بنگر که چون است

The whole condition of the world is upside down.
If thou art wise, be aware that is it so.

If that was the condition of traditional Islamic society centuries ago, what would Shabistarī say of today's world? Even in traditional times sages compared the conditions of their own society to that of the ideal society, or what Fārābī called *al-madīnat al-fāḍilah* or the Virtuous City.

کسی کو باب لعن و طرد و مقت است
پدر نیکو بد، اکنون شیخ وقت است

He who is the gate of curse, rejection and opposition,
His father was good; now he is the Shaykh of the moment.

This verse is a harsh criticism of some of those who claimed religious and spiritual authority during the period in which the author lived.

خضر می‌کشت آن فرزند طالح
که آنرا بد پدر با جدّ صالح

Khidr was killing that wicked progeny,
Who had a father with a righteous ancestor.

This is a reference to the story of Moses and Khiḍr (Q. 18:65–82), when Khiḍr took a young boy and killed him, Moses being very upset because he did not understand the intention of the act that Khiḍr was performing. In that story, Moses represents exoterism and Khiḍr esoterism. *Jadd*, which has been translated here as "ancestor," also means "grandfather."

کنون با شیخ خود کردی تو ای خر
خری‌را کز خری هست از تو خرتر

Now, with thy Shaykh, thou hast done o donkey [an asinine act]
Is there an ass who in being asinine is more asinine than thee?

This is strong criticism of one who takes an unqualified person as his or her spiritual master.

چو او «لا یعرف الهرّ من البرّ»
چگونه پاک گرداند تورا سرّ

Since he does not "distinguish one thing from another" (*lā ya'rafu 'l-hirr min al-birr*),
How can he purify thy spiritual secret (*sirr*)?

"He" in the first stanza is in reference to the unqualified so-called master. The Arabic phrase *lā ya'rafu 'l-hirr min al-birr* is a proverbial expression used also in Persian. Secret (*sirr*) in the second hemistich is a technical Sufi expression referring to man's inner spiritual reality.

و گر دارد نشان باب خود پور
چه گویم چون بود «نورٌ علی نور»

If the son has the characteristics of his father,
What can I say, it is "light upon light."

This verse continues the sarcastic tone of the verses above. The words "light upon light" are of course a reference to the Light Verse in the Quran (Q. 24:35), which has entered into everyday Persian to mean "so much the better."

پسر کو نیکـرای و نیکـبخت است
چو میوه زبده اندر سر درخت است

A son who is of good thought and good fortune,
Is like choice fruit at the top of the tree.

No matter what family background one possesses, if one entertains that which is true and good, one is like a good fruit clinging to the top of the fruit tree.

ولیکن شیخ دین کی گردد آن کو
نداند نیک از بد بد ز نیکو؟

However, could he become the Shaykh of religion, if he,
Does not know the good from the bad and the bad from the good?

"He" in the first hemistich refers to a person who wants to become an authentic spiritual master. How can such a person become a master if he cannot distinguish good from evil?

مریدی علم دین آموختن بود
چراغ دل ز نور افروختن بود

To become a disciple was learning the science of religion;
It was lighting the lamp of the heart.

Using past tense, Shabistarī wants to refer to what the authentic tradition was in days of old. It was to learn the science of religion in depth and to illuminate the heart through spiritual practice.

کسی از مرده علم آموخت هرگز؟
ز خاکستر چراغ افروخت هرگز؟

Has anyone ever learned knowledge from the dead?
Has a lamp ever been lit by means of ash?

To learn knowledge from the dead of course refers to operative esoteric knowledge and not ordinary knowledge, which we often learn from the works of those who have died. The transmission of esoteric knowledge and guidance needs an authentic living master. It must be added, however, that there are in Sufism certain masters who can guide the living despite being physically dead, but such figures cannot be considered to be dead spiritually.

مرا در دل همی آید کز این کار
ببندم بر میان خویش زنّار

In my heart there continues to come [the desire], in this matter,
To tie a belt (*zunnār*) around my waist.

The verse refers of course to Christian monasticism but is metaphorical language to describe devoting oneself fully to the spiritual life.

نه زان معنی که من شهرت ندارم
که دارم لیك از وی هست عارم

Not in the sense that I am not famous;
For I am, yet I am embarrassed that I am so.

The spiritually accomplished may remain unknown, but they could also be famous and well-known. Shabistarī adds that he belongs to the second category but not only is not proud of this but also embarrassed by it. An authentic master seeks neither fame nor fortune.

شریکم چون خسیس آمد در این کار
خمولم بهتر از شهرت به بسیار

Since my partner became stingy in this matter,
My becoming humbled is much better than being famous.

This verse again emphasizes the importance of humility and the refusal to court fame.

دگرباره رسید الهامی از حقّ
که بر حکمت مگیر از ابلهی دقّ

Once again, an inspiration came from the Truth,
That from a fool do not expect wisdom.

One of the characteristics of wisdom, given by God, is to be able to know where to seek and find authentic wisdom—and not to expect to find it in a fool.

اگر کنّاس نبود در ممالک
همه خلق اوفتند اندر مهالک

If there were to be no well-diggers (*kannās*) in various countries,
All the people would be in a calamitous state.

A *kannās* is a person who digs wells to be used primarily for bathrooms, a job seen to be of low social status. If, however, even such a lowly job did not exist, the result would be a disaster. What Shabistarī is implying is that you need all kinds of people to make a world, and that it is not possible in practice to have a society constituted of only the wise and the sagacious.

بود جنسیّت آخر علّت ضمّ
چنین آمد جهان والله اعلم

Similarity of nature is the cause of people gathering together;
The world is like that, and God knows best.

The first hemistich is a Persian verse of the English proverb, "Birds of a feather fly together," but it can also be interpreted in a grammatical sense: that is, the world is also like the words of the Arabic alphabet, with different declensions depending on what part of speech affects the other.

ولی از صحبت نااهل بگریز
عبادت خواهی از عادت بپرهیز

But flee from discourse with someone unworthy (*nā-ahl*),
If thou wantest to worship (*'ibādat*), avoid habit (*'ādat*).

Nā-ahl can also mean someone who is not of your ilk, so to speak—someone who does not follow the right principles, or someone who is not naturally inclined to do something positive. In Arabic and Persian script, the words for worship (*'ibādat*) and habit (*'ādat*) are written in a very similar way, with just the letter *bā'* distinguishing them. To avoid habit here means both bad habits and a particular act that is done on a whim. It does not refer to good habits such as daily prayers, which should, however, become habitual but always done with good intentions and awareness.

نگردد جمع با عادت عبادت
عبادت میکنی بگذار عادت

One cannot add worship and habit.
If thou worshippest, put aside habit.

This verse follows the message of the previous verse. Obviously, if we perform our prayers every day, it becomes a habit. But what Shabistarī is saying is that it should never become just a habit in the sense that you are merely performing it automatically, in the same way that you get up every morning, brush your teeth, have breakfast, and go to work. Every time you pray is a new chapter of your meeting with God. It should not be seen as just a habit. A human example of this reality can be seen when a young man and a woman meet each other and fall in love. Every time they see each other it feels special and not a boring repetition. The relation with God should be like falling in love for the first time. *'Ibādat* should never be just habit. To be in the habit of performing the daily prayers is a very good thing, but the act of prayers should always be something fresh, not just carrying out an old, tired ritual, as some people claim about religious rites. Obviously, each time we pray must be fresh like the early morning breeze. For over seventy years I have performed my prayers continuously. If there were not something fresh every time in performing these prayers, I wouldn't be able to continue. In every prayer there is new life, a fresh meeting with God.

An Indication of Christianity

ز ترسائی غرض تجرید دیدم
خلاص از ربقهٔ تقلید دیدم

I saw the purpose of Christian monasticism (*tarsā'ī*) to be catharsis (*tajrīd*);
I saw it to be freedom from the bonds of imitation.

When he says Christian monasticism, (*tarsā'ī*) he means a life devoted to spirituality and based on *tajrīd*, which means "spiritual catharsis." The term "catharsis" should be understood in its original sense in classical Greek, meaning "disentanglement from potentiality and materiality," not in its modern psychological and mental sense.

جناب قدس وحدت دیر جان است
که سیمرغ بقارا آشیان است

The exalted Sacred Presence of Divine Unity is the monastery (*dayr*) of the soul,

Which is the nest of the Griffin of subsistence (in God).

Continuing with the symbol of the Christian monastery, Shabistarī reminds us that it (the *dayr*) is the Divine Presence itself, where the Griffin (*Sīmurgh* in Persian and *al-'Anqā'* in Arabic) resides. I have already explained the symbolism of the *Sīmurgh* and remind you of 'Aṭṭār's *Manṭiq al-ṭayr* and the symbolism of the *Sīmurgh* therein.

ز روح الله پیدا گشت این کار
که از روح القدس آمد پدیدار

This matter became evident through the Spirit of God,
Which became manifest (*padīdār*) through the Holy Spirit.

Let me add here that *Rūḥullāh* (*Rūḥ Allāh*), the Spirit of God, is also used as a proper name, especially in Persian, but sometimes has been considered as contentious by some people. This issue became prominent when Ayatollah Ruhullah Khomeini came to power, and suddenly the word Ruḥullah, which we always had as a proper name in Persian, became known all over the world. This term is not usually used as a proper name in the Arab world. But Ruḥullah as a proper name does not mean God's Spirit in the literal sense. We have a spirit, and it is the highest element of our being—but the Spirit of God is not the highest reality of God. The Spirit is below God's Essence. As a *ḥadīth* states, *awwalu mā khalaqa'Llāh al-rūḥ,* "The first thing that God created was the Spirit," and the Quran states, *al-rūḥ min amri rabbī*, "The Spirit is from the Command of my Lord" (Q. 17:85). In Islamic prophetology, *Ruḥullāh* is considered to be a title of Christ.

So, "This matter became evident through the Spirit of God" means the Spirit that God had created, not the Spirit of God seen in analogy to our spirit. It is important to be very careful about this matter. In metaphysics and theology, it is important to understand this distinction especially since Christianity speaks all the time about the Holy Spirit, the Holy Ghost as one of the hypostases of the Trinity along with Father and Son. There has been much complicated discussion about this matter. In Islam, where there is no Trinity, this matter is much simpler. In the Islamic context one should not put *Ruḥullāh* above the Divine Essence, Names and Qualities as we put our *ruḥ* above the rest of our being.

In the first hemistich *padīdār* translated as "evident" means also "visible" or "manifested."

هم از الله در پیش تو جانی است
که از قدّوس اندر وی نشانی است

There is also a soul in thee from God;
Which has a sign in it from the Sacred (*al-Quddūs*).[9]

Our soul is not derived from our body but is created by God, and thereby bears a sign of the sacred within itself. *Al-Quddūs,* the Sacred, is one of the revealed Divine Names.

اگر یابی خلاص از نفس ناسوت
درآیی در جناب قدس لاهوت

If thou becomest free from thy lower soul (*nafs-i nāsūt*).
Thou wilt arise into the Presence of the Exalted Sacred Divinity (*lāhūt*).

Terms such as *nāsūt, malakūt,* and *lāhūt* are common Sufi expressions often not properly translated into English in scholarly works. They are traditional descriptions of states of being. *Nāsūt* is related to the word *nās*, which means "human being," "man." So, *nāsūt* is the world of man. And then you have *malakūt*, *jabarūt*, *lāhūt,* and *hāhūt* referring to the hierarchical states of being, with *hāhūt* signifying the Divine Essence Itself. *Nafs-i nāsūt* means, therefore, the "ordinary soul," before the soul's ascent to higher states of being.

هر آن کس کو مجرّد چون ملک شد
چو روح الله بر چارم فلک شد

Whoever reaches catharsis (*mujarrad*) has become like the angel,
Like *Rūḥullāh*, he has gone to the fourth heaven.

The fourth heaven in Islamic astrology is the station of Christ, and the title of Christ is *Rūḥullāh*. So, this verse is a reference to that abode. *Mujarrad*, again, means to be in a state of catharsis (*tajrīd*), of being removed from potentiality and materiality.

Illustration

بود محبوس طفل شیرخواره
به نزد مادر اندر گاهواره

A breastfed child is a prisoner,
Before its mother, in the cradle.

This verse wishes to emphasize the utter reliance of a baby upon its mother, who symbolizes here biological functions in everyday ordinary life.

چو گشت او بالغ و مرد سفر شد
اگر مرد است همراه پدر شد

When he has become a grown-up and a man who journeys,
If he is a man, then he would follow his father.

Of course, these verses are symbolic. As the mother symbolizes here the guide and help for ordinary human life, the father symbolizes spiritual guidance in the journey toward catharsis of the soul. These references are not to be taken literally. In human life a mother can also be a spiritual guide and a father a person incapable of giving intellectual and spiritual guidance.

عناصر مرتورا چون امّ سفلی است
تو فرزند و پدر آباء علوی است

The [four] elements are like thy mother, in the lower world.
Thou art the child, and thy father is the 'fathers' of the world above.

"'Fathers' of the world above" is reference to realities of the archetypal world above, which are the sources of the realities in the world below.

از آن گفته است عیسی گاه اسرا
که آهنگ پدر دارم به بالا

It is for that reason that Jesus said at the time of his ascension,
"My intent is to reach my father (*āhang-i pidar dāram*) above."

Āhang means literally melody, but in the expression *āhang-i pidar dāram* it means metaphorically "to have the intent to reach my father."

تو هم جان پدر سوی پدر شو
بدر رفتند همراهان بدر شو

Thou also, o soul of the father, turn towards the father;
Others in company have already left; so leave.

"To turn toward the father" means to turn to the spiritual and intellectual dimension of existence. "So leave" means leave ordinary life and undertake the spiritual journey.

اگر خواهی که گردی مرغ پرواز
جهان جیفه پیش کرکس انداز

If thou wantest to become a flying bird,
Cast the world of the carcass before the vulture.

To travel upon the spiritual path and fly in the heaven of the Spirit one must throw away that lower soul, whose earthly weight prevents the bird of the soul from spiritual flight.

به دونان ده مر این دنیای غدّار
که جز سگ را نشاید داد مردار

Give to those of a lowly [spiritual] station (*dūnān*) this contentious world
(*dunyā-yi ghaddār*),
Because dead cadavers should not be given save to a dog.

The word *dūnān*, literally "those who are low," is not to be taken as an individual appraisal and not a social one. It is used here from the point of view of the knowledge and practice of spirituality and of the intention of walking toward God. *Ghaddār* means contentious, full of struggle or opposition.

نسب چبود؟ تناسب را طلب کن
به حقّ رو آور و ترک نسب کن

What is genealogy (*nasab*)? Seek harmony (*tanāsub*).
Turn to the Truth and leave genealogy behind.

"What is genealogy?" means of what good is genealogy and boasting that, "I am the son of so and so"? *Nasab* and *tanāsub* come from the same root in Arabic, and Shabistarī is playing poetically on that fact. To turn to the Divine Truth, one must leave genealogy behind. Do not say I am spiritually worthy or superior because I am the son or daughter of this or that notable person. Leave all that self-appraisal aside and turn toward God.

به بحر نیستی هر کو فرو شد
«فلا انساب» نقد وقت او شد

Whoever has become immersed in the ocean of nonexistence,
"There is no kinship" becomes a description of his time.

"Of his time" means his or her state of being. "There is no affinity" is in reference to the Quran, "And when the trumpet is blown, there shall be no kinship between them that Day, nor will they question one another" (Q. 23:101).

هر آن نسبت که پیدا شد ز شهوت
ندارد حاصلی جز کبر و نخوت

Whatever affinity (*nisbat*) appears through [animal] passion (*shahwat*),
Has no result except haughtiness (*kibr*) and self-aggrandizement (*nikhwat*),

If affinity related to animal passion dominates the self-identity of a person, it only leads to pride and egotism.

اگر شهوت نبودی در میانه
نسب‌ها جمله می‌گشتی فسانه

If passion were not to exist in the middle,
All the claims of genealogy would become but a tale.

"All the claims of genealogy would become but a tale" means that the person involved and in fact everybody else would not take them seriously.

This criticism of genealogy should not obviously be taken as denial of the positive aspects of one's biological, psychological, and religious heritage.

چو شهوت در میانه کارگر شد
یکی مادر شد آن دیگر پدر شد

When passion became operative, in the middle,
One person became the father, the other the mother.

Shabistarī is of course referring here to the conjugal union leading to procreation.

نمی‌گویم که مادر یا پدر کیست
که با ایشان به عزّت بایدت زیست

I am not saying who [your] mother or father is,
For thou shouldst deal with them with kindness.[10]

نهاده ناقصی‌را نام خواهر
حسودی‌را لقب کرده برادر

An imperfect person is named sister,
A jealous one titled brother.

Shabistarī is drawing attention to imperfections of close relatives to whom ordinary people often cling, and criticizing such an attitude from a spiritual point of view.

عدوی خویش‌را فرزند خوانی
ز خود بیگانه خویشاوند خوانی

Thou callest thine enemy thy son.
He who is alien to thee, thou callest thy relative.

The first hemistich echoes the Quranic diction that your children are your enemies,[11] and the second again draws attention that people still call those who are their blood kin "relatives," although they are spiritually alien to a seeker of the truth.

مرا باری بگو تا خال و عم کیست
وز ایشان حاصلی جز درد و غم چیست؟

Tell me, who is the maternal aunt, who is the paternal uncle (or aunt);
And what results from them, except pain and sorrow?

'Amm translated here as "paternal uncle" implies also *'ammah* or paternal aunt. These verses seek to cover the whole chain of close biological relatives.

رفیقانی که با تو در طریق‌اند
پی هزل ای برادر هم رفیق‌اند

[Even] friends who claim to be with thee on the spiritual path,
Are also only friends in jest (*hazl*), o brother.

The author criticizes even some who claim to be one's fellow travelers on the Sufi path, warning the serious seeker that such people could be friends only in jest and not true friends. So, Shabistarī is extending his criticism even to some who claim to follow the path to God (*ṭarīq*).

به کوی جدّ اگر یک دم نشینی
از ایشان من چه گویم تا چه بینی؟

If thou sittest down with them in the quarter of seriousness (*jidd*) for a moment,
About them what can I say of what thou seeth?

In the first hemistich *jidd* could also be interpreted as a reference to a serious form of poetry or saying, while its opposite *hazl* means a form of poetry or saying that is in jest.

همه افسانه و افسون و بند است
به جان خواجه کاینها ریشخند است

All are stories, magical tales and things that bind together (*band*).
By the soul of the Prophet, these are all things to fool you.

Band can also mean simply a line of poetry, implying that it is inconsequential.

به مردی وارهان خودرا چو مردان
ولیکن حقّ کس ضایع مگردان

Let thyself go in manliness, like [real] men,
But never tread upon the rights of others.

"[Real] men" refers to an authentic spiritual person. Being manly does not mean bullying people and being aggressive. It also does not mean to tread upon or threaten the rights of others.

ز شرع ار یک دقیقه ماند مهمل
شوی در هر دو کون از دین معطّل

If for one minute thou wert to put aside the Divine Law,
Thou wouldst be kept waiting (*mu'aṭṭal*) in both worlds for religion.

Having said all that he did above concerning various forms and modes of outwardness, Shabistarī now returns to remind us in the strongest terms of the importance of following the Divine Law (*shar'*). This is one of many verses that reveals the pertinence and significance of the *Sharī'ah* for Sufism.

حقوق شرعرا زنهار مگذار
ولیکن خویشتنرا هم نگهدار

Therefore, never leave aside the rights of the Divine Law,
And at the same time control thyself.

Here, the author again emphasizes the importance of following the Divine Law, to which he adds the necessity of self-control and self-restraint.

زر و زن نیست الّا مایهٔ غم
به جا بگذار چون عیسی بن مریم

Gold and wife are nothing but the source of sorrow.
Leave the two aside like Jesus, son of Mary.

Gold and wife is a general metaphor for the worldly impediments to advancing in the spiritual life. For a woman, "wife" could be replaced by "husband." Gold indicates, needless to say, worldly wealth and possession. In the second hemistich, the case of Christ is given as the ideal example because he had no spouse nor any worldly wealth.

حنیفی شو ز قید هر مذاهب
درآ در دیر دین مانند راهب

Become a follower of the primordial religion (*ḥanīfī*) [free] from the condition of religious schools;
Come into the monastery of religion like a monk.

Ḥanīf (pl. *ḥunafā'*) means to be in a primordial state. There were people even before the rise of Islam who were primordial monotheists, and the Prophet himself was one of the *ḥunafā'* even before he became a prophet. The Prophet was never a polytheist even before Gabriel appeared to him. He did not go from polytheism to monotheism but believed always in the one God. The Islamic belief is that in all ages gone by there were a number of people who were *ḥunafā'*, who naturally turned to the one God, going back to the Prophet Adam.

"Come into the monastery of religion like a monk." This stanza is a praise of Christian monasticism but implies more generally to become detached from the world. The first hemistich should not be taken literally as becoming a monk and does not negate the *ḥadīth, lā ruhbāniyyah fi'l-islām* (there is no monasticism in Islam) meaning monasticism as an institution.

ترا تا در نظر اغیار و غیر است
اگر در مسجدی آن عین دیر است

If what thou hast in thy mind is others and otherness,
Even if thou art in a mosque, it is like being in a monastery.

The first hemistich concerns concentration on what is important and avoiding dispersion. "It is like being in a monastery" is used here in a negative sense in contrast to the verses above.

چو برخیزد ز پیشت کسوت غیر
شود بهر تو مسجد صورت دیر

When the dress of otherness is lifted from thee,
For thee the mosque takes on the form of a monastery.

When the dress of otherness is removed, outward form disappears and only the inner reality remains so that mosque and monastery appear as the same, that is, the inner reality of religions is one.

نمی‌دانم به هر حالی که هستی
خلاف نفس کافر کن که رستی

I do not know, but in whatever condition thou art,[12]
Act against the infidel soul so as to be liberated.

This is universal advice to combat the lower soul (*al-nafs al-ammārah bi'l-sū'*) in order to gain spiritual deliverance and felicity.

بت و زنّار و ترسائی و ناقوس
اشارت شد همه بر ترک ناموس

The idol, the belt, Christian monasticism, and the church bell,
All are references to leaving behind the Law (*nāmūs*).

Nāmūs originally in Arabic meant "to hide," to "veil." But the Greek meaning of *nomos* also became an Arabic and Persian word, and that is why we have the term *nawāmīs al-anbiyā'* (the laws of the prophets). So, *nāmūs* means also "Divine Law." "All are references to leaving behind the Law" means leaving behind exoterism and the external aspect of the Law—but not abandoning its practice as earlier verses have also indicated—and turning only to the esoteric, inner meaning.

اگر خواهی که گردی بندهٔ خاصّ
مهیّا شو برای صدق و اخلاص

If thou wilt be [God's elite] (*khāṣṣ*) servant,
Prepare thyself for truthfulness (*ṣidq*) and sincerity (*ikhlāṣ*).

Khāṣṣ can also be taken to mean special or choice. Truthfulness and sincerity are very important virtues and qualities, which are cardinal in *taṣawwuf*.

برو خودرا ز راه خویش برگیر
به هر لحظه درآ ایمان ز سر گیر

Go and free thyself from thy path.
At each moment begin faith anew.[13]

"Go and free thyself from thy path" means free thyself from the path of ordinary life of forgetfulness of God that thou hast been following. There is no guarantee that with the next breath we shall not lose our faith. So, this constant renewal of spirituality is essential to all religions, and that is why Shabistarī stated above so strongly that religious faith should not become just a habit but should be constantly renewed.

به باطن نفس ما چون هست کافر
مشو راضی بدین اسلام ظاهر

Since inwardly our soul is an infidel,
Do not be satisfied with this external Islam,

Many consider themselves Muslim but their Islamic faith is only outward, while their inner being is in rebellion like that of an infidel. So, a spiritual seeker should not be satisfied with only the outward practice of Islam. If he were to be so, he would not be a real spiritual seeker.

ز نو هر لحظه ایمان تازه گردان
مسلمان شو مسلمان شو مسلمان

Every moment make thy faith fresh anew.
Become a Muslim, become a Muslim, become a Muslim.

This is yet another famous verse of Persian poetry. Its message is that one should not take faith for granted. Every moment one should return to God anew. At every moment the Reality of God should be experienced above and beyond the reality of our *nafs* and also of the world. Every moment we should become in a sense "a new" Muslim (*jadīd al-islām*) and surrender to God. There is not just a horizontal continuity in the spiritual life. There is also a vertical relationship we have at every moment with God, one that is to be renewal at all times.

بسی ایمان بود کان کفر زاید
نه کفر است آن کزو ایمان فزاید

There is many a [superficial] faith from which infidelity is born;
That infidelity from which faith is born is not infidelity.

Faith that is outward can lead to inner infidelity, while outward infidelity can lead to inner faith.

ریا و سمعه و ناموس بگذار
بیفکن خرقه و بربند زنّار

Ostentation, reputation and the external law, leave them aside.
Cast away thy Sufi dress and tie the Christian belt.

The first hemistich warns the spiritual seeker of being pretentious, seeking to be reputable in the eyes of worldly people and observing only the externals of the *Sharī'ah* while neglecting the inner meaning. The second hemistich does not mean leaving Sufism and becoming a Christian monk but to cast aside the outward and devote oneself to the inward.

چو پیر ما شو اندر کفر فردی
اگر مردی بده دلرا به مردی

Like our spiritual teacher (*pīr*), become in infidelity an individual;
If thou art a [real] man, surrender thyself to a man.

In the first hemistich "infidelity" means, of course, going beyond the outer meaning of faith to its inner reality. In the second hemistich "real man" means a spiritual person, while the second reference to man means "spiritual master."

مجرّد شو ز هر اقرار و انکار
به ترسازاده‌ای دل ده به یک بار

Become separated (*mujarrad*) from every confession and denial.
For once give thy heart to the child of a Christian (*tarsāzādah*).

Mujarrad as catharsis has been explained early in this commentary. "The child of a Christian" here symbolizes Abrahamic esoterism.

An Indication of the Christian Child

بت ترسا بچه نوری است باهر
که از روی بتان دارد مظاهر

The idol of the Christian child is a shining light,
That possesses manifestations from the face of idols.

"Idol" in this verse must, of course, be understood as a symbol of Divine Names and Qualities and not in any way associated with idol worship in its ordinary sense, which the Quran criticizes so strongly.

کند او جمله دلهارا وشاقی
گهی گردد مغنّی گاه ساقی

[That reality] makes all the hearts good news.
Sometimes it appears as a singer, sometimes as a pourer of wine.

زهی مطرب که از یک نغمهٔ خوش
زند در خرمن صد زاهد آتش

Long live the musician who with one beautiful melody,
Sets fire upon the harvest of a hundred ascetics!

"Beautiful melody" refers to spiritual music that reflects supernal realities and burns away the shell of mere asceticism.

زهی ساقی که او از یک پیاله
کند بیخود دو صد هفتاد ساله

Long live that Saki, who from one cup,
Makes two hundred septuagenarians lose themselves!

The Saki is the spiritual master who with one cup of true knowledge and love of God makes so many even old men and women become drunk spiritually and lose their ordinary self-centered consciousness.

رود در خانقه مست شبانه
کند افسون صوفی‌را فسانه

At night he goes into the Sufi center drunk;
He makes the magic of the Sufi a tale.

This verse is still in reference to the Saki, who goes in a state of spiritual drunkenness into the *khānaqāh* where his presence is magical. The second hemistich could also be understood to mean being present as a living master, he will make people see the magic of the usual tales told about Sufis as empty tales.

وگر در مسجد آید در سحرگاه
نبگذارد در او یک مرد آگاه

And if at early dawn, he comes into the mosque,
He will not leave a single aware man therein.

The second hemistich means that the Saki will not leave anyone in his or her apparent state of wakefulness and awareness, which is not real awakening and awareness but an illusion from which he saves them.

رود در مدرسه چون مست مستور
فقیه از وی شود بیچاره مخمور

He goes into a school, like a hidden drunkard,
The jurisprudent (*faqīh*) will become helpless through him drunk.

The spiritual power of the authentic Sufi master is such that he is able to make even the exoteric scholar, usually opposed to esoterism, fall into a state of spiritual drunkenness.

ز عشقش زاهدان بیچاره گشته
ز خان و مان خود آواره گشته

From his love, ascetics have become helpless,
Having fled from their household and home.

The Saki's power is such that it makes those who are mere ascetics feel helpless and flee from their ordinary conditions of life.

یکی مؤمن دگررا کافر او کرد
همه عالم پر از شور و شر او کرد

It is he who made one person faithful, the other an infidel,
It is he who filled the world with commotion and excitement (*shūr-u sharr*).

Here, *sharr* does not mean evil. Rather, *shūr-u sharr* is a common Persian expression meaning commotion and excitement.

خرابات از لبش معمور گشته
مساجد از رخش پر نور گشته

The taverns of ruin have become built from his lips.
The mosques from his face have become full of light.

Not only is the esoteric aspect of religion or Sufism based upon words issuing from the lips of the Saki, but even the exoteric aspect or the mosque becomes full of light through his presence.

همه کار من از وی شد میسّر
بدو دیدم خلاص از نفس کافر

All my [spiritual] work became possible through him,
In him I saw freedom from the infidel concupiscent soul.

The verse turns from the master or Saki to the disciple who is speaking here in the first person and asserts that only through a spiritual master can one become freed from the stranglehold of the ego.

دلم از دانش خود صد حجب داشت
ز عُجب و نخوت و تلبیس و پنداشت

My heart was covered by a hundred veils through my knowledge,
As a result of womanizing, haughtiness, falsification and presumptions.

The verse starts with the many veils that cover the soul of fallen man. Knowledge here does not mean principial or traditional knowledge of reality but derivative and self-centered knowledge. The second hemistich mentions some of the causes of this veiling.

درآمد از درم آن بت سحرگاه
مرا از خواب غفلت کرد آگاه

In early morn that idol came through my door;
She made me aware of the dream of negligence.

The meaning of idol or *but* as theophany has already been explained. It is that theophany that awakens us from the dream of forgetfulness of God and His Commands.

ز رویش خلوت جان گشت روشن
بدو دیدم که تا خود کیستم من

From Her face, the inner retreat of [my] soul became illuminated;
Through Her I saw who I was.

Only God's Grace can enable us to discover who we really are beyond all the accidents of our terrestrial existence. Only the Self within us can know the Self.

چو کردم در رخ خوبش نگاهی
برآمد از میان جانم آهی

When I cast a glance upon Her beautiful Face,
From my heart there arose a sigh.

When one has a theophanic vision, one cannot but sigh looking at our own fallen state. We realize what we have been missing in life and seek to become what we should really be.

مرا گفتا که ای شیّاد سالوس
به سر شد عمرت اندر نام و ناموس

She told me, "O duplicitous impostor (*shayyād-i sālūs*),
Thy life has passed in preserving thy name and formal religion (*nāmūs*)."

Shayyād means someone who cheats, who is duplicitous and does not speak the truth. *Sālūs* also means someone with pretension, who puts on a false act, an impostor. *Nāmūs* here is in reference not to *nomos* (*nāmūs*), but to formal exoteric religion. In general, it could also refer to the women in one's family, but here Shabistari has exoteric religion in mind..

ببین تا علم و کبر و زهد و پنداشت
ترا ای نارسیده از که واداشت

Look, how knowledge, haughtiness, asceticism and presumptions,
From what they prevented thee, o thou who hast not arrived.

The first hemistich repeats the obstacles in the soul that prevent spiritual advancement. *Nārisadah* in the second hemistich can also mean "unripe" or "immature." Knowledge here means exoteric and outward knowledge not ma'rifah.

نظر کردن به رویم نیم ساعت
همی‌ارزد هزاران ساله طاعت

Looking at my face for half an hour,
Is worth thousands of years of devotion.

To behold the Face of the Beloved for even a short time is spiritually more precious than a whole lifetime of ordinary devotion that, although positive, is limited by the veil of separation from the One.

علی‌الجمله رخ آن عالم آرا
مرا با من نمود آن دم سراپا

Finally, that Face that decorates the world.
Revealed myself to me, that moment from head to foot.

"That Face that decorates the world" is, of course, a reference to *wajh Allāh*, the Face of God, which is present wherever one turns. And it is that Face that reveals to us our whole being, enabling us to know who we really are.

سیه شد روی جانم از خجالت
ز فوت عمر و ایّام بطالت

The face of my soul turned dark from shame,
From wasting my life and days in falsity.

When we hear the call of the Beloved, we become shameful for having spent our precious life here on earth in frivolity and falsehood.

چو دید آن ماه کز روی چو خورشید
که ببریدم من از جان خود امّید

When that beauty with a face like the Sun saw,
That I had cut hope from my own soul,

This verse sets the condition for the Saki to turn to the soul of one who has opened his or her heart to the Divine.

یکی پیمانه پر کرد و به من داد
که از آب وی آتش در من افتاد

She filled a cup and gave it to me;
From whose liquid, fire engulfed my being.

The fire within the Divine Wine sets the soul of those who drink it on fire as well. The poet plays with the similarity of the redness of wine, the fiery state it creates when drunk, and the qualities of fire that transform the soul.

کنون گفت از می بی‌رنگ و بی‌بوی
نقوش تختهٔ هستی فرو شوی

Then She said [to me], "With the wine that has no color nor smell,
Wash away the forms written upon the tablet of existence."

The spiritual wine offered by the Saki is beyond form, free of any color or odor, and it is with this wine that one should wash away the world of form and limitations from one's existence.

چو آشامیدم آن پیمانه‌را پاک
در افتادم ز مستی بر سر خاک

When I drank that cup completely,
I fell through drunkenness upon the earth.

To fall upon the earth in a drunken state means to go beyond the self-asserting ego and ordinary consciousness, all a result of drinking that cup of Divine Wine.

کنون نه نیستم در خود نه هستم
نه هشیارم نه مخمورم نه مستم

Now, I neither am nor am not within myself,
I am neither aware, nor inebriated, nor drunk.

Having drunk the cup given by the Saki, man goes beyond the dichotomy between sobriety and drunkenness.

گهی چون چشم او دارم سری خوش
گهی چون زلف او باشم مشوّش

Sometimes, I have, like Her eye, a happy mental state;
Sometimes, like Her hair, I am entangled.

گهی از خوی خود در گلخنم من
گهی از روی او در گلشنم من

Sometimes, as a result of my own nature, I am in hell (*gulkhan*).
Sometimes, through Her face, I am in the rose garden (*gulshan*).

These lines again describe the often opposing states of the wandering soul before it becomes attached to the firm rope (*ḥabl al-matīn*) of Sufism. *Gulkhan* is another name for hell. *Gulshan* of course means "rose garden," but here it means "paradise."

On the Conclusion of the Book

از آن گلشن گرفتم شمّه‌ای باز
نهادم نام اورا گلشن راز

From that Rose Garden I receive an open drop of perfume;
I named it the *Rose Garden of Divine Mysteries.*

Even the title of this work came to Shabistarī through inspiration. And the verse reveals that the Rose Garden is in reference to the Celestial Garden where the mysterious roots of all beings reside.

در او از راز دل گلها شکفته است
که تا اکنون کسی دیگر نگفته است

In it from the secret of the heart flowers have bloomed,
Which no one else has mentioned before.

This verse is direct reference to the fact that there are esoteric truths in the *Gulshan-i rāz* not to be found in the works of others who came before Shabistarī.

زبان سوسن او جمله گویاست
عیون نرگس او جمله بیناست

Its lily-of-the-valley tongue is all telling;
The eyes of its narcissus are all seeing.

Both hemistiches refer to characteristics of the *Gulshan-i rāz.*

تأمّل کن به چشم دل یکایک
که تا برخیزد از پیش تو این شک

Meditate with the eye of the heart each one,
So that this doubt will be uplifted from thee.

It needs the inner eye, the organ of metaphysical vision, to understand this work. If each verse is seen with this inner eye, doubt about the truth of the nature of things will be removed, and one reaches the station of certainty.

ببین منقول و معقول و حقائق
مصفّی کرده در علم دقائق

See [how] the transmitted and intellectual sciences and truths,
Have been lined up in the science of subtleties.

If one has penetrating insight, one will see how the sciences and sapiential truths are explained in it by means of subtle knowledge.

به چشم منکری منگر در او خوار
که گلها گردد اندر چشم تو خار

Do not cast the eye of denial upon it with contempt,
For [then] in thy eye flowers become thorns.

If one looks upon this work with rejection and contempt, the flowers of gnosis appear as thorns.

نشان ناشناسی ناسپاسی است
شناسائی حقّ در حقّ شناسی است

The sign of ignorance is ungratefulness;
Awareness of the Truth is knowledge of the Truth.

The unqualified and ignorant person is ungrateful for the gift of the *Gulshan-i rāz*, while to know the Truth brings with it principial knowledge.

غرض زین جمله آن کز ما کند یاد
عزیزی گویدم رحمت بر او باد

The purpose of all (*jumlah*) [that is written] is that someone dear would remember us;
A dear one would say, "May God bless his soul."

Jumlah here refers to the whole text of the *Gulshan-i rāz*. Shabistarī is asking the person who benefits from this work to ask God's blessings for the author.

به نام خویش کردم ختم و پایان
الهی عاقبت محمود گردان

I have brought [the work] to an end and termination with my name.
O God, at the end make me the object of Thy blessing (*maḥmūd*).

The first name of Shabistarī being Maḥmūd, he asks God to make him *maḥmūd*, which means literally "one who receives God's blessings."

Tamma hādha'l-sharḥ bi-mannihi wa karamihi
Seyyed Hossein Nasr
5 Dhu'l-ḥijjah 1443 A.H.

Glossary of Persian and Arabic Technical Terms

'adam	nonexistence, nothingness
'adl	justice
'aks	reflection, picture
'ālam al-khalq wa'l-amr (Arabic)	the world of creation and Divine Command
'āmmah	ordinary people
'awāmm	ordinary people (as opposed to *khawāṣṣ*, elites)
'aql	intelligence, intellect, reason
'araḍ (pl. *a'rāḍ*)	accident (in the sense of the nine Aristotelian accidents)
'awn	help
'ayān	manifest
'ibrat	a lesson
'iffat (Arabic, *'iffah*)	temperance, shyness, chastity
'illat (Arabic. *'illah*, pl. *'ilal*)	cause
'ilm	knowledge
'unṣur (pl. *'anāṣir*)	element
āfāq (sing. *ufuq*)	the horizons, the macrocosm
ākhirat	the other world, the Hereafter
al-ḥaqīqah al-muḥammadiyyah (Arabic)	the Muḥammadan Reality
al-ḥayyiz al-ṭabī'ī (Arabic)	the natural place (of each element)
al-insān al-kāmil (Arabic)	the Universal Man
al-mawālīd al-thalāthah (Arabic)	the three kingdoms (mineral, plant and animal)
al-nūr al-muḥammadī (Arabic)	the Muḥammadan Light
ālā	blessings, kindnesses
anāniyyat (or Arabic, *anā'iyyah*)	I-ness
anfus (sing. *nafs*)	souls, the microcosm
aṣl	root, principle, origin, source
astaghfiru'Llāh	"I ask forgiveness of God"
athīr	ether, the "fifth element," *quinta essentia*
āyah (pl. *āyāt*)	sign [of God], verse [of the Quran]
baqā'	subsistence (through God)
barakah	grace, blessing
basīṭ	simple
basṭ	expansion

bāṭil	false, in vain
bāṭin	inward, hidden, esoteric
but	idol
chishm-i dil	the eye of the heart
dā'irat al-nubuwwah (Arabic)	the cycle of prophecy
dā'irat al-walāyah/wilāyah (Arabic)	the cycle of *walāyah/wilāyah*
dam	breath, moment, nearness, proximity, intimacy
dargāh	threshold, court, Sufi lodge
darwīsh	spiritually poor, a follower of the Sufi path
dhāt	essence, the Divine Essence
dhawq	taste, spiritual intuition, sapiential knowledge
dhikr	remembrance, invocation
dil	heart
dilrubā	stealer of hearts
dunyā	this world, the lower world
faḍl	virtue, knowledge, generosity, bestowal, grace
fakhr	pride, bragging, refinement
falak (pl. *aflāk*)	astronomical heaven, star, planet, sky, the orbit in which a star or planet moves
falak al-aflāk (Arabic)	the supreme sphere, the outermost cosmic sphere = *falak al-aṭlas*
falak al-aṭlas (Arabic)	the supreme sphere, the outermost cosmic sphere
fanā'	annihilation (in God)
faqīr (pl. *fuqarā'*)	poor, an aspirant on the Sufi path
farḍ (pl. *farā'iḍ*)	obligatory acts of worship
fayḍ	emanation, manifestation, grace
fi'l (pl. *af'āl*)	act, action
fikr, *fikrat*	thought, meditation
fiṭrat (Arabic, *fiṭrah*)	primordial nature
gul	flower, rose
gulshan	garden, rose garden
ḥadīth qudsī	"holy *ḥadīth*," a saying uttered by the Prophet in which God speaks in the first person
ḥāl (pl. *aḥwāl*)	state, particularly a spiritual state or state of the soul
ḥamd	praise
ḥanīf (pl. *ḥunafā'*)	primordial monotheist

ḥaqīqat (Arabic *ḥaqīqah*)	truth, the Truth
ḥaqq	truth, right, the Divine Truth
ḥayrat (Arabic, *ḥayrah*)	bewilderment
hayūlā (Arabic, *hayūlā'*)	prime matter, *materia prima*
hunar	art, virtue
ḥusn	goodness, beauty
huwaydā	apparent, manifest
i'tibārī	contingent
i'tidāl	balance, equilibrium
iḥsān	kindness, generosity, making beautiful, excellence, virtue
ijmāl	the whole, synthesis
imkān	contingency, possibility
inshirāḥ-i ṣadr	expansion of the breast
ism al-Af'āl (Arabic)	Name of the Divine Acts
ism al-Dhāt (Arabic)	Name of the Divine Essence
ism al-Ṣifāt (Arabic)	Name of the Divine Attributes
isrā'	the Night Journey of the Prophet (from Makkah to Jerusalem, which was followed by the *mi'rāj*)
istighfār	asking forgiveness (of God)
jafr	the science of the numerical symbolism of letters of the Arabic alphabet
jahl	ignorance
jalāl	majesty
jam'	synthesis, addition, multiplicity, assembly, collectivity, collectedness
jamāl	beauty
jān	soul, spirit, life, dear
jawhar	substance (in the sense of the Aristotelian category)
jism-i laṭīf	subtle body
kashf	unveiling, discovery, spiritual intuition
kawn	existence
kawnayn	the two worlds
khānaqāh	Sufi center
khātam al-anbiyā' (Arabic)	the Seal of Prophets
khawāṣṣ	elites
khirad	reason, intellect, wisdom
kithrat	multiplicity

kufr	infidelity
kun (Arabic)	the Divine Command "Be!"
laṭā'if (sing. *laṭīfah*)	the subtle centers of the human being
lawḥ	tablet, the (Guarded) Tablet
luṭf	kindness, gentleness, mercy
mā siwā'Llāh	all that is other than God, i.e. the created order
ma'ād	return, i.e., the return to God, eschatology
ma'nā	meaning, inner meaning, inner reality, the esoteric dimension
ma'rifat (Arabic, *ma'rifah*)	knowledge, gnosis
mabda'	origin, the Origin
māddah	matter
maḥabbat (Arabic, *maḥabbah*)	love
māhiyyat	quiddity, essence
man	the Persian first person pronoun, "I"
maqām	station (on the spiritual path)
maqṣad	aim, purpose
mard-i tamām	the complete man
maṣdar	place of issuing, source; noun of action
mashhad	place of witness, the burial site of a saint
mast	drunk
mastī	drunkenness
mathnawī	a genre of poetry consisting of rhyming couplets of which *Gulshan-i rāz* is an example
maẓhar (p. *maẓāhir*)	locus of manifestation, the place of *ẓuhūr* (manifestation), reflection, theophany, symbol
mi'rāj	the Celestial Ascent of the Prophet (from the Temple Mount in Jerusalem, through the Seven Heavens and to the Divine Presence), spiritual ascent
mithāl	sample, example, image, symbol
muḥdath	having temporal origination
mujarrad	being in a state of catharsis, separated from materiality and potentiality
mumkin	contingent, possible
munājāt	supplications, intimate discourses with God
murakkab	compound
muṭlaq	absolute

muṭrib	troubadour, musician
nabī	prophet
nafas al-Raḥmān (Arabic)	the Breath of the All-Compassionate
nafs	self, itself, soul, sometimes used as an abbreviation of *nafs-i ammārah*, "the soul that incites to evil," i.e., the lower self or ego
nām	name
namād	symbol
namūd (or *nimūd*)	appearance
naqsh	pattern
nash'ah	state of being
nawāfil (sing. *nāfilah*)	recommended or supererogatory acts of worship, i.e., acts of worship beyond that which the Divine Law makes obligatory
naẓar	rational discourse, opinion, vision
nubuwwat (Arabic, *nubuwwah*)	prophecy
paydā'ī	state of being visible, being manifest
qabḍ	contraction
qadīm	ancient, eternal
qahr	dominion, power, punishment
qalam	pen, the Pen
qiyās	syllogism, analogy
qudrat (Arabic, *qudrah*)	power
qurrat al-'ayn (Arabic)	the coolness of the eyes (i.e. something very precious), "the light of the eye"
rak'at (Arabic, *rak'ah*, pl. *rak'āt*) (Arabic)	a cycle of the daily canonical prayers
rāz	mystery, secret
rubūbiyyah	lordship
rūḥ	spirit
rukn (pl. *arkān*)	column, foundation, element
sālik	traveler
samā'	hearing, audition, the Sufi concert and its accompanying sacred dance
ṣanā'at (Arabic, *ṣinā'ah*, pl. *ṣanāyi'*)	craft, skill
sāqī	saki, the cup-bearer, the wine-pourer
sha'n	state (of being), station, task
shāhid	lit. witness, a beautiful youth present at Sufi gatherings
shahīd	martyr
shakhṣ	individual being

sharī'at (Arabic *sharī'ah*)	Divine Law
shaṭḥ (p. *shaṭaḥāt*, *shaṭḥiyyāt*)	theophanic locution, ecstatic utterance
Shayṭān	Satan, the Devil
shuhūd	witnessing
shukr	gratitude
ṣifat	attribute
sirr	secret, mystery, the inner reality of the heart
sukr	drunkenness, intoxication
ṣūrat	form (in either the Aristotelian sense, as opposed to matter (*māddah*), or the Sufi sense, as opposed to inner meaning (*ma'nā*)
ta'ayyun	determination (in a metaphysical sense, e.g., determination or delimitation of being)
ta'dīl	straightening, balancing, "the happy mean," avoiding excesses, equilibrium, being in the middle
ta'wīl	hermeneutics
ta'yīd	Divine Help, Divine Affirmation
ṭab' (pl. *ṭabāyi'*)	nature (also in the sense of the four natures: wet, dry, hot and cold)
tadabbur	learning, gaining experience, controlling one's thought
tadhakkur	reminding, recollection
tafṣīl	details, the analysis of something
taḥayyur	bewilderment
taḥṣīl-i ḥāṣil	to attain that which has already been attained
tajallī	theophany
tajdīd al-khalq fī kulli'l-ānāt (Arabic)	the renewal of creation at every moment
tajrīd	catharsis of the soul, detachment of the soul from the material realm, disentanglement from potentiality, materiality and imperfection
tamaththul	symbolism
tamthīl	illustration, symbol
tamyīz	discernment
tanzīh	to go beyond, transcendence
taqwā	reverence, fear of God, piety
ṭarīqat (Arabic, *ṭarīqah*)	the Sufi way, the Sufi path, Sufi order
taṣawwuf	Sufism

taṣawwur	conceptualization, concept
taṣdīq	affirmation, assent, judgment
tashbīh	to be like, similitude, analogy, likeness, immanence
tawakkul	trust (in God)
tawfīq	succor, granting success
tawḥīd	unity, Divine Unity
ṭawr (pl. *aṭwār*)	stage, state
thawābit	the fixed stars
waḥdat	unity
waḥdat al-wujūd (Arabic)	the unity of Being
wahm	apprehension
wājib	necessary
walāyah/wilāyah	initiation, spiritual guidance, sanctity, rule
walī (pl. *awliyā'*)	friend [of God], saint
wiṣāl	to reach, to unite, to attain, to embrace, to have reached the desired goal
wujūb	necessity
wujūd	being, existence
ẓāhir	outward, manifest, exoteric
zuhd	asceticism
ẓuhūr	manifestation, appearance

Notes

Compiler's Introduction

1. This month corresponds to December 1317 or early January 1318 CE. See below, "On the Purpose of the Composition of this Book and its History."

2. On 16 Shawwāl, 718/December 1, 1318. See Leonard Lewisohn, *Beyond Faith and Infidelity* (Irvine: UCI Jordan Center for Persian Studies, 2020), 26.

3. Lewisohn, *Beyond Faith and Infidelity*, 16.

4. See Maḥmūd Shabistarī, *Mahmud Schebisteri's Rosenflor der Geheimnisse*, ed. Joseph von Hammer-Purgstall (Pest and Leipzig, 1880); *The Dialogue of the Golshan-i-Raz or Mystical Garden of Roses*, trans. E. A. Johnson (London, 1887); *Gulshan i Raz = The Mystic Rose Garden of Sa'd Ud Din Mahmud Shabistari*, trans. E. H. Whinfield (Islamabad; Lahore: Iran Pakistan Institute of Persian Studies; Islamic Book Foundation, 1978); *The Secret Rose Garden of Sa'd Ud Din Mahmūd Shabistarī*, trans. Florence Lederer (London: J. Murray, 1920).Robert Abdul Hayy Darr, *Garden of Mystery: The Gulshani-i Raz of Shabistari* (London: Archetype, 2007). For further information see Hamid Algar, 'GOLŠAN-E RĀZ,' *Encyclopædia Iranica*, XI/1, 109–11, available online at http://www.iranicaonline.org/articles/golsan-e-raz.

5. Lewisohn, *Beyond Faith and Infidelity*, 10.

6. Trans. Lewisohn in *Beyond Faith and Infidelity*, 1–2.

7. Ibid., 13.

8. See ibid., 2.

9. See ibid., 51–59.

10. See ibid., 30–51. On the works attributed to Shabistarī, see also Ṣamad Muwaḥḥid (ed.), *Majmū'ah-yi āthār-i Shaykh Maḥmūd Shabistarī* (Tehran: Kitābkhānah-yi Ṭahūrī, 13645 S.H. [1986]), 7–12.

11. For further information concerning this figure see Mīr Harawī, *Nuzhat al-arwāḥ*, ed. and intro. Najīb Māyil Harawī (Mashhad: Zawwār, 1392 A.H. [1972]).

12. See below, "On the Book and its Composition."

13. The fact that this is poem is written in the form of *mathnawī* means that each verse is composed of two rhyming hemistiches. The meter *hazaj maḥdhūf* means that each hemistich has the following arrangement of long and short syllables: . — /. — /. — , often pronounced *mafā'īlun-mafā'īlun-fa'ūlun* or more colloquially, *ta-tan-tan-tan/ta-tan-tan-tan/ta-tan-tan*.

14. It is also important to note that a great many commentaries have been written on this work, such that by the sixteenth century close to thirty commentaries had been written on the text. See Lewisohn, *Beyond Faith and Infidelity*, 17.

15. See below, "On the Book and its Composition."

16. Muḥammad ibn Yaḥyā Lāhījī and Maḥmūd Shabistarī, *Mafātīḥ al-i'jāz fī sharḥ Gulshan-i rāz* ed. Ghulāmriḍā Kaywān Samī'ī (Tehran: Maḥmūdī, 1958); Maḥmūd Shabistarī 1976. *Gulshan-i rāz, az āthār-i Ḥazrat-i Shaykh Maḥmūd Shabistarī. Bā taṣḥīḥ wa muqaddimah wa ḥawāshī wa ta'līqāt-i Jawād Nūrbakhsh*, ed. Javād Nūrbakhsh (Tehran: Intishārāt-i Khānqāh-i Ni'mat Allāhī, 1976).

[Exordium]

1. Ed. This is a traditional formula that marks the transition between the opening sections of praise and the introductory comments to the work. The phrase means literally "then what comes after."

2. الا یا ایهّا الساقی اَدِر کأساً و ناوِلها
   که عشق آسان نمود اوّل ولی افتاد مشکلها
   Khwājah Shams al-Dīn Muḥammad Ḥāfiẓ Shīrāzī, *Dīwān-i Khwājah Shams al-Dīn Muḥammad Ḥāfiẓ Shīrāzī*, eds. Muḥammad Qazwīnī and Qāsim Ghanī (Tehran: Kitābkhānah-yi Zawwār, 1320 S.H. [1941]), 2.

3. Fairly recently I published a complete translation and commentary on the *Tao Te Ching* in Persian. Laozi, *Tā'ū tih chīng: Ṭarīq wa-faḍā'il-i ān*, English trans. Toshihiko Izutsu and Seyyed Hossein Nasr; Persian trans. and comm. Seyyed Hossein Nasr (Tehran: Intishārāt-i Iṭṭilā'āt, 2021). The Persian text has been in turn translated into English by M. Faghfoory as *A Sufi Commentary on the Tao Te Ching: The Way and Its Virtue* (Louisville: Fons Vitae, 2025).

4. Here the Nūrbakhsh edition has been preferred. For this hemistich, the Kaywān Samī'ī edition has,
   در آدم شد پدید این عقل و تمییز
   "There appeared in man intellect and discernment."

5. The best essay written on this matter in English is by the late Toshiko Izutsu, "The Concept of Perpetual Creation in Islamic Mysticism and Zen Buddhism," in *Mélanges offerts à Henry Corbin*, ed. S. H. Nasr (Tehran: Institute of Islamic Studies, 1977) 115–48; reprinted in Izutsu, *Creation and the Timeless Order of Things* (Ashland: White Cloud Press, 1994), 141–73.

6. These three works are *Ḥaqq al-yaqīn fī ma'rifat rabb al-'ālamīn*, *Gulshan-i rāz,* and *Sa'ādat-nāmah.* On these works and a discussion of other works attributed, most likely erroneously, to Shabistarī see Lewisohn, *Beyond Faith and Infidelity*, 15–59. See also Muwahhid ed., *Majmū'ah-yi āthār-i Shaykh Maḥmūd Shabistarī*, 7–12.

7. See Seyyed Hossein Nasr, *Islam in the Modern World: Challenged by the West, Threatened by Fundamentalism, Keeping Faith with Tradition* (New York: HarperOne, 2010), 418n2.

8. هفت شهر عشق‌را عطّار گشت
   ما هنوز اندر خم یک کوچه‌ایم
   While this verse is not found in the major editions of Rūmī's works, it is commonly attributed to him by the oral tradition.

Question [1]

1. Śrī Ramana Maharshi, *Who Am I?: Nān Yār? of Bhagavān Śrī Ramana Maharshi; a New Translation*, 11th ed. [N.T.] (Tiruvannamalai: T. N. Venkataraman: 1968).

2. See for example, Q. 20:19.

3. See for example, Muḥyi al-Dīn ibn al-'Arabī, *al-Futūḥāt al-makkiyyah*, vol. 2 (Cairo: Bulāq, 1911), 267–68.

4. See *The Study Quran*, eds. Seyyed Hossein Nasr et al., commentary on 24:35. Cf. William Chittick, *The Self Disclosure of God* (Albany: State University of New York Press, 1998), 59 and 129.

5. Cf. Q. 17:44.

6. The Nūrbakhsh edition has been preferred here for the second hemistich. The Kaywān Samī'ī edition has
   نیابد اندر او تغییر و تبدیل
   "No change and transformation is found within it."

7. Here the Nūrbakhsh edition has been preferred. The Kaywān Samī'ī edition has
ز نابینائی آمد راه تشبیه
"It was from blindness that came the way of similitude."

8. Ananda K. Coomaraswamy, "On the One and Only Transmigrant" Supplement to the *Journal of the American Oriental Society* 64 (1944): 19–43.

Question [2]

1. Here the Nūrbakhsh edition is preferred. The Kaywān Samī'ī edition has
سیاهی گر ببینی نور ذات است
"Blackness, if thou wert to see, is the Light of the Divine Essence."

2. This title, found in some editions, is not included by Samī'ī.

3. The Nūrbakhsh edition is preferred here. The Kaywān Samī'ī edition has the variant: طاقت و تاب.

4. Here the Nūrbakhsh edition is preferred. The Kaywān Samī'ī edition has وز او, "And through it . . ."

5. The other version of this title that appears in some manuscripts is:
به دیده دیده‌را هرگز که دیده است
"Who has even been able to see with the eye that which sees."

6. This title is found in the Kaywān Samī'ī edition but is not found in other editions of the text.

7. See William A. Graham, *Divine Word and Prophetic Word in Early Islam: A Reconsideration of the Sources, with Special Reference to the Divine Saying or Hadîth Qudsî* (The Hague: Mouton, 1977), 69–72.

8. Martin Lings, *A Sufi Saint of the Twentieth Century*, 3rd ed. (Cambridge, UK: Islamic Texts Society, 1993), 37.

9. دل هر ذره‌را که بشکافی
آفتابیش در میان بینی
Hātif Iṣfahānī, *Kulliyyāt-i Dīwān-i Hātif-i Iṣfahānī*, ed. Muḥammad 'Abbāsī (Tehran: Fakhr-i Rāzī, 1362 S.H. [1983]), 20.

10. Here the Nūrbakhsh edition is preferred. The Kaywān Samī'ī edition has: در اسما meaning, "In the Names."

11. See Michael Behe, *Darwin's Black Box: The Biochemical Challenge to Evolution* (New York: Free Press, 1996).

12. Here the Nūrbakhsh edition is preferred. The Kaywān Samī'ī edition has: در نقطهٔ خال meaning, " . . . in the point of the mole," which would refer to Shabistarī's discussion of the symbolism of the face in the final sections of the book.

13. See Seyyed Hossein Nasr, *Islamic Philosophy from its Origin to the Present: Philosophy in the Land of Prophecy* (Albany: State University of New York Press, 2006), 72.

14. The word is thought to derive from the Avestan *mərəγō saēnō* 'the bird Saēna.' See Hanns-Peter Schmidt, 'Simorġ,' *Encyclopaedia Iranica* (July 20, 2020), https://www.iranicaonline.org/articles/simorg.

15. Farīdu'd-Dīn 'Aṭṭār, *The Speech of the Birds: Concerning Migration to the Real (Manṭiqu'ṭ-ṭair)*, trans. Peter Avery (Cambridge, UK: Islamic Texts Society, 1998); Farid ud-Din Attar, *The Conference of the Birds*, trans. Dick Davis and Afkham Darbandi Harmondsworth (Middlesex, UK: Penguin, 1984).

16. I have translated part of the climax of this poem in the "The Flight of Birds to Union: Meditations upon 'Aṭṭār's *Manṭiq al-ṭayr*'" in *Islamic Art and Spirituality*, in which the event of identity, you might say spiritual identity, takes place. Seyyed Hossein Nasr, "The Flight of Birds to Union: Meditations upon 'Aṭṭār's

Manṭiq al-ṭayr," in *Islamic Art and Spirituality* (Albany: State University of New York Press, 1987), 98–113.

17. See Marco Pallis (Thubden Tendzin), *The Way and the Mountain: Tibet, Buddhism, and Tradition*, ed. Joseph A. Fitzgerald (Bloomington: World Wisdom, 2008), 1–28.

18. See Henry Corbin, *Corps spirituelle et terre céleste, de l'Iran mazdean à l'Iran shî'ite* (Paris: Buchet/Chastel, 1979); idem., *Spiritual Body and Celestial Earth—From Mazdean Iran to Shî'ite Iran*, trans. Nancy Pearson (Princeton: Princeton University Press, 1977).

19. The Nūrbakhsh edition has the variant,
چو خورشید عیان بنمایدت چهر
"When the manifest Sun shows its face to thee,"

20. For this verse, the variant found in the Nūrbakhsh edition is preferred. The Kaywān Kaywān Samī'ī edition has:
نشستی چون زنان در کوی ادبیر
نمی‌داری ز جهل خویشتن عار
"Thou art sitting like women in the quarter of misfortune,
Thou dost not become ashamed of thine own ignorance."

21. For further discussion of the role of and attitudes toward women in medieval Sufism see Annemaria Schimmel, *Mystical Dimensions of Islam* (Chapel Hill: University of North Carolina Press, 1975), 426–35; Rkia Cornell, ed. and trans., *Early Sufi Women (Dhikr an-Niswa al-Muta'abbidāt aṣ-Ṣūfiyyāt)*, by Muḥammad ibn al-Ḥusayn al-Sulamī (Louisville, KY: Fons Vitae, 1999), 15–20 and 54–70, and Sachiko Murata, *The Tao of Islam A Sourcebook on Gender Relationships in Islamic Thought* (Albany: State University of New York Press, 1992).

22. Shabistarī may be referring to a *ḥadīth*, which some consider weak, "The religion of infirm old people behooves you," though in this *ḥadīth* "the religion of infirm old people" is clearly something positive, implying simple and sincere faith.

23. Seyyed Hossein Nasr, "The Wedding of Heaven and Earth in Astrology," Chapter 9 in *An Introduction to Islamic Cosmological Doctrines*, rev. ed. (Albany: State University of New York Press, 1993), 151–65.

24. Giorgio de Santillana and Hertha von Dechend, *Hamlet's Mill: An Essay Investigating the Origins of Human Knowledge and Its Transmission through Myth* (Boston: David R. Godine, 1977).

25. Cf. Maḥmūd Shabistarī, *Gulshan i Raz = The Mystic Rose Garden of Sa'd Ud Din Mahmud Shabistari*, trans. E. H. Whinfield, 24.

26. Titus Burckhardt, *Clé spirituelle de l'astrologie musulmane d'après Mohyiddin Ibn 'Arabī* (Milan: Archè, 1974); idem., *Mystical Astrology According to Ibn 'Arabi*, trans. Bulent Rauf (Louisville: Fons Vitae, 2001).

27. For this verse, the variant found in the Nūrbakhsh edition is preferred. The Kaywān Samī'ī edition has:
کلام حق همی ناطق بدین است
که باطل دیدن از ضعف یقین است
"The Word of God speaks precisely of this,
"For to see falsehood is weakness of certitude."

28. I.e. in place of *ḥikmat ay khām*, "wisdom, o unripe man."

29. Nasr, *An Introduction to Islamic Cosmological Doctrines*, 75–83 and 151–65.

30. Here the Nūrbakhsh edition is preferred. The Kaywān Samī'ī edition has
فروغ جانور از صدق و اخلاص
"The splendor of the [realm of] animals on the basis of truth and sincerity,"

31. See above, in the "Answer" to "Question [1]."

32. See Q. 7:12.

33. See René Guénon, *The Great Triad* (Hillsdale: Sophia Perennis, 2001), 46–52.

Question [3]

1. For this verse, the variant found in the Nūrbakhsh edition has been preferred. The Kaywān Samī'ī edition has:
   یکی ره برتر از کون و مکان شو
   جهان بگذار و خود در خود جهان شو
   "Choose the path beyond the world of existence (*kawn*) and place (*makān*),
   "Leave the world behind and become the world within thyself."

2. For this verse, the variant found in the Nūrbakhsh edition has been preferred. The Kaywān Samī'ī edition has:
   بود هستی بهشت امکان چو دوزخ
   من و تو در میان مانند برزخ
   "Being is Paradise and contingency like Hell,
   "I and thou are in the middle, like Purgatory (*barzakh*)."

3. For this hemistich, the variant found in the Nūrbakhsh edition has been preferred. The Kaywān Samī'ī edition has:
   من و تو چون نماند در میانه
   "When I and thou no longer remain in the middle . . ."

4. For this verse, the variant found in the Nūrbakhsh edition has been preferred. The Kaywān Samī'ī edition has:
   چو صافی گشت غین تو شود عین
   "When it becomes pure, thy *ghayn* (otherness) becomes the *'ayn*."

Question [4]

1. Here the text has been edited in preference over the Kaywān Samī'ī version, which reads
   که تا انسان کامل گشت مولود
   "In order that the Universal Man should be born."

2. در پرتو تو علی ولی شد
   آئینهٔ حقّنما علی شد

3. See Lewisohn, *Beyond Faith and Infidelity*, which deals at length with this perplexing subject from the Sufi point of view.

4. For this hemistich the Nūrbakhsh edition has the notable variant,
   به زیر قبه‌های ستر مستور
   "Under the domes of the hidden secret [of God]"

5. Leviticus, 23:40.

6. Syed Abdul Wahhab, *The Shadowless Prophet of Islam: Being a Treatise on Spiritual Aspects of the Prophet's Life and Spiritualism of Islam as Taught by Him*, 2nd ed. (Lahore: Kashmiri Bazar, 1962).

7. For this verse the Nūrbakhsh edition has been preferred. The Kaywān Samī'ī edition has:
   نبی چون در رسالت بود اکمل
   بود از هر نبی ناچار افضل

"The Prophet, since he was the most perfect in messengerhood,
"Is higher than any prophet."

8. See, for example, Henry Corbin, *En Islam iranien: Aspects spirituels et philosophiques*, (4 vols., Paris: Gallimard, 1971–73).

Question [5]

1. For this hemistich the Nūrbakhsh edition has been preferred. The Kaywān Samī'ī edition has,
   که با وی آدمی همچون بهیمه‌است
   "For with it man is like a wild beast."
2. Ḥāfiẓ Shīrāzī, *Dīwān-i Khwājah Shams al-Dīn Muḥammad Ḥāfiẓ Shīrāzī*, eds. Muḥammad Qazwīnī and Qāsim Ghanī, 216.
3. Literally meaning "setting up" or "establishing," the *iqāmah* is worded similarly to the call to prayer with the addition of the words, "the prayer has been established," and is generally recited at a lower volume.

Question [6]

1. For this hemistich the Nūrbakhsh edition has been preferred. The Kaywān Samī'ī edition has,
   «الست بربّکم» ایزد کرا گفت؟
   "To whom did God say, 'Am I not your Lord?'"
2. مطرب آغازید پیش ترک مست
   در حجاب نغمه اسرار الست
   Mathnawī, 6:703. See Jalal al-Dīn Rūmī, *The Mathnawi of Jalālu'ddīn Rūmī*, ed. and trans. Reynold A. Nicholson, vol. 5 (Leiden: Brill 1933), 313.
3. Frithjof Schuon, *From the Divine to the Human*, trans. Gustavo Polit and Deborah Lambert (Bloomington, IN: World Wisdom, 1982), 97.
4. For this hemistich the Nūrbakhsh edition has been preferred. The Kaywān Samī'ī edition has,
   تو بشنیدی برو باخود بپرداز
   "Thou hast heard it, go and work on thyself."

Question [7]

1. *Luke*, 17:21.
2. Yaḥyā ibn Ḥabash Suhrawardī, *The Philosophical Allegories and Mystical Treatises*, ed. and trans. W. M. Thackston (Costa Mesa: Mazda, 1999), 99–100.

Question [8]

1. As stated by the early Sufi Rabi'ah al-'Adawiyyah.
2. See S.H. Nasr, "The Question of Existence and Quiddity and Ontology in Islamic Philosophy," chap. 4 in *Islamic Philosophy from its Origin to the Present,* 63–84.

Question [9]

1. The Kaywān Samī'ī edition has *būd-u nābūd* (existence and nonexistence) here, but the variant *būd-i nābūd* (the existence of this nonexistence) has been preferred.
2. See *Mathnawī*, 1:602, Jalāl al-Dīn Rūmī, *The Mathnawī of Jalālu'ddīn Rūmī*, ed. and trans. Reynold A. Nicholson, vol. 1 (Leiden: Brill 1925), 38.
3. Here, Shabistarī may be referring to a reported *ḥadīth*, "The Qadarites [i.e. the proponents of free will] are the Magians of my community."
4. This verse may be a reference to Iblīs.
5. As such, this verse may be a reference to Adam.

Question [10]

1. See Wolfgang Smith, *Cosmos and Transcendence: Breaking through the Barrier of Scientistic Belief*, 2nd rev. ed. (San Rafael: Sophia Perennis, 2008); and Smith, *The Wisdom of Ancient Cosmology: Contemporary Science in Light of Tradition* (Oakton: The Foundation for Traditional Studies, 2004), 83103.

Question [11]

1. Muṣliḥ ibn 'Abdallāh Sa'di Shīrāzī, *Gulistān*, ed. Nūr Allāh Īzadparast (Tehran: Dānesh Press, 1376 S.H. [1997]), 2.
2. Ṣadr al-Dīn Qūnawī, *I'jāz al-bayān fī ta'wīl umm al-Qur'ān*, ed. M. Ahmed (Hyderabad: N.P., 1988).
3. "I ask forgiveness of God."
4. Schuon, *From the Divine to the Human*, 97.
5. This verse is one of a small number of instances in this section in which a previous verse is repeated in the same or similar form.
6. Henry Corbin, *The Man of Light in Iranian Sufism*, trans. Nancy Pearson (New Lebanon: Omega Publications, 1994), 121–31.
7. This is another instance of the repetition of a previous verse.
8. Henry Corbin, *Terre céleste et corps de la résurrection: De l'Iran mazdéen à l'Iran shī'ite* (Paris: Buchet-Chastel, 1960). English translation as *Spiritual Body and Celestial Earth*, by Nancy Pearson (Princeton, NJ: Princeton University Press, 1977).
9. "Knowledge only saves us on condition that it enlists all that we are, only when it is a way and when it works and transforms and wounds our nature even as the plough wounds the soil." Frithjof Schuon, *The Essential Frithjof Schuon*, ed. Seyyed Hossein Nasr (Bloomington, IN: World Wisdom, 2005), 116.

Question [12]

1. See S. H. Nasr, "The Contemporary Islamic World and the Environmental Crisis," *Sophia: The Journal of Traditional Studies* 13, no. 2 (Winter 2007–2008): 23.

Question [13]

1. Ibn al-ʻArabī, *The Tarjumán al-ashwáq: A Collection of Mystical Odes*, ed. and trans. Reynold A. Nicholson (London: Royal Asiatic Society, 1911).
2. Here the text has been edited in preference over the Kaywān Samīʻī version, which reads
چو سوی لفظ و معنی گشت نازل
"When the inner meaning and the external expression descended."
3. For this hemistich, the Nūrbakhsh edition has been preferred. The Kaywān Samīʻī edition has:
ز چشمش خاست بیداری و مستی
"From Her Eyes have arisen wakefulness and drunkenness."
4. Here the Nūrbakhsh edition has been preferred. The Kaywān Samīʻī edition has:
از آن کردند نامش آب حیوان
"That is why they have named it 'the water of life.'"
5. Here the Nūrbakhsh edition has been preferred. The Kaywān Samīʻī edition has:
ز تاریکی زلفش روز و شب کن
"Through the blackness of Her Hair, pass day and night."

Question [14]

1. در خرابات مغان نور خدا می‌بینم
این عجب بین که چه نوری ز کجا می‌بینم
Ḥāfiẓ Shīrāzī, *Dīwān-i Khwājah Shams al-Dīn Muḥammad Hāfiẓ Shīrāzī*, ed. Muḥammad Qazwīnī and Qāsim Ghanī, 245.
2. As Rūmī says,
"Before there was in this world the cup, grape and wine,
"From the Eternal Wine, our soul was already drunk.
"We were beating in the Baghdad of the cosmos (of the soul) the drum of 'I am the Truth',
"Before there was all this commotion and rebellion of Ḥallāj."
پیش از آن کاندر جهان جام و می و انگور بود
از شراب لا یزالی جان ما مخمور بود
ما به بغداد جهان کوس انا الحق می‌زدیم
پیش از آن کاین گیر و دار و فتنهٔ منصور بود
Nothing could be clearer than this poem from the Dīwān-i Shams of Mawlānā. To indicate the deeper meaning of these terms, the poem also points to the preeternal nature of the soul; the reality of soul beyond time.
Mawlānā Jalāl al-Dīn Rūmi, *Kulliyyāt-i Dīwān-i Shams*, ed. Badīʻ al-Zamān Furūzānfar (Tehran: Rād Press, 1374 S.H. [1995]), 304.
3. For this hemistich the Nūrbakhsh edition has been used. The Kaywān Samīʻī edition has:
شراب و شمع ذوق و نور عرفان
"Wine and candle of tasting and the light of gnosis."
4. Here, the Nūrbakhsh edition is preferred. The Kaywān Samīʻī edition has:
مگر از مکر خود یابی امانی
"Unless thou wilt be able to be free from thine own deception."
5. Here, the Nūrbakhsh edition is preferred. The Kaywān Samīʻī edition has,
جهان و جان در او شکل حباب است
"The world and the spirit in him are in the form of a bubble."

6. For this verse, the Nūrbakhsh edition is preferred. The Kaywān Samī‘ī edition has:
ز عکس او تن پژمرده جان گشت
ز تابش جان افسرده روان گشت
"From Her Image, the decrepit body became spirit.
"From the casting of Her Light, the sad soul began to flow."

7. For this verse, the Nūrbakhsh edition is preferred. The Kaywān Samī‘ī edition has:
یکی از بوی دردش عاقل آمد
یکی از رنگ صافش غافل آمد
"One person, simply smelling the dregs, became wise (*‘āqil*),
"Another from its pure color became negligent."

8. The order of this verse and the previous verse is reversed in the Kaywān Samī‘ī edition. Here, the order in the Nūrbakhsh edition is the preferred version.

9. For this hemistich, the Nūrbakhsh edition is preferred. The Kaywān Samī‘ī edition has:
زهی دریا دل و رند سرافراز
The meaning is almost identical.

Question [15]

1. مسلمان گر بدانستی که بت چیست
بدانستی که دین در بت‌پرستی است

2. Here Kaywān Samī‘ī also includes a variant:
یقین کردی که دین در بت‌پرستی است
"He would be certain that religion is idol-worship."

3. For this hemistich the Nūrbakhsh edition has been preferred. The Kaywān Samī‘ī edition has,
کاز او کفر حقیقی شد پدیدار
"For from him real *kufr* has become manifest."

4. In the exact wording, probably for the sake of meter, Shabistarī is combining the wording of Q. 6:91 with the synonymous first words of this verse: "So leave them (*fa-dharhum*) to indulge in idle talk and play until they meet the Day that they are promised." (Q. 70:42)

5. Cf. Q. 67:3.

6. For this verse the Nūrbakhsh edition has been preferred. The Kaywān Samī‘ī edition has:
ز ابلیس لعین بی‌شهادت
شود پیدا هزاران خرق عادت
"From the cursed Devil (Iblīs), without testification,
"A thousand miracles (*kharq-i ‘ādat*) appear."

7. See René Guénon, *The Reign of Quantity and the Signs of the Times* trans. Lord Northbourne (Hillsdale: Sophia Perennis, 2004), 260–66.

8. This verse does not exist in the Kaywān Samī’ī edition but has been included from the Nūrbakhsh edition.

9. The Nūrbakhsh edition has been preferred here. The Kaywān Samī‘ī edition has:
که از روح القدس در وی نشانی است
"Which has a sign in it from the Holy Spirit."

10. For this hemistich the Nūrbakhsh edition has been preferred. The Kaywān Samī’ī edition has:
که با ایشان به حرمت بایدت زیست
"For thou shouldst live with them with respect."

11. See Q. 64:14.

12. For this hemistich the Nūrbakhsh edition has been preferred. The Kaywān Samī'ī edition has:
نمی‌دانم به هر جائی که هستی
"I do not know, in whatever place thou art."

13. For this hemistich the Nūrbakhsh edition has been preferred. The Kaywān Samī'ī edition has:
به هر یک لحظه ایمان دیگر گیر
"In every moment take up new faith."

Selected Bibliography

Arberry, A. J. *Sufism: An Account of the Mystics of Islam*. London and New York: Routledge, 2008.

Corbin, H. *En Islam iranien*, 4 vols. Paris, Gallimard, 1971–72.

Ilāhī Ardabīlī, H. *Sharḥ-i gulshan-i rāz*. Tehran: Markaz-i Nashr-i Dānishgāhī. 1375 A. H. solar.

Lāhījī, M. *Mafātīḥ al-i'jāz fī sharḥ gulshan-i rāz*. Tehran: Maḥmūdī, 1958.

Lewisohn, L., ed. *Beyond Faith and Infidelity: The Sufi Poetry and Teachings of Mahmud Shabistari*. Richmond, UK: Curzon, 1995.

———. *The Legacy of Medieval Persian Sufism (1150-1500)*. Oxford: Oneworld, 1999.

Nasr, Seyyed Hossein. *The Garden of Truth: The Vision and Practice of Sufism, Islam's Mystical Tradition*. New York: HarperOne. 2007.

———. *Sufi Essays*, 3rd ed. Chicago: Kazi, 1999.

——— . *What is Metaphysics? Ruminations on Principial Knowledge and Some of Its Applications*. Sheffield: Equinox, 2025.

Nicholson, R.A. *The Mystics of Islam*. London and Boston: Routledge and K. Paul, 1975.

Rypka, J. *History of Iranian Literature*. Translated from the German by P. van Popta-Hope. Dordrecht: D. Reidel Publishing, 1968.

Schuon, F. *Sufism: Veil and Quintessence*. Translated by Mark Perry, Jean-Pierre Lafouge, and James S. Cutsinger. Edited by J. Cutsinger. Bloomington, IN: World Wisdom, 2006.

Shabistarī, Maḥmūd. Darr, R. A., trans. *Garden of Mystery*. Cambridge, UK: Archetype, 2007.

———. Lederer, F., trans. *The Secret Rose Garden of Sa'd ud dīn Maḥmūd Shabistarī*. London: J. Murray, 1920.

——— . Whinfield, E. H., trans. *Gulshan i Raz: The Mystic Rose Garden: Sa'd ud Din Mahmud Shabistari*. London: Trübner & Co., 1880.

——— . Yate, A., trans., *The Secret Garden*. Blanco, TX: Zahra, 2018.

Selected Bibliography

Index

'Abbāsī, Muḥammad, 293n2.9
'Abd al-'Aẓīm, Ḥaḍrat-i, 66
Abdul Wahhab, Syed: *The Shadowless Prophet of Islam*, 123, 295n4.6
Abraham, 67, 111, 123
Abrahamic: esoterism, 275; forms of esoterism, 97; religions, 40, 183, 210; sacred history, 55; sanctity, 126; traditions, 162; world, 4, 124
the Absolute Truth (*kull-i muṭlaq*), 30, 99
Abū Jahl, 171
Abū'l-Khayr, Abū Sa'īd, 37
Achaemenid period, 59
al-'Adawiyyah, Rābi'ah, 296n8.1
Adam, 8, 15, 55, 56, 81, 91, 105, 110, 116, 119, 120, 122, 123, 138, 139, 180, 192, 205, 228, 231, 232, 272, 297n9.5
Advaita Vedanta, 8, 99, 142
Afghanistan, xi, 28
Africa, Central and South, 61
al-Aḥad, 15, 16, 69
Ahrīman, 168, 169
Ahūrāmazdā, 168, 169
al-Ākhir, 14, 95
Akhlāq-i nāṣirī (of al-Ṭūsī), 185
'ālam al-amr, 11
'ālam al-kawn. See *kawn*
'ālam al-khalq, 11, 283
'ālam al-khalq wa'l-amr, 11, 283
'ālam al-khayāl, 62; *see also khayāl*
'ālam al-ta'yyunāt, 211
Aleppo, 134
Alexander the Great, 46
Algar, Hamid, 291n4
'Alī ibn Abī Ṭālib, 69, 113, 121, 122, 126, 127, 255
al-'Alīm, 79, 176
Allāh, passim
the All-Powerful, 5, 6
the Alps, 60
the Americas, 61
Amīn al-Dīn, Shaykh, xi
ana'l-Ḥaqq, xii, 19, 143-146, 151
anamnesis, 139
angel, passim
the Angel of Death (*Malak al-Mawt*), 202, 204
the Anglo-Saxon world, 98
anima mundi, 159
anthropology, 61, 81
anthropos, 74, 114
Antichrist, 261-262
'aql, 8, 15, 30, 36-38, 141, 146, 162, 193, 245, 283; *see also* intellect; *khirad*; Universal Intellect
Aquinas, St. Thomas, 33, 44, 183
the Arab world, 7, 37, 106, 267
Arabia, xi, 124, 125
Arabic, passim
Arabic Sufi poetry, 18, 219
Arberry, Arthur John, 129, 301
arc of ascent, 119, 166
arc of descent, 119, 166
archetype, 11, 40, 44, 73, 89, 103, 196-198, 207, 220, 268
Ardabīlī, Ilāhī, 301
Aristotelian: accidents, 283; categories, 41, 150, 198, 285; causes, 89; cosmology, 53, 189; ethics, 183-184; form, 58, 85-86, 155, 187, 207, 288; matter, 58, 85, 155; philosophy, 85; syllogism, 31
Aristotelianism, 44
Aristotle, 41, 44, 150, 155, 156, 183, 185, 198, 208
'arūḍ, 24
the Ash'arites, 150
Asia: Northern, 61; Western, 60, 61
aṣl, 13, 52, 88, 283
'Aṣṣār, Sayyid Muḥammad Kāẓim, 18
astrology and astronomy, traditional, 72, 73, 75-80, 90, 158, 188, 189, 268, 284; Aquarius, 76, 78; Aries, 72, 76, 78; Cancer, 76, 78; Capricorn, 76, 78; the Earth, 6, 28, 39, 40, 47, 61-63, 71-73, 75, 77-80, 83, 84, 87, 89, 90-92, 95, 118, 128, 134, 137, 138, 154, 157-160, 176, 184, 188, 189, 199, 203, 210, 212, 227-229, 244, 247, 250, 269, 278, 279; the Footstool, 76, 77; Gemini, 76, 78; the heavens, 12, 62, 63, 71, 74-78, 80-83,

90, 92, 107, 111, 118, 158, 188, 189, 227, 228, 237, 240, 244, 268, 286; horoscope, 73, 78; Jupiter, 77, 78, 158, 188, 189; Leo, 76, 78; Libra, 76, 78; Mars, 77, 78, 80, 158, 188; Mercury, 77, 78, 80, 158, 188; the Moon, xi, 63, 67, 72, 77-79, 83, 112, 114, 138, 158, 188, 189, 207, 236; Pisces, 76, 78; planets, 72, 73, 75-79, 82, 83, 90, 158, 188, 189, 284; Sagittarius, 76, 78; Saturn, 77, 78, 158, 188; Scorpio, 76, 78; the solar system, 53, 75, 188; spheres, 12, 76, 78, 80, 83, 157, 158, 161, 188, 284; the sublunar region, 77, 83-85, 189; 75, 81-83, 186, 158, 187; the Sun, 34, 35, 46, 48, 49, 53, 63, 67, 72, 77-79, 90, 92, 112, 114, 117, 122, 123, 125, 137, 138, 157, 158, 180, 188-190, 203, 220, 278; Taurus, 76, 78; Venus, 63, 77, 78, 158, 188; Virgo, 76, 78; *see also* Zodiac
astrophysics, 189
ātash-gardān, 13-14, 216
Ātman, 9, 40, 88, 97, 99, 126, 149
atom, 53, 54, 57, 138, 243
'Aṭṭār, Farīd al-Dīn, xii, 24-25, 37, 59, 60, 61, 267, 293n2.15-16
Australia, 61
Avery, Peter, 281n2.15
Avestan, 293n2.15
Avicennan: faculty psychology, 14; philosophy, 18, 33, 153; ontology, 156; *see also* Ibn Sīnā; Peripatetic philosophy
al-Awwal, 14, 95
Azerbaijan, xi, 20, 103

Bahā' al-Dīn Āmulī, Shaykh, xi
baḥr hazaj maḥdhūf, xii, 291n13
baqā', 115, 205, 208, 283
Barfield, Owen: *Saving the Appearances*, 147
Basṭāmī, Bāyazīd, 167
the Ba'th Party, 206
al-Bāṭin, 35, 95, 230
Behe, Michael: *Darwin's Black Box*, 54, 293n2.11
Beijing, 106
Being (being), 5, 6, 9, 10-12, 27, 30, 32-36, 43, 47-50, 56, 57, 59, 60, 63, 73, 78, 85-89, 91, 94, 97, 99-102, 105, 107, 117, 119, 120, 124, 129, 130, 132, 134, 137-139, 141, 143, 145, 147, 148, 151, 153, 154, 156, 157, 160-164, 167, 175, 195-199, 201, 207-209, 215, 217, 219, 220, 226-228, 234, 235, 241, 242-244, 247, 253-257, 267, 268, 270, 274, 278, 279, 287, 288, 295n3.2; *see also Kun! fa-yakūn*; *wujūd*
Belgium, 106
the Beloved, 130, 167, 226-230, 232, 233, 235, 236, 241, 245, 249, 278
Bernier, François, ix
the Bible, 89, 118; *see also* Christianity; the New Testament; the Old Testament
Bilāl, 255
al-Bīrūnī, Abū Rayḥān, 80
black light, 46-48, 124, 148
Bodhidharma, 126
Britain, 7, 98, 147, 254
the Buddha, 126
Buddhism, 40, 51, 126
Burckhardt, Titus, 79, 105; *Clé spirituelle de l'astrologie musulmane d'après Mohyddîn ibn 'Arabî*, 79, 294n2.26

Cairo, 87, 161
California, 254
Catholicism, 185, 195-196, 210, 221
the Central Asian School of Sufism, 209
Chardin, Jean, ix
chemistry, 83
China, 72, 184; *see also* Zodiac, Chinese
Chittick, William, 292n1.4
Christ, 4, 15, 46, 55, 56, 61, 66, 78, 100, 111, 123, 126, 128, 140, 185, 258, 267, 268, 272; as Logos, 15; as Messiah, 258
Christian: cosmology, 83, 189; doctrine of incarnation, 37, 38, 146, 147; monastery, 102, 266, 267, 272, 273; monasticism, 265, 266, 272, 273; monk, 184, 185, 253, 257, 272, 274; mysticism, 4, 8, 184; philosophy, 44; theology, 38, 41, 51, 145, 195, 196; thought, 63
Christianity, xii, 4, 8, 19, 35, 38, 41, 44, 51, 63, 83, 108, 124, 145, 147, 183-185, 189, 195, 196, 202, 210, 251, 253, 254, 256, 257, 258, 265-267, 272-275
circulus vitiosus, 33
The Cloud of Unknowing, 8
coincidentia oppositorum, 85
Confucianism, 51
the Communist Party, 106

consciousness, 9, 10, 29, 57, 63, 100, 102, 104, 109, 138, 162, 184, 199, 201, 229, 242, 248, 250, 275, 279
contingent, passim; *see also imkān/mumkin*
Coomaraswamy, Ananda, 24; "On the One and Only Transmigrant", 39-40, 293n1.8
Corbin, Henry, 61, 127, 209, 211, 292n5, 294n2.18, 296n4.8, 297n11.6,8, 301
Cornell, Rkia, 294n2.21
cosmology, vii, xii, 7, 11, 12, 20, 40, 53, 58, 59, 61, 70, 72, 73, 79, 83, 84, 134, 157, 158, 161, 188, 189, 210, 216
the Creator, 107, 205, 216, 244, 254
The Crest Jewel of Discernment (of Shankaracharya), 8
Cusa, Nicholas of, 85

dā'irat al-nubuwwah, 119, 126, 284; *see also nabī; nubuwwah/nubuwwat*
dā'irat al-walāyah/wilāyah, 119, 126, 284; *see also walāyah/wilāyah*; *walī, awliyā'*
Damascus, 7
Damavand (Mount), 60
Dante, 15, 211
Dār al-Kutub al-Miṣriyyah, 161
Darr, Robert Abdul Hayy, ix, 291n4, 301
Darwinian evolution, 7, 54, 89, 108, 119
Davis, Dick, 293n2.15
the *Day of Alast*, 95, 138, 139, 140
Day of Judgement, 64, 144, 172, 200, 201, 209, 210
Day of Resurrection, 62, 199-201, 203, 209
Delhi, 106
Descartes, René, 9; *Meditations*, 9
the Devil, 55, 89, 91, 132, 133, 242, 259, 260, 288, 299n15.6; *see also* Iblīs; Shayṭān
dhikr, 12, 30, 94, 131, 184, 199, 226, 243, 284
Divine: Abode, 69, 259; Acts, 3, 11, 15, 44, 285; Affirmation, 32, 288; Beauty, 39, 43, 57, 131, 193, 219-221, 230, 232, 234; Bounty, 161, 205, 206; Command, 6, 11, 13, 86, 91, 124, 168, 176, 206, 267, 277, 283; Emanation, 5, 206; Essence, 8, 15, 33, 34, 36, 41, 43-48, 99, 101, 124, 137, 140, 146, 147, 151, 165, 195, 226, 233, 267, 268, 284, 285, 293n2.1; Generosity, 5; Grace, 27, 170, 177, 206, 227, 277; Help, 27, 32, 88, 206, 242, 288; Knowledge, 3, 5, 11, 51, 79, 81, 137, 169, 172, 176, 186, 243; Law, 31, 168, 172, 179, 255, 272, 273, 287, 288; Light, 5, 35, 36, 44-49, 51, 53, 64, 99, 110, 124, 137, 138, 151, 163, 164, 167, 170, 187, 211, 239, 244, 245, 293n2.1, 299n14.6; Love, 3, 43, 51, 160, 190; Mysteries, 5, 8, 27, 142, 143, 219, 234, 250, 280; Names, passim; Power, 5-7, 43, 73, 74, 79, 87, 89, 107, 117, 169, 227, 228, 230; Presence, 4, 13, 27, 33, 36, 40, 45, 48, 54, 68, 119, 144-146, 159, 171, 181, 192, 210, 213, 227, 231, 236, 240, 241, 244, 266, 267, 286; Principle, 12-14, 33, 40, 56, 115, 145; Qualities, passim; Reality, passim; Self, 10, 40, 88, 94, 100, 135, 142, 151, 153, 163, 277; Succor, 27, 206; Threshold, 45, 57; the Throne, 5, 54, 71, 74, 75, 112, 143, 234; Truth, passim; Virtue, 5
The Divine Comedy (of Dante), 15
Divine Unity, science of, xi
Dīwān-i Ḥāfiẓ (of Ḥāfiẓ), 3, 292n2, 296n5.1, 298n14.1, 2
Diwān-i Shams (of Rūmī), 292n14.2
Druids, 40

Eckhart, Meister, 8, 126, 195
ecology, 84
Egypt, xi, 22, 135
England, 40, 61, 125
English, passim
environmental crisis/degradation, x, 127
esoteric (*bāṭin*), xii, 15, 22, 41, 44, 52, 62, 69, 97, 107, 112, 113, 115, 126, 127, 134, 151, 155, 162, 179-181, 186, 199, 204, 205, 207, 221, 226, 230, 255, 256, 263, 264, 273, 275-277, 280, 284, 286; *see also al-Bāṭin*
the Eternal, 13, 215
Eurasia, 124
Europe, 60, 61, 98, 209
exoteric (*ẓāhir*), 17, 41, 47, 124, 170, 179, 180, 184, 196, 207, 239, 276-278, 289; *see also al-Ẓāhir*
eye of the heart, 8, 38, 280, 284

fanā', 115, 155, 203, 224, 284
al-Fārābī, Abū Naṣr, 263
female/feminine, xii, 7, 64-66, 88, 97, 101, 107, 151, 191, 192, 219, 221, 226, 229
Fermi, Enrico, 53
fiat lux. See Kun! fa-yakūn

Fīhi mā fīhi (of Rūmī), 129
the Fountain of Life, 46, 233
France, ix, 73, 124
free will, 52, 83, 108, 166-169, 172, 297n9.3
the French, ix, 98
French language, 4, 9, 58, 71, 145, 219
Fuji (Mount), 60
Fujiyama, 60
Furūzānfar, Badīʻ al-Zamān, 298n14.2
Fuṣūṣ al-ḥikam (of Ibn ʻArabī), ix, 134
al-Futūḥāt al-makkiyyah (of Ibn ʻArabī), 292n1.3

Gabriel, 45, 46, 68, 272
Gaia hypothesis, 159
Galileo, 54, 189
géographie imaginaire, 61
geography, 61, 92, 106, 124, 183; ancient, 61; Greek, 61; medieval, 61; Muslim, 61
German language, ix, 3, 130, 135, 301
Germans, 73, 98, 126, 149, 184, 223
Germany, 209
al-Ghaniyy, 212
Ghanī, Qāsim, 292n2, 296n5.2, 298n14.1
al-Ghazzālī, Abū Ḥāmid, xi, 37, 50, 86, 150
gnosis, xi, 8, 10, 20, 21, 38, 51, 73, 115-117, 129, 130, 132, 139, 160, 164, 175, 239-243, 256, 281, 286, 298
God, passim
Graham, William, 293n2.7
Greece, 72
Greek (language), 31, 44, 61, 77, 85, 86, 139, 150, 155, 195, 266, 273
the Greeks, 60, 61, 83
Greek philosophy, 149, 210; *see also* Aristotle; Neoplatonism; Peripatetic philosophy; Plato
Guénon, René, 39, 60, 92, 262, 295n2.33, 299n15.7
Gulistān (of Saʻdī), 199, 297n11.1
gynecology, Quranic, 108

ḥadīth, passim; *qudsī*, 50, 52, 118, 131, 243, 284; collections, 50, 181
Ḥāfiẓ, Shams al-Dīn, 3, 18, 28, 120, 122, 154, 191, 219, 239, 262, 292n2, 296n5.2
hāhūt, 267, 268
Ḥāʼirī, Hādī, x
al-Ḥallāj, Manṣūr, xii, 17, 102, 125, 143, 144, 151, 249, 298n2
Hamadan, 134
von Hammer-Purgstall, Joseph ix, 291n4
Ḥaqīqah, 115, 116, 117, 239, 285
al-Ḥaqq, 145; *see also ana'l-Ḥaqq*
Ḥaqq al-yaqīn fī maʻrifat rabb al-ʻālamīn (of Shabistarī), xi, 292n6
Harawī, Mīr Ḥusayn (Hirawī Sayyidī-yi Ḥusaynī), ix, xi, xii, 20, 175, 291n11
Harawī, Najīb Māyil, 291n11
Harmondsworth, Afkham Darbandi, 293n2.15
ḥayrah/ḥayrat, 29, 37, 96, 212, 285
Heidegger, Martin 223
Heraclitus, 149
Herat (Harat), xi, 20, 134
Hidden Treasure, 50, 51, 107
Ḥikmat al-ishrāq (of Suhrawardī), 28
Hindu: astronomy, 77; civilization, 73; cosmology, 40, 161; Law, 97; metaphysics, 9, 63, 88, 97, 97, 149
Hinduism, 7, 9, 40, 51, 60, 63, 73, 77, 88, 97, 99, 126, 149, 157, 161, 184, 185, 193, 254, 256
the Himalayas, 19, 60
history, passim; of philosophy, 149-150; of science, 72, 189; sacred, 55, 121, 123
Hume, David, 150
ḥurūf shamsiyyah, 79
ḥurūf qamariyyah, 79
Ḥusayn, Imam, 135
Huwa, 14, 15, 95, 97, 99, 101, 146, 150, 151, 156, 206
52, 95
huwiyyah/huwiyyat, 101, 103

Iblīs, 91, 259, 297n9.4, 299n15.6; *see also* the Devil; Shayṭān
Ibn ʻAbbās, 62
Ibn ʻArabī, Muḥyī al-Dīn, ix, xi, xii, 27, 29, 32, 35, 63, 79, 94, 105, 106, 121, 125, 126, 131, 134, 154, 162, 217, 219, 225, 233, 292n1.3, 294n2.26, 298n13.1
Ibn Khaldūn, 37
Ibn Rushd (Averroes), 37, 86
Ibn Sīnā (Avicenna), 5, 12, 14, 18, 21, 37, 44, 53, 56, 86, 89, 102, 134, 153, 156, 197; *see also* Avicennan
Ibn Turkah, Ṣāʼin al-Dīn, 37

Ibn Taymiyyah, 121
idol worship, xii, 19, 221, 251, 253-256, 273, 275, 277, 284, 299n15.2
Idrīs (Enoch), 111
Ikhwān al-Ṣafā', 61
Ilāhī-Qumsha'ī, Mahdī x
'ilm-i wirāthat, 181, 182
imkān/mumkin, 33, 47, 56, 102, 107, 153, 162, 285, 286
India, ix, 4, 7, 9, 28, 29, 37, 40, 45, 60, 61, 65, 67, 72, 92, 126, 184, 192
Indian languages, 4, 45, 92
Indian Ocean, 61
Indo-European languages, 3, 6, 97
Indo-Iranian languages, 130
al-Insān al-kāmil (of 'Abd al-Qādir Jīlī), 105
intellect, passim; the First Intellect, 5; the Second Intellect, 5; *see also 'aql*
the intelligible world, 11, 222
Iran, passim
the Iranian Revolution, 113
Iraq, 37, 106, 206
Isfahan, 28, 219
Isfahānī, Hātif, 53, 293n2.9
Isfarāyinī, Nūr al-Dīn, xi
al-Ishārāt wa'l-tanbīhāt (of Ibn Sīnā), 21
Ishrāqī (Illuminationist) philosophy, 28, 33, 37, 44
Islamic: anthropology, 81; art, passim; astrology and astronomy, 72, 73, 77, 79, 189, 268; jurisprudence, x, 72, 276; languages, xii, xiii, 31, 86, 192, 222, 239, 255; Law, 66, 108, 132, 180, 224; Peripatetic philosophy, 37, 44; philosophy (*falsafah/ḥikmah*), passim; theology. *See kalām*; thought, 37, 38, 55, 58, 63, 131, 153, 159, 168, 201, 255; world, x, 38, 65, 66, 72, 125, 133, 206, 227; *see also* Zodiac, Islamic
Ismā'īlī, 121
isrā', 68, 240, 285
Israel, 237
Italian (language), 145, 219
Italians, 98
Italy, 85, 209
Ithnā 'asharī Shi'ism, 121
Ithnā 'asharī Shi'ite philosophy, 121
Izutsu, Toshihiko, 292n3, 292n5

jabarūt, 11, 267
al-Jabbār, 80, 118
Jābulqā and *Jābulsā*, 59-62
jāhiliyyah, 255
jān-i jānān, 4
Japan, 60, 124, 135
Jassās, 262
Jerusalem, 68, 240, 285, 286
Jewish: cosmology, 83; mysticism, 239
Jīlānī, 'Abd al-Qādir, 125
Joseph, 22
Judaism, 4, 51, 124, 183, 185
Junayd, 125
Jung, Carl Gustav, 73

Ka'bah, 102, 113, 219, 255
kalām, 37, 41
Kant, Immanuel, 150
Kashmir, 19, 295
kawn, 5, 6, 69, 100, 119, 285, 295n3.1
Kaywān Samī'ī, Ghulāmriḍā: edition of the *Gulshan-i rāz*, xiii, 291n16, 292n4, 292n1.6, 293n1.7, 293n2.1, 3, 4, 6, 10, 12, 294n2.20, 295n3.1-4, 295n4.1, 7, 296n5.1, 296n6.1, 4, 297n9.1, 298n13.2-5, 298n14.3-5, 299n14.6-9, 299n15.2, 3, 6, 8-10, 300n15.12-13
Kepler, Johannes, 189
Khaḍir. *See* Khiḍr
khalwah, 113
kharābāt, xii, 236, 239, 246
khayāl, 62, 154, 162, 217
Khayyām, 'Umar, 25, 53, 81
Khiḍr, 233, 263
khirad, 38, 100, 141, 177, 285; *see also 'aql*
Khomeini, Ayatollah Ruhullah, 267
Khunjī, Amīn al-Dīn 'Abd al-Salām, xi
Khurāsān, xi, 20, 24, 26, 48, 97, 103
Kitāb al-mawāqif (of al-Niffarī), 129
Knesset, 102, 237
Krishna, 126
Kun! fa-yakūn, 6, 11, 89, 286
Kubrā, Najm al-Dīn, 209
Kubrawī Sufi order, xi
Kurdistān, 190

Lāhījī, Muḥammad ibn Yaḥyā, xiii, 19, 72, 88, 291n16, 301
lāhūt, 267
Lao Tzu, 140, 292n3

al-Laṭīf, 159
Latin, passim
lawḥ, 7, 286
lawḥ al-'adam, 6
The Laws of Manu, 97
Lederer, Florence, 291n4, 301
Lewisohn, Leonard, xi, 291n2-3, 291n5-6, 291n14, 292n6, 295n4.3, 301
Lings, Martin, 52, 293n2.8
logic, 29-32, 150, 170
The Lord's Prayer, 4
Lucknow, 28

macrocosm, 52, 73, 75, 78, 87, 98, 201, 203, 283
al-madīnat al-faḍīlah, 263
the Magians, 297n9.3
Maharshi, Śri Ramana, 9, 29, 97, 292n1.1
the Mahdī, 127, 128
māhiyyah, 11, 33, 156, 197, 286
Majnūn, 160, 185
Makkah, 123, 240, 285
malakūt, 267
male/masculine, 7, 16, 52, 66, 97, 101, 105, 107, 191, 219, 226
Manicheism, 254
Manṭiq al-ṭayr (of Farīd al-Dīn 'Aṭṭār), 24, 59-61, 267, 293n2.15, 293n2.16
maqām, 16-17, 21, 83, 112, 115, 131, 202, 233, 241, 286
Mary, the Virgin, 65, 272
Mashhad, 25, 48, 103
master (*khwājah/pīr/shaykh/ustād*), ix, x, xi, 9, 18, 20, 21, 23, 26, 29, 34-37, 53, 54, 64, 68, 81, 72, 81, 82, 87, 88, 90, 91, 100, 103, 104, 106, 114, 119, 122, 123, 126, 133, 134, 162, 184, 188, 209, 243, 246, 250, 255, 262-265, 274-277, 291n10, 291n16, 292n2, 296n5.2, 298n14.1
mathnawī (rhyming couplets), xii, 24, 286, 291n13
Mathnawī-yi ma'nawī (of Rūmī), ix, 24, 113, 138, 296n6.2, 297n9.2
Mawlawiyyah Order, 249
the Mazdeans, 168; *see also* Zoroastrianism
medieval period, 61, 71, 210, 294, 301
Meru (Mount), 60
Mesopotamia, 72, 73, 184; *see also* Zodiac, Mesopotamian
metacosm, 60
metaphysics, passim
metric system, 97, 98
Michelangelo, 44
the Michelson-Morley experiment, 189
microbiology, 54
microcosm, 52, 73, 75, 78, 88, 92, 98, 201, 203, 283
Mīr Dāmād, 215
mi'rāj, 45, 46, 69, 78, 112, 123, 240, 285, 286
modern: education, 72; science, 54, 73, 84, 85, 89, 197, 201; *see also* physics, modern; psychology, modern
modernism, passim
the Mongols, 25
Morocco, 106, 184
Moses, 31, 32, 67, 68, 111, 123, 126, 140, 144, 229, 240, 263
the Muḥammadan Light, 15, 123, 271, 283
the Muḥammadan Reality, 15, 16, 95, 120, 125, 243, 283
muḥdath, 18, 215, 286
Mullā Ṣadrā. *See* Shīrāzī, Ṣadr al-Dīn
Munājāt (of Khwājah 'Abd Allāh Anṣārī), 134
Murata, Sachiko, 294n2.21
Mūsā al-Kāẓim, Imam, 126
Muslim India, 28
Muslims, passim
Mu'tazilite, 40
Muwaḥḥid, Ṣamad, 291n10, 292n6

nabī, 112, 114, 121, 287; *see also dā'irat al-nubuwwah*; *nubuwwah/nubuwwat*
nafas al-Raḥmān, 7, 11, 12, 74, 287
Nagarjuna, 126
al-Najāh (of Ibn Sīnā), 156
Names and Qualities, passim; *see also* Divine
Nasafī, 'Azīz al-Dīn: *Insān-i kāmil*, 105
Nāṣir-i Khusraw, 61
nāsūt, 267, 268
Nayshapur, 25
Neoplatonism, 5, 67
Neo-Vedanta, 254
New York, 106
Nicholson, Reynold A., 105, 219, 296n6.2, 297n9.2, 298n13.1, 301
Nicomachean Ethics (of Aristotle), 183, 185
the Nile, 54
Noah, 111

nubuwwah/nubuwwat, 112, 113, 119, 121, 126, 127, 175, 284, 287; *see also dā'irat al-nubuwwah*; *nabī*
Nurbakhsh, Javad, 27, 80; edition of the *Gulshan-i rāz* of, xiii, 80, 291n16, 292n4, 292n1.6, 293n1.7, 293n2.1, 3, 4, 10, 12, 294n2.19, 20, 27, 30, 295n3.1-4, 295n4.4, 7, 296n5.1, 296n6.1, 4, 298n13.3-5, 298n14.3-5, 299n14.6-9, 299n15.3, 6, 8-10, 300n15.12-13

the Old Testament, 240; *see also* the Bible; Christianity
Olympus (Mount), 60
Oppenheimer, J. Robert, 53

Pakistan, 7, 28, 192
Pallis, Marco (Thubden Tendzin): *The Way and the Mountain*, 60, 294n2.17
Paris, 106
Parmenides, 149
Pascal: *Pensées* (*Meditations*), 4
Peripatetic philosophy, 33, 37, 44, 58; *see also* Islamic, Peripatetic philosophy
Persia, passim
Persian: language, passim; literature, passim; poetry, passim; Sufism, passim; Sufi literature, passim; *see also* Zodiac, Persian
the Persian Gulf, 176, 177
the Persian-speaking world, ix, 28, 134
phainómenon, 44
phallic symbol, 7
Pharaoh, 229, 260
phenomenology, 41
philosophy, passim; Eastern, 198; rational, 33, 37, 38; Western, 33, 150, 195, 198
physics: celestial, 189; modern, x, 83; Newtonian, 189; terrestrial, 189
Plato, 10, 44, 254
Platonic ethics, 183
Platonic Ideas, 10, 184, 196, 197
Platonism, 10, 44, 183, 187, 196, 197
postmedieval Western theology and philosophy, 210
prakriti, 7
Pre-Socratic philosophers, 149
prime matter, 85, 86, 155, 156, 285
the Prophet, passim; 'Abd Allāh, 107; Aḥmad, 15-16, 69, 112, 131; *khātam al-anbiyā'*, 16, 120, 285; *Khwājah*, 68, 123, 262; Maḥmūd, 131, 133, 281; Muḥammad, ix, 15, 16, 95, 126, 127, 131, 171; Muṣṭafā, 111, 113; *see also* the Muḥammadan Light; the Muḥammadan Reality; the Prophetic Reality
the Prophetic Reality, 15, 113, 125
prophetlogy, 56, 78, 119, 122, 125, 233, 267; *see also nubuwwah/nubuwwat*
Protestants, 185
psychology, 5, 132, 135, 166, 203, 270; Avicennan, 14; Jungian, 73; modern, 266
purusha, 7
Pythagoreanism, 10

the Qadarites, 297n9.3
qadīm, 18, 215, 287
Qāf (Mount), 6, 58, 59, 60
qāfiyah, 24
al-Qahhār, 44, 144
qalam, 6,7, 287
qānūn, 31
Qāṭīghūriyās (of Aristotle), 150
al-Qayṣarī, Dāwūd, 37
Qazwīnī, Muḥammad, 292n2, 296n5.2, 298n14.1
qiyās, 31, 170, 287
Qom, 66
quantum mechanics, 189
al-Quddūs, 267
quintessentia, 83, 189
Qūnawī, Ṣadr al-Din, 205, 297n11.2
the Quran, passim; *see also The Study Quran*
al-Qur'ān al-tadwīnī, 69
al-Qur'ān al-takwīnī, 69
qurrat al-'ayn, 135, 258, 287

al-Raḥīm, 3, 70
al-Raḥmān, 3, 4, 7, 11, 12, 54, 70, 71, 74, 143, 159, 234, 287
Rakhsh, 191, 192, 258
Rama, 126
rationalism, 32, 37, 38, 73, 100, 110, 141
Red Sea, 24
reincarnation, 10, 39-40, 117, 120
Renaissance, 209
al-Riḍā, Imam 'Alī, 48, 103
rind, 191, 245, 250
Rome, 44

Rūmī, Mawlāna Jalāl al-Dīn, ix, 24, 25, 28, 37, 61, 86, 113, 122, 125, 126, 129, 138, 167, 207, 219, 220, 244, 292, 296n6.2, 297n9.2, 298n14.2
Russia, 106
Rustam (of the *Shāhnāmah*), 258
Rypka, Jan, 301

Sa'ādat-nāmah (of Shabistarī), xi, 292n6
Sa'dī, Muṣliḥ al-Din, 28, 199
al-Ṣādiq, Imam Ja'far, 39, 113
saki, 3, 241, 275-279, 287
San Francisco, 106
Sanskrit, 3, 7, 51, 109, 145
de Santillana, Girogio and Hertha von Dechend: *Hamlet's Mill*, 73, 294n2.24
sanyasin, 185
Schimmel, Annemarie, 294n2.21
Schmidt, Hanns-Peter, 293n2.14
Schuon, Frithjof, 8, 39, 60, 139, 208, 296n6.3, 297n11.4, 297n11.9, 301
Scotland, 150
the Sea of Oman, 176
Second World War, 254
secularism, 32, 34, 60
Seljuq period, 37
Shabistar, xi
al-Shādhilī, Shaykh Abū'l-Ḥasan, 106, 122
the *shahādah*, 97, 103, 131, 143, 145, 146, 191, 226
shāhid, 18, 103, 104, 225, 226, 239, 240, 287
shāhid-bāzī, 18, 240
Shāhnāmah (of *Firdawsī*), 258
Shakespeare, 63, 66
Shankaracharya, 8, 88, 99, 126, 149
Sharī'ah, 102, 115-117, 131, 168, 172, 184, 186, 221, 223, 239, 255, 272, 274, 288
shaṭḥ, 125, 248, 259, 288
Shayṭān (Satan), 89, 91, 124, 133, 159, 166, 193, 242, 288; *see also* the Devil; Iblīs
al-Shifā' (of Ibn Sīnā), 156
Shi'ism, 104, 113, 121, 126, 127
Shi'ite Imams, 21, 39, 48, 49, 103, 113, 126, 135, 211
Shi'ite Sufis, 113
Shīrāzī, Ṣadr al-Dīn (Mullā Ṣadrā), 37, 62, 63, 130, 135, 149, 197, 209, 215, 217
shirk, 171, 255
Shiva, 7
Siberia, 61
silsilah, xi, 230
Simnānī, 'Alā' al-Dawlah, 209
Sīmurgh (*al-'Anqā'*, Griffin), 58-61, 215, 267
Sinai (Mount), 111
Smith, Wolfgang, 189, 297n10.1
Socrates, 139
Socratic dictum, 91
the Source, 15, 119, 153, 163, 164, 190, 195, 227, 232, 242, 245, 256, 257
Spain, 106
Stoicism, 159
The Study Quran, 292n1.4
Sufi: cosmology, passim; literature, passim; metaphysics, passim; order, xi, 43, 113, 126, 192, 249, 288; philosophy of language, xii
Sufis, passim
Sufism (*taṣawwuf*), passim; theoretical, ix, x, xi, xiii
Suhrawardī, Yaḥyā ibn Ḥabash, 28, 37, 61, 62, 97, 146, 150, 154, 189, 197, 217, 296n7.2
Sumerian Tablets, 73
the *Sunnah*, 175
Sunnism, 113, 127
the Supreme Cause, 7, 171
Switzerland, 60
Syria, 106, 206

Ṭabāṭabā'ī, 'Allāmah Muḥammad Ḥusayn, x
Tabriz, xi, 14
Tabrīzī, Ḥajjī Amīn al-Dīn (Ḥajjī Dādā), xi
Tahdhīb al-akhlāq (of Miskawayh), 185
tahlīl, 143
tajdīd al-khalq fī kulli'l-ānāt, 12, 199, 288
tanzīh, 39, 41, 55, 288
The *Tao Te Ching*, 4, 292n3
Taoism, 4, 184, 292n3
Ṭarīqah, 115-117, 224, 239, 288
Tarjumān al-ashwāq (of Ibn 'Arabī), 219, 298n13.1
tasalsul, 33
tashbīh, 39, 55, 289
tawḥīd, 13, 41, 109, 171, 241, 246, 289
Tehran, 7, 60, 66, 98
Tehran University, 14, 30
theophany, 6, 36, 40, 43, 67-69, 90, 94, 104, 107, 116, 120, 125, 140, 206, 211, 219,

220, 221, 228, 231, 232, 239, 253, 259, 277, 286, 288
the Three Kingdoms (*al-mawālīd al-thalāthah*), 71, 85, 157, 158, 165, 210, 283
traditionalists, 19, 39, 128
the Transcendent Supreme Principle, 13
transmigration, 10, 40
Turk, 37, 138
Turkey, xi, 192
Turkish language, 4, 24, 60, 92
al-Ṭūsī, Naṣīr al-Dīn, 56, 185, 262

Umm-i Hānī, 69
United States, vii, x, 254
Universal Being, 195, 197
Universal Intellect (*'aql-i kullī*), 70, 88, 243
Universal Man / perfect man / complete man, passim
Universal Soul (*nafs-i kullī*), 70, 88, 191, 243
University of Chicago, 53
Urdu, 45, 60, 92

Vedanta, 8; *see also* Advaita Vedanta
Virginia, x

wādī al-ṭuwā (the Sacred valley of Ṭuwā), 32, 67, 144; *see also wādī-yi ayman*
wādī-yi ayman (the Valley of the Right), 31-32, 144, 240; *see also wādī al-ṭuwā*
waḥdat al-wujūd, 161, 215, 289
Wahhabism, 121
al-Wāḥid, 44, 144
walāyah/wilāyah, 67, 112, 113, 119, 121, 126, 127, 175, 284, 289; *see also dā'irat al-walāyah/wilāyah* and *walī, awliyā'*
walī, awliyā', 17, 112-114, 120, 121, 125, 126, 243, 289; *see also walāyah/wilāyah*
Washington, DC vii, x, xiii
Whinfield, Edward Henry, ix, 291n4, 294n2.25, 301
wine, 3, 18, 81, 212, 213, 221, 228, 231, 232, 237, 239, 240-245, 247-250, 275, 287, 298n14.2-3
the World Egg (*Hiranyagarbha*), 161
wujūb, 33, 289
wujūd. *See* Being

Yate, Asadullah, 301
Yazdān, 168, 169
Yazīd ibn Mu'āwiyah, 3
Yemen, 92

al-Ẓāhir, 35, 95, 230
Zodiac, 72, 73, 76-79; Babylonian, 72, 73; Chinese, 72; Greek, 72; Islamic, 72, 73; Persian, 72; Roman, 72; Mesopotamian, 72, 73
Zoroastrianism, 60, 168, 169
zunnār, 251, 253, 264

www.ingramcontent.com/pod-product-compliance
Lightning Source LLC
Chambersburg PA
CBHW060242240426
43673CB00048B/1940